I0140020

EXCEL

IN

CRE

BY

LIVINUS WESONGA

Ariba Book Publishers

Christian Religious Education – KCSE revision
Copyright © 2014

All rights reserved by **Livinus Wesonga**

No part of this book may be reproduced or transmitted in any form or by any means, graphic, electronic, or mechanical including photocopying, recording, taping or by any information retrieval system, without permission in writing of the publisher.

Ariba Book Publishers

P.O Box 503–40600

Siaya –Kenya

Website: www.aribabp.com

Email: admin@aribabp.com

ISBN: **978-9966-1818-2-4**

First published 2014

Printed by: **Susmo Enterprises**

        P.o Box 345-00511

        Nairobi

PREFACE

Excel in CRE book is written to assist both learners and teachers in Secondary Schools to prepare for the Kenya Certificate of Secondary Education. It aims at meeting the requirements of both the Kenya National Examinations Council and the Kenya Institute of Curriculum Development syllabi. It also conforms to the current setting trend in Christian Religious Education, both Papers 1 and 2. It is complete with examination tips to guide learners, especially candidates, on how to tackle exams in the subject.

The purpose of the book is to guide learners in identifying the areas that are examined in Paper 1 and 2, since it outlines the topics in the order in which they are examined in each of the two Papers. It aims at providing insight to the learners and to equip them with the necessary knowledge with which to relate with God, themselves and with others in the society. It builds moral values in the learner.

This book ends with past KCSE papers, from 2006 to 2013, Papers 1 and 2, plus their marking schemes. This content should guide the learner to test his/her ability to answer KCSE questions, and to even know the marking points of each question tested previously.

SARAH WALIAULA

EXAMINER, CRE PAPER 1

ACKNOWLEDGEMENT

I would like to greatly appreciate dear my parents, Nicholas and Anne, who have been of invaluable support, and whose advice I have always cherished to live by. My sincere gratitude goes to Rt. Rev. Bishop Emmanuel Okombo, my brothers and sisters, who have always challenged me by their success, inspiration and humility. All I can I say to my professional mentor, Mr. Mutenyo Michael, whom I really admire his character, hardwork and wisdom, is may the good God bless you abundantly. I am indebted to my colleagues and great friends, Robert Okapel, Andrew Ondieki, Otieno Wanga, Sarah, Consolata, Susan Ombima, Amos Kiprotich, James Nyaga, David Aswani, Jonam Indeke, David Maina and many more whom I may not be able to mention here, but may they accept my gratitude. Many thanks to my students at St. Monica Chakol Girls High School, who always gave me a reason to do quality work in preparing lesson notes and to research widely, which later culminated in this book. To the Publishers, editors and all those who contributed to the success of this work in one way or another, where I cannot individually thank them, I say, may God life up His countenance on you. Lastly, I give thanks to our Almighty God who provided the energy and determination throughout the writing of this book. May His name be exalted forever.

EXAMINATION TIPS

1. Read the instructions on the cover page carefully before turning to the questions. CRE, both papers 1 and 2 contain 6 questions, each carrying 20 marks, of which the candidate should answer 5 questions in the order of his/her ability.

2. Read each question carefully in order to understand its requirements. There are two types of questions:

    a. Closed ended/restricted questions: these require that a candidate should give only the number of points specified for in the question. No marks are awarded for extra points beyond the specified number.

    b. Open ended/Unrestricted questions: these require that the candidate give as many points as possible. However, candidates need to check on the marks allocated to such questions so as not to waste time in answering them.

3. Number your work properly, in the same way as the questions are numbered in the question paper e.g. a, b, c,

4. Present your work in good handwriting and be neat.

5. Choose questions wisely and start by answering questions that will earn the candidate maximum marks e.g. 20 marks.

6. Write answers in prose/continuous manner, arranging them in set paragraphs.

7. Avoid giving one-word answers, the candidate should express his/her answers in statement form, trying to support their points.

8. The candidate should develop more than one idea in a paragraph. This is possible because the candidate is writing answers in prose, so as he/she is thinking about an answer, he/she develops another one to complement what he/she already has written.

9. The candidate should avoid using abbreviations e.g. RSV, 1st Cor, but say Revised Standard Version, 1st Corinthians.

10. Answering of particular points requires good mastery of content to organize work in paragraphs. Lack of adequate information result in repetition of points which will disadvantage the candidate.

11. Candidates need to be keen throughout the session while dealing with different questions.

12. In preparation for the exam, candidates should read the Revised Standard Version Bible, particularly St. Luke's Gospel, in order to perform well in Paper 2.

Frequent terms used in questions

- **Describe, relate, and narrate**: these require the candidate to tell the story as it is. Do not give explanations or interpretations, they are not required.

- **Identify, give**: answer the questions by telling the examiner the right answers to the questions.

- **State**: in brief, tell the examiner what you know about the question in statement form.
- **Outline**: give a brief overview.
- **Explain**: look at the question keenly, then tell the examiner what you know about it in a convincing way. Such questions sometimes have two sides, identify the point, then give details about it.
- **Lessons learnt about**: this means characteristics, virtues, qualities. For example:

   Question: What lessons do Christians learn about God from the creation stories? (5 marks)

   The answers include: God is omnipotent, God is good, God is powerful, God is omnipresent

- **Lessons learnt from**: This explains the relevance, significance of an event. Example:

   Question: What lessons do Christians do Christians learn from the incident when cleansed the temple. (5 marks)

   The answers include: Christians should respect the House of God, Christians should have courage like Jesus to condemn evil practises e.t.c. Hence, candidates should begin their answers by "Christians should…"

- **Ways**: such questions require candidates to show how Christians or the parties in question are practically involved e.g.

   Question: Show the ways in which the elders promote harmony and mutual responsibility in traditional African communities. (8 marks)

   The answer should begin by: Elders acted as spokesmen and reconciled warring parties.

   Question: Give ways in which the church is helping in maintaining peace in Kenya. (6 marks)

   Answer: Through preaching peace, condemning all kinds of discrimination and creating awareness.

   Candidates should at all times give positive answers to questions.

- **Activities, events, actions**: Candidates should look at what was happening in a particular story and give the events as they were happening e.g.

   Question: Give five actions from the life of Abraham which show his faith in God. (Genesis 12, 15. 17, 19, 22)

   In the answers, Genesis 12, 15, 17, 19 and 22 indicates that answers should only come from the chapters indicated. No mark will be awarded outside the brackets of the verses.

- Questions on similarities and differences:

   Use in both… for similarities

   Use whereas, while, or but for differences.

   Differences should come out clearly from the same point.

13. Several questions in CRE require candidates to exercise their reasoning abilities e.g. How can Christians help church leaders to perform their duties effectively?

A candidate must reason out and find answers from their understanding of the content of the subject.

The use of the Bible as a text book or for reference is very important. This is because it brings out the ideas as they occurred and words used are most appropriate for answering descriptive questions.

TABLE OF CONTENTS

PAPER ONE

PAPER TWO

Topic 1: INTRODUCTION TO CRE

MEANING OF CRE
- It is the study of God's self-revelation to human beings through the person of Jesus Christ, scriptures and the Holy Spirit.

REASONS WHY CRE IS TAUGHT IN SCHOOLS
- It enables students get a better understanding of God.
- It enables students acquire principles of Christian living.
- It enables students appreciate their own religion and that of others.
- It enables students contribute to the achievement of the national goals of education.
- It helps students form a bridge for further studies and career development.
- It enables students have a better understanding of the bible.
- It helps students identify answers to some life's questions for instance why people die.
- It enables students contribute to the development of the whole person i.e. spiritual, moral, emotional and physical development.

National Goals of Education in Kenya include:
- To foster nationalism, patriotism and promote national unity.
- To promote social, economic, technological and industrial needs for development.
- To promote individual development and self-fulfilment.
- To promote sound moral and religious values.
- To promote social equality and responsibility.
- To promote respect for and development of Kenya's rich and varied cultures.
- To promote international consciousness and foster positive attitude towards other nations.
- To promote positive attitudes towards good health and environmental protection.

In what five ways can teaching of C.R.E enhance national unity in Kenya?
- It teaches about the universal brotherhood through Adam and Eve.
- Develops oneness in Christian unity.
- It teaches equality of human kind before God.
- It imparts the virtue of love which brings unity.
- It teaches about the destiny of man.

How does the teaching of CRE in secondary schools promote international consciousness?
- It helps one to respect other people's cultures.
- It helps one to appreciate the universality of God.
- CRE teaches that human beings have one origin and destiny.

- It teaches about love, respect and unity.
- It teaches social moral values which strengthen unity among citizens.
- Through the study of CRE, people learn that they are equal before God.
- It teaches on the importance of understanding oneself and appreciating others.
- It teaches on tolerance.

Topic 2: THE BIBLE

THE BIBLE AS THE WORD OF GOD (Hebrews 1: 1 – 2; 2 Timothy 3: 16; Revelation 22: 18)

Give reasons why the Bible is referred to as the Word of God

- The Bible is the inspired word of God.
- The authors of the Bible wrote under the influence of the Holy Spirit.
- God took part in the writing of the Bible e.g. he wrote the Ten Commandments.
- It contains the true message of God for daily living.
- God reveals himself to Christians through historical events in the Old and New Testaments.
- Through the Bible, God communicates His will to Christians.

Why is the Bible is referred to as Good News?

- Bible has a message of hope.
- Contains messages of reconciliation.
- Through it man gets salvation from his fallen state.
- It gives an answer to the suffering of man.
- It gives a man revelation of mysteries.
- Through it God communicates his will to man.
- It brings mankind closer to God.
- Makes human beings to be aware of their destiny.

Give reasons why Christians refer to the Bible as a holy book.

- It talks about God who is holy.
- The writers were inspired by God.
- It calls for spiritual purity.
- It is the word of God.
- It is used in worship and adoration.
- It contains laws of what God expects of us.
- Its presence signifies God's presence.
- It is a summary of the salvation history of mankind.
- It is the core of Christian's faith.
- It is the mirror and guide to Christianity and its tenets.
- It is reserved for special uses like worship.
- It is a source of Christian's instructions.

Why do Christians read the Bible?

- It is the word of God.
- It provides moral and spiritual guidance.
- Helps them to discover the will of God.
- Reading it is an aspect of worship.

- It is the basis of Christian doctrines/teachings and practices.
- It gives guidance on relationships among human being.
- Christians come to discover who they are.
- Helps human beings to understand the universe and their relationship to it.
- It helps in spiritual development and maturity.
- It is a source of inspiration.
- It helps human beings to understand the meaning of their lives and relationship to God and to one another.

Identify various ways that Christians use the Bible.

- For swearing in people in court that they will say only the truth.
- It is used as a major text book in CRE.
- It is used as a part of worship in churches.
- They read it to know the will of God.
- To instruct new converts in spiritual matters.
- To give people the meaning of their life and how to relate with each other.
- To establish the basis of Christian doctrine and practices.
- To explain man's destiny in life.

Give the ways in which Christians use the Bible to spread the good news.

- Christians read the Bible to others.
- Bible is used for instructing and teaching new converts on Christian doctrine/teachings.
- Used for preaching and teaching on different issues.
- Bible is used as the main text book in teaching and learning of Christian Religious Education in schools and Colleges.
- Used as a reference book in the general search of knowledge.
- Hymns are composed from the Bible.
- Christians distribute Bibles to individuals to read the word of God.
- Christians translate the Bible into vernacular so that many people can read and understand in their own language.

In which ways do Christians use print media to spread the gospel?

- Publishing Christian literature.
- Distributing Christian literature free.
- Reading the Bible and other Christian literature.
- Using Biblical stories to produce Christian programmes in electronic media.
- Teaching using CRE text books.
- Selling Christian literature to institutional and public.
- Advertising Christian issues in the newspaper.

HUMAN AUTHORS (2 Peter 1:20-21)

- God used various human authors/writers to write His message which is found in the different books in the Bible.

- Some of the authors were prophets, kings, scribes, apostles and some disciples.
- The writers lived at different times in history.
- Some of the human authors are Moses, Solomon, David, Isaiah, Paul, Peter, Samuel, Mark, Luke, John e.t.c.
- The Bible was written after the death and resurrection of Jesus.

Reasons why the Bible was written after the death and resurrection of Jesus Christ
- There was need to write an orderly account of Jesus.
- There was need for a text to combine both Old and New Testaments.
- There was rapid expansion of the church.
- It was intended to counter the rise of false teachings which confused the Christians.
- Christians had waited for long for the second coming of Jesus Christ which was not forthcoming.
- The death of many eye witnesses led to the need to write so that we preserve Jesus teachings.
- The writing material on which the work was recorded was available.
- They had the Holy Spirit which inspired them to write.

Literary forms used by the authors of the Bible are;-
- The use of narratives/prose form e.g. Genesis.
- Religious epics e.g. Exodus.
- Legal expressions/legislative texts e.g. Leviticus.
- Prophetic speeches e.g. Jeremiah.
- The use of prayers e.g. Nehemiah.
- The use of poetic devices e.g. Psalms.
- The use of wise sayings e.g. Proverbs.
- Philosophical essays e.g. Job.
- The use of love songs e.g. Song of Songs.
- Epistles e.g. Romans.
- Biographies/Gospel e.g. St. Luke.

MAJOR DIVISIONS OF THE BIBLE
The Bible contains 66 books divided into two major divisions:
- The Old Testament and
- The New Testament.

THE OLD TESTAMENT
The Old Testament has 39 books subdivided into four groups.
- Law Books/Torah/Pentateuch e.g. Genesis, Exodus, Leviticus, Numbers and Deuteronomy.
- Historical books e.g. Joshua, Judges, Ruth, 1and 2 Samuel, 1 and 2 Kings, 1 and 2 Chronicles, Ezra, Nehemiah, and Esther.
- Poetic books/writings e.g. Job, Psalms, Proverbs, Ecclesiastes, and Songs of Solomon.

- Prophetic books are divided into two
  a. Major Prophets e.g. Isaiah, Jeremiah, Lamentations, Ezekiel and Daniel.
  b. Minor Prophets e.g. Hosea, Joel, Amos, Obadiah, Jonah, Micah, Nahum, Habakkuk, Zephaniah, Haggai, Zechariah, and Malachi.
- In some Bibles used by Catholics, the Old Testament has an additional 7 books, which are considered part of the Holy Scripture and are referred to as deuterocanonical books or Apocrypha e.g. Tobit, Judith, 1 & 2 Maccabees, Wisdom, Ecclesiasticus and Baruch.

THE NEW TESTAMENT

It has 27 books in number subdivided into five groups:
- Biographical books/Gospels e.g. Matthew, Mark, Luke, and John.
- Historical book e.g. Acts of the Apostles which records the origin and development of the early church.
- Pauline epistles/letters – These are letters written by Paul to various churches e.g. Romans, 1 and 2 Corinthians, Galatians, Ephesians, Philippians, Colossians, 1 and 2 Thessalonians, 1 and 2 Timothy, Titus and Philemon.
- General Epistles e.g. Hebrews, James, 1 and 2 Peter, 1, 2 and 3 John, and Jude.
- Prophetic book/Apocalypse – it carries prophesies on the world to come. This is the book of Revelation.

THE BIBLE AS A LIBRARY

Reasons why the Bible is referred to as a library

- It contains many books under one cover, a total of 66 books.
- The books are arranged according to subjects e.g. books of law, historical books, wisdom writings, prophecy, biography, epistles.
- The books are written by different authors.
- The books are written in different styles such as poetic, prophetic speeches, letters, prayers, philosophical essays, wise sayings and songs.
- The books are arranged in an orderly manner to develop the theme of God's plan of salvation for humankind.
- Different books of the Bible are addressed to different groups of people.
- The books were written at different times in human history.
- The books were written in different places.

THE TRANSLATIONS OF THE BIBLE FROM THE ORIGINAL LANGUAGES (HEBREW AND GREEK) TO THE LOCAL LANGUAGES

Describe the translation of the Bible from original to the local languages

- The Old Testament was originally written in Hebrew.
- The New Testament was written in Greek, the official language in the Roman Empire.
- The Old Testament was translated from Hebrew to Greek, this translation is called Septuagint.
- In the 4th Century AD, Jerome translated the Bible into Latin, this translation is known as vulgate.

- In 1384, John Wycliffe translated the Bible into English.
- In the 19th Century, Johann Ludwig Krapf, a German missionary translated the Bible into Kiswahili.
- In Kenya the Bible has been translated into more than 29 local languages e.g. Gikuyu, Kamba, Dholuo, Kimeru, Kalenjin and Luhya.

Reasons why the bible was translated from original languages to local languages
- In order to enable the word of God to reach more people in their own language.
- In order to train local people to take up leadership roles.
- In order to increase the demand for formal education.
- To facilitate the expansion of the church.
- To indigenize Christianity.
- To encourage research into African language/culture.
- In order to establish local bible translation society e.g. Bible society of Kenya

Versions of the Bible used in Kenya today
- Good News
- Revised Standard Version
- The African Bible
- Jerusalem Bible
- The Gideon's International Version
- Common Bible
- New English Bible
- New International Version
- New Living Bible
- New King James Version

The effects of the translation of the Bible into African languages
- It led to the development of local languages.
- Local people could read the Bible in their own languages.
- The word of God reached more people in their own languages.
- It led to the establishment of more schools to cater for the growing need for education.
- Led to formation of independent churches as Africans could read and interpret the Bible.
- Africans became more actively involved in the church.
- Africans began exercising leadership in the churches.
- Africans became critical of certain issues preached by missionaries e.g. equality, love, monogamy e.t.c.
- It led to mass evangelism since more Africans were converted into Christianity.
- There was demand for more Bibles leading to establishment of local printing presses.
- Missionaries began to appreciate the African culture, thus reducing suspicion between them and Africans.
- Africans rediscovered their own cultural identity e.g. dancing styles, local languages, musical instruments e.t.c.

- Africans understood themselves better and became more aware of their own human dignity.
- It led to the establishment of Bible translation societies e.g. Bible society of Kenya.

Highlight eight ways in which the Bible translation has facilitated the spread of Christianity in Kenya

- Many people can now read the Bible in their own vernacular languages.
- The Bible has become a useful resource for learning in school and for adult education.
- It has led to the expansion of the church.
- It has led to emergence of African independent churches and schools.
- It enabled the missionaries to learn the local languages for faster spread of Christianity.
- Africans are able to discover certain contradictions on issues e.g. racism, equality, polygamy etc.
- It has made it possible for Africans to participate actively in Evangelism e.g. as pastors, priests, evangelists e.t.c.
- It has contributed to the spirit of ecumenism as several denominations have emerged.
- It has contributed to the development of African theology e.g. study of African religions

In what ways do Christians use the Bible to spread the gospel?

- Christian literature quotes the bible as a reference book.
- Christian songs /hymns are derived from the bible.
- Preaching/teaching from the bible by religious leaders.
- By reading the bible to others.
- By using it for instructions guidance.
- By translating it into local languages for people to read/understand it.
- Distribution of the bible to those who do not have it.
- The bible is used as a reference /main resource material in search for religious knowledge.
- The bible is a resource material in teaching CRE in schools and colleges.
- The bible is used in taking of oaths to prove its authenticity.

Topic 3: CREATION AND THE FALL OF MAN
THE BIBLICAL ACCOUNTS OF CREATION AND THEIR MEANING (Gen 1 and 2)
Describe the first account of creation as recorded in Genesis 1
- In the beginning God created the heavens and the sky.
- The earth was without form, was void and had darkness.
- On the first day God created light and separated it from darkness and called it day and night respectively.
- On the second day He created the sky/firmament.
- On the third day, He created dry land/earth, seas, oceans and vegetation.
- On the fourth he created the heavenly bodies.
- On the fifth day he created sea creatures and birds.
- On the sixth day, God created animals, creeping creatures and human beings.
- On the seventh day God rested.

Describe the second account of creation as recorded in Genesis 2
- God made the earth and heavens.
- He formed man out of dust.
- He breathed into his nostrils the breath of life and man became a living being.
- God planted the Garden of Eden in the East.
- God made every tree to grow out of the ground.
- He also made the tree of life in the midst of the garden and the tree of knowledge of good and evil.
- He made a river to flow out of the garden and divided it into four rivers.
- God put man in the Garden of Eden to till it and keep it.
- He told man to eat from every tree apart from the tree of knowledge of good and evil.
- The Lord saw that it was not good for man to be alone.
- He made every beast of the field and every bird of the air and brought them to man.
- He told man to name them.
- The man was happy and called her woman.

Why is man considered the climax of God's creation?
- He was created in God's image and likeness.
- He has God's breath.
- He was created to have fellowship with God and communicate with God.
- He was given free will, conscience, knowledge and intelligence to choose between right and wrong.
- He was given the responsibility to rule over and manages all the creation of God.
- Man was blessed and commanded to multiply and fill the earth.
- Man was given responsibility to name the rest of the animals and creation.

- Man was created last after everything else had been created for his use.
- Man was given a helper and companion.
- Man was moulded by God himself.

How do human beings fail to carry out responsibilities given to them by God?

- By deciding to remain unmarried.
- By not worshipping him and observing the Sabbath.
- Not guarding the land from erosion.
- Failing to conserve the environment e.g. by keeping it clean.
- Through deforestation/cutting vegetation and not planting trees.
- Mining and excavations leading to open ground prone to erosion.
- Preventing pregnancy by using contraceptives or not procreating.
- Committing murder and capital punishment.
- Pollution of the environment.
- Through abortion.
- Through sexual immorality e.g. prostitution, lesbianism etc.

Give the ways in which Christians continue with God's work of creation.

- Caring for and conserving the environment.
- Through procreation.
- Respecting and protecting human rights.
- Making just laws and condemning unjust or oppressive laws.
- Through coming up with technology that enhances life.
- Provision of education for development.
- Preaching peace to promote unity.
- Training people for and providing employment opportunities.
- Being creative and innovative.
- Helping the needy.

How has man interfered with God's work of creation?

- Through deforestation or cutting down of trees.
- Pollution of water, air and soil.
- Abortion, killing and murder.
- Test tube babies or artificial fertilization.
- Use of contraceptives.
- Through genetic engineering.
- By practicing pervasive sexual behaviours.
- Through environmental degradation.

ATTRIBUTES OF GOD FROM THE BIBLICAL CREATION ACCOUNTS (Gen 1 & 2)

- God is omnipotent, almighty and all-powerful.
- God is omniscient, all-knowing.

- God is omnipresent.
- God is good and everything he creates is good.
- God is orderly as He creates in stages.
- God is transcendent and man can never understand him fully.
- God is merciful.
- He is powerful as he brings things to existence by his spoken word.
- God must be obeyed.
- God is full of blessings.
- God is the sole creator.
- God is the provider as he gives man everything he needs.
- God is loving and caring, understanding as he understood Adam and Eve.
- God is a spirit; the Bible says "the spirit of God was hovering over the waters".

Lessons that Christians learn from the Genesis stories of creation
- God is the creator of the universe.
- God sustains his creation.
- Everything that God created is good.
- Human beings were created in the image and likeness of God.
- Human beings should observe the Sabbath as a day of rest and worshipping God.
- Human beings were put in charge of God's creation.
- Human beings should procreate as a way continuing with the work of creation.
- Man was created to worship God.
- Plants and animals were created for the benefit of man.
- God ordained work so man must work.
- The woman was created to be man's companion.
- Marriage was ordained by God.

SIMILARITIES AND DIFFERENCES BETWEEN THE FIRST AND SECOND ACCOUNTS OF CREATION
SIMILARITIES
Explain the similarities in Genesis 1 and 2
- In both accounts God is acknowledged as the creator.
- In both accounts God created the living and non-living things.
- In both accounts human beings share in the life of God.
- Marriage is ordained by God in both accounts.
- In both accounts God gave responsibilities and privileges to humankind.
- In both accounts God is self-existent.
- In both accounts human beings are superior to the rest of the creation.
- In both accounts human beings are created both male and female.

DIFFERENCES BETWEEN THE FIRST AND SECOND ACCOUNTS OF CREATION

- The first account is orderly and takes place according to days while there is no specific structure of days in the second account.
- In the first account plants were created before man while in the second account they came last.
- In the first account God rested on the seventh day while in the second account there is no indication of rest.
- In the first account male and female are created at the same time while in the second account the female was created last and from man's rib.
- In the first account man was created out of nothing while in the second account he was created out of dust.
- In the first account marriage is for procreation while in the second account it is for companionship.
- Creation is by word in the first account while in the second account God moulded man from dust and breathed the breath of life into him.
- The second account omits the creation of the firmament, creeping creatures, heavenly bodies and fishes which are included in the first account.
- Planting of the Garden of Eden and the making of the rivers is described in the second account which is omitted in the first account.

TEACHINGS FROM THE BIBLICAL ACCOUNTS OF CREATION (Genesis 1 and 2)

- Human beings are the most important of God's creation.
- Human beings are co-creators with God, in transforming the world for their benefit.
- Human beings have the responsibility to look after God's creation.
- Creation is by deliberate will of God and not by accident.
- Plant, animals, sunshine and rain were created for the benefit of human beings.
- Man and woman are companions hence, they are social beings.
- Work and leisure are God's gifts to humankind.
- Human beings were created to obey and have faith in God and live in fellowship with Him.
- Both human beings and the environment share the same origin.
- The human race is one in origin and destiny.
- Marriage is a divine, blessed and sacred institution ordained by God.

State the instructions given to man by God in the creation stories.

- Man was told to control or have dominion over all creation of God.
- To till the land and subdue it.
- To procreate and fill the earth.
- To name every creature.
- To be companions to each other, man and wife.
- To complement each other (man & wife).

- To choose between good and bad (evil).

The relationship between Human beings and God in the second Biblical account of creation

- Human beings have the spirit of God in them.
- Human beings are to obey God.
- Human beings get their provisions from God.
- Human beings are to take care of God's creation.
- God wants human being to work.
- Human beings are co-creators with God.
- God wants human beings to lead a comfortable life, hence He provides for their needs.

Give the relationship between man and woman according to the Genesis Accounts of creation.

- Both were created by God and given the breath.
- They have to marry and procreate.
- They are companions and they complement each other.
- Both are equal before God.
- They are to take care of creation, hence they are co-workers with God/continue with creation.
- Both are to die.
- They are to obey and worship God and have a personal relationship with God.

Explain the relationship between the environment and human beings in Genesis creation stories

- They were both created by God.
- Both have the same destiny.
- Their relationship is interdependent.
- Man has a role to conserve the environment.
- The environment has a role to provide for the needs of man.
- Man has the duty to protect the environment.
- The environment provides a home for man.

TRADITIONAL AFRICAN VIEW OF CREATION

- Each African community believes that God is the creator.
- Each community has different names given to God to explain His creation work e.g. creator, moulder, maker of heavens e.t.c.
- Africans believe the universe and everything in it is created and ordered by God.
- God created and placed people in different areas like plains, lakeshores and plateaus.
- God's creation activity still goes on in the universe as e.g. through new births.

Write down the teachings about God from the Traditional African myths of creation.

- God is self-existent.
- He is the sole creator.

- He is all-powerful or omnipotent.
- He is good and gives everything that is good to man.
- He demands obedience from human beings.
- He is a protector.
- He is eternal and ever-living/immortal.
- He punishes evil doers hence He is a just God.
- God is a spirit and is therefore not represented by images or idols.
- He is the provider of all the needs of human beings.
- He is supreme.

State the similarities between the Biblical and traditional African myths about the origin of man and the universe.
- In both God is the sole creator.
- In both God is eternal and immortal.
- In both, death occurs as a punishment to sin or evil.
- In both God is all powerful.
- In both God creates from nothing.
- In both God provides for and sustains the creation.
- In both God created man and woman for procreation.
- In both God is a source of goodness.

THE BIBLICAL TEACHING ON THE ORIGIN OF SIN AND ITS CONSEQUENCES (Gen. 3: 4; 6 – 9; 11)

Explain the causes of the origin of sin as recorded in Genesis 3
- Man disobeyed God's command not to eat from the tree of knowledge of good and evil.
- Humankind yielded to the temptations of Satan like Eve did.
- Lack of trust in God's good intentions.
- Due to weak faith, Adam and Eve were easily misled by Satan.
- Lust for material gain, pleasure and power.
- It was due to human weakness that Adam accepted the offer of the fruit from his wife Eve without resisting.
- It was a rebellion against God.
- Due to greed and desire to be like God, humankind fell into sin.

List the consequences of Adam and Eve's disobedience to God.
- Adam and Eve were expelled from the Garden of Eden.
- The ground was cursed.
- Woman would feel pain during delivery.
- Woman became subordinate to man.
- Man would sweat and toil to earn a living.
- There would be enmity between human beings and snake.
- Death penalty was passed on humankind.
- Humankind was alienated from God.

- Human beings became prone to sin.
- The serpent was cursed.
- Sin strained the relationship between man and woman.

What is the origin of sin according to Genesis 3; 4: 6 – 9; 11?

- Disobedience to the will of God.
- Temptation by Satan.
- Desire for worldly glory/materialism
- Human weakness, violence, drunkenness
- Jealousy, rivalry e.g. Cain
- Lust.
- Anger e.g. Cain
- Lack of self-control, uncontrolled desires
- Pride e.g. the building of Tower of Barbell.
- Free will.

How did the temptation by Satan lead to the fall of humankind?

- It made man want something which was not his, that is, to be like God/know good and evil.
- They doubted the nature of God as a result … the serpent portrays God as a liar by assuring Adam and Eve that they cannot die.
- Man mistrusted God and lost their relationship.
- They were cheated, hence, disobeyed God by eating the forbidden fruit in disregard to God's warning.
- Temptation made man develop greed for knowledge and power that belongs to God alone.
- As a result of temptation man rebelled against God after listening to the serpent's advice.

Give reasons why it is important for Christians to obey God.

- Obedience brings blessings.
- To avoid God's punishment.
- God expects them to do so.
- It is a command from God.
- It makes them to live in harmony with others.
- God alone is to be obeyed and worshiped.
- To maintain a good relationship with God.

GOD'S PLAN OF SALVATION (Genesis 3: 15)
Give the Biblical evidence that God had a plan for the salvation of human kind.

- He looked for Adam and Eve in the Garden of Eden.
- He provided them with a means to find food after throwing them out of the garden.
- God made Adam and Eve clothes from skin and clothed them.

- God cursed Satan who tempted Eve and gave human kind power over snake.
- God chose Abraham and made him the father of faith.
- God chose prophets to bring people back to the covenant way of life.
- God sent Jesus to bring salvation to free humanity from the bondage of sin.
- He saved Noah and the family during the flood.
- He chose Israel as a Holy Nation through whom other Nations would receive God's salvation.
- He promised a new covenant through prophet Jeremiah.
- He sent very many prophets to his people.

Explain the steps that God took to heal the broken relationships with mankind after the fall of man

- He looked for Adam and Eve to find out where they were.
- He made garments of skin for Adam and Eve then clothed them.
- He gave man power over the serpent.
- He provided Adam and Eve means to find food after chasing them out of the Garden of Eden.
- God called Abraham and made a covenant with him.
- God chose Israel as a holy nation and gave them Ten Commandments to guide them.
- God sent prophets to guide and correct his people.
- God provided a New Covenant with mankind through prophet Jeremiah.
- God sent a Messiah who died on the cross for the sins of mankind.
- God sent the Holy Spirit to guide people in the church.

TRADITIONAL AFRICAN CONCEPT OF EVIL

Explain the African understanding of evil

- Africans believe God did not create evil.
- When the ancestors are offended by the living they can cause evil.
- Some communities attribute evil to evil spirits.
- They also believe that magicians cause evil.
- Sin results due to lack of respect to the elders.
- It is a result of breaking of oaths.
- It results from breaking of taboos.

Mention the causes of evil in Traditional African Society

- It is caused by evil spirits.
- Disobedience to elders, parents and older relatives leading to curses.
- Breaking of oaths or wills.
- Failure to honour rituals, taboos, customs, norms and ancestors.
- It is caused by evils such as murder, incest and rape.
- Killing of sacred animals
- It is caused by magic, sorcery or witch craft
- It is acquired or inherited from parents.

What are the consequences of breaking taboos in traditional African communities?

- Barrenness.
- Drought.
- Wars
- Epidemics.
- Poverty
- Illness
- Physical or mental handicap in children
- Disasters e.g. earthquakes, floods
- Unstable families
- Rebellious children.

SIMILARITIES AND DIFFERENCES BETWEEN THE TRADITIONAL AFRICAN CONCEPT OF EVIL AND THE BIBLICAL CONCEPT OF SIN

SIMILARITIES

- In both cases God did not create evil.
- In both cases evil is caused by external forces.
- In both cases evil originated from the disobedience of human beings.
- In both cases sin and evil lead to punishment of the offender.
- In both cases it leads to suffering and hardship.
- In both cases evil destroys the relationship between God and human beings.
- In both cases God is the custodian of morality, law and order, which are tools against evil.
- In both cases evil destroys the relationship between human beings.
- In both cases it leads to death.

DIFFERENCES

Explain the differences between African concept of evil and biblical concept of sin

- Biblically there is eternal punishment for wrong doers while in African concept punishment is immediate in the physical world.
- Africans believe in collective punishment unlike in the bible that talks about individual punishment.
- Traditionally, suffering is a result of doing evil while biblically it is not always true.
- Traditionally, African religion does not have an opportunity of a saviour which is provided for in the Bible through Jesus Christ.
- Biblically sinners go to hell and those who repent their sins go to heaven while traditionally the dead join the spirits, there is no heaven no hell.
- Biblically sin originated from the heart while in traditional African society external forces are believed to cause evil.

Topic 4: FAITH AND GOD'S PROMISES: ABRAHAM

BACKGROUND TO THE CALL OF ABRAHAM (GENESIS 11: 24-32; 12:1-9)

- Abraham lived in the city of Ur near River Euphrates.
- His father's name was Terah, a Semite.
- They were semi-nomadic people.
- His father was a moon worshipper.
- Initially, he was called Abram which was later changed to Abraham and his wife was Sarai, later changed to Sarah.
- He had two brothers, Haran and Nahor. Haran had a son called Lot, Abraham's nephew.
- Terah left Ur for Canaan with his son Abraham, Sarah, Abraham's wife and his grandson Lot.
- They settled in Haran where Terah eventually died.

THE CALL OF ABRAHAM

- While living in Haran, God called Abraham at the age of 75, after the death of his father.
- Abraham was told to leave his native land, his relatives and father's home and go to a land that God would show him.
- God promised Abraham many things such as descendants, blessings and fame.
- Abraham left Haran together with his wife Sarah, nephew Lot and servants together with his livestock.
- He arrived in Canaan and settled at Shechem.
- God appeared to him at Shechem and Abraham built an altar for God at Shechem.
- He later moved to Bethel where he built another altar for God. He built another altar at Negeb.

Give reasons why Abraham was called by God.

- God wanted to reveal himself to the Israelites.
- To begin God's plan of salvation.
- It was the new beginning of rescuing human beings from sin.
- It was in order to teach the meaning of faith in God.
- So as to make him the father and founder of God's chosen people.
- God intended to teach us that he is merciful and forgiving.
- He wanted to give Abraham the land of Canaan.
- He wanted to separate Abraham from moon worshippers.
- In order to begin the worship of one God.

What lessons can Christians from the call of Abraham?

- Christians learn that God communicates to people like He spoke to Abraham.
- Christians learn that God takes the initiative to restore the broken relationship with humankind.

- Faith is better expressed in actions, like Abraham left his land to go to an unknown land.
- Christians learn that God expects obedience from man.
- Christians learn that God works through men of faith.
- Christians learn that God calls anyone despite his/her background.
- Christians learn that God rewards those who obey him.

In what ways does God speaks to us today?
- Through dreams.
- Through visions.
- Through nature.
- Through historical events.
- Through one's conscience.
- Through the Holy Spirit.
- Through the Bible.
- Through Jesus Christ.

DEFINITION OF THE TERM FAITH IN GOD (HEBREWS 11: 1-6)
- Faith is the complete trust or confidence in somebody or something.
- It is the firm belief without necessarily having logical proof.
- Biblically, faith is based on complete trust, belief and obedience to God, the creator.

A) ABRAHAM'S ACTS OF FAITH IN GOD (GENESIS 12:1 -9; 15: 1-6; 17:23-24; 21: 1-7; 22: 1-19)
Give evidence that Abraham had faith in God
- Abraham believed in God whom he never knew.
- He chose to worship an unknown God amidst polytheists.
- He readily accepted and went to an unknown land when God called him.
- He accepted to make a covenant with God without questioning.
- He was ready to sacrifice his only son God at Mt. Moriah.
- He believed in God's promise of a son despite his old age and that of his wife Sarah.
- He accepted to change his name from Abram to Abraham and his wife's from Sarai and Sarah.
- He accepted to be circumcised in old age as a sign of the covenant with God.
- He built altars in many places to worship God e.g. at Bethel, Shechem and Negeb.
- He sacrificed animals and birds to God to God in the covenant making.

B) THE IMPORTANCE OF FAITH IN CHRISTIAN LIFE TODAY
What is the importance of faith to Christian's life today?
- Through faith a Christian becomes acceptable to God.
- It is through faith that God's promises are fulfilled to Christians.
- Faith makes Christians' hope for the kingdom of God become a reality.
- For Christians, faith in Jesus is the foundation of their faith.
- Christians should be prepared to face difficult situations as a test of their faith.

- Through faith Christians are spiritual descendants of Abraham as long as they remain obedient and faithful to God, through Jesus Christ.
- Faith gives Christians the courage to submit their lives to God totally and even take risks for the sake of their belief in God.
- Faith enables Christians to persevere in prayer.
- Faith makes Christians part of the kingdom of God.

THE MOUNT MORIAH EXPERIENCE

- God told Abraham to take his son, Isaac, to Mt. Moriah and offer him as a burnt sacrifice.
- Abraham took his son, two of his servants and firewood and went to the place where God told him.
- When Abraham came near the mountain, he told the servants to remain behind, as he went with Isaac.
- Isaac carried the wood and he took fire in his hands and a knife and they went together.
- Isaac asked him where the lamb for the sacrifice was and Abraham answered that the Lord would provide.
- When they came to a place where God had told him, he made an altar, arranged wood in order and bound Isaac and laid him on the altar upon the wood.
- When Abraham was about to slay his son, an angel of the Lord called him and told him not to lay his hand on Isaac.
- Abraham lifted his eyes and saw a ram behind him.
- He took the ram and offered it as a burnt offering.
- He called the place "the Lord will provide".
- God promised to bless Abraham because of this.
- He went back home with his servants and Isaac.

From the Mt. Moriah experience what lessons did Abraham learn about God?

- God did not want a human sacrifice.
- God sometimes tests man.
- God created human life and wants to preserve it for it is precious.
- God cannot be easily understood by man.
- God understands human feelings.
- God cannot be likened to gods who are greedy for human sacrifice.
- God is loving and merciful.
- God is the provider because he provided a lamb for a sacrifice.

Give the reasons why some Christians have lost faith in God today

- Their prayers are not answered.
- Some Christians suffer and die and yet non-Christians prosper and lead good lives.
- There is prolonged poverty, starvation, famine and drought
- Wrangling in Church leadership
- Bad examples by Church leaders due to corruption and sexual immorality.

- Some leaders fail to condemn evils in society hence compromising abuse of justice by leaders.

How do Christians show their trust in God today?
- Reading the Bible.
- Praying to Him and fasting.
- Practicing sacraments e.g. baptism.
- Calling upon His name when in danger.
- Observing the Sabbath
- Helping the needy, sharing with the poor and carrying out charitable works.
- Attending church services, meetings, workshops and fellowships.
- Observing religious ceremonies and rituals.
- Giving guidance to others.
- Caring for the environment.
- Condemning evils and injustices in society.
- Keeping God's laws or obeying Gods commandments.
- By giving offerings and tithes to God.
- Evangelizing, preaching and witnessing Christ.
- Through worshipping Him.

GOD'S PROMISES TO ABRAHAM AND THEIR RELEVANCE TO CHRISTIANS TODAY (GENESIS 12: 2-3; 15:1-21; 17:1-8; 17:15-18)

List the promises that God gave to Abraham

- God would give him a land to dwell in.
- He would make Abraham's name great.
- He would establish an everlasting covenant with Abraham and his descendants and that He shall be their God.
- He promised to protect Abraham.
- God promised to give him and his wife Sarah a son of their own.
- He promised to make Abraham's descendants a great nation.
- Abraham's descendants would be enslaved for 400 years in a foreign land but God would free them and deliver them back to their land with great possessions.
- He would make Abraham's descendants kings.
- God promised to bless Abraham.
- He would bless those who blessed Abraham.
- He promised to curse those who cursed Abraham.
- He promised to bless the people through Abraham.
- He promised to let Abraham live for long and die in peace.

Explain the ways in which God fulfilled the promises he made to Abraham

- God gave him and his descendants the land of Canaan as he had promised.
- Through Abraham there has risen a great nation, Israel.
- God promised Abraham many descendants which is fulfilled in the Christians who look to Abraham as the father of faith.
- Abraham was promised a son and he bore Isaac.
- God promised to deliver Abraham's descendants from slavery after 400 years. Moses led the Israelites out of Egypt back to Canaan.
- God promised to make an everlasting covenant with Abraham, which is fulfilled in Jesus' death and resurrection.
- Abraham died in peace at old age as God had promised.
- God promised to bless the people through Abraham, which is fulfilled in Jesus Christ the saviour of mankind.

What is the relevance of God's promises to Abraham to Christians today?

- The promise that God would protect Abraham shows that God continues to protect Christians in all circumstances.
- God values a personal relationship with humankind.
- The promises are a continuation of God's plan of salvation.
- Through these promises God reveals his intention to redeem the broken relationship between him and man.
- Christians acknowledge Abraham as the source of blessings to all mankind.
- The promise of the land of Canaan is fulfilled to Christians through the promise of an eternal kingdom.

- Abraham's name has remained great as the father of faith.

MEANING OF THE TERM COVENANT

- A covenant is a solemn agreement between two people or groups of people.
- It's sometimes referred to as a 'pact' or 'treaty'.
- The term covenant can also be defined as an agreement between two or more people or parties that were separated before.

There are two types of covenants:

i. Conditional covenant – it involves two equal parties e.g. between two people or between two countries.
ii. Unconditional covenant – it involves two unequal parties where one is greater e.g. between God and man or between citizens and the President or King.

State the elements or characteristics of a covenant

- A covenant involves two or more parties.
- There must be a binding agreement in the covenant.
- Promises or oaths must be made.
- It must have a physical sign or symbol.
- It must have witnesses.
- There must be a ceremony to accompany the covenant.
- The covenant must be sealed.
- There are serious consequences should the covenant be broken.

GOD'S COVENANT WITH ABRAHAM AND ITS IMPORTANCE (GEN 15: 1 – 19)

Describe the covenant between Abraham and God (Gen 15:1-17)

- Abraham was disturbed because he did not have an heir.
- He asked God to give him an assurance that his own son will be his heir.
- God responded showing him the stars in the night and the sand on the ground. He told him that the two represent the number of his descendants.
- Abraham wanted further assurance that God will fulfil His promise.
- Abraham was told to bring sacrificial animals: a 3 year-old heifer, a 3 year-old she goat, a 3 year-old ram, a turtle dove and a young pigeon.
- He cut the animals into halves and arranged them opposite each other in rows but he did not cut the birds.
- He drove away the birds of prey that came to the carcasses.
- At sunset, Abraham fell into deep sleep and thick darkness came over him.
- A smoking firepot with flaming torch appeared and passed between the pieces of meat.
- Abraham was promised that his descendants would be given the land of Canaan from the boarders of Egypt to River Euphrates.

Name five animals used in God's covenant with Abraham

- A heifer, 3 years old

- A she-goat, 3 years old.
- A ram, 3 years old.
- A turtle dove
- A young pigeon.

Mention the signs used in the Abrahamic covenant
- Countless stars in the sky at night.
- Change of names e.g. from Abram to Abraham.
- Smoking firepot.
- Flaming torch.
- Circumcision.

COVENANTS IN MODERN LIFE AND THEIR IMPORTANCE
Give examples of modern day covenants
- Marriage
- Baptism
- Oath of loyalty e.g. by the President, Members of Parliament
- Contracts of employment
- Circumcision.
- Ordination.
- Contracts singed when buying land.
- Agreements signed by students when being admitted in schools.

Explain the importance of Modern day covenants.
- Modern day covenants promote peace.
- They help Christians to be organized as order is promoted.
- Covenants such as trade agreements help countries to develop economically.
- Unity between people is promoted for instance through reconciliation.
- Covenants enable people to develop trust in relationships.
- They promote understanding in the society.
- People are enlightened of their rights.
- Religious covenants encourage people to have the right relationship with God.
- Commitment to Christian principles enables people to face and overcome emerging daily challenges that are part of life.
- Secular covenants remind and encourage office bearers to serve the nation in the spirit of total loyalty.

Give reasons why Christians should keep covenant agreements
- To imitate God who kept his covenant with Abraham.
- Life depends on keeping covenants.
- In order to establish God's relationship with others in society.
- So that one can be trusted.
- It ensures peace and stability in society.

- It ensures justice is done in society.
- It ensures unity of purpose by those partaking in it.
- It is a sign of seriousness in what one is doing.
- It ensures commitment to Christian principles so that they can face and overcome daily challenges.

CIRCUMCISION

- God promised to make an everlasting covenant with Abraham and his descendants.
- Abraham was expected to obey and do what was right and pleasing to God.
- As a sign of obedience to the Lord, God commanded Abraham to circumcise all males of eight days old, including slaves born in their homes and those brought from foreigners. Those who failed would be considered as outcasts.
- As part of the covenant the name "Abram" was changed to Abraham while Sarai's name was changed to "Sarah".
- Abraham was circumcised at the age of 99.
- On the same day his son Ishmael was also circumcised.
- From that day, all Jewish children were to be circumcised on the eighth day.
- Circumcision became a mark of identity for all true Jews, the chosen people of God in the covenant.

A) THE IMPORTANCE OF THE CIRCUMCISION TO ABRAHAM AND HIS DESCENDANTS (GENESIS 17: 1 – 16).

- It was an outward sign of inner faith in God.
- It was a physical sign that Abraham and his descendants had entered into a covenant with God.
- Circumcision was a mark of identity for the Jews as a people of God.
- It confirmed Abraham's faith and obedience to God.
- It is a continuous reminder of God's covenant with Israel.
- It served as an assurance of God's blessings.
- It was a sign that the Israelites were a chosen people of God.
- It was a sign of Israelites' unity in God.
- It showed the Israelites' acceptance of Yahweh as the true God and their willingness to obey him.

B) COMPARE THE JEWISH AND AFRICAN PRACTICES OF CIRCUMCISION.
SIMILARITIES
Explain the similarities between the African traditional circumcision and the Jewish circumcision

- In both cases circumcision has a religious significance.
- In both cases there is shading of blood.
- In both cases it is performed by religious specialists.
- In both cases circumcision is performed in sacred places.
- In both cases it is a mark of identity.

- In both cases it gives one a new status.

DIFFERENCES

Explain the differences between Jewish and traditional African practices of circumcision.

- Jewish circumcision is performed on an eight day old baby while Africans circumcise an adolescent.
- Initiates acquire new status and responsibilities in African society but not in Jewish, where the initiate is still a small child.
- Only males are circumcised among Jews but some African societies circumcise both male and female.
- African circumcision tests courage and bravery while the Jewish practice tests faith and commitment to God.
- Circumcision for the Jews is in obedience to God's command while in African societies it is in obedience to the customary laws.
- There's seclusion of initiates in the traditional African practice of circumcision but not in Jewish community.

How a Christian facing difficulties can be encouraged from the life of Abraham.

- Christians should learn not to doubt God but always remember that God is there and he fulfils his promises.
- They should be prepared to face very difficult situations.
- They should learn to be patient and wait upon God's promises.
- They should continue having faith in God even in tough or difficult circumstances of life.
- They should be alert and listen to what God is saying.
- They should be ready to give up everything and work for God as proof of their faith.
- They should respond to God through complete obedience.
- They should have faith in Jesus which gives power to overcome all temptations.

Topic 5: SINAI COVENANT: MOSES

BACKGROUND TO THE CALL OF MOSES (Genesis 37: 1 – 36, 50: 1 – 26)

- Moses was born at a time when the Pharaoh in Egypt had issued an order to have all Israelite male children killed by being drowned in River Nile.
- His mother hid him for three months.
- When she could no longer hide him, she made a waterproof basket, laid the child inside and placed it among the reeds at the bank of River Nile.
- At River Nile, Moses was rescued and adopted by the Pharaoh's daughter.
- He grew up at the Pharaoh's palace where he was given the best education and training of the time.
- One day, Moses killed an Egyptian as he was defending an Israelite, as a sign of identifying himself with his people, the Israelites.
- When he learned that the Pharaoh had discovered what he had done, he ran to the wilderness of Midian to escape punishment.
- In Midian he lived with a priest, Jethro, as a shepherd and married his daughter, Zipporah.

Outline the ways in which Moses was prepared by God to be the future leader of the Israelites

- He was rescued by the Pharaoh's daughter as a baby who made him discover that his protection is with God.
- He grew up in Pharaoh's palace where he learnt the art of leadership and administration.
- He was nursed by his own mother and caused him to know his identity as an Israelite.
- His flight from Egypt through the desert taught him how to cope with hardship.
- Through his escape to Midian, he learnt the geographical routes in the desert.
- His life as a shepherd taught him the virtue of patience with the stubborn Israelites.
- His marriage to Zipporah and having children made him a responsible person and it prepared him to lead the wider Israelite family.
- At the burning bush he got a personal experience with God and learnt to trust in Him.
- He got spiritual training at Jethro's house from Jethro the priest.
- His knowledge of being a Hebrew helped him to learn his people are suffering which made him concerned about their delivery from Egypt.

What was the role of Moses in the history of the Israelites?

- He received God's call with a mission to liberate the Israelites.
- He performed extra-ordinary miracles for the purpose of overpowering Pharaoh to release to Israelites.
- He led the Israelites throughout the wilderness during the Exodus.
- He mediated between God and the Israelites who complained and asked him for provisions.

- He led the Israelites into making the Sinai covenant with God.
- He was given 10 commandments by God to guide the Israelites to live according to the covenant.
- He sought God's providence for Israelites e.g. manna and water
- He made the Israelites renew the covenant with God.
- He protected Israelites against hostile desert tribes e.g. the Amalekites.
- He led them during the crossing of the Red sea.

THE CALL OF MOSES (EXODUS 3: 1 – 22)

Describe the call of Moses.

- Moses was in the wilderness tending to the flock of his father-in-law, Jethro.
- He saw a burning bush that was not being consumed at the foot of Mt. Sinai.
- He moved closer to see why the bush was burning but not being consumed.
- God called him and commanded him to remove his shoes because the ground on which he was standing was holy.
- God identified himself as the God of Abraham, Isaac and Jacob.
- God told Moses that he had heard the cry of his people in Egypt and he had chosen him to go and rescue them.
- Moses inquired the name of the God sending him and he was told it is "I AM WHO I AM".
- Moses was reluctant to go back to Egypt but he was given Aaron as his spokesperson and was enabled to perform signs.
- He finally accepted and went to Egypt to carry out the task.

How did Moses demonstrate his obedience to the God of Israel?

- When asked to remove his sandals during his call, he obeyed.
- When asked to throw down his rod, to pick it up, to put his hand in his pocket, and remove it, he obeyed.
- He accepted to carry out God's instructions in Egypt which led to the ten plagues that faced the Egyptians.
- He struck the waters of the Red Sea with his rod and a way was provided for the Israelites.
- In the provision of food and water for the Israelites as they journeyed through the wilderness, Moses obeyed God's instructions.
- He prepared the Israelites to meet with God as instructed at Mt. Sinai.

State five lessons Moses learnt about God from his call.

- Yahweh is God of history.
- God fulfils his promises.
- God is loving and caring.
- God is holy.
- God is beyond human understanding (transcendent).

- God chooses whomever he wills to carry out his plans.
- God expects total obedience and faith.
- God is all-knowing/omniscient.
- God uses events to reveal himself.
- God punishes the enemies of his people.

THE TEN PLAGUES (EXODUS 7: 14 – 11: 1– 10)

List the plagues that God brought to Egypt before the Israelites could be released.

- **Turning water into blood** – Moses was commanded by God to tell Aaron to strike the waters of the Nile with his rod and the water turned into blood. It meant that all the source of life was contaminated, since Egyptians depend on R. Nile as a source of water.
- **The plague of frogs** – the Lord commanded Moses to tell Aaron to stretch his hand over the streams, canals and ponds and there were frogs all over the land of Egypt.
- **The plague of gnats** – the gnats (small two-winged biting flies) covered the land, people and animals.
- **Plague of flies** – Flies came to the land of Egypt in swarms and invaded Pharaoh's palace, and the houses of his officials while there were no flies I the houses of Israelites.
- **Plague of death of livestock** – God sent a plague that killed all the Egyptian animals, however, the animals of the Israelites were not affected.
- **Plague of boils** – Moses and Aaron were told by God to cast ashes into the air and this act produced sores and open wounds on the Egyptians and their animals.
- **Plague of hail** – A severe hailstorm came upon Egypt which destroyed everything that was left in the open and all people who had not taken shelter were killed. All trees and plants were destroyed.
- **Plague of locusts** – Locusts came upon their land.
- **Plague of darkness** – the Lord sent darkness over the whole land of Egypt. No one could see anything or anyone for three days.
- **Death of Egyptian first born sons** – the first born sons of the Egyptians and those of their animals were killed starting with the Pharaoh's son to the son of the slave in Egypt.

What attributes of God do Christians learn from the ten plagues?

- He is a God of justice.
- God punishes sin/evil or he is a moral God.
- He is a God who defends the weak.
- God is tolerant and gives time for the people to repent
- He is a loving and caring God
- God is Almighty.
- God is forgiving.
- God is determined to fulfil his plans no matter how difficult the task seems.
- God expects total obedience to his commands.
- God is faithful and keeps his promises.
- God is merciful and he sees the suffering of his people.

THE PASSOVER (EXODUS 12:1-31)

- The tenth plague involved the killing of the first born sons of the Egyptians and those of their animals.
- God instructed Moses to make preparations in readiness for the day of the tenth plague.
- Moses called all the elders of Israel and gave them the following instructions:

Outline the preparations that Moses asked the Israelites to make in readiness for the Exodus.

i. Each man had to choose for his family a one-year old lamb or goat, without blemish. The animal being young signified the innocence of the sacrifice, while an animal without blemish signified purity of the sacrifice.

ii. The chosen animal was to be killed and its blood smeared on the doorposts of the Israelites' houses. This was to distinguish the Israelites' houses from those of the Egyptians so that the angel of death would spare them when he killed the first-born sons of the Egyptians.

iii. The animal was roasted whole, with its legs and inner parts. This signified that the Israelites were in a hurry since roasting was the quickest method of cooking.

iv. The meat was eaten that night with unleavened bread and bitter herbs since there was no time to ferment the dough. Bitter herbs signified the bitter experience of slavery in Egypt.

v. They were to eat the meal while readily dressed up and after packing their luggage to signify that they were in a hurry.

vi. The Israelite women were to ask for jewellery, silver and clothing from the Egyptian women. These items acted as compensation for the free labour that the Israelites had given in Egypt.

vii. All the people were to remain indoors until morning in order to be protected from the angel of death.

viii. The Passover was to be celebrated annually and its significance taught to the coming generations.

- On the night of the Passover, the angel of death passed over the Israelites' houses, killing first-born sons of the Egyptians and spared the Israelites.
- Pharaoh's son was also killed.
- This led to the wailing and mourning all over Egypt.
- This plague, of the killing of the first-born sons of the Egyptians and those of their animals made the Pharaoh to release the Israelites.
- He called Moses and Aaron and commanded them to take the Israelites out of Egypt.
- On that night, the Israelites left Egypt for the wilderness led by Moses towards Mt. Sinai.
- The journey from Egypt to the wilderness by the Israelites is what is called the 'Exodus' which means 'going out'.

THE EXODUS
A) THE CROSSING OF THE RED SEA (EXODUS 14: 5 – 31)
- Moses led the Israelites out of Egypt towards Mt. Sinai.
- God led them during the day in a pillar of cloud and during the night in a pillar of fire.
- On realizing this, the pharaoh took chariots, horsemen and soldiers and pursued the Israelites hoping to bring them back because he did not want to lose the slave labour.
- When Pharaoh's army came close to the Israelites, they were afraid and angry at Moses and started complaining to Moses.
- God ordered Moses to stretch out his hand over the Red Sea that was ahead of them.
- A strong wind separated the water in the Red Sea and the Israelites crossed it on dry ground.
- The water began to flow back while the Egyptian soldiers were crossing the sea and it filled their path so they could not turn back.
- God told Moses to hold out his hand over the sea and the water flowed over the Egyptians until all of them died.

B) PROVISION OF WATER (EXODUS 15: 22 – 29; 17: 1 – 6)
- The Israelites went through the desert towards Mt. Sinai and the people were thirsty.
- The Israelites wondered why Moses had brought them in the wilderness to suffer.
- Moses sought God's guidance.
- At Marah, the bitter waters were turned sweet after God told Moses to throw a tree into the water.
- At Rephidim, God told Moses to strike a rock with his rod and water flowed from it.

C) PROVISION OF MANNA AND QUAILS (EXODUS: 16: 1 – 35)
- The Israelites lacked food while in the wilderness.
- They complained and murmured to Moses.
- God provided manna and each morning the people gathered a whole day's portion and quails which came in large flocks.

D) DEFEAT OF THE AMALEKITES (EXODUS 17: 8 – 16)
- The Israelites were attacked by a hostile desert tribe called Amalekites.
- Moses was too old to fight, so he asked Joshua, Son of Nun, to lead the people to battle.
- Moses stood on a hill with his hands held out to God in prayer.
- Whenever the Israelites saw his hands held up, they knew God was in control, but whenever Moses got tired and put his hands down, they lost hope and the Amalekites began to win.
- Aaron and Hur held up Moses' hands and eventually the Israelites won.

Show how God cared for the Israelites during the Exodus liberated Israelites from slavery in Egypt
- He helped the Israelites to cross the Red sea.

- He made the Egyptian soldiers to perish in Red sea.
- Provided water, manna and quails to satisfy their needs.
- Helped the Israelites to defeat the hostile desert tribes e.g. Amalekites.
- Led Israel by a pillar of fire at night and pillar of cloud during day time.
- He gave Israelites Ten Commandments to guide them on how to relate among themselves and with God.
- He accepted to renew the covenant with Israel after breaking it and forgave Israel after they worshipped the golden calf.
- He dwelt among the Israelites through the Ark of the Covenant.
- He provided leaders e.g. Moses and Joshua.

THE MAKING OF THE SINAI COVENANT (EXODUS 19; 24: 1 – 8)

Preparation for the covenant

- God called Moses to the mountain and asked him if the Israelites were willing to obey Him.
- God promised to make them his people, a kingdom of priests, and a holy nation if they accepted to obey him.
- Moses came down the mountain and told the Israelites what the Lord had said.
- The Israelites promised to do what the Lord had spoken.
- God promised to meet the Israelites on the third day.
- They prepared to meet God by abstaining from sex, purifying themselves, washing their clothes and marking boundaries on the mountain
- On the third day, God appeared to them in form of thunder, lightning, earthquake, trumpet, thick cloud, fire and smoke and the people were frightened.
- Moses went up the mountain and was given the Ten Commandments.
- He came back from the mountain and told the people about the laws which were to guide them as a covenant people.
- All the people answered in one voice that they will do all the words that the Lord had spoken.

The sealing of the covenant

Describe the ceremony prepared during the sealing of the covenant between God and the Israelites at Mt. Sinai Genesis 24: 1 – 8

- Moses prepared a special ceremony to seal covenant.
- He built an altar at the foot of Mt. Sinai.
- Young men sacrificed oxen as fellowship offering.
- Moses took half of the blood of the animals and put it in basin.
- Half of the blood was sprinkled on to the altar, a place of meeting with God.
- Moses then read the book of the covenant to the Israelites.
- Moses took the blood in the basin and sprinkled it on the people.
- Moses then told the people that the blood had sealed the covenant.

In which ways did God manifest Himself when he came to meet the Israelites?

- Pillar of cloud/thick cloud
- Earthquakes
- Trumpet blast
- Thunder
- Lightning
- Pillar of fire during the night
- Smoke /fire

THE BREAKING OF THE SINAI COVENANT (EXODUS 32: 1 – 35)

Describe the breaking of the covenant by the Israelites

- Moses went up the mountain to receive the written Ten Commandments from God, leaving Aaron in charge of the people.
- When Moses delayed coming back, the Israelites became impatient and restless.
- The asked Aaron to make them a god that would lead them for they did not know what had happened to Moses.
- Aaron asked them for jewellery, smelted it and moulded a golden bull calf for them to worship.
- They also built an altar for the god.
- They offered burnt and peace offerings to it and indulged themselves in eating, drinking and sex, hence sinning before God.
- God revealed to Moses that the Israelites had broken the covenant.
- He threatened to destroy them but after Moses interceded for them, God changed his mind.
- As Moses came down the mountain, he found Israelites singing and dancing around the golden bull calf.
- He got annoyed and he threw down the stone tablets on which the Ten Commandments were written.
- Moses took the golden calf, burnt it into powder, mixed it with water and made the Israelites drink.
- He called those who had not sinned and ordered them to take their swords and kill those who had sinned.

Outline reasons why Israelites broke their covenant with God at Mt. Sinai

- Moses delayed on the mountain when he went to meet God, he stayed for forty days.
- Israelites thought Moses was dead.
- They were restless and impatient.
- They thought God had abandoned them at the foot of the mountain.
- The Israelites desired to go back to the old superstitious life of Egypt.
- They wanted a visible god.

What is the significance of Moses throwing down the stone tablets?
- Israel had disobeyed God.
- Israel had broken their covenant with God.
- God had also in turn broken his covenant with God.
- God will no longer protect them until they repent and turn back to him.
- God will destroy those who will not repent.

Give the results of the breaking of the covenant
- Moses smashed the stone tablets on which the Ten Commandments were written.
- Moses melted the golden calf into powder and forced the people to drink it.
- Moses ordered for the killing of the people who had participated in the worship of the calf.
- Those who repented were forgiven.
- Moses made other stone tablets and God re-wrote the Ten Commandments.

Teachings about God during the breaking of the Sinai covenant
- God is a jealous God since He does allow the worship of other gods.
- He is a just God for he punishes sin.
- He is merciful since He forgave the Israelites their after they worshipped idols.
- He is almighty, His power exceeds all other powers.
- He is holy and hates sin.
- He is faithful to his promises.
- He is the only one to be worshipped.
- He is slow to anger.

Outline the ways in which errant members are rehabilitated in churches today
- Through guidance and counselling.
- Preaching forgiveness to them.
- Denying them some privileges e.g. Pastors are demoted/sacraments/Holy communion.
- Visiting them.
- Praying for them/interceding for them.
- Assisting those who are materially weak/poor.

How do modern Christians demonstrate obedience to God in their lives?
- Accepting the call of God to serve him in any capacity.
- They face opposition in their work without giving up.
- Respecting the teachings of God to avoid judgment and punishment.
- Being bold enough to proclaim God's message despite the consequences/evangelization.
- They don't work for pay.
- They lead holy and righteous lives in accordance to the laws of God.
- They are ready to serve God even if they are not religious people.
- Using their wealth to serve God and to help the needy/orphans/widows.

THE RENEWAL OF THE SINAI COVENANT (EXODUS 34: 1 – 35)

- The renewal of the covenant came after Moses pleaded with God not to destroy the Israelites after they broke the covenant.
- God spared the Israelites.
- He commanded Moses to cut two stone tablets and go up the mountain.
- He them told Moses that he would make a covenant with Israelites again.
- God gave the Israelites conditions to fulfil with the renewal of the covenant.
- He promised to protect and preserve the Israelites, bless them and make them prosperous.
- He asked Moses to write the commandments on the new stone tablets which showed that the covenant between God and Israelites was now renewed.

Outline the conditions given to the Israelites during the renewal of the Sinai Covenant

- To obey what God commands them.
- Not to make any treaty with the people of the land where they were going.
- Not to worship any idol/other gods.
- To keep the feast of the unleavened bread.
- To rest on the seventh day.
- Not to intermarry with foreigners.
- Not to make cast idols.
- To offer to God the first fruits of their crops.
- To dedicate their first born male children and first born male of their domestic animals to God.
- To destroy the places of worship for idols.

THE TEN COMMANDMENTS (EXODUS 20: 1 – 17)

Outline the commandments given to the Israelites.

- You shall have no other gods before me.
- You shall not make for yourself a graven image.
- You shall not take the name of the Lord your God in vain.
- Remember the Sabbath and keep it holy.
- Honour your father and mother for your days may be long.
- You shall not kill.
- You shall not commit adultery.
- You shall not steal.
- You shall not bear false witness against your neighbour.
- You shall not covet your neighbour's property or wife.

Explain the moral teachings contained in the Ten Commandments

- They stress on respect for parents and elders.
- They stress that people should respect God's name and not use it in vain.
- They stress on love for God and other people in the society.
- They tell us to respect other people's property and not to steal.

- They want us to speak the truth all the time.
- They want us to be faithful to our marriage partners.
- They want us to be contented with what God has given us and not covet.
- They direct us to work hard for six days then rest on the seventh day.
- They direct us to respect and preserve human life.
- They direct us to worship only one true God and not to be involved in devil worship.

Reasons why some children disobey the commandment "Obey your parents"

- Affluence/ riches i.e. when children earn more than their parents they disregard them.
- Permissiveness in the society which allows children to act the way that pleases them.
- Urbanization which affects /influences children negatively.
- Traditional values like respect towards parents are decaying.
- Poor role models from parents.
- Drug abuse/alcoholism.
- Exposure to pornographic literature.
- Poor parental discipline/removal of cane from schools.
- Western influence and education i.e. when children get modern education they become proud and disobey parents.
- Negative peer influence from the environment.

Give six reasons why Christians should not covet their neighbours' property

- It's a caution against greed/selfishness.
- It instils the virtues of hard work/honesty.
- It creates satisfaction/contentment amongst them.
- It's a way of self-control.
- To avoid the deliberate will or wish to possess what is coveted.
- To create trust in God and in his providence.

THE WORSHIP OF GOD BY THE ISRAELITES IN THE WILDERNESS
State the ways in which the Israelites worshipped God in the wilderness during the Exodus

- They approached God's altars with respect/reverence.
- All men presented themselves to God three times in a year.
- They celebrated yearly festivals e.g. the Passover, the Pentecost and feast of tabernacles to honour God.
- They kept the Ten Commandments to guide them in their daily lives to God.
- They gave offering of various articles such as silver, gold and bronze to God.
- They observed the Sabbath as day of worship.
- They said prayers to God.
- They worshipped Yahweh as the only God.
- They built altars for God where they sacrificed the holocaust and communion sacrifices.
- They sang and danced to God.
- They paid tithes.

- They moved from place to place with the Ark of the Covenant where the stone tablets containing the Ten Commandments were kept.

State five ways Christians worship God today.

- They read the Bible.
- Priests interpret the scriptures for them.
- They attend church service on Sundays.
- They observe important events in the history of Christianity e.g. Easter, Christmas e.t.c.
- They sing songs of praise and dance to God.
- They undergo baptism.
- They give offerings to God.
- They lead exemplary Christ-like lives/lead moral lives.

Identify the ways in which Christians observe the day of worship.

- Preaching to others.
- Repenting their sins.
- Going to church.
- Visiting the needy.
- Engaging in Bible study
- Giving church contribution and offerings.
- Participating in singing for the Lord.
- Attending fellowships.
- Reading Christian literature.
- Listening to preaching.
- Offering guidance and counselling services.
- Resting from routine work.

How are people initiated into Christian worship today?

- They are given Christian induction into Christian living.
- They are encouraged and taken through Bible study lessons.
- They undergo baptism/confirmation.
- Some are anointed with oil.
- They are allowed to partake the holy communion/Eucharist.
- Fellowship and pastoral visit are made to them by church leaders.
- They are introduced to the members of the congregation.
- They are counselled and taught Christian values.
- They are taught their duties and responsibilities.
- They are taught catechism to prepare them for baptism.

ISRAELITES NEW UNDERSTANDING OF THE NATURE OF GOD

Outline the new understanding Moses gave the Israelites about the nature of God from the Exodus

- He is a God of their fore fathers, Abraham, Jacob and Isaac.

- He is more powerful than other gods for He led them across the Red Sea on dry land.
- God is holy; He restricted people going up Mt. Sinai to avoid contact with people.
- He is the provider; He gave food/manna/quills etc.
- He is a personal God, for he initiated covenant ceremony on Mt. Sinai
- He is a just God, for He punished idol worshipers
- God demands total obedience; He gave instruction during the renewal of the Sinai covenant.
- God is omnipresent, He moved with the Israelites in a pillar of cloud/fire.
- God is jealous, expressed in the commandments.

Explain the problems that Moses faced as he led the Israelites during the Exodus.

- When the Israelites saw the Egyptian army following them they panicked and turned against Moses.
- The Israelites were hungry in the wilderness.
- They encountered hostile desert tribes who attacked them.
- Lack of water and food in the desert.
- Israelites started practicing idolatry, hence breaking God's commandments.
- Attacks by wild animals and snakes.
- The stubbornness of Pharaoh who was not ready to let the Israelites leave.
- His spokesman, Aaron, was a weak leader who allowed idolatry.
- The journey across the desert was long and tiresome.
- He had to settle disputes among the people he was leading.

Outline the leadership qualities a modern Christian leader should learn from Moses.

- A leader should have confidence in God.
- He should be courageous/brave.
- He should be wise/educated/talented/intelligent.
- He should be humble/compassionate/loving.
- He should obey/respect God.
- He should be determined/endure.
- He should be diplomatic.
- He should be inquisitive.
- He should be patient.

Identify the occasions during the exodus when the Israelites lost faith in God.

- When they were pursued/followed by Pharaoh's soldiers.
- When they lacked water/food in the wilderness.
- When attacked by diseases.
- When attacked by snakes.
- When Moses stayed for a long time on the mountain/made a golden calf.
- When Moses died.

Topic 6: LEADERSHIP IN ISRAEL: DAVID AND SOLOMON

- Leadership refers to the way in which a community is ruled or controlled e.g. some communities in traditional African society were ruled by kings, chiefs or elders.
- After the Israelites settled in Canaan, they were ruled by judges for over 200 years, with the first judge being Joshua, who took over after Moses died in the wilderness.
- The judges were appointed by God, but God remained the sovereign ruler, hence they were referred to as a theocratic nation, that is, a nation ruled by God.
- Examples of judges in Israel included Othniel, Ehud, Shamgar, Deborah, Gideon and Prophet Samuel.

The duties of these judges were both political and religious e.g.

i.   They led Israelites to war against their enemies.
ii. They settled disputes among Israelites.
iii. They led the Israelites in worship e.g. they offered sacrifices on behalf of the people.
iv. Some judges acted as prophets.
v.   They offered sacrifices on behalf of the people.
vi. Some anointed kings e.g. Samuel anointed King David and Saul.
vii. They ruled the nation on behalf of God.

State the duties performed by Samuel in Israel after his call and until his death
- He anointed kings e.g. Saul and David.
- He judged among the people.
- He prophesized God's plan for the future.
- He reminded the people of the covenant way of life.
- He condemned social injustices and corruption in Israel.
- He brought to the king's attention their mistakes c.g. king Saul.
- He preached the worship of God/monotheism.
- He led in offering sacrifices to the Lord.
- He led the Israelites to war against their enemies.
- He took care of the tabernacle and the Ark of the Covenant of the Lord.
- He performed a priestly duty in the house of the Lord e.g. he replaced Eli the priest.

REASONS FOR KINGSHIP IN ISRAEL (1 SAMUEL 8: 1-9)
God continued to be the ruler of the Israelites through judges, however, a time came when they decided to have an earthly king to rule over them.

Outline the reasons why the Israelites demanded for a King in Israel (1 Sam 8: 1 – 9)
- Samuel's sons, Joel and Abijah, were corrupt and took bribes hence they lacked good leadership qualities.

- They wanted a warrior king who could lead them to war and bring victory to Israel.
- They wanted to be like their neighbouring nations who had kings.
- They wanted a stable political government ruled by law and order.
- Samuel had grown old and weak and hence could not lead.
- They wanted a human leader whom they could see and approach.
- They needed a leader to guide them in justice.

REASONS AGAINST KINGSHIP IN ISRAEL (1 SAMUEL 8: 10 – 20)

The elders of Israel approached Samuel to appoint for them a king. Samuel was disturbed and prayed to God for guidance. God told him to listen to the voice of the people, for it was not Samuel they were rejecting but Yahweh, who was their unseen ruler. God told Samuel to give the Israelites strict warnings and explain how the king would treat them for example:

- The king would forcefully recruit the Israelites' sons to serve in his army.
- The king would take their daughters to be his perfumers, cooks and bakers.
- The king would take their land and vineyards for government use.
- The king would introduce forced labour.
- The king would overtax them to maintain their army.
- The king would make them slaves.
- Their demand was seen as a rejection of Yahweh as their unseen King.
- Israel would become like other nations which did not know Yahweh and then they would cease to be a covenant people.
- Yahweh would reject them if they cried to him.

KING SAUL'S FAILURES (1 SAMUEL 13: 8 – 14; 15: 7 – 25)

Background

- The elders went to Prophet Samuel and asked him to appoint for them a king.
- Samuel prayed to God seeking his guidance and God told him to obey the people's voice.
- God sent Samuel to anoint Saul, son of Kish from the tribe of Benjamin to become king over Israel.
- Samuel poured oil on Saul's head and the people shouted 'long live the king'.
- Saul therefore became the king of Israel.
- Samuel told the Israelites that they would remain God's people and the king of Israel would be the servant of God.
- Samuel explained the rights and duties of the king and wrote them in a book and laid it before the Lord.
- Even though Saul was God's own choice and led won several wars, he had a number of weaknesses that led to his failure and final rejection by God.

State the failures of King Saul as the first king of Israel

- He was impatient and offered a sacrifice to God instead of waiting for Samuel.

- He broke the law of Herem of total destruction of a conquered enemy when he spared the best sheep, lambs, cattle and other good things intending to offer them as sacrifice to God.
- The spirit of God left him and was replaced by an evil spirit that tormented him.
- He disobeyed God's prophets.
- He was jealous and plotted to kill David because David was getting popular with the Israelites.
- He consulted a medium so as to communicate with Samuel who had died, thereby showing lack of faith in God.
- He committed suicide when he realized that Philistines would defeat his army in battle.
- He spared King Agag of the Amalekites

LESSONS LEARNT FROM KING SAUL'S FAILURES
Lessons Christians learn from the King Saul's failures
- Christians should be patient and not lose hope.
- Christians should obey God's commands.
- Christians should have faith in God and be God-fearing.
- Political leaders should listen to advice from church leaders.
- Christians should not turn against rivals and should accommodate people who have different opinions or views from theirs.
- Christians should learn to be sincere in worship.
- Christians should not shed innocent blood or take away lives.
- Christians should learn to respect each other's position in society.
- Christians should not to be greedy for material possessions.
- Christians should learn to repent when they make mistakes and accept correction.

Factors that prevent political leaders from performing their duties efficiently in Kenya today
- Inability to live up to the expectations of the electorate.
- Ridicule from those who are discriminated against/looked down upon.
- Divisional conflicts along parties.
- Insecurity in some areas/threats especially during campaigns.
- Lack of adequate forum to meet and address the problems facing their electorate.
- Conflicting ideologies resulting in undesired decisions.
- Personal differences.
- Inadequate funds to initiate development projects to help their electorate.
- Inadequate infrastructure.
- Corruption in the government.

KING DAVID'S IMPORTANCE:
- After God rejected Saul as king of Israel, Samuel was guided by God to go to the home of Jesse, who had eight sons, to anoint one of them, who God would show him.

- The seven sons of Jesse were brought before Samuel, one at a time but God told Samuel that he had not chosen any of them.
- The youngest son, David, a shepherd was brought before Samuel and God told him to anoint him.
- Samuel anointed David with Olive oil before his brothers.
- David had to wait until the death of Saul before becoming the king of Israel.
- He was employed to serve King Saul to be playing a lyre and a harp to sooth him whenever he was possessed by an evil spirit.
- Later, Saul and his sons were killed in a battle against the Philistines.
- David mourned their death and then became the next king of Israel and ruled for over 40 years.
- He succeeded as king because he knew and obeyed God in all his undertakings and is remembered as the greatest king and founder of Israel because of his achievements.

KING DAVID'S ACHIEVEMENTS AS KING OF ISRAEL (1 SAMUEL 16: 1 – 23; 2 SAMUEL 6:1 – 15)

- He was appointed by God and filled with God's Holy Spirit.
- He recognized God's supremacy in his leadership respecting Prophets and consulting them before he acted.
- He captured the city of Jerusalem from Jebusites and made it his administrative headquarters.
- He made Jerusalem a religious centre by bringing the Ark of the Covenant.
- He recognized the unity of Israel by uniting twelve tribes together.
- He initiated the idea of building the temple in Jerusalem.
- He was knowledgeable, eloquent, generous, patient and kind to his people.
- He established a powerful nation, though military conquest and boundary expansion.
- He was a skilled diplomat who established good international relations with the neighbours.
- He increased state wealth by promoting local and regional trade.
- He composed and recited Psalms which were adopted in scriptures used for worship.
- He was a charismatic leader and shrewd administrator who sought advice from wise men.
- He established the longest serving dynasty in Israel that lasted for over 400years

Give the ways in which King David promoted the worship of Yahweh in Israel.

- David brought the Ark of the Covenant in Jerusalem.
- He made Jerusalem a Holy city by centralizing worship.
- He composed songs and Psalms that are used in worship.
- He respected prophets of God e.g. Prophet Nathan.
- He repented his sins to God whenever he made mistakes.
- He called himself the servant of Yahweh/God.
- He had the initial plan of God to build the temple For God.
- He advised his son Solomon to obey the commandments of God.
- He prayed to God before carrying out any task/exercise.

- He was chosen by God through public ministry.

How did the kings of Israel promote the worship of God?

- Kings destroyed the altars of other gods e.g. Baal and Asherah.
- Kings set examples to the people e.g. repenting sins, worshiping God.
- Some kings killed false priests e.g. King Jebu.
- Some built places of worship for God e.g. Solomon.
- Some kings refused to form political alliances with neighbouring Kings showing that they trusted in God.
- They called the whole nation to repentance of King Josiah.
- They sought advice from Gods' prophets e.g. David sought Nathan's advice.
- Brought religious reforms e.g. Josiah.

Identify the lessons that modern Christian leaders can learn from the leadership of King David

- Modern leaders should learn to appreciate that all authority is from God.
- Leaders should foster unity in their countries.
- Leaders should protect their states from external aggression.
- Political and religious leaders should respect one another.
- They should acknowledge God in all their achievements.
- They should choose wise advisors to advise them on administrative issues.
- They should respect religious leaders and consult them whenever necessary.
- They should accept correction when they make mistakes.
- They should trust in God.
- They should obey the commandments of God.
- They should be brave and courageous.
- They should seek God's guidance for leadership.

DAVID AS AN ANCESTOR OF JESUS CHRIST (2 SAMUEL 7: 1 – 29; LUKE 1: 26 – 33)

- David wanted to build a temple for God after he built his palace in Jerusalem.
- He felt that it was not right for the Ark of the Covenant to continue dwelling in a tent while he himself lived in a magnificent palace.
- David consulted Prophet Nathan to find out whether it was in order to do so and Nathan approved of the idea.
- However, God told Nathan that David was not to build a house for God.
- Instead, God made to David some divine promises through Prophet Nathan.

Outline the promises God gave to David through Prophet Nathan

- God promised to protect David's descendants from all enemies.
- He will give Israel land to dwell in.
- David's son will build a temple for God.
- God would be a father to David's son.

- David's dynasty would last forever.
- God would raise an heir from David's house to establish an everlasting kingdom.
- He would make David's name famous among all other leaders of the earth.
- God would always support David's Son.

These promises were fulfilled when Solomon, David's son and successor, built the temple for God and brought and prosperity to Israel.

The promises made to David were also fulfilled in the New Testament through the coming of Jesus Christ in the following ways:

- Joseph, the foster father of Jesus is a descendant of David, confirmed when the Angel Gabriel is sent to a girl betrothed to Joseph, from the house of David. (Luke 1: 26 – 27)
- The angel in his annunciation message to Mary says that Jesus will be king like his ancestor David. (Luke 1: 32 – 33)
- Zachariah in his Benedictus says God has raised up a saviour descended from the house of David. (Luke 1: 69)
- Jesus was born in Bethlehem which was also the birthplace of David. (Luke 2: 4)
- The blind man at Jericho hailed Jesus as the son of David and looked to him to restore his sight. (Luke 18: 38)
- During his triumphant entry into Jerusalem Jesus was hailed by the crowd as the Messiah descended from David. (Matthew 21: 9)
- In their preaching and sermons, Peter and Paul made references to Jesus as a descendant of David (Acts 2:29 – 35, 13: 25)

What is the relevance of God's promises to David to Christians today?

- Jesus has established the kingdom of God on earth.
- The kingdom of Jesus is everlasting.
- Christians call God their father as He promised to be the father to David and his descendants.
- God continues to protect his people as He had promised David.
- David is still famous today through Jesus, his descendant.
- Christians consider themselves as spiritual descendants of David through Jesus.

QUALITIES OF A GOOD LEADER DRAWN FROM KING DAVID'S LEADERSHIP

- Courage/bravery: David was a courageous military commander who led his people to wars. Leaders should be ready to die with and for their subjects in case of any attacks or challenges.
- Faith: He was God-fearing and consulted God before undertaking any task. All leaders should realize that authority comes from God and that they are servants.
- Gratitude: He always thanked God for any successes or favours he received from God. Leaders should thank God for their successes and avoid being boastful.

- Loyalty: David sought the acceptance of the people even though he was appointed by God. Leaders should be loyal to their subjects according to the oaths by which they swear.
- Justice: David never practiced tribalism or nepotism. Those in authority should avoid discriminating against others on any basis such as ethnicity, religion e.t.c.
- Wisdom: he chose wise elders to advise him. Leaders should pray for wisdom to administer their subjects.
- Humility: He accepted his mistakes and repented his sins. Both church and political leaders should accept positive criticism change where necessary.
- Forgiving: He spared Saul's life though Saul had attempted to kill him. Modern leaders should accommodate their political rivals and also forgive their offenders.

KING SOLOMON'S ACHIEVEMENTS AND FAILURES (1 KINGS 3 – 12)

- Solomon was anointed by Zadok, the Priest in the presence of Prophet Nathan and the Royal bodyguards, to succeed his father David as king of Israel.
- Before King David died, he advised his son Solomon to:
  i. Be confident and determined.
  ii. Do what the Lord God commands him.
  iii. Keep the Laws of Moses.
- David added that if Solomon obeyed God, the Lord would fulfil the promise He made to make David's descendants rule forever.

KING SOLOMON'S ACHIEVEMENTS

What were the achievements of King Solomon?

- He was a successful trader/merchant by establishing and developing trade with neighbouring countries.
- He built up a professional army and equipped them with horse drawn chariots.
- He developed diplomatic relations with foreign countries by marrying the daughters of the kings of those countries.
- He was a wise man, as he judged difficult cases and settled disputes fairly.
- He built a beautiful temple for God in Jerusalem, which lasted for seven years, hence making Jerusalem a centre for worship.
- He brought the Ark of the Covenant to the temple in Jerusalem.
- He composed 3,000 proverbs and 1,005 songs which are used in the worship of God.
- He expanded the geographical boundaries of Israel.

FAILURES OF KING SOLOMON

- He married many foreign wives who worshipped other gods, hence disobeying God's warning to the Israelites not to intermarry with foreigners.
- He built temples for the pagan gods worshipped by his wives.
- He also participated in worshiping the pagan gods.
- He introduced forced labour when he forced men of Israel to work during the building of his palace and the temple.

- He killed his own half-brother Adonijah because he suspected Adonijah could be his rival to the throne, hence committing murder.
- He practiced nepotism, by exempting his tribesmen, Benjamin and Judah, from the forced labour.
- He introduced high taxation in Israel. The tax required was too high and a heavy burden for the ordinary Israelite.
- He valued himself more that God when he spent only seven years in building the temple but took thirteen years in building his own palace.
- He was extravagant in the way he used the wealth that belonged to the state of Israel and maintained a high standard of living.
- He sold part of Israelite territory to the King to the king of Tyre in repayment for a debt he was unable to pay.
- He hired pagan craftsmen who designed, decorated and furnished God's temple.

Show how King Solomon fulfilled Samuel's prophecy about kingship in Israel.
- He enslaved the Israelites by using forced labour during the construction of the temple and his palace.
- He overtaxed the Israelites to provide for his palace.
- He grabbed their properties and gave to his officials.
- He forced their sons to be members of his army.
- He took their daughters and made them his concubines.
- He married many foreign wives who brought idolatry into Israel.
- He killed his half-brother Adonijah.
- He made treaties with other nations, which was against the spirit of the Sinai covenant.
- He sold part of Israelites land to settle his debts.

Factors that led to the failure of the kings that succeeded David in their leadership
- They lacked faith in God.
- They were dishonest and never consulted God before undertaking their activities.
- They married foreign wives who brought foreign influence.
- They disobeyed God's command by marrying foreign wives.
- They practiced idolatry.
- They oppressed the poor thus destroying the law of brotherhood.
- They subjected the Israelites to forced labour and slavery.
- They did not go according to the Law of Moses.
- They took part in pagan festivals.
- They encouraged syncretism.
- They built temples for worshipping idols.
- They shed innocent blood.

Why do political leaders in Kenya fail to perform their duties effectively?
- Lack of leadership skills.
- Lack of obedience in God.

- Lack of faith/ trust in God.
- Some of them were chosen through corrupt means.
- Tribalism.
- Conflicts among themselves on issues affecting the government.
- They are not loyal to their leaders and subjects.
- Failure to accept their mistakes and change for the better.

THE DEATH OF SOLOMON AND THE DIVISION OF THE KINGDOM (1 Kings 12)

- After King Solomon's death, his son Rehoboam succeeded him.
- Rehoboam went to the north of the country to be accepted publicly as the King of Israel.
- The elders of the ten tribes of the North led by Jeroboam, son of Nebat, met Rehoboam at Shechem.
- The elders told Rehoboam that they were willing to accept him as their king if he was less harsh than his father.
- Being young, Rehoboam consulted his fellow young men who advised him to be harsher than his father.
- He followed the advice from the young men and gave an unwise answer to the elders, threatening them that he would be harsher than his father.
- The elders were angry with his harsh reply and rebelled against him.
- They made northern tribes made Jeroboam their king, and was called Israel.
- Rehoboam was left with two tribes of Judah and Benjamin, and became Judah.
- Judah retained Jerusalem as its capital city.
- Jeroboam fortified two cities, Shechem and Penuel, from where he ruled Israel in turns. He finally settled at Tirzah, in the North.
- Later he changed the capital city of Israel to Samaria.

IMPORTANCE OF THE TEMPLE IN ISRAEL

Give the reasons why the temple of Jerusalem was considered an important place for the Israelites

- It symbolized the presence of God in Israel since the Ark of the Covenant that was kept in the temple.
- It was a place of worship e.g. offering sacrifices.
- Dedication of their firstborn sons was done in the temple.
- It was a residence for priests and Levites.
- Jewish religious festivals were celebrated in the temple e.g. Passover, Pentecost e.t.c.
- It was a learning centre since teachers of the law taught in the temple.
- Purification of mothers took place in the temple.
- It acted as a court where Jewish religious cases were handled.

Topic 7: LOYALTY TO GOD: ELIJAH

THE SPREAD OF IDOLATRY
- Idolatry is the worship of idols and an idol is an image representing a god.
- The Israelites had been forbidden from worshipping idols.
- They were also not to intermarry with foreigners and not to make any treaties with foreigners.
- The covenant and the commandments were therefore meant to prepare them against the temptations they would face in the Promised Land that they were going to inherit.
- However, when the Israelites settled in the new land they were influenced by the local Canaanite religion and the influence on them was great and they started to fall away from the worship of Yahweh.

What circumstances led to the spread of idolatry in Israel?
- Kings like Jeroboam encouraged idol worship by setting up temples for worshipping idols.
- The religious schism between the Israel and Judah contributed to spread of idolatry.
- They were influenced by the local Canaanite religion which was polytheistic in nature.
- King Jeroboam married a Phoenician Princess, Jezebel, who introduced Baalism in Israel.
- They had not forgotten the worship of idols which they practiced in Egypt.
- The transition from a pastoral life to agricultural life after settling in Canaan made them to start performing Canaanite rituals to bring rain and fertility of animals and human beings.

A. THE LOCAL CANAANITE RELIGION
The Israelites worshipped God in a simple portable house called Tent of meeting on their journey to the Promised Land. When they got to Canaan, they found that the Canaanites had permanent temples for their gods. This made them feel inferior before their neighbours hence were influenced into idolatry.

The characteristics of the local Canaanite religion include:
- It was a nature religion, that is, related to the forces of nature e.g. rain and drought.
- The aims of the religion were to ensure continued fertility of land, flock and people.
- It was cyclic, that is, seasons repeated in contrast to Yahweism, which was linear.
- It comprised a family of gods e.g. El was the high god or king, his wife was Asherah, the goddess of fertility.
- Symbols were used to represent each god.
- They practised temple prostitution.
- They built high places of worship under sacred trees and hill tops.

- They offered human sacrifices to their gods.
- They celebrated festivals and feasts e.g. feast of unleavened bread, feast of weeks.

B. THE SCHISM BETWEEN JUDAH AND ISRAEL (1 KINGS 12: 25 – 33)

Schism refers to a division within or separation from an established church or religion. King Jeroboam contributed to the spread of idolatry, by making sure that the people of his kingdom did not have any links with the people of Judah.

Describe the religious schism between Judah and Israel

- When Solomon was king of Israel, he oppressed the people through over-taxation, forced labour e.t.c hence the people were dissatisfied.
- When his son Rehoboam took over, people wanted him to be less harsh than his father, Solomon.
- Rehoboam, being young, he consulted his fellow youths who advised him to be more harsh than his father.
- Hence, Jeroboam, one of the senior army officials, led the elders of Israel to rebel against Rehoboam.
- Ten tribes led by Jeroboam split and formed the Northern kingdom, called Israel.
- The two Southern tribes, Benjamin and Judah, remained loyal to Rehoboam and formed the Southern Kingdom, called Judah.
- The Temple of Jerusalem remained in the South.
- The southern kingdom remained under the Davidic rule until the Babylonian exile.
- Jeroboam built two temples in the north, at Bethel and at Dan, where he put two golden calves to represent Yahweh.
- King Jeroboam prevented the people of the Northern Kingdom from going to worship in the south at Jerusalem.
- The kings of the Northern kingdom who came after Jeroboam continued to worship these idols e.g. kings Omri and Ahab.

*It is this split in worship that is referred to as schism.

How did King Jeroboam contribute to the spread of idolatry in Israel?

- He built two temples at Bethel and Dan, and placed two golden calves to act as the visible representation of Yahweh.
- Jeroboam ignored Jerusalem as a centre of worship and set up two rival places of worship at Dan and Bethel, hence destroying the idea of the covenant brotherhood and unity amongst Israel which David had achieved.
- He made Israelites to offer sacrifices to the two golden calves representing Yahweh.
- He built other places of worship on hilltops thus copying the practices of the surrounding nations.
- He chose priests from ordinary families to serve Yahweh at the centres of worship, yet priests were supposed to come from the tribe of Levi.
- He instituted religious festivals or feasts in the month of his choice.
- He burnt incense at the altar of idols, thus breaking the first commandment.

Give the reasons that contributed to schism between Judah and Israel.

- It was a punishment for Solomon's sins.
- Jeroboam had built two worship places at Dan and Bethel.
- Solomon's rule was oppressive in the form of forced labour, high taxes and slavery.
- Rehoboam rejected the request of the people even after being advised by the elders.
- Solomon's great development in the South at the expense of the North, which brought tension between the Northern and Southern kingdoms.
- Solomon had also exempted the inhabitants of Judah from paying taxes.
- Jerusalem city belonged to the Southern division.
- Ten tribes preferred the rule of Jeroboam while two tribes remained under the rule of Rehoboam.

C. KING AHAB'S MARRIAGE WITH THE PHOENICIAN PRINCESS

- When Ahab's father, Omri, then, King of Israel died, he arranged a marriage between his son and the daughter of the King of Phoenicia (Tyre) called Jezebel.
- This was against God's warning that Israelites were not to intermarry with other nations because they would be influenced into idolatry.
- Jezebel was a strong follower of the Phoenician religion.
- When Ahab became king of Israel, he allowed his wife to introduce her religion to Israel.
- She imported the Phoenician gods and 450 Baal prophets and supported them.
- Ahab built a temple for the worship of Baal.
- Jezebel started campaigning to substitute Yahweism with that of Baal and so Baalism became the official state religion.

Failures of King Ahab

- He broke the first commandments by allowing idol worship.
- He killed the prophets of God.
- He allowed his wife Jezebel to bear false witness against Naboth.
- He coveted Naboth's vineyard.
- He killed Naboth/ broke law against murder.
- He broke the law that forbids stealing by taking Naboth's vineyard.
- He failed to protect the weak/poor as demanded by the law.

THE EFFECTS OF IDOLATRY IN ISRAEL

- It led to the development of syncretism, that is, the worship of Yahweh alongside other gods.
- Former places of worship for the Canaanite gods were turned into places of worship for Yahweh without removing the Canaanite symbols such as altars.
- The Canaanite agricultural calendar was adopted by Israel for the timing of the Passover feast.
- Names of Canaanite gods were also used for Yahweh, e.g. El the name of the father of all gods was applied to Yahweh.

- Parents began naming their children after Baal.
- Baalism was declared a compulsory state religion.
- Queen Jezebel ordered the destruction of the altars of Yahweh.
- Yahweh's prophets were killed, and some went into hiding.
- The 450 Baal prophets were made the officials of the royal court in order to protect the Baal religion.
- God raised up prophets like Elijah to help bring back the Israelites to the Covenant way of life.
- Famine and drought befell Israel leading to the people's suffering.
- Corruption and social injustices became widespread, a rejection of the covenant way of life.

ELIJAH'S FIGHT AGAINST:
A) FALSE RELIGION (1 KINGS 18: 17 – 46)

Following the spread of idolatry in Israel, God sent prophet Elijah to return the people back to the covenant way of life. He fought against false religion in the following ways:

- He openly rebuked King Ahab for promoting Baalism in Israel.
- He announced a three and a half year drought as punishment from God for idolatry.
- He repaired the altar of Yahweh to restore the true worship and rededicate the Israelites to Yahweh.
- He killed the prophets of Baal who spread idolatry in Israel.
- He appointed Elisha as a prophet to continue with the prophetic crusade.
- He prophesied the death of Ahab and his family as punishment for promoting idolatry.
- He called for a contest on Mt. Carmel between him and the prophets of Baal to prove the supremacy of Yahweh over Baal and to prove who the true God is.

Describe the contest on Mt. Carmel

- Elijah asked King Ahab to summon all Israel together with the 450 prophets of Baal.
- All the people assembled at Mount Carmel.
- Elijah challenged the people to decide on the true God to be worshipped between Baal and Yahweh.
- Elijah asked people to bring two bulls, one for the prophets of Baal and another for Elijah.
- He ordered the Baal prophets to offer the sacrifice first, but they were not to light fire. The god that would respond with fire was the true God.
- The Baal prophets took the bull and sacrificed, they prayed, danced and shouted but there was no fire.
- At noon, Elijah started mocking them, asking them to pray harder.
- Elijah then gathered all the people around him and prepared an altar.
- He dug a trench round the sacrifice.
- He cut the bull into pieces and laid it on the wood and ordered the Baal prophets to pour water on the sacrifice until the trenches were full.
- Elijah prayed to God to prove that he is the true God.

- Fire then came down and burnt the sacrifice.
- When the people saw this, they fell on their knees and worshipped God.
- Prophet Elijah then ordered the killing of Baal prophets.
- He also told Ahab to go and eat and drink, for the rains would come down.

Lessons about God that the Israelites learnt from the Mt. Carmel contest

- Yahweh is a living God.
- Yahweh is powerful.
- He is holy.
- He is faithful to his promises.
- He punishes those who break his laws.
- God forgives.
- God answers prayers.
- God calls people to repentance.

Forms of idolatry that threaten Christianity today

- Devil worship.
- Sexual immorality/pleasure of sex.
- Alcohol and drug abuse.
- Greed for money and wealth.
- Greed for power.
- Education.
- Careers and employment.
- Love of popular culture.
- Media influence/internet/facebook.
- Desire of high status.

Mention any seven factors that lead people away from the worship of God today

- Materialism.
- Permissiveness in society.
- Mass media.
- Corruption.
- Urbanization.
- Threats to human dignity.
- Confusion from religious pluralism.
- Oppression.
- Social immorality.
- Drug abuse/alcoholism.
- Scientific discoveries /technological innovations.
- Poverty.
- Education.

Roles that Christians play in the restoration of true worship in Kenya today

- Christians courageously condemn evils being committed in the church.
- By upholding the teachings of the Bible.
- Christian leaders can use their authority to protect/uplift the poor and the weak.
- Christians can defend the cause of the poor/orphans/widows.
- Christians ought to lead a life of prayer all the time.
- Christians need to put their confidence in God so as to overcome temptations.
- Being ready to perform whatever task that is given to them in church.
- Being honest in giving information that affects others.
- Avoid modern idolatry at all costs/valuing God above all things.

B) CORRUPTION (1 KINGS 21).

Explain how prophet Elijah fought against corruption among the people of Israel as contained in 1 Kings 21

- Naboth, a farmer, had a vineyard next to Ahab's.
- Ahab coveted it and asked Naboth to sell it to him but he declined.
- Ahab was disturbed that he fell sick, he could neither eat nor drink.
- Jezebel planned a corrupt scheme to ensure that Ahab possessed the vineyard.
- Jezebel forged letters using the king's seal accusing Naboth of two great sins; blasphemy and treason.
- The punishment for both mistakes was stoning to death.
- Jezebel bribed some youth to be her witnesses against Naboth before all people.
- Naboth was condemned to death together with his entire family who would have inherited the vineyard.
- Ahab was happy and took Naboth's vineyard.
- Elijah was angered by Ahab's action and went to the palace and declared God's judgement on Ahab and Jezebel.

List the various forms of corruption today

- Tribalism.
- Bribery.
- Cheating in business.
- Stealing,
- Robbery with violence.
- Dishonesty.
- Misuse of public property.
- Grabbing personal and public land.

Give the effects of corruption in Kenyan society today.

- There is an increase in crime.
- The public has lost trust/faith in the government and leaders.
- There is an increase in poverty and has widened the gap between the rich and the poor.
- There is a high level of inflation.

- Lack of quality services in all areas of life.
- Inefficient people are hired/employed.
- It has led to disillusion and poor morale of workers.
- It has led to strikes and riots among workers.
- It has created unemployment due to inability to create jobs and has promoted laziness.
- It has led to sexual immorality, leading to STIs and HIV/AIDS.
- It has given the country a negative image globally.

How can Christians help to reduce/curb corruption in Kenya today?

- Use of life-skills e.g. creative thinking, critical thinking and decision making.
- Praying for the corrupt to change their behaviour.
- Setting a good example by acting as role models for others.
- Educating the people on the evils of corruption.
- Reporting those who are engaged in corrupt practices to the relevant authorities.
- Participating in making laws to curb the vice.
- Fighting for just and fair wages and good working conditions.
- Supporting and practicing fair distribution of wealth and resources.
- Giving heavy punishment to the offenders.

REASONS WHY ELIJAH FACED DANGER AND HOSTILITY AS A PROPHET OF GOD

Why did Elijah face danger and hostility in his work?

- He had pronounced a three and a half year drought in Israel.
- He openly condemned King Ahab for taking Naboth's vineyard.
- He hid in the wilderness where he faced dangers from wild animals.
- He killed 450 prophets of Baal.
- He faced starvation for lack of food and water in the wilderness.
- By the time Elijah was a prophet, Baalism had become the official state religion in Israel.
- He was greatly discouraged and lost hope.
- All other prophets had been killed except him and some had gone into hiding.
- Jezebel swore to kill him the way he had killed the 450 prophets.

What would Prophet Elijah condemn if he came to Kenya today?

- Bribery and corruption.
- Murder
- Violence
- Thuggery /robbery /theft.
- Suicidal acts.
- Rape
- Idolatry.
- Immorality.
- False accusation/witness

- Nepotism/tribalism.
- Misuse of public property
- Deceit/deception.

Why do Christian leaders face opposition today?
- When they condemn evils.
- When they are poor role models.
- Due to doctrinal differences.
- Rivalry for leadership.
- Political interference.
- Different religions.

LIFE SKILLS THAT HELP FIGHT CORRUPTION:

Life skills are positive abilities that enable an individual to deal effectively with the b demands and challenges of everyday life. They help individuals make informed decisions in life and avoid risky behaviour.

CRITICAL THINKING: Critical thinking is ability to analyse the merits and demerits of an   action.

CREATIVE THINKING: It is the ability to explore new ways of handling issues.

DECISION MAKING: It is the ability to think and come up with a solution or way forward to an issue or difficult situation. It is about making choices: choosing to do something or say one thing instead of another.

ASSERTIVENESS: It means demanding your rights and communicating your views while respecting other people. It is the ability to express your desires, feelings, opinions, values and beliefs and demand your rights clearly and firmly without violating another person's rights or hurting their feelings.

Lessons Christians learn from the leadership of Prophet Elijah
- Christian leaders should remain courageous/ firm in condemning any form of social injustice in society like Elijah.
- Christians should remain faithful/ loyal to God/ practiced monotheism just like Elijah.
- Christians should not despair in their missionary work.
- They should remain prayerful to God in faith and God will answer their prayers like Elijah at Mt. Carmel contest.
- Christians should be persistent like Elijah was in their struggle against injustice.
- They should not give false evidence against their neighbours like Jezebel and Naboth.
- God is able to establish an intimate relationship with his faithful like Elijah.

Topic 8: SELECTED OLD TESTAMENT PROPHETS AND THEIR TEACHINGS

DEFINITION OF THE TERMS: 'PROPHETS' AND 'PROPHECY'

- The term **prophet** is derived from a Greek word "**propheters**" which means 'one who speaks or proclaims'.
- It also comes from a Hebrew word '**nabi**' which means 'God's spokesman' or one who proclaims the will of God.
- A prophet can also be referred to as seer, man of God, servant of God, messenger of God, watchman, shepherd, custodians of God's law, mediators etc.
- A prophet is a person who receives messages from God through visions, dreams or prayers and then tells people what God has revealed to him.
- **Prophecy:** This is uttering God's revelation about the future. It is also the utterance or statement by a prophet or prophetess aimed at predicting future happenings.

CATEGORIES OF PROPHETS

Outline the categories of Old Testament prophets

- **Early Old Testament Prophets** – they appeared early in the history of Israel as a nation e.g. Moses, Elijah, Samuel, Nathan, and Elisha.
- **Professional prophets** – acted as clerks in courts, assisting Kings to know God's will. They earned their living through prophecy. These were true prophets and they therefore never gave prophecies in favour of what kings wanted to hear. E.g. Samuel was given a small silver coin as a token by Saul for his prophecy. (1 Sam 9: 8 – 20)
- **Canonical Prophets** – are prophets whose prophecies are recorded and preserved under books bearing their names. They are categorized into two:
    i. Major Prophets: are considered major because their books are long as compared to the minor prophetic books e.g. Jeremiah, Ezekiel, Isaiah, and Daniel.
    ii. Minor Prophets: are referred to as minor because their books are short and hence contain less information e.g. Amos, Micah, Zephaniah, Haggai, Zechariah, Nahum, Hosea, Joel, Habakkuk, Obadiah, Malachi and Jonah.
- **Non-canonical prophets** – prophets whose oracles/messages have been compiled by other authors e.g. Elijah, Nathan and Elisha.
- **True prophets** – they acted on behalf of God and they upheld the covenant way of life.
- **Cultic Prophets** – they carried out religious activities in shrines. They assisted the priests in carrying out their duties and their life depended on the institution of priesthood.
- **Prophetesses** – they are female/women prophets e.g. Miriam, sister of Moses, Huldah, and in St. Luke's Gospel there is prophetess Anna.
- **False prophets** – they claimed to speak in the name of Yahweh but their message never came to pass. They always were opposed to what the true prophets of Yahweh stood for.

IMPORTANCE OF PROPHETS

Explain the roles played by the Old Testament prophets in Israel

- They spoke on behalf of God, were messengers of God, used to reach to His people.
- They foretold the future events especially those that affected the people e.g. wars, exile, the New Covenant by Jeremiah e.t.c.
- They guided and counselled the kings and people whenever they went against the covenant way of life.
- They warned people of God's impending judgement especially if they did not change their evil ways.
- They called people back to repentance.
- They gave messages of hope to people for salvation despite God's judgement e.g. Jeremiah.
- They condemned the evil in society e.g. Amos condemned corruption, dishonesty e.t.c.
- They made the people understand the nature of God e.g. Prophets Jeremiah, Amos, Isaiah showed that God is kind, loving, holy and merciful.
- They offered sacrifices to God.
- They anointed kings e.g. Samuel anointed Kings Saul and David.
- They interpreted the visions and dreams from God.

Give reasons why God sent prophets in Israel

- To teach people about God's true nature.
- To act as mediators between God and the people.
- To condemn the social evils in Israel.
- To anoint leaders and Kings.
- To warn people of God's coming judgement for their sins.
- To teach the people the covenant way of life.
- To announce the restoration of Israel for those who repent.
- To guide kings and people.
- To condemn idolatry and promote monotheism.

Identify various ways through which the Old Testament prophets communicated their messages to the people

- Singing or lamentations e.g. Amos sang a funeral song.
- Through story telling/narratives.
- Preaching sermons e.g. Jeremiah's temple sermon.
- Letters e.g. Jeremiah
- Through poetry e.g. Isaiah
- Use of vivid words e.g. Amos
- Use of direct words or quotes e.g. "thus says the Lord".
- Symbolic actions e.g. Jeremiah carried an ox-yoke.
- Lifestyle e.g. Hosea was to marry a prostitute, Jeremiah remained single.
- Some wrote down their messages e.g. Jeremiah instructed a scribe Baruch to write down his message.

- Through miracles e.g. Elijah's $3^{1}/_{2}$ years drought.

THE CHARACTERISTICS OF PROPHETS

Outline the characteristics of a true prophet in Israel.

- They were called by God.
- They responded to God's call in faith and obedience.
- They were given specific tasks to carry out.
- They received God's revelation in the form of dreams, visions and symbolic actions.
- They faced opposition and persecution in their work.
- They acknowledged God as the only true God and kept to the covenant way of life.
- They acted as mediators between God and his people.
- They spoke with authority from God e.g. thus says the Lord.
- They were courageous and delivered God's message without fear.
- Their prophesies came to pass or were fulfilled.
- They performed miracles.
- They never prophesied for material gain.
- They were morally upright.

Outline the features/characteristics of false prophets in Israel.

- They prophesied from their own imaginations and filled people with false hope.
- Some were paid by servants of kings and only said what pleased the king.
- They lived immoral lives.
- They gave messages that people wanted to hear e.g. preached peace when there was no peace.
- They challenged the work of true prophets and gave messages that carried untruths.
- False prophets had no personal knowledge of God.
- They received no visions or dreams from God.
- The false prophets used evil forces like magic to call upon the spirits.
- They expressed themselves without authority before God and men.
- Their prophecies were not in line with the divine revelation.
- False prophets prophesied for payment against the covenant that the Israelites had with God.
- They served other gods and not Yahweh e.g. Baal.

THE WRITING OF PROPHETIC MESSAGES

- Prophetic messages were collected and written over a long period of time, not in one sitting.
- The messages were written in different styles and subjects.
- Some messages were written by prophets themselves following God's command for example Isaiah 30: 8, Isaiah is instructed to write on a tablet, same to Jeremiah in Jeremiah 36:2
- The disciples of the prophets wrote down what they gathered from their leader for example Isaiah 8: 16.

- Some messages were preserved by prophets' disciples as oral traditions, who later passed them to the people. Isaiah 8: 16.
- Some of the prophetic messages were preserved and passed on through oral tradition.
- Some messages may have been written down from the memories of those who heard the prophets' message.

CONTENT OF THE PROHETIC MESSAGES

There are three different kinds of messages in the prophetic books:

i. Prophetic sayings which were in form of poetic passages carrying some teaching, prediction, threat or a promise (Isaiah 28, 29: 13 – 14; Amos 1: 3, 3: 2).
ii. Narratives told in the first person, in which the prophet relates his own personal experience (Isaiah 6; Jeremiah 1).
iii. Narratives in the third person, which recounts events in the prophet's life, or conditions in which the prophet worked.

RELATIONSHIP BETWEEN THE OLD TESTAMENT PROPHECIES AND THE NEW TESTAMENT

- Isaiah's prophesy that a virgin will bear a son called Immanuel (Isaiah 7:14) is fulfilled in the conception of Mary and later giving birth to a son called Immanuel.
- The prophecies of prophets Jeremiah and Ezekiel of God making a new covenant with each individual, is fulfilled in the Last Supper and in Jesus' death and resurrection. Every Christian has a personal relationship with God through Christ.
- All the teachings and prophecies of the Old Testament was the basis on which the New Testament laid for example Jesus in Matt 5: 17 says He came to fulfil the Law of Moses but not to abolish it.
- The Old Testament prophets condemned insincere worship and elaborate sacrificial rituals. Likewise, Jesus condemned outward observance of the Law in the New Testament.
- Micah 5: 2 states that the messiah will be born in the city of David which is fulfilled in Luke 2: 4 which says Jesus was born in Bethlehem the city of David.
- Nathan's prophecy about a descendant of David establishing an everlasting Kingdom (2 Sam 7:13-14) is fulfilled by Angel Gabriel's message during the annunciation of the birth of Jesus.
- Joel's prophesy (Joel 2:28) about the descending of the Holy Spirit is fulfilled on the day of Pentecost (Acts 2) when the disciples are filled with the Holy Spirit.
- Prophet Isaiah prophesied about the suffering servant of Yahweh is fulfilled in the suffering and death of Jesus Christ.
- Malachi 4: 5 states that there would be a forerunner of the Messiah which is fulfilled in John the Baptist who prepares the way for Jesus.
- Jesus himself read Isaiah 61:1 – 2 and said that the scripture was fulfilled in his coming.

SIMILARITIES AND DIFFERENCES BETWEEN THE TRADITIONAL AND THE OLD TESTAMENT PROPHETS AND THEIR RELEVANCE TO CHRISTIANS TODAY

SIMILARITIES

In what ways were the Old Testament prophets similar to the African prophets?

- Both possessed spiritual or divine powers that ordinary people did not have.
- Both were mediators between people and a Supreme Being/God.
- Both performed the role of healers both physical and spiritual healing.
- Both received their revelations in form of dreams, visions and trances which were considered supernatural.
- Both expected to be people of high integrity and moral standards and be obedient to God's call.
- Both warned people of impending dangers and foretold the future.
- Both condemned social injustices.
- Both were consulted to reveal and interpret God's message to the people.
- Both prophets had charismatic personalities.

DIFFERENCES

Highlight the differences between the traditional African and Old Testament prophets.

- The traditional African prophets received their powers from spirits and ancestors while Old Testament prophets were appointed and received theirs from God.
- The traditional African prophets were highly respected and obeyed while the Old Testament ones faced opposition most of the time.
- The prophecies of the traditional African prophets have been preserved and passed on mainly through oral traditions while the Old Testament ones were recorded and preserved in written from.
- Some of the Old Testament prophets had an idea of a glorious Messiah who would come while the traditional African prophets have no concept of the Messiah.
- The traditional African prophets recognized and worshipped many gods and goddesses while the Old Testament ones stressed on monotheistic religion, that is, worship of only one God.
- The traditional African ones limited their messages to their communities while the Old Testament ones gave the messages to the Israelites and the whole world.

Explain the relevance of Old Testament prophets today.

- Christians learn to condemn evil in the society.
- Christians are called to be God's people in spreading His words today.
- Christians should stand firm and be committed in the faith.
- Christians should fight for the rights of the downtrodden, poor, and defenceless today.
- Christians learn to endure hardships today.
- Christians learn to always obey God's call.

- Christians learn that they are the new Israel hence should a permanent relationship with God.
- They should prophecy for the glory of God.
- They should lead holy lives.
- Christians need to learn to be courageous and bold irrespective of the consequences just as the prophets were.
- As the prophets, the Christians should provide hope for the people in times of suffering.
- Christians learn to pray to God for wisdom and guidance to conquer temptations and hardships.
- Christians learn that they can face persecution and rejection because of their stand just as the prophets.

State the ways in which a Christian can know a false prophet today.

- If their words never come to pass.
- If he practices magic.
- If his teachings are not in line with the Bible.
- When he asks for payment.
- If he condones sin and evil.
- If his life does not bear a fruit of the spirit.
- If he speaks about things that do not exist.

How did Jesus fulfil the roles of a prophet?

- Jesus taught people on their duties to God.
- Jesus proclaimed judgment of God on sinners.
- Jesus condemned sin and evil.
- He taught on the universality of God.
- Jesus performed miracles.
- He had disciples through whom the people got his teachings.
- He was rejected and persecuted for the gospel.
- He taught people and asked them to repent.
- He led an exemplary life.
- He warned people of coming disasters and asked them to repent and foretold the future.
- He reminded people on their social responsibilities.

Topic 9: AMOS

BACKGROUND TO PROPHET AMOS

Historical background

- He came from a village called Tekoa, near Jerusalem in Judah, the Southern Kingdom.
- Prophet Amos was a shepherd by profession who owned sheep and goats.
- He also grew sycamore trees.
- He also was in charge of other shepherds.
- He prophesied during the reign of King Uzziah of Judah and king Jeroboam II of Israel.
- He was a native of Judah but was sent to proclaim God's message to the people of the Northern Kingdom of Israel.

Political Background

- The prophetic ministry of Amos fell during the time when Jeroboam II was the king of Israel.
- During this time, Israel lived securely from outside attacks because Jeroboam II was a warrior and had expanded the political borders of Israel and made the nation secure from attacks of her neighbours.
- However, this situation changed, when the Assyrian empire became the most powerful nation in the region.
- The king of Assyria wanted to expand his empire with the aim of conquering Egypt.
- The smaller states that lay between Assyria and Egypt e.g. Israel and Judah were in danger of being conquered.
- Amos understood that God would use Assyria as his instrument to punish Israel for her sinfulness.

Social background

- Israel was prospered economically due to the stability that existed during the reign of Jeroboam II.
- However, the wealth of the nation was in the hands of a few rich people.
- There was a wide gap between the rich and the poor.
- The rich lived a luxurious life and spent extravagantly while the poor lacked basic needs.
- The poor were exploited and oppressed by the wealthy land owners.
- Wealth was in the hands of the royal family and his officials.
- The merchants were dishonest and used false scales in their businesses.
- Bribery and corruption was rampant in law-courts whereby the poor were denied justice (Amos 5:7-10)
- The powerful and wealthy were hypocrites and showed off by offering large sacrifices in the name of Yahweh yet they had broken His covenant.

State the ways in which the rich oppressed the poor during prophet Amos time

- Merchants overcharged the poor with high interests.
- The poor were sold into slavery for a piece of sandals or silver for failing to pay their debts.
- The poor were denied justice in law courts because they could not bribe judges.
- Temple prostitutes came from the poor families.
- The poor were cheated in business deals by using faulty weighing scales.
- Food sold to the poor was unfit for human consumption.
- The poor were forced to work on the rich people's farms for little or no pay.
- The land for the poor was grabbed by the rich.
- The rich lived in extreme luxury feasting as the poor starved.

Religious background

- The Israelites continued to worship God.
- Bethel, Gilgal and Samaria were the main centres of worship.
- Israel worshipped Yahweh alongside other gods like Sakkuth and Kaiwan (Amos 5:26).
- There was religious hypocrisy because the worshippers of Yahweh were unjust and they oppressed the poor.
- They observed external practices rather than doing from the heart.
- The few existing priests and prophets were paid to condone the evils of the rulers.
- Religious ceremonies and costly sacrifices were offered at the expense of the poor.

THE CALL OF AMOS (AMOS 1: 1; 3: 8; 7: 10 – 15)

- Before his call he was a shepherd and dresser of sycamore trees.
- He received his call in form of a vision.
- He was sent to proclaim God's message to the people of Israel, the Northern Kingdom.
- His task was to condemn the evils such as social and economic injustices and idolatry which existed in Israel at the time.
- As a result of these evils, Amos pronounced severe punishment from God on both the king and the nation of Israel.
- He said that Jeroboam would die by the sword and the nation of Israel would be sent to exile in Assyria.
- His message about judgement angered the priests who worked in favour of the rulers, for example, Amaziah, the high priest ordered him to leave Israel and go back to Judah, his birth place.
- Amos responded to Amaziah's threat by stating that he was not a professional prophet but was a shepherd and tender of sycamore trees.
- He added that God had called him and commanded him to prophesy to the Northern kingdom.

Lessons that Christians learn from the call of Amos

- Christians learn that God can call anybody to serve him, regardless of their status.
- Just like Amos, Christians should respond to God's with obedience.
- Christians should condemn the evils that exist in the society with courage like Amos did.

- Christians should be ready to work anywhere because God's work goes beyond any boundaries, like Amos was sent by God to prophesy in Israel, which was not his own.
- Christian leaders learn that they should not practice hypocrisy in order to please the rulers like Amaziah the priest did.
- Christians learn that they should not give up in their service to God despite opposition.
- Christians learn that sinners will be punished like Jeroboam and the Israelites were.

THE VISIONS OF AMOS (AMOS 7: 1-9; 8:1:3; 9:1-14)
Name and explain the significance of the visions of Amos.
(i) Swarm of locusts (Amos 7:1-3)

- Amos saw God sending a swarm of locusts which destroyed all plants and food in the land.
- Amos cried to God to have mercy on his people.
- This vision symbolized the impending famine that would strike Israel.
- Amos' prayer was answered and God lifted the punishment away.

(ii) The vision of a great fire (Amos 7:4-6)
- Amos saw a supernatural fire that consumed the waters and land.
- Amos pleaded again and God answered his prayer.
- This vision showed that God was going to destroy Israel by sending a supernatural fire.

(iii) The vision of the plumb line/crooked wall (Amos 7:7-9)
- Amos saw a crooked wall being checked with a plumb line.
- This time Amos didn't plead with God for forgiveness.
- The visions showed that Israelites were crooked and God had checked their hearts and found them not right.
- As a plumber destroys a crooked wall so would God destroy Israel.
- It meant that punishment was inevitable because Israel had sinned against God.

(iv) The vision of a basket of ripe fruits (Amos 8:1-3)
- Amos saw a vision of a basket of ripe summer fruit at the end of the fruit harvest.
- Amos did not pray again.
- The vision implied that the time was now ripe for Israelites to be punished by destruction.

(v) Vision of the destruction of the altar (Amos 9: 1 – 4)
- Amos saw the Lord standing by the altar.
- He then ordered for the destruction of the temple and its pillars.

- Every wicked person would be killed and could not hide.
- This vision meant that the shrines at Bethel and Dan would be destroyed because they were the centres of evil. No one would escape the punishment no matter where they hide.

THE TEACHINGS OF PROPHET AMOS

A. SOCIAL JUSTICE AND RESPONSIBILITY (AMOS 2: 6 – 8; 3: 9 – 12; 4: 1 – 3; 5: 10 – 15; 6: 1 – 8; 8: 4 – 6)

- Social justice refers to fair dealings in our interactions with other people.
- Responsibility means being accountable for our actions towards others. It shows how our actions affect the people we interact with.
- The commandments that God gave the Israelites were to guide them in their relationship with Him and fellow human beings.
- The Israelites were supposed to appreciate that every person was created in God's image and is equal in his eyes and therefore, no Israelite was supposed to despise or oppress his/her neighbour.
- In his teaching about social justice and responsibility, Amos condemned the social injustices that existed in Israel.

What are the teachings of prophet Amos on social justice and responsibility?

i. Oppression of the poor – The poor were oppressed by the rich and were made slaves until they could pay for their debts. They took excessive shares of the harvest of the poor. The rich therefore showed no value to the poor. Amos told them that God was going to punish them because of the unjust ways of acquiring and spending their wealth.

ii. Corruption and Bribery - Amos condemned the judges for abusing justice and judging cases in favour of the rich. The poor people's cases could not be heard because they were unable to bribe the judges.

iii. Dishonesty – Amos condemned the wealthy merchants who valued their business rather than religious festivals. They used false scales and sold poor quality goods to the poor. They also charged wheat at high interest rates.

iv. Sexual Immorality and Temple prostitution – Amos condemned sexual immorality which was prevalent in Israel. For example a father and a son could share the same girl sexually. They also practiced temple or cultic prostitution which made the temple unholy. Amos warned them that God's punishment was inevitable.

v. Greed and luxurious living – Amos condemned and warned those living luxuriously at the expense of the poor. The wives of the rulers forced their husbands to rob the properties of the poor to get luxuries like strong drinks. Amos warned that such people would face God's punishment.

vi. Robbery and violence – The prophet warned that those who practiced violence would be destroyed the same way an animal caught by a lion is destroyed.

vii.   Idolatry – The Israelites worshiped other gods, and offered sacrifices to them. Amos warned them that they were breaking God's covenant.

viii.   Slavery – the poor people who were unable to pay debts were sold into slavery by the rich. The merchants and rich land owners made them work like slaves and as slaves the poor were harshly treated. This was against the Law, which prohibited an Israelite from using a fellow Israelite as a slave.

Explain the relevance of Amos teachings on social justice and responsibility to Christians today.
-   Christians learn that God will and reward all those that obey his law.
-   Christians are called to practice what they preach and to condemn hypocrisy.
-   Christians should be just in their dealings with one another.
-   Christians should not pursue luxuries and self-indulgence when others lack basic needs.
-   They should condemn corruption and uphold justice.
-   They should bear in mind that every evil committed will be punished by God.
-   They should be aware of the dangers associated with wealth since it can divert their attention from God.
-   They should be ready at any time when called to do God's work.
-   They should prepare for the judgement day by being obedient to God's word.
-   They should not indulge themselves in activities that are harmful to their faith.

How is the church promoting social justice in Kenya today?
-   Condemning social injustices.
-   Advising the government in promoting social justice.
-   Helping the needy.
-   Preaching social justice.
-   Reporting cases of injustices to the authority.
-   Participating in movements against social injustice.

B. HYPOCRITICAL RELIGION IN ISRAEL (AMOS 4: 4 – 5; 5: 4 – 5, 5: 21 – 27)
Why was Amos against the Israelite way of worship?
The Israelites practiced the following evils which Amos condemned:
-   They practiced idolatry by worshipping other gods e.g. Sakkuth and Kaiwan, the Assyrian gods.
-   Worshippers went to holy places to satisfy their own desires other than pleasing God.
-   Worshippers were making offerings to show off, and not out of love for God.
-   The offerings which the Israelites made at the holy places did not reflect holy lives.
-   They practiced religious syncretism, where they worshipped Yahweh alongside idols.

Explain the teachings of Amos on Hypocritical Religion in Israel. (Amos 4:4-5, 5:21-27).

- Bethel and Gilgal were the most important places of worship in Israel and the people thought that by going to these high places of worship would please God. Amos told them that true worship meant living one's life in accordance with God's law.
- Amos demanded that worship rituals be purified because they had been contaminated with pagan thoughts and practices.
- Amos told them that God would not accept their worship while they practiced injustice.
- Amos warned them of the coming punishment of being taken to exile because of their idolatry.
- Amos demanded that they conduct the religious ceremonies in purity and return to the covenant way of life.
- He stated that true religion is practicing justice and righteousness.

List the religious evils condemned by Prophet Amos.

- Human sacrifice.
- Idolatry.
- Temple prostitution.
- Syncretism.
- Insincere worship.
- Empty sacrifices.

What is the relevance of Amos teaching on hypocritical religion to Christians today?

- Amos stresses on justice and righteousness as features of true religion. Christians should live right regardless of the church they attend.
- Church leaders need to rehabilitate the poor, widows and the sick for them to fit in society.
- Christians should shun luxurious living to help those who are in poverty.
- Like Amos, Christians should condemn hypocrisy in the church where some members do good in order to be praised.
- Christians' ways of worship must be in line with the teachings of Jesus and reflect their way of life.
- Christians must turn away from gods and worship God through Jesus.

Identify the ways in which Christians practice hypocritical religion.

- They are insincere in their worship as they engage in elaborate religious rites yet they are unjust and always oppress the poor.
- They give empty offerings as their aim is to show off and not out of love for Yahweh.
- They practice religious syncretism by combining aspects of Christianity with those of their diverse African religious heritage.
- They practice idolatry by worshipping money, material wealth etc.
- Their actions go against covenant way of life by exploiting the poor and engaging in bribery to pervert justice.

- Some Christians practice sexual immorality.
- Some Christians practice drunkenness.
- Some Christians are dishonest in their business dealings as they evade taxes, use false scales etc.

What are the forms of idolatry that threaten Christianity today?

- Material wealth.
- Devil worship.
- Crave for leadership positions/power.
- Belief in witchcraft.
- Personal appearance/beauty/handsomeness.
- Sexual immorality.
- Work/job/career/profession.
- Drugs and substance abuse.
- Leisure/sports.
- Political personalities.

C. JUDGMENT AGAINST ISRAEL AND OTHER NATIONS (PUNISHMENT AND REPENTANCE) (AMOS 1: 3-5; 5:1-17; 6: 7; 8: 9)

- In the Old Testament, judgment refers to the punishment that God would subject to individuals and nations with a view to reforming or changing them.
- Judgement is meant to make or enable individuals and nations to repent and turn to God.
- Punishment came as a result of people committing certain evils, both social and religious.

JUDGEMENT AND PUNISHMENT AGAINST OTHER NATIONS

Prophet Amos prophesied judgement and punishment to the following nations and for the following reasons:

- **Syria (Damascus) (Amos 1: 3 – 5)** – they mistreated pregnant women of Gilead during their war with Israel. God would destroy the whole nation by sending divine fire on their land.
- **Philistia and Gaza (Amos 1: 6 – 8)** – they sold their fellow citizens as slaves to Edom. God would send his divine fire to burn down her palaces.
- **Tyre/Phoenicia (Amos 1: 9 – 10)** – the king of Tyre sold Israelites as slaves to Edom. God would send fire to destroy Tyre.
- **Edom (Amos 1: 11 – 12)** – The Edomites attacked Jerusalem, killed its citizens and carried some into slavery. God would destroy them with fire.
- **Ammon (Amos 1: 13 – 15)** – were cruel to the pregnant women of Gilead during the war with Israel. The king and his subjects would be sent into exile.
- **Moab (Amos 2: 1 – 3)** – they raided the royal graves and burnt the bones of the dead kings of Edom, which meant total destruction of the royal family. This was after they defeated the Edomites in war. Moab would be destroyed by divine fire.

JUDGEMENT AND PUNISHMENT AGAINST ISRAEL (Amos 2: 4 – 16; 3: 1 – 2)

- Being chosen people of God, the Israelites did not expect that they would be judged and punished like other nations.
- However, they were going to be punished for the sins they had committed.
- Amos pronounced divine judgement on the people of Israel because of the social injustices and religious sins they had committed. They had broken God's covenant in the following ways:

i. They enslaved the poor, orphans and widows.
ii. They practiced bribery in law courts.
iii. They practiced sexual immorality was rampant such as temple prostitution.
iv. They charged high interest rates on loans borrowed by the poor.
v. Land grabbing was widespread in Israel.
vi. They practiced idolatry and religious hypocrisy.
vii. Judah would also be punished because she had broken the covenant treaty with God.

Forms of punishment Amos prophesied for Israel and Judah

- Israel would be surrounded by the Assyrians, who would destroy the people and their land.
- They would be attacked by an epidemic.
- There would be an earthquake that would destroy the houses of the rich and the poor.
- Famine of the word of God – Spiritual famine or hunger for God's word.
- There would be an eclipse and the land would be covered in darkness.
- There would be drought leading to painful thirst.
- The altars at Dan and Bethel would be destroyed.
- Those who will hide will be carried to exile in Assyria.

What is the relevance of prophet Amos message on judgment to Christians?

- God will judge evil and punish the wrongdoers.
- Christians should be courageous as they face life situations.
- God is universal and will pass judgement on all nations.
- Christians have to put God's teachings into practice to avoid false holiness.
- God hates sin which is why he judges all nations.

State the evils condemned by prophet Amos in Israel

- Oppression of the poor.
- Corruption and bribery.
- Dishonesty.
- Sexual immorality.
- Drunkenness.
- Pride in material possessions.
- Insincere worship.
- Empty sacrifices.

- Syncretism.
- Idolatry.

What lessons do we learn about God from the teaching of Amos on judgment and punishment?

- God is universal/judges all nations; He expects people to be morally and spiritually upright.
- God hates evil; He condemned the Israelite and other nations for disobeying him.
- God is merciful since through Amos he promised that the remnants shall remain after punishment and restore them back to Himself.
- God is concerned about people's welfare e.g. he speaks on behalf of the pregnant women.
- God gives prosperity to those who sincerely turn to him and serve him.
- He is a just God because he passes judgement to those who sin against him.
- God's people should behave in a way to match their religious holiness by putting God's teachings in practice.
- God is supreme hence leaders are not above the law of God.
- He expects people to live according to the will of God to avoid judgement.

D. ISRAEL'S ELECTION (AMOS 2:9 -11; 3:1-2; 9: 7)

- Election is a concept in the Bible referring to God choosing people to serve his purpose in the world.

Amos taught the following about Israel's election:

- Israel's election was due to Yahweh's love for their forefathers and not because she merited it. She could lose this priviledge to any other nation if she became proud and selfish.
- The election placed on Israel a responsibility to make God known to other nations.
- Israel would be punished severely if she failed to meet this responsibility.
- Amos reminded them of how God liberated them out of slavery in Egypt.
- God made the Israelites his own chosen race by making a Covenant with them at Mt. Sinai.
- God gave them a special land to inherit, laws to guide them and prophets and priests to lead them in the Covenant way of life.
- However, God's continued favour to them would be determined by their obedience to Him.

Relevance of the teachings of Amos on Election for Christians

- Christians are the chosen people of God as Peter refers to them as a chosen people, a royal priesthood, a holy nation, and God's own people.
- Christians are chosen to proclaim the Good News of God.
- Christians should understand that God's election is not a guarantee of getting into the kingdom of God.
- Christians have to understand the moral responsibility that goes with election.

- Through Jesus Christ, Christians have entered into a special covenant relationship with God.
- As disciples of Jesus, Christians should implement Jesus' commands through teaching, healing and other charitable works.

E. THE DAY OF THE LORD (AMOS 5: 18 – 20; 6: 3 – 5; 8: 7 – 13)

The Israelites had the following expectations about the day of the Lord:

- God would realize His covenant promises e.g. making them prosper and peaceful and crown her with glory and honour.
- God would revenge against her enemies, and fight on her behalf and make them victorious.
- They expected that God would punish the wicked nations with disaster.
- They thought that on this day, Israel would be safe from her enemies.
- They thought God would exalt them above all nations of the earth.

However, Amos reversed their expectations about victory and happiness that would accompany the Day of the Lord. Amos declared that on the Day of the Lord, God would punish Israel for their sins and breaking of His covenant with them.

What is the day of the Lord and what did prophet Amos teach about it?

- The day of the Lord will be a day when God's anger will be rekindled upon Israel because of their sins.
- It would be a day of doom and darkness and not light.
- He taught that it's a day of terror and disaster against the rich land owners and rulers.
- It will be a day with heavenly signs such as the eclipses. The sun would go down at noon and darken the earth.
- It would be a day when sorrow and weeping over the ruined farms and buildings by the earthquake.
- It will be a day of mourning and every home will observe the rites of mourning e.g. wearing sack clothes, shaving their heads and hymns of joy would turn into songs of mourning.
- Israel would be defeated by her enemies.
- It will be a day of famine and drought when they will hunger for the word of God.

What is the relevance of Amos' teaching on the day of the Lord?

- To Christians, the day of the Lord is the second coming of Christ, which is, the end times.
- Christians should understand that the day of the Lord will be a day of judgment.
- Christians should await, expect and hope for it.
- Nobody knows the exact day and time when Jesus will come back hence Christians should be ready at all times.
- On that day everybody will give an account of his/her actions.
- Christians should prepare for this day by living an upright life.
- On this day the sinners will be punished and the righteous will be rewarded.
- The day of the Lord shall be accompanied with signs.

F. THE REMNANT AND RESTORATION (AMOS 9: 8 – 15)

- The word remnant refers to a small number that survives destruction. It is to refer to the small number of the faithful Israelites who would survive God's punishment.
- Although Amos pronounced destruction on Israel due to their sins, he however felt there was some hope for those who would sincerely repent and turn to God.
- Through the faithful remnants, the promises of God would be fulfilled and blessings would come to the nations.
- Amos gives a message of hope for the future restoration of the people of Israel, which would come only after God's judgement.

Describe the teaching of Amos on remnant and restoration.

- God would re-unite Judah and Israel into one strong Davidic Kingdom.
- God would raise a descendant of King David to rule over Israel forever.
- The nation of Israel would be peaceful and prosperous.
- The Israelites would never be taken into exile again.
- God would bring the exiles back to their land.
- The people would rebuild their cities so that the remnants can occupy them.
- The land would be productive/grapes will be in abundance and wine would be plenty.
- The people would grow food and harvest it.

How is the teaching on Remnant and Restoration relevant to Christians today?

- Christians should learn to stand by the teachings of Jesus even if everyone is doing evil for they in turn will be the remnant.
- Christians especially the youth should shun immorality and drug abuse because the body is the temple of God.
- Christians are the today's remnant and so they should live exemplary lives.
- Christians are the remnant whom God continues to use in the world.
- Christians need to know that the remnants are only those who choose, to live a righteous life.
- The Christians will enjoy eternal life in paradise just as the Israelites did after destruction.

What did prophet Amos condemn in the Northern Kingdom?

- Mistreatment of the less privileged in the society.
- Women who were living luxurious lives.
- Wealthy traders who overcharged their goods.
- Murder.
- Cult prostitution.
- Exploitation of the poor.
- Bribery.

State five lessons a Christian can learn from the religious message prophet Amos had for the people of the Northern Kingdom

- They should be courageous and condemn all forms of evils in the society.
- They should avoid insincere worship by being humble before God during worship and leading exemplary lives.
- They should be willing to confess their sins and ask for forgiveness to avoid punishment.
- They should know that God is a universal God and makes moral claims on everybody despite his nationality.
- They should preach against and avoid sexual immorality, drugs and alcohol abuse.

Give the basic teaching of Amos

- His theme was divine judgment of sin.
- He emphasized social justice, "let justice run down like waters and righteousness like a mighty stream.
- Social justice was inseparable from piety.
- He called the people to repent and reform.
- He foretold the destruction, and desolation that was among the Israelites.
- He concludes by setting up of the Messiah's Kingdom and spiritual happiness of the Kingdom of Israel.

What are the characteristics of God according to Amos?

- He is Holy and righteous.
- He is the sustainer.
- He is a just God.
- He is a universal God.
- He is the creator.
- He is super natural.

What are the similarities in the prophetic ministry of prophets Amos and Jeremiah?

- Both taught on the universality of Yahweh.
- Both pronounced their messages fearlessly.
- Both of them had their prophecies come to pass, though they were rejected.
- Both proclaimed God's judgement but gave hope that He would not destroy them forever.
- They both believed in Yahweh as a righteous and forgiving God.
- They both forbade hypocritical worship and insisted on true worship.
- They both foretold of natural calamities and harsh punishments to those who don't repent.
- They both condemned evils of their day and told people to turn to God by repenting.
- They both received opposition in their work.
- They received God's support in their prophetic Ministry.
- They responded in faith and obedience to God's calling.

Give four reasons why Amos was against the Israelite way of worship.

- They had broken their covenant with God.
- They worshiped idols.
- They exploited one another.
- Their worship was external.
- Their sacrifices and offerings were a show off.
- Their worship was syncretic in nature.

Topic 10: JEREMIAH

POLITICAL, SOCIAL AND RELIGIOUS BACKGROUND OF PROPHET JEREMIAH

Political background

- Jeremiah started his ministry as a prophet in Judah during the thirteenth year of the reign of King Josiah
- Jeremiah prophesied for a period of 40 years, during which five kings Josiah, Jehoahaz, Jehoakim, Jehoaichin and Zedekiah ruled over Israel.
- At this time, Assyria was the super power in the region and had conquered the Northern Kingdom, Israel, and was therefore a threat to Judah.
- However, fourteen years after he began his prophecy, the Assyrian empire finally collapsed when Nineveh, her capital city, was destroyed by the Babylonians.
- In 609 BCE, Judah fought Egypt, and King Josiah was killed when the Egyptian army attacked Judah.
- For several years, Judah was controlled by Egypt because the power of Assyria had declined and Egypt was gaining greater power in the Middle East.
- Egypt was defeated by Babylon led by King Nebuchadnezzar.
- Consequently, Judah came under the rule of Babylon.
- Babylon invaded Judah and finally destroyed her.
- Jeremiah prophesied during this time of political instability.
- Judah was ruled by King Zedekiah under whose reign the city of Jerusalem and its temple were destroyed and people taken to exile.
- Jeremiah witnessed poor social conditions, neglect of the poor, the innocent were murdered, adultery and many other evils existed.

Social background

- The people of Judah had forgotten the Covenant Way of Life.
- They did not live as brothers and sisters as required in the Mosaic Law.
- Jeremiah identified the following social evils among the people of Judah:
  i. The orphans, widows and aliens were oppressed, exploited and denied their rights.
  ii. The rich acquired wealth through unjust means.
  iii. Sexual immorality such as adultery was rampant in the society.
  iv. The innocent were murdered.
  v. Bribery and corruption were practiced in law courts.
  vi. Priests and false prophets told lies, they cheated people that all was well while it was not, thus misleading them.
  vii. Rulers had failed to lead people to the Covenant Way of Life and, therefore, led them astray.
- Jeremiah observed that the society was morally corrupt and the people did not want to acknowledge their sins.
- It is this state of affairs that made Jeremiah to address the social evils in his teachings.

Religious background

During Jeremiah's time religion was corrupted because the people had broken the Sinai covenant. The people had done the following:-

- People worshipped idols in the temple (Jeremiah 7: 30 – 31, 19: 5).
- Kings had married foreign wives who led them into idol worship.
- King Manasseh had opened up pagan shrines and installed idols in them (2 king 2:16).
- They did not listen to the messengers of God.
- The rich enriched themselves at the expense of the poor.
- Priests and false prophets told lies to the people.
- They practiced syncretism

The worship of idols continued until the time of King Josiah who introduced religious reforms in Judah which were supported by Jeremiah. However, King Josiah's reforms did not succeed in changing the hearts of people since the people stopped worshipping Canaanite gods in public but continued to worship them in private.

Explain the reforms King Josiah made in Judah during the time of prophet Jeremiah

- He abolished the worship of Baal.
- He ordered the repair of the temple of God.
- He burnt foreign objects in the temple.
- He led a national ceremony to renew the covenant faith.
- Human sacrifice was stopped.
- Temple prostitution was stopped.
- He discontinued consultation of mediums.
- Passover feast was reinstated.

PERSONAL LIFE AND THE CALL OF JEREMIAH (JEREMIAH 1)

Give an account of Jeremiah's personal life. (Jeremiah l)

- Jeremiah was born in the village known as Anathoth, near Jerusalem.
- He was a son of priest called Hilkiah, who was a priest in Anathoth.
- Jeremiah was well-educated and had a deep knowledge of the Law of Moses and the prophetic teachings since he was from a priestly family, even though he was not a priest.
- He was called by God when he was still a young man.
- He was isolated from the society since he didn't marry and he didn't attend social gatherings.
- He was rejected by his people because of his prophetic mission, which involved pronouncing judgment on his own people for their sinfulness.
- He was imprisoned for prophesying coming punishment.
- He died probably in Egypt as a man of God.

Describe the call of Jeremiah (Jeremiah 1)

- Jeremiah was called when he was still young man during the reign of King Josiah in 627BC.

- The call was in form of a dialogue instructing Jeremiah that he had been appointed to be a messenger of God.
- God instructed him to pronounce the judgment of God to Judah.
- God touched his lips to symbolize He was the one going to put words in Jeremiah's mouth.
- Jeremiah responded positively and God promised to be with him.
- Jeremiah saw two visions:
  i. The first was a branch of almond tree to mean that God was watching to ensure that his words came to pass.
  ii. The second vision was of a boiling pot facing the North. This symbolized that God would appoint a nation from the North (Babylon) to execute his judgment.
- God then directed Jeremiah to go and tell the people about the revelation.

EVILS ADDRESSED BY PROPHET JEREMIAH
Name and explain the evils addressed by Jeremiah.
a) NECROMANCY (Jeremiah 14:14; 27: 9)
- It is the act of consulting mediums, or practicing divination, magic or sorcery and also consulting the spirits of the dead.
- Jeremiah warned King Zedekiah against listening to diviners, mediums or soothsayers who were advising him to rebel against the Babylonians.
- Necromancy was condemned in the Law of Moses.

Give the reasons why Jeremiah condemned necromancy in Judah
- It indicated lack of faith in God.
- It gave false messages which did not come from God.
- It was a form of deception that led people away from God.
- It polluted the true worship of God.
- It showed lack of knowledge of one God.
- It brought God's punishment upon people.

b) DISHONESTY/DECEPTION (Jeremiah 3, 4, 5, 7, 9)
- This is falsehood, insincerity and lack of moral values.
- The priests and prophets spoke lies and led people astray. They cheated the people by telling them that God was not going to punish them.
- The people of Judah were also dishonest in their worship since they worshipped God alongside other gods.
- Jeremiah called upon the people to be sincere, pure in heart, repent in truth, show integrity and purify their hearts. He also condemned their external religious practices.

c) FALSE PROPHECY (HANANIAH)
- Jeremiah challenged the false prophecies of Hananiah who had prophesied that Judah would be victorious and will break the rule and power of the Babylonians and the exiles will return to Judah.

- On the contrary, Jeremiah proclaimed that God would use the Babylonians to punish the people of Judah for their unfaithfulness and sinfulness.
- He also predicted Hananiah's death which was fulfilled.

d) HUMAN SACRIFICE
- The people of Judah had started worshipping many idols and were even offering their children to these idols at the Valley of Ben Hinnom.
- Jeremiah condemned offering human sacrifices, which was copied from the Baal religions.
- The Law of Moses forbids murder because human life is sacred.

e) IDOLATRY (JEREMIAH 2; 3; 4; 5; 7; 9; 10; 23; 28)
- Jeremiah condemned idolatry which was practiced in the following ways:
  i. The Israelites built altars for the worship of idols.
  ii. They kept idols in the Temple of Yahweh.
  iii. They offered human sacrifices.
  iv. Prophesying in the name of Baal.
  v. They practiced temple prostitution which defiled the temple of Yahweh.
- Jeremiah ridiculed idols as being powerless since idols cannot answer people's prayers.
- He described idolatry as forsaking God's love and defiling the holy land.

List the lessons that Christians can learn from Jeremiah's teaching on evil and false prophets.
- Christians should be honest in their worship of God instead of mere outward show of religion.
- Christians should be aware that there are true and false prophets.
- Christians should not practice human sacrifice for it is wrong and it does not wipe sins.
- Christians should have courage and be firm in their principles when faced with opposition.
- They should be truthful and faithful in their vocations.
- They should condemn all sorts of evil in society.
- They should be governed by laws of God.
- They should condemn destruction of human life and violence in general.

How can Christians show respect to God's places of worship?
- Giving church offering.
- Contributing to the establishment and maintenance of their church building.
- Keeping the places of worship (church) clean.
- Respecting the church leaders.
- Attending worship sessions.
- By condemning evil particles committed in church.

THE TEMPLE SERMON (JEREMIAH 7: 1-8: 1-3)

A sermon refers to the interpretation of God's word by a priest, pastor or lay leaders.

Describe Jeremiah's Temple Sermon

- Jeremiah gave his sermon at the gate of the Temple of Jerusalem as commanded by God.
- He told the people to change their ways of life and to stop the evils they were practicing.
- He told them to stop exploiting and oppressing the aliens, widows and orphans.
- He warned them against idolatry murder of innocent people.
- He also told the people that they were insincere in their worship since they broke the commandments and engaged in evil then proceeded to the temple to worship Yahweh.
- Jeremiah told them that God would destroy Jerusalem and the Temple just like he destroyed the shrine at Shiloh if they continued with their evil ways.
- He also condemned them for worshipping idols by offering sacrifices to those idols.
- He accused them of being stubborn and rebellious and since they had refused to heed to the teachings of the prophets.
- Due to their sinfulness, Jeremiah prophesied that Jerusalem and its people would be destroyed.
- He prophesied God's judgement on Israel when many people would lose their lives and their corpses would be unburied and eaten by vultures.
- None of them would escape the punishment. The few who would survive would be taken to exile.

Give reasons why Jeremiah gave the sermon at the gate of the temple

- King Jehoiakim shed innocent blood despite the advice from prophets.
- Israelites continued with Baal worship.
- Israelites practiced idolatry.
- Pagan gods and idols were put in the temple.
- People were hypocritical in their worship.
- There was moral decay among the Israelites.
- Israelites allowed false prophets to thrive.
- There was widespread oppression and exploitation of the poor.
- They had false belief and a false sense of security about the temple.
- Social injustice was widespread.

Identify seven evils condemned by prophet Jeremiah in the temple sermon.

- Hypocrisy in worship/insincere worship
- Syncretism
- Idolatry/worship of false gods
- False security in the temple
- Offering of human sacrifices
- Sexual immorality such as adultery and incest.
- Telling lies/dishonesty

What can modern leaders learn from Jeremiah's sermon in the temple?

- Christians need to have a personal relationship with God.
- Christians should rely on God rather than consulting spirits.
- Christians should condemn idolatry.
- Christians should avoid false prophets.
- Christians should condemn destruction of life.
- Priests and church leaders should be firm in their faith.

RELEVANCE OF JEREMIAH'S TEACHINGS ON EVILS AND FALSE PROPHETS TO CHRISTIANS TODAY

- Christians should have total trust in God's providence.
- Christian leaders should preach the truth about divine judgement on sinners and avoid of giving people false hope.
- Christians should be honest and fair in their dealings with others.
- Christians should be sincere in worship and avoid hypocrisy in worship.
- Christians should be aware of false prophets and preachers who may come in the name of Jesus in order to lead people astray.
- Christians should condemn social evils that exist in the society and churches today.
- They should lead morally upright or exemplary lives for others to emulate.
- Christians should call sinners to repentance for them to avoid divine judgement.
- Christians should avoid idolatry e.g. worship of material wealth, devil worship e.t.c.

TEACHINGS ON JUDGMENT AND PUNISHMENT (JEREMIAH 5:12–18; 6: 1–30; 7: 30–8:1–17; 10: 17–25; 14: 1–18; 15:1–9; 16:16 –18; 17:1–13; 21: 1–14; 25: 1–38; 39: 1 – 10)

Judgement refers to the punishment and destruction that befell individuals, communities and nations as a result of disobeying God's commandments. God's punishment was meant to correct those who had done evil.

God's punishment befell Israelites due to their failure to observe the covenant way of life.

a) Causes of the Judgement and punishment

- The rich oppressed the poor, widows and aliens.
- Offering human sacrifices contrary to God's commandments.
- They defiled the temple by placing images of idols in it.
- The people did not follow the teachings of the prophets.
- Priests and prophets spoke lies preaching peace when there was no peace.
- They practiced idolatry.
- Judah had sinned against God and had disobeyed His Commandments.
- The people practiced necromancy, that is, consulting mediums and acts of divination.
- The people of Judah worshipped God using foreign religious rituals, used in worshipping idol gods. They refused to turn back to God through repentance
- The rulers and religious leaders led people astray, away from the Covenant Way of Life

b) How God would punish Judah

- Judah would be attacked by a nation from the North, that is, Babylonian.
- All the people would be carried to exile and Judah would remain without inhabitants.
- Drought would come upon the people of Judah, which would cause a lot of suffering to human beings and animals.
- He would destroy Jerusalem contrary to the expectations of the people.
- Judgement would be preceded by signs such as lack of peace, terror, starvation and earthquakes.
- Judah would be surrounded by an enemy who would attack her severely.
- The bones of the leaders would be exhumed and spread on the ground in humiliation.
- Many corpses will be unburied and ravaged by vultures and beasts.
- Not even the righteous servants of God could intervene on behalf of the Israelites to prevent them from the inevitable punishment.
- God would use Babylon to also destroy other nations for disobedience and killing their leaders.
- God would in turn punish the Babylonians who oppressed His people of Judah after the exile.

c) Forms of Punishment for Judah

As a result of their disobedience to Yahweh, the People of Judah experienced punishment in the following ways:

- The city of Jerusalem was captured and came under the rule of Babylon.
- Zedekiah's sons, government officials and many other people died during the Babylonian invasion.
- King Zedekiah was blinded and taken to Babylon as a prisoner of war.
- The temple and the buildings of Jerusalem were completely destroyed.
- The Babylonians stole everything of value from Jerusalem and the temple.
- All the people of Jerusalem were taken to exile in Babylon as slaves.
- The vineyards and fields of those who had gone to exile were given to the poor by the Babylonians.

Which evils would Prophet Jeremiah condemn in Kenya today?

- Idolatry.
- Sexual immorality.
- Struggle for power.
- Corruption/bribery.
- Exploitation of the poor by the rich.
- Devil worship.
- Desire for wealth/materialism.

What can Christians do to avoid God's punishment?

- Obeying God's commandments.
- Preaching the Good News of Jesus to others.

- Condemning all evils in society.
- Responding to God's call to serve others.
- Assisting the needy and the disadvantaged.
- Praying.
- Avoiding temptations.
- Repenting their sins.
- Living exemplary lives/be role models.
- Asking for guidance from the Holy spirit

SYMBOLIC ACTS RELATED TO JUDGEMENT AND PUNISHMENT (JEREMIAH 13; 16; 18; 19; 24; 27)

Give the significance of the symbolic acts related to judgment and punishment.

a) **The linen waist cloth** (Jer 13:1 – 11): God instructed Jeremiah to buy a linen waist cloth and wear it. After which he was instructed to hide it in the rocks in river Euphrates. On retrieving it after some days, it was spoilt and useless. This symbolizes how Israel was once close to God but now they had turned against him. The rotting of the cloth symbolized the punishment they would face and make them useless.

b) **Jeremiah's Life** (Jer 16): Jeremiah was commanded by God neither to marry nor have a family. This signified that the coming judgement would disrupt the normal family life.

He was also not to enter any house where a funeral was being held or mourn or show sympathy to the bereaved. This signified that God had withdrawn his blessings, love and pity and that there would be no time to mourn the dead and the remnants would have no one to comfort them.

Jeremiah was also restricted from entering a house where there was feasting which meant that the time for feasting and happiness was over and it would be replaced by suffering and grief.

c) **The potter and his clay** (Jer 18): Jeremiah was instructed to visit a potter's house. He watched the potter make his clay pots. He observed that whenever the pot had defects, the potter would press the clay into a lump and mould another pot. This illustrated the relationship between God and his people. The potter represented God while the clay represented people. This signified that God had authority to tear down a nation or build a nation in the same way a potter could mould or destroy a pot.

d) **The Earthen flask** (Jer 19): God instructed Jeremiah to buy an earthen flask and smash it publicly, in the presence of priests and elders. This signified that God would destroy Jerusalem and Judah as Jeremiah did to the flask.

e) **The vision of two baskets of figs** (Jer 2 - 4): Jeremiah saw a vision of two baskets of figs. One basket had good fruits while the other had spoilt fruits. The good fruits represented the exiles who were taken to Babylon and would be restored back to their home.

The bad fruits represented the King Zedekiah and the survivors who fled to Egypt. Since this group had defied God's word, God would send judgement to them until they were all destroyed.

f) **Wooden ox yoke** (Jer 27): God wanted Jeremiah to make a yoke and wear it around his neck during the start of the reign of King Zedekiah. This signified the coming subjection of Judah under Babylonian rule. God would use Nebuchadnezzar to bring judgment upon the nations.

THE FALL OF JERUSALEM AND THE EXILE OF THE ISRAELITES (JEREMIAH 39)

Describe the fall of Jerusalem and exile of the Israelites (Jer 39)

- The destruction of Jerusalem took place in 587 BC during the reign of King Zedekiah.
- King Nebuchadnezzar of Babylon laid siege on Jerusalem, and smashed the army of Judah, and broke into the wall of Jerusalem.
- Zedekiah, his sons and officials were captured by the Babylonians and taken to Riblah, in Syria.
- Zedekiah's sons were executed in his presence. He was then blinded, chained and sent captive to Babylon.
- Nebuchadnezzar's officials took their seats in the middle gate entering the city.
- The villages and the royal palace were burnt down. Solomon's temple was demolished and its treasures looted.
- The people of Judah were captured and Judah made the province of Babylon with Gedaliah as its governor.
- The poor people were spared and given fields and vineyards to cultivate.
- Prophet Jeremiah was spared and was treated well by Nebuchadnezzar. He was asked to choose whether to stay in Judah or go to Babylon and he chose to remain in Judah.
- The people who remained in Judah continued to live in their stubbornness since they did not understand that the fall of Jerusalem and the exile were due to their unfaithfulness to God.
- And so they were punished.
- In exile, the Israelites went through a time of spiritual purification.

Explain the circumstances which led to the exile of Israelites in Babylon.

- The Babylonians had become the most powerful nation.
- Israelites had forsaken the covenant way of life and that was the punishment.
- In 589 BC the Babylonians broke into the city and destroyed it including the temple of Jerusalem.
- In 587 BC the Babylonians army returned to Judah and surrounded the city of Jerusalem.
- Nebuchadnezzar defeated the Egyptians in 605 BC and was crowned the king so there were no obstacles preventing him to conquer other small nations.

SUFFERING AND LAMENTATIONS OF JEREMIAH (JEREMIAH 11: 18 – 23; 12:1 – 6; 15: 10 – 21; 17: 14 – 18; 18: 18 – 23; 20: 1 – 6; 26; 37; 38)

a) **The plot against Jeremiah's life (Jeremiah 11: 18 – 23; 12: 1 – 6)**
- Jeremiah's relatives and friends from his hometown, Anathoth, planned to kill him because he relayed God's message of judgement to them.
- Jeremiah prayed to God for revenge against his enemies and also lamented wondering why God allowed the wicked to prosper and the dishonest to succeed.
- God encouraged him to stand firm and continue preaching his message even when the situation worsened.

b) **Jeremiah's lament about his isolation (Jeremiah 15: 10 – 21)**

- Jeremiah was isolated and suffered loneliness due to his work that involved pronouncing judgement and punishment on the people of Judah for their sinfulness.
- At this stage he despaired because he felt that the work he had done was futile and felt that God had abandoned him.
- However, God promised Jeremiah that if he remained steadfast and repented for doubting God, he would be forgiven and would be allowed to continue with God's work.

c) **Jeremiah's lament on the people's mockery (Jeremiah 17: 14 – 18; 18: 18 – 23)**
- The people mocked Jeremiah because his prophecies had not been fulfilled.
- They also tried to kill him arguing that even if they killed him, God would always raise up other prophets.
- Jeremiah further lamented to God that the people he was interceding for had turned against him.

d) **Jeremiah's torture by Pashhur (Jeremiah 20: 1 – 6)**
- Jeremiah's preaching on judgement was rejected by Pashhur, the priest, who had Jeremiah arrested, beaten and chained overnight and later chased from the temple gates.
- However, this did not stop Jeremiah, since he pronounced judgement for Pashhur, his family and the people of Judah who would be exiled in Babyon.

e) **Jeremiah's arrest and trial (Jeremiah 26)**
- For having prophesied the destruction of the Temple and city of Jerusalem, Jeremiah was arrested by the priests and false prophets of Jerusalem and accused of blasphemy.
- Jeremiah defended himself when he was brought before the princes in three ways:
    i. He argued that his message was from God, this meant that he was God's true prophet.
    ii. His message was conditional and therefore if the people repented and reformed their ways, God would not send disaster to them.
    iii. He warned them if they sentenced him to death, they would be guilty of the murder of an innocent person.
- After listening to Jeremiah's defense the officials were convinced that his message was from God and therefore they set him free.

f) **Jeremiah's imprisonment (Jeremiah 37; 38)**
- Jeremiah was arrested when he tried to leave Jerusalem to go back to hometown, Anathoth, to claim his share of the family land. He was accused of deserting his people to join the Babylonians.
- This accusation amounted to treason, an offence which was punishable by death.
- Jeremiah was brought before the princes who beat him up and demanded for his execution.
- He was detained in an underground cell where he remained for several days.
- Later on he pleaded with King Zedekiah to release him from the dungeon.
- King Zedekiah did not release him but ordered that he be placed in the palace courtyard where he stayed being fed on bread and water daily.
- Jeremiah continued giving the same message to the court officials that they must surrender to the Babylonians.

- This made the court officials even angrier with Jeremiah.
- They had him lowered into a dry well with ropes for him to starve to death.
- He however was rescued by Ebedmelech, an official of the king, who begged the king to rescue Jeremiah.

The relevance of Jeremiah's suffering and lamentations to Christians

- Christians learn that as Jeremiah they will be rejected by their families and communities for the sake of the gospel.
- Christians should be ready to face persecution for the sake of Christ, but persistence in prayer will see them victorious.
- Christians learn that their messages will not always be accepted by the people.
- Christians should draw security and protection from God for deliverance from enemies.
- Christians are encouraged to pray for their persecutors and not exercise vengeance.
- Christians learn that tribulations and suffering are meant to strengthen their faith.
- Christians learn to be faithful through difficult times in their spiritual life.
- Christians should always tell the truth about God's will regardless of the consequences.
- Christians should pray for their enemies and leave vengeance against their enemies to God.

How can Christians help church leaders to perform their duties effectively?

- Giving financial/material help.
- Advising or counselling them on various issues.
- Encouraging them in their work.
- Participating fully in church activities and functions.
- Giving tithes and offerings faithfully.
- Praying for them.
- Respecting them.
- Practicing and obeying the word of God.
- Defending them from unfair criticism.
- Providing training opportunities for them.

Cite the problems prophet Jeremiah encountered in his Ministry

- He was rejected by his family and relatives.
- He was accused falsely.
- Israelites rejected his message (refused to repent).
- He faced death threats.
- He suffered loneliness and solitude.
- The scroll was burnt by King Jehoiakim.
- He was beaten by court officials.
- He was banned from going to the temple.
- He was referred to as a traitor and insulted, mocked and ridiculed.
- He was imprisoned.
- Had difficulties in convincing the people that this message was true.

- He went through spiritual struggle in his relationship with God.

THE SYMBOLIC ACTS RELATED TO HOPE AND RESTORATION (Jeremiah 24: 11 – 32: 1 – 14)

Due to stubbornness of the people of Judah and their refusal to listen to Jeremiah's call to repentance, God punished them by sending them into the Babylonian exile.

However, God still loved his people and was still faithful to his promises.

The period of suffering in exile was meant to be a period of reflection, transformation and readiness to turn to Yahweh.

God was ready to receive them back if they repented their sins.

God used Jeremiah to give the exiles hope and to bring them back to their homeland.

The symbolic acts that Jeremiah used to give hope to the people include:

a) The two Baskets of figs (Jeremiah 24: 1 – 10)
- Jeremiah saw a vision of two baskets of figs. The first basket contained good figs while the other contained bad ones.
- The good figs represented all the people of Judah who willingly submitted to the Babylonians.
- God promised to watch over and preserve them as a remnant, to protect them and restore them back to their homeland.

b) The Wooden Ox yoke (Jeremiah 27, 28)
- The wooden yoke symbolized the perseverance of the Jews in the exile in Babylon.
- The yoke would be broken and they will no longer be under foreign rule.
- God would restore them back to their homeland.

c) The Letter to the Exiles (Jeremiah 29)
- The exiles in Babylon were in a state of despair as they thought that Yahweh had deserted them or was powerless in the face of the Babylonian gods.
- Jeremiah therefore wrote a letter of encouragement to the exiles. In his letter he encouraged them in the following ways:
  i. They should build houses and settle down.
  ii. They should plant their gardens and eat their produce.
  iii. They should marry and bear children and increase in number.
  iv. They should live in peace in the Babylon and promote the welfare of their masters.
  v. They should not to listen to false prophets who lied to them that they would return back to Jerusalem quickly.
  vi. They would be restored back to their land after 70 years in exile.
  vii. They should trust in God and not to give up.

d) Jeremiah Purchases Land (Jeremiah 32: 1 – 15)
- Jeremiah bought land from his cousin Hanamel, in Anathoth as he was commanded by God.
- This was a sign that there was hope that God would bring back his people to Israel from where they had been taken into exile.
- Jeremiah told Baruch to seal the title deeds and keep them in clay jar for preservation for the future so that the land could be claimed again.

- This showed that even if the exiles stayed for a long time they would return to Judah, reclaim their property and their normal life would be restored. Houses, fields and vineyards would again be bought by the people of Israel in the land.

THE NEW COVENANT (JEREMIAH 23:1 – 8; 24; 29; 30; 31; 32; 33)

- The Israelites broke the covenant law despite constant reminders from God's prophets to return to the Covenant way of life.
- God therefore used other ways of establishing a permanent relationship with his people.
- This would be done through the establishment of a new and everlasting relationship as prophesied by prophet Jeremiah.
- Jeremiah prophesied about a New Covenant in order to give hope to the people of Judah who would be punished through exile.

The New Covenant foreseen by Prophet Jeremiah would have the following characteristics:

Outline the characteristics of the New Covenant as foreseen by Jeremiah the Prophet

- The law would be written in people's hearts.
- There would be personal knowledge of God.
- There would be forgiveness of sins.
- There would be personal responsibility for sin.
- It would bring a new community of God's people.
- God would take the initiative of establishing the covenant.
- The new community would be ruled by the righteous one from the Davidic family/dynasty.
- The Israelites would be given new hearts.
- This covenant would be an everlasting one/would not be broken.
- It would mark a new beginning/ a new era.

What lessons can Christians learn from prophet Jeremiah's teaching on new covenant?

- Christians should internalize the law of God and keep it in their hearts.
- They should have personal relationship with God.
- There is forgiveness of sins if one repents.
- Christians have an everlasting relationship with God.
- Those who repent their sins have a new beginning.
- They need to have faith in God.
- They should obey and practice the law of God.
- The new covenant is fulfilled in Jesus Christ.

Outline the ways in which the covenant foretold by Jeremiah is different from the Sinai covenant

- In Jeremiah's new covenant, laws were to be written in people's hearts whereas in the Sinai covenant laws were written on stone tablets.
- While the Sinai covenant had repeatedly been broken, Jeremiah's would last forever.

- In Jeremiah's covenant, there would be personal knowledge of God while in the Sinai Covenant, there was need for a mediator.
- In the new covenant there would be spontaneous forgiveness of sins through repentance of sin, whereas in the Sinai covenant, sins were carried forward to the next generation.
- In the new covenant, there would be personal responsibility for sin while in old, sin was a collective responsibility.
- The Sinai covenant was meant for one nation (Israel) while that of Jeremiah was for all humankind.

In what ways did Jesus fulfil the New Covenant foretold by Jeremiah?
- He began a new people, the Christians.
- He gave them a new will, a new spirit and a new heart.
- Through him, the whole Christian community has known God.
- They can get forgiveness through Christ.
- God dwells in people's hearts.
- Through him, people have a personal knowledge of God.
- He inaugurated the new covenant at the last supper sealed by his blood on the cross, his blood washed away people's sins.
- On the day he died, the curtain tore into two enabling people to have a direct link with God.

RELATING THE TEACHING OF JEREMIAH TO THE NEW TESTAMENT AND CHRISTIAN LIFE TODAY

Relate the teachings of Jeremiah to the New Testament and Christians' life today
- Jeremiah condemned the evils performed by the leaders. Christians should not mislead people but be examples to others.
- As Jeremiah was called to serve God so are the Christians. They are supposed to respond positively. Jesus also called his disciples and commissioned them to preach the good news.
- Jesus and his disciples were persecuted in the same way Jeremiah suffered. Christians are called to endure suffering as part of their calling.
- Like Jeremiah, Christians are called to denounce the evils in our society e.g. sorcery, abortion, rape, child molestation etc.
- Repentance is an important feature in Christianity. Christians are required to repent and call others to repentance which leads to forgiveness and eternal life.
- Jeremiah condemned hypocritical worship. Jesus condemned the hypocrisy of the Pharisees. Christians must not pretend to serve God with their outward piety rather they should serve God honestly.
- Jeremiah condemned idol worship. St Paul stresses that gods are powerless. Jesus states that no man can serve God and the mammon at the same time. Christians learn to give God all their priority.

- Jeremiah's prophecy of the new covenant is fulfilled in the life and ministry of Jesus. The new covenant makes the Christians have a personal relationship with God, with his laws written in their hearts.
- Jeremiah predicted judgment and punishment. Jesus tells off the Jewish leaders of their hypocrisy and pronounced judgement against them. Christians learn that they will be punished and judged on the judgement day. No evil will be spared.
- After exile Jeremiah gave hope to the Israelites. God would restore the remnant. Jesus gives us hope of eternal life if we believe in God.
- Jeremiah predicted the fall of Jerusalem and destruction of the temple. Jesus also prophesied the same. This showed that security is not the temple as the Israelites believed. Christians are called to hope in Jesus as their security.
- The righteous king that Jeremiah predicted was fulfilled in the coming of Jesus who establishes God's kingdom which will last forever.
- Christians learn to listen to the messages given to the servants of God.
- Christians learn the need for prayer when faced with difficulties.

Show how prophet Jeremiah fulfilled the characteristics of an Old Testament prophet.
- He received this call from God.
- He accepted this call.
- He was brave and courageous.
- He acted as the mediator between God and Israel.
- He used signs and symbols to pass his message.
- He saw visions.
- He was faithful to God.
- He stood for the covenant way of life.
- He foretold future happenings.
- He was God's spokesman.

Give ways which shows that God showed concern for Israel through Prophet Jeremiah
- He prophesied of a new covenant that could make everyone responsible for his sins.
- Jeremiah's letter to exiles was full of messages of hope.
- Jeremiah prophesied of a righteous king from Davidic lineage who would rule forever with justice.
- Jeremiah taught that God's punishment was a corrective measure through which they could learn and return to God.
- He prophesied that God would punish the Israelites for their sins but forgive them if they repented.
- During his call God told him that he would destroy Israel but restore them as His people.

In what ways are the teachings of Jeremiah similar to those of Jesus?
- Both condemned hypocrisy.
- Both corrected the attitude towards the temple/challenged false belief about the temple.
- Both give the message of hope and restoration.
- Jeremiah's message about the new covenant through Jesus' death.

- Both warned people against false prophecy.
- Both touch on the theme of God to a universal saviour and a just judge.
- Both condemned idolatry and emphasized on the worship of one true God.
- Both their personal life was symbolic e.g. Jeremiah divine judgment upon Judah.

Topic 11: NEHEMIAH

POLITICAL, RELIGIOUS AND SOCIAL BACKGROUND TO NEHEMIAH

a) Political background

- Nehemiah started his mission at a time when the Israelites were still in exile in Babylon.
- In exile, the Israelites were oppressed politically.
- The Babylonians were later conquered by King Cyrus of Persia.
- The Israelites welcomed this with great joy because they saw this as a source of liberation.
- King Cyrus allowed the Israelites to return to Judah and reconstruct the walls and the temple of Jerusalem.
- He offered them grants in aid and encouraged the Jews who remained in Babylon to contribute to the cost of those returning to Judah.
- He ordered for the return of all valuables e.g. gold and silver plates and cups that had been stolen from the temple when the temple was destroyed.
- The temple and the wall were rebuilt under the leadership of Nehemiah amidst strong opposition.
- This restored a sense of political pride among the Israelites.
- However, the Israelites remained subject to the Persians and continued to pay tribute.

Socio-Economic background

- During the exile the Israelites were settled in various places and there was deep social uprooting.
- They had lost their social influential status.
- They were integrated into the Babylonian society.
- They engaged in economic activities and some became rich.
- Others were appointed as leaders e.g. Nehemiah and Ezra.
- During the time of returning to Judah, a number of them did not return home because of the riches they had accumulated.
- Those who returned to Judah had been influenced by the foreign culture of their rulers and neighbours.
- Men married foreigners and had children of mixed decent.
- They also found that their land partly occupied by foreigners and which caused a lot of hostility between those who returned and the foreigners.
- The rich and powerful oppressed the poor and the less fortunate.

c) Religious background

- In exile the Babylonians allowed the Israelites to go on with their religious activities and community life.
- The exile became a period of spiritual purification.
- On returning to Judah, they had a new zeal to worship God and they rebuilt the altar under the leadership of Zerubabel for offering sacrifices.

- They also built the temple led by Haggai and Zachariah and it was dedicated to God by Ezra.
- Under the leadership of Ezra, they renewed their covenant with God with great rejoicing.
- Nehemiah led the Jews in rebuilding the wall of Jerusalem amidst opposition from non-Jews.
- Nehemiah also led all the religious reforms and the cleansing of the temple and ensured people followed the Law of Moses.

Why did the Persian government allow the rebuilding of the temple?

- It was wealthy having its own land, workforce and its own money to lend loans.
- It contributed to economic development of the Persian Empire.
- The Persian officers ensured that the priests pay tribute to the Persian Empire.
- Priests were custodians of the legal traditions in the region.
- The Priests and the temple contributed to the maintenance of law and order.
- The priests helped in the implementation of the local traditional laws in the region.
- The priesthood served as custodians of the laws in the region.

Describe the religious traditions observed by the Israelites during the Babylonian exile.

- Circumcision was carried out to distinguish Israelites from the Babylonians and it also helped to retain its value as a sign of the covenant.
- They observed the Sabbath.
- They chanted Psalms during worship.
- They observed the Mosaic Law and they valued the book of Deuteronomy which gave them the belief that sacrifices should only be made in Jerusalem. The exiles hence never offered sacrifices as a means of worship.

OCCASIONS WHEN NEHEMIAH PRAYED (NEHEMIAH 1:4 – 11; 2: 4 – 8; 4: 4 – 9; 5: 19; 6; 9; 13: 14; 22; 29; AND 31)

Before Nehemiah approached the king to seek permission to go back to Judah, he fasted and prayed and his prayer has the following characteristics:

- It showed that there was a strong bond between Nehemiah and the Jews.
- It has various elements that are found in the religious traditions of the Israelites such as the Exodus and the Covenant which God made with Israelites at Mt. Sinai.
- Nehemiah begins his prayer by praising God.
- He asked God to hear his concerns for his people and for God to see their suffering.
- Nehemiah referred to himself as a humble servant of God.
- Nehemiah confessed with humility the sins of his fathers and those of his generation.
- Nehemiah sought God's help, asking God to grant him mercy before the king.
- He interceded for the Israelites, reminding God of His promise to restore the people to their homeland if the repented.

Identify and explain the occasions when Nehemiah prayed.

- Nehemiah prayed when he learnt about the suffering of Jews back in Judah and the ruined state of Jerusalem. He asked God to forgive the sins of His people.
- Nehemiah prayed before approaching the king to ask for permission to go back to Jerusalem to rebuild Jerusalem.
- Nehemiah prayed when he was ridiculed by Sanballat while reconstructing the wall of Jerusalem, he asked God to punish him and his associates.
- Nehemiah prayed when his enemies conspired to attack Jerusalem so as to stop the construction work, he asked for protection from his enemies.
- Nehemiah prayed for strength to finish the rebuilding task after Sanballat accused Him of planning to overthrow the king of Persia.
- Nehemiah prayed for God to remember his good deeds when he learnt that Eliashab the priest had defiled the temple. He had let Tobiah a foreigner to reside in the temple.
- Nehemiah prayed when he realized that people were not keeping the Sabbath.
- Nehemiah prayed when the people broke the marriage laws and for the priests to uphold the covenant.
- Nehemiah prayed for divine protection when Shemaiah tried to frighten him telling him to hide in the temple because of a plot to kill him.

IMPORTANCE OF PRAYER IN CHRISTIAN LIFE

Explain and appreciate the importance of prayer in Christian life.

- Christians pray to express their faith in God and that they are dependent on God.
- Christians pray to thank God for his blessings.
- Christians pray to make their requests known to God.
- Christians pray to strengthen their relationship with God and remain close to him.
- Christians pray so as intercede for others.
- Christians pray to God for forgiveness of their sins and others.
- Christians pray for God to help them solve difficult circumstances.
- Christians pray to know God's will on a particular issue.
- Communal prayer binds/unites the Christian community together as believers in Christ.
- Prayer strengthens a Christian to face challenges in life.

Identify four types of prayers used by Christians today.

- Petition/supplication – asking God for our needs.
- Confession/penitentiary – asking God for forgiveness of our sins.
- Thanksgiving – thanking God for the good he has done to us.
- Intercessory prayer – praying for the needs of others.

Occasions when Christians should pray

- Christians pray when faced with difficulties
- When they do not understand certain scriptures Christians pray for God's revelation.
- When they are inadequate and sinful Christians repent.
- They repent when they want God to perform a miracle for them.

- They pray when they want to thank God for the blessings they have received.
- They pray when they want to intercede for others.

GOOD LEADERSHIP QUALITIES (NEHEMIAH 1; 2; 4; 5; 6, 7)
Explain the good leadership qualities that Nehemiah possessed.

- Being prayerful – He prayed and sought God's guidance before undertaking any task.
- Trust/faith in God – He was God fearing and always saw himself as a servant of God.
- Patriotism – He loved his country and people so much that he went back to rebuild the walls of the city.
- Dedication/ commitment/Hard work – He did not give up the tasks despite the obstacles he faced.
- Courage – He faced the King and asked for permission to go back home/ he was never discouraged by threats and opposition from his enemies.
- Team spirit – He joined his workers in the rebuilding site and worked.
- Wisdom – He used wisdom to see the tricks of his enemies e.g. when Shemaiah threatened him and told him to hide in the temple.
- Justice/compassion – He showed love for his people when he condemned the rich for oppressing the poor.
- Planning/organizational skills – Before embarking on the reconstruction he inspected the broken walls and prepared the materials for work.
- Role model – He often led by example e.g. he was prayerful, trusting to God e.t.c.
- Honesty – He never kept anything away from God or the people.

RELEVANCE OF NEHEMIAH'S LEADERSHIP TO CHRISTIANS TODAY
Identify the relevance of Nehemiah good leadership qualities to Christians today.

- Christians should be concerned about the welfare of others.
- Christians should be organized and good planners of their tasks.
- Christians should be role models/lead by example.
- Christians should be committed/ work selflessly.
- Christians should be patient and caring/should listen to people's problems.
- Christians should initiate socio-economic and political reforms in the society.
- Christian should obey and uphold the country constitution.
- Christians should practice justice and honesty always.

PROBLEMS FACED BY NEHEMIAH (NEHEMIAH 3:5; 4; 5; 6; 13)
Describe the problems that Nehemiah faced during his mission (Neh 3, 4, 5, 6, 13).

- **Opposition from enemies**: Sanballat and his servant Tobiah led others in opposing Nehemiah's construction work. They plotted attacks against Jerusalem and wanted to kill the builders which caused panic among them. However with Nehemiah's prayers they overpowered them.
- **Disloyalty and lack of cooperation**: Some nobles of Tekoa objected to work as constructors claiming it was too demanding. They later repented and agreed to work.

- **Death threats**: Sanballat made a plot with a prophet called Shemaiah to cheat Nehemiah to hide in the temple because Jerusalem was going to be attacked. If he had done this could have been killed there.
- **Oppression of the poor**: Because of famine in Jerusalem the rich overtaxed people and charged them high interest on loans. This made him loose popularity among the poor even though he sacrificed his rights to the poor.
- **Defiling/misuse of the Temple**: The temple had been defiled by letting a foreigner called Tobiah to live in it. The Levites also were not being given their sacrificial shares as required by the law.
- **Violation of Sabbath laws**: The Sabbath law had been broken because people went to farm, trade and transact their businesses. Their tithes were not being taken to the storehouse of God.
- **Foreign influence**: After the exile, people had intermarried with the non-Jews, this was, against the law of God. The foreign women influenced their men to worship their idols which made the Jews unclean.

What can the Christians learn from the experiences of Nehemiah?

- Christians must expect opposition as they try to spread the gospel, but they learn to be brave as Nehemiah was.
- Christians learn to be prayerful and trust in God for restoration of the less privileged in the society.
- Christians have a responsibility of condemning the evils in their societies. They should preach justice for all.
- Christians should avoid any form of activity that can render them and others unclean spiritually.
- Christians have the responsibility of reminding political leaders of their responsibilities towards the people. They should discourage corruption, oppression, immorality e.t.c.
- Christians are required to fight for justice and the less privileged in the society.
- Christians should come up with ways of solving the problems affecting the people.
- Christians learn that a call from God involves hardship and opposition but with God's help they can overcome.

Lessons a Christian leader can learn from the problems faced by Nehemiah

- They should be prepared to face opposition as they preach the gospel.
- They should have faith in God and persevere as they carry out their duties.
- They should fight for the rights of the poor in the society and their wealth to benefit others.
- They should learn how to correct wrongdoers.
- They should learn to condemn all forms of injustice e.g. corruption.
- They should be ready to forgo their personal interests for the sake of God's kingdom.

RELEVANCE OF NEHEMIAH'S EXPERIENCES TO CHRISTIANS TODAY
What is the relevance of Nehemiah's experiences to the Christians?
- Christians should be committed to serving the people like Nehemiah did.
- Christians should display courage and strength in the face of difficulties and persevere in their work.
- Christians should use their time and resources to serve others and God.
- A Christian should be honest like Nehemiah.
- Should be compassionate to those who are suffering.
- Christians should lead by example and be role models.
- Christians should pray to God for guidance in their undertakings and be dependent on God.
- Christians should be selfless and be mindful of others' welfare.
- Christians should condemn all forms of evil and injustices in the society.
- Christians should take practical measures to solve problems affecting people

RENEWAL OF THE COVENANT (NEHEMIAH 8 – 12:1-26)
Describe the renewal of the covenant
- It was held in Jerusalem, in the seventh month.
- It was led by priests and other religious leaders.
- The people assembled in the public square in Jerusalem.
- Ezra read the law book to the people.
- The people performed the ritual of raising and lowering their heads as a sign of repentance.
- They cried out in guilt when they realized that they had failed to observe the law but were calmed down by Ezra, Nehemiah and the Levites.
- They were told to return back to their homes and celebrate for it was a holy day.
- On the following day, they erected tents/booths and lived in them for seven days – feast of booths.
- They held a day of confession where they fasted and wore sack clothes.
- They separated themselves from foreigners and made vows to keep the law.
- Ezra led people into prayer of confession where they repented their sins.
- The covenant was sealed by the Israelite leaders who signed the agreement.
- Nehemiah redistributed the people to settle in Jerusalem and other areas.

Identify the major steps taken in the renewal of the covenant
- People gathered in the public square
- Ezra read the law book
- People performed the ritual of raising and lowering their heads in repentance.
- They celebrated the feast of booths.
- They held a day of confession.
- The leaders signed the agreement to seal the covenant.
- The people were redistributed to settle in Jerusalem and other areas.

Outline the promises that the Israelites made during the renewal of the covenant at the time of Nehemiah

- They promised to live according to God's law, obeying all his commands and requirements.
- They would not intermarry with foreigners.
- They would not buy anything on the Sabbath or any other holy days.
- Every seventh year they would cancel debts according to the Mosaic Law.
- Every seventh year they would let the land rest.
- They would contribute annual expenses and ensure the Temple is not neglected.
- They would provide sacrifices and offerings for the temple.
- They would arrange for wood to be brought for the purpose of burning sacrifices and offerings in the temple.
- They would offer the first fruits of their harvest to God.
- They would dedicate their first born sons and flock to God.
- They would pay tithes.

Lessons that Christians learn from the renewal of the covenant

- Christians should repent for it renews one's relationship with God.
- Human beings are sinners and sometimes they fail to meet God's expectations of moral life.
- Christians should set aside time to worship God.
- Christians should avoid situations that lead them to sin.

DEDICATION OF THE WALL OF JERUSALEM (NEHEMIAH 12:27-47)

Describe the dedication of the wall of Jerusalem

- When the wall was completed the Jews were overjoyed.
- Nehemiah invited Levites who were custodian of Israelites religion.
- He also invited Priests, political leaders and the Israelites.
- Singers were also invited and they came with cymbals, harps & lyres.
- Priests and Levites purified themselves, the people, and the walls.
- The gates and the walls were also purified.
- Nehemiah brought leaders (Princes) of Judah upon the wall, and then divided the people into two groups who gave thanks and then went into a procession
- The first group led by Ezra moved towards the right, followed by musicians, civic officials, and half the community leaders and priests blowing trumpets and Levites with musical instruments.
- The second group went to the left led by Nehemiah.
- Two groups finally converged at the temple, where there was singing, sacrifices and rejoicing.
- Nehemiah then chose people to be in-charge of tithes, offerings and contributions and ensure they are handled well
- The city was once more seen as the city of God.

Reasons why it was important to rebuild the broken walls of Jerusalem
- To symbolize the physical/spiritual, restoration of the people of Israel from exile.
- To signify new beginning in the Israelites new relationship, with God.
- To fulfil the prophecies of preserving the remnant.
- To enhance the Israelites self-esteem.
- To enhance their privacy/avoid shameful exposure to passers-by.
- Enhance physical security.

NEHEMIAH'S FINAL REFORMS (NEHEMIAH 13)
- Separation from foreigners: Israelites separated themselves from people of foreign descent. He brought order in marriage by cursing and beating men who had married foreign wives. He made them to swear that they would not allow foreign marriages.
- Purification of the temple: Nehemiah threw Tobiah out of the temple along with his belongings because he was a foreigner. According to Mosaic Law this defiled the temple.
- He ordered for the cleansing of the temple and its use for rightful religious functions.
- Levites and other temple workers were given back their positions. They had been denied their dues for upkeep and so they had resolved to farming so as to take care of themselves. He appointed new people to be in charge of temple contributions and gave the Levites and singers back their duties.
- Observance of the Law of Moses: Nehemiah ensured that the Sabbath law was kept and that trading activities were not carried out on this day. He appointed Levites to close the gates of Jerusalem during the Sabbath and to keep it guard.
- Nehemiah purified the office of priesthood and Levite by maintaining that it was a holy and respectable office.
- Nehemiah's stand on intermarriage was firm. He even ensured that those who had intermarried divorced. He stated that foreign women had caused the downfall of great kings like Solomon. He condemned such marriages and the people who had done so.

How did Nehemiah restore the independence of Israelites through religious reforms?
- He cleansed the temple by expelling Tobiah from the temple.
- He restored the Levites to their rightful duties in the temple.
- He stopped the Israelites from marrying foreigners.
- He reinstated the true worship on the Sabbath by abolishing business activities.
- He led the people in the renewal of the covenant.
- He improved their tithing system.
- He gave the singers their rightful position in the temple.
- He purified the priests and the people as a sign of making them fit for God's service.

Why it is difficult to have reforms in Kenya.
- Lack of political will by leaders.
- There is a lot of corruption.

- Tribalism is rampant.
- The institutions are weak and unable to carry out meaningful reforms.
- There are too many political parties without clear reforms agenda.
- Selfishness and lack of vision among the reformers.
- Lack of adequate finances to restructure economy.

TEACHINGS FROM NEHEMIAH'S EXEMPLARY LIFE TO ST. LUKE'S GOSPEL AND THE CHRISTIAN LIFE TODAY

Relate the exemplary life of Nehemiah to St. Luke's Gospel and Christian life today.

- Prayer: Nehemiah's success was based on his prayerfulness before approaching any issue. He prayed for strength, guidance, decision making etc. St. Luke's gospel emphasizes the importance of prayer. Jesus prayed constantly and taught his disciples too. Christians need to be persistent in prayer and apply humility, forgiveness and intercession
- Nehemiah sacrificed some of his personal rights to the poor and condemned any form of oppression against such people. Jesus' miracles and death is a sign of compassion for his people. Christians learn to practice compassion towards the needy.
- Condemnation of evil – Nehemiah condemned all forms of evils of his time. Jesus in his ministry condemns evil against God and man. Christians are called to condemn evil practices of their time e.g. corruption
- Reformer - Nehemiah brought reforms in the life of his people. He led the people in the renewal of the covenant. Jesus is the maker of the new covenant which reconciles man to God. Christians learn the need for repentance always in order to be reconciled with God.
- Courage and bravery: Nehemiah faced much opposition from his people while bringing reforms in Israel. Jesus too was opposed by his people including the Scribes and Pharisees. Both Jesus and Nehemiah did not give up in accomplishing their mission. Christians should be courageous whenever they encounter obstacles in their Christian life,
- Nehemiah observed the law of God. Jesus too followed the law and stressed that he had come to fulfil it. Christians too should follow the commandments of God in reverence.
- Nehemiah condemned discrimination of any kind. Jesus is a universal leader who encompasses the poor, and all irrespective of colour or race. Christians must condemn all forms of discrimination and preach equality.

Give the similarities in the life and experiences of Nehemiah and Jesus Christ.

- Both purified the temple.
- Both led prayerful lives.
- Both had compassion for the people/ weak/poor.
- Both were reformers.
- Both led exemplary lives/holy lives.
- Both came to restore the worship between God and the people.
- Both faced opposition in their ministry from close relatives.

Explain five teachings Christians can learn about patriotism from the characters of Nehemiah

- They should have great love for their country.
- They should participate in development projects of their country as Nehemiah did.
- They should be mindful of the welfare of other citizens and cater for their needs.
- They should promote justice as Nehemiah condemned those who exploited the poor.
- They should be ready to defend their country in the event of external aggression.
- They should defend the values of their country and avoid bad foreign influence.
- They should be law abiding citizens and respect the constitution of the country.
- They should pay taxes promptly to enhance development.
- They should recognize and respect public national days like Nehemiah did for Sabbath.
- They should participate in national elections by praying and choosing good leaders.

Topic 12: SELECTED ASPECTS OF AFRICAN RELIGIOUS HERITAGE
AFRICAN CONCEPT OF GOD, SPIRITS AND ANCESTORS

GOD
- Traditional African communities believe in God, a Supreme Being, who is the creator and sustainer of all things.
- He is the creator of the universe and all that it contains.
- Through His creation activity, Africans have formulated ideas about the nature of God. These ideas concern his real being and his activities.

Describe the African beliefs about the nature of God in Traditional African Communities.

The following are some of the attributes of God as understood by the African peoples:
- **God is the creator** – Africans believe the world was created by God and that God existed from the beginning. God is the source of life, the visible world, human beings and the spirits.
- **God is a provider** – God provides for His creation, for example, He gives rain to crops to grow, provides water and food to human beings and animals e.t.c.
- **God is merciful** – God is believed to deliver the people from situations like danger, illness, difficulty or anxiety.
- **God is holy and pure** – Africans believe God has no blemish hence they approach Him with reverence, fear, respect and honour.
- **God is all powerful (omnipotent)** – God is thought to be Almighty and shows his strength over all things, both living and non-living.
- **God is all-knowing (omniscient)** – God is believed to know and understands all things and nothing can be hidden from Him.
- **God is omnipresent** – God is present everywhere all the time in the universe.
- **God is transcendent** – Africans believe God is beyond human comprehension and cannot be limited.
- **God is a spirit** – God is believed to be a spirit and is invisible.
- **God is everlasting/eternal** – God never changes, is same always and he never dies.
- **God is good** – Africans understand God as good, he is neither evil nor the author of evil. His goodness is seen in the fact that he created the world and he sustains and provides for his creation.

SPIRITS
- In the hierarchy of beings, spirits come second after God.

- Some of the spirits are believed to have been created by God as spirits, while others are spirits of people who died long ago and are no longer remembered by the living.
- The spirits are subordinate to God and depend upon him.
- God sometimes uses them to perform certain things such as causing floods and lightning.

There are various types of spirits:

a. **Nature spirits:** they are of two types:
i.   Spirits of the sky – are associated with objects and forces of the sky like the sun, moon, stars, rain, thunder and lightning.
ii.   Earth spirits/nature spirits – are connected with natural phenomena e.g. hills, mountains, rocks, forests, lakes and rivers. Some are also connected with certain animals, insects, and diseases. These spirits are believed to control forces of nature. Some are manipulated by human beings for good or evil purposes.
b. **Human spirits** – these are can be categorized into two:
i.   Ghost spirits – these are spirits of people who died long ago and have been forgotten. People fear ghosts because they cause harm to the living when they possess them e.g. diseases like madness.
ii.   Ancestral spirits. They are also referred to as living dead. They are spirits of people who died recently and are still remembered vividly by the people. They are believed to appear to the living in visions and dreams and also possess people. They are believed to be close to their clans and families and are generally interested in their welfare unless they are offended by the living in a particular way.
c. **Divinities**: this is a category of spirits between God and the spirits. Divinities are believed to have been created by God as spirits and they represent his activities on earth. In the hierarchy of beings, divinities appear below God and above other spirits.

ANCESTORS
- Ancestors are forefathers and foremothers or founders of the African clans and tribes.
- They are people who died recently and whose names and identity are still remembered by the family and or clan members.
- They are also referred to as the living dead.
- They are concerned with the welfare of the people.
- They are close to their immediate families, which they belonged while still alive.
- They speak the language of human beings when they appear to them either in a dream or a vision.

AFRICAN UNDERSTANDING OF THE HIERARCHY OF BEINGS

HIERARCHY OF BEINGS
Africans believe that the universe consists of two parts: the visible (the earth) and the invisible (sky). The sky is regarded as the home of God.

The universe has a specific order of created beings with God, the Creator, occupying the highest rank/position.

This ordering is what is referred to as the hierarchy of beings and it consists of:

Describe the traditional African understanding of the Hierarchy of beings.

- At the top of the hierarchy is God, the Supreme Being, who is the creator and sustainer of human beings and all other things.
- The divinities come second and they control the forces of nature in the universe.
- The common spirits are third and this comprises the spirits of human beings who died along ago.
- Fourth are the ancestors or the living dead, who are still remembered by the living.
- Human beings come fifth; they include both the living and those who are yet to be born/the unborn.
- Sixth are living things e.g. animals and plants. They are used by human beings in their natural and religious life as food and sacrifices.
- The last category comprises non-living things such as rocks, rivers and all other lifeless objects.

```
        ┌──────────┐
        │   GOD    │
        └────┬─────┘
             │
             ▼
      ┌──────────────┐
      │  DIVINITIES  │
      └──────┬───────┘
             │
             ▼
        ┌──────────┐
        │ SPIRITS  │
        └────┬─────┘
             │
             ▼
  ┌────────────────────────┐
  │ LIVING DEAD (ANCESTORS)│
  └───────────┬────────────┘
              │
              ▼
      ┌────────────────┐
      │  HUMAN BEINGS  │
      └───────┬────────┘
              │
              ▼
      ┌────────────────┐
      │ LIVING THINGS  │
      └───────┬────────┘
              │
              ▼
      ┌────────────────┐
      │   NON-LIVING   │
      │    THINGS      │
      └────────────────┘
```

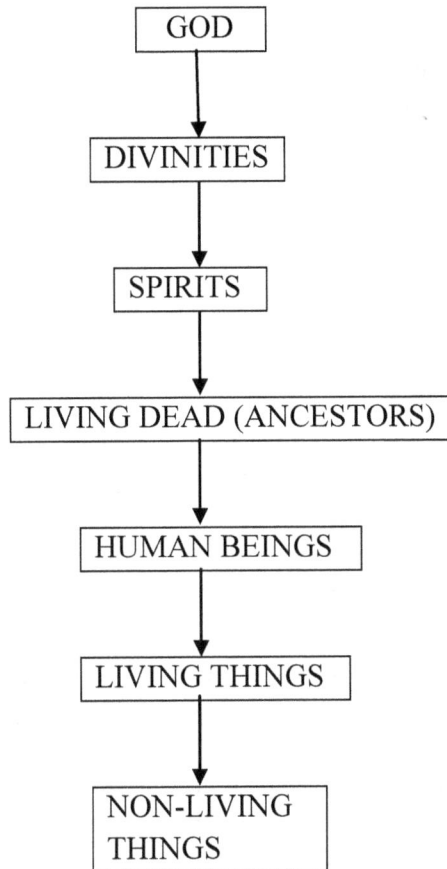

The inter-relationship of all things, living and non-living

According to the African view of the universe, all created beings depend on each other and on God.

What is the inter-relationship between God and Human Beings

The purpose for which God created the universe is seen in how human beings depend on God. Most African communities recognize this dependence in various aspects

- Human beings depend on God for essential requirements of life e.g. rain, air and sunshine.
- Human beings are less powerful than God.
- They have to obey the laws and commandments given by God.
- Human beings are punished if they do not obey God's commandments while those who obey the commandments do prosper in their lives.
- Human beings must offer sacrifices to God to maintain a good relationship with him.
- Natural calamities like drought, floods and earthquakes are believed to be controlled by God and are beyond people's power.

Explain the inter-relationship between Human Beings and animals

- Human Beings use some animals as food e.g. cows, and goats provide meat and milk.
- Some domestic animals like cattle and goats are used to pay dowry.
- Possession of the domestic animals is seen as a sign of prestige and wealth.
- The skins of these animals can be used as clothes and for making musical instruments like drum.
- Some of the animals are used as sacrifices to God.
- Animals are also used as payment for a fine by an offender to God and the ancestors, and the offended person.

The inter-relationship between Human Beings and plants

- Some plants like vegetables are used for food.
- Pastoralists and those who rear animals depend on grass and foliage for their livestock.
- Trees are used for fuel and for building purposes.
- Some trees are used as sacred places for worship.
- Certain plants are used for medicinal purposes.
- In some communities plants are also used as totems.

Explain the relationship that exists between Human beings and non-livings things

- Non-living things like rain, rocks and rivers are given a religious significance e.g. rain is considered a blessing from God.
- Natural phenomena like thunder are seen as God's movement or God's voice.
- Rocks and mountains are considered as dwelling places for the spirits and the ancestors.
- They are used to construct houses and homes.
- Some non-living things are used as worshipping places e.g. mountains, rocks, rivers e.t.c.

THE ROLE OF GOD, SPIRITS AND ANCESTORS
ROLE OF GOD

The roles that God plays in the world and in people's lives include:

- God cares about human beings and can be invoked.
- God is the giver and sustainer of life.
- God protects human beings from evil.
- God is the guardian of the moral and ethical order. He punishes those who do evil.
- As a powerful being, God controls the spirits that are more powerful than human beings.
- God gives order to the universe and controls it.
- God communicates with special people like healers, medicine people, kings, priests and prophets through dreams, visions and trances.

ROLE OF SPIRITS

Spirits are believed to play a very important role in the lives of the living e.g.

- Some spirits are invoked by witches and magicians to cause harm to others and are associated with sicknesses and bring suffering to human beings.

- Some spirits help diviners, mediums, medicine persons and other religious specialists to do their work by giving them important information on how to handle people's problems.
- Spirits relay human requests to God and relay back God's response to humans during calamities e.g. drought, famine, floods e.t.c.
- More powerful spirits are appealed to by human beings to get rid of mischievous spirits.
- Spirits provide humans with explanations of the many mysteries which they find in the universe.
- Spirits receive/welcome the dead into the spirit world.
- Spirits such as divinities help God to control phenomena such as rain, floods, lightning e.t.c.

ANCESTORS

State the roles of the ancestors towards the living in Traditional African Communities

- They are guardians/head of their families as seen when they are invited to ceremonies.
- Ancestors encourage, bless and strengthen people during the rites of passage.
- They welcome those who die into the spirit world.
- They are the guardians of the customs and traditions of families and communities.
- They convey people's wishes to God and vice versa.
- They protect the community against harmful spirits.
- They advise the living members on both religious and cultural issues through dreams and visions.
- They warn family or community members of the impending danger.

RESPONSIBILITY OF THE LIVING TOWARDS GOD, SPIRITS AND ANCESTORS

Responsibility of the living towards God

- To worship God. God is to be worshipped all times and everywhere.
- Thank God for having given them life and for sustaining and maintaining them.
- To give offerings and sacrifices to God.
- Taking care and respecting the sacred places where God lives or is worshipped e.g. shrines.
- Taking care of the creation e.g. animals, birds and the environment.
- Teach the children about God and instil in them religious values.
- To present their needs and those of the community to God in prayer.

What is the responsibility of the living towards spirits in traditional African communities?

- Sharing their food and drinks with the spirits by pouring libation to them.
- Making sacrifices and offerings to appease them.
- Praying to God through them.
- Building shrines for them to act as centres for meeting between the living and the spirits.
- To respect sacred objects like trees, mountains, hills, rivers, caves e.t.c. which the spirits are believed to abode for God and spirits.
- Teaching children about them.
- Inviting them to social functions like circumcision.

- Singing and dancing to them/Compose songs in their honour.
- To consult spirits before major undertakings to avoid misfortunes.

Responsibility of the living towards the ancestors/living dead

- Naming children after them, in order to bring them back to life.
- During celebrations e.g. the rites of passage the ancestors are invited to join and participate.
- Sacrificing to them to appease them whenever they feel that the ancestors are unhappy with them.
- Sharing food and drinks with them by pouring libation and leaving food for them.
- Protecting ancestral land.
- To accord proper burial rites to the ancestors as a sign of respect.
- To preserve society's culture because this is an act that is pleasing to the ancestors.
- To obey and respect the wishes of the ancestors which are revealed through dreams, visions and trances.

TRADITIONAL AFRICAN WAYS OF:
A) WORSHIPPING GOD:

- Worship refers to the various ways in which man relates to God. Worship expresses submission to God.
- In African religion, only God is to be worshipped. Spirits and ancestors are venerated.
- Therefore, African religion is strictly monotheistic.
- God is worshipped at all times and in every place.

In traditional African communities God is worshipped in the following ways:

- Prayers were said while kneeling or facing some natural phenomena e.g. mountains, moon, or while raising hands.
- Giving sacrifices and offerings. Sacrifices involved slaughtering of animals or birds without blemish, while offerings involved giving foodstuffs, milk, water or honey to God.
- Singing and dancing to God during worship.
- Building shrines for God.
- Pronouncing blessings and curses in the name of God.
- Through invocations where God's name is called to cause blessing to people. An invocation is a short informal prayer e.g. "Help me, Oh God"
- Consulting prophets about God's will.

The places where God was worshipped are

- Community shrines
- Graveyards
- In caves.
- Under sacred trees
- At the river banks, lakes, mountains, near rock e.t.c.

Reasons why God was worshipped

- To thank God for various reasons such as blessings and successes.
- To ask God for needs and blessings e.g. food, health e.t.c.
- To appease God and spirits.
- To request for the removal of calamities e.g. an epidemic.
- To recognize our dependence on God
- To fellowship with God and share the joys and perplexities of life.

In what ways did the African communities use the environment to demonstrate their belief in God?

- Using the land and other resources responsibly and with reverence.
- Setting aside sacred places, trees and building of shrines for worship of God.
- They set aside totems regarded as sacred e.g. animals, birds and reptiles.
- They prayed while facing the sun, moon, mountains and objects that were regarded as the sign of God's presence.
- Use of soil during oathing or cursing ceremonies and when blessing and making of covenants.
- Protecting the land as it was given by God.
- Sharing of resources from the land.
- Offering to God the resources and produce from the land.
- Pouring of blood onto the ground during initiation and during covenant making.
- Burning of sacrifices to God so that the smoke ascends to heaven.

B) VENERATING AND COMMUNICATING WITH SPIRITS AND ANCESTORS

Venerating ancestors means to give due respect to the ancestors.

Africans venerated ancestors in the following ways:

- Though naming their children after the ancestors.
- Africans make offerings to ancestors during the rites of passage, mainly to invite them to join and participate in the ceremony.
- Pouring libations in form of beer, milk, honey in order to share drinks with them.
- Inviting them during ceremonies e.g. rites of passage.
- Maintaining graves of the dead and respecting their burial places.
- Praying to God through them.
- Teaching children about them and their culture.
- Building shrines for the ancestors at home to ensure that the spirits are part of the family.
- Communicating to them through diviners.
- The ancestors are remembered by mentioning their names during prayers.

COMMUNICATION WITH THE SPIRITS

- People come to know what the spirits want through religious specialists.
- Religious specialists are sacred persons who were mainly concerned with the official worship of God and veneration of ancestors.
- Such specialists were priests, prophets, diviners, medicinemen and elders.

- The religious specialists link human beings with the spirit world.
- Mediums and diviners may become "spirit-possessed" through various means e.g. through:
  i. Sitting quietly in a place
  ii. Singing
  iii. Dancing
  iv. Clapping of hands
  v. Falling in a trance
- The possessed person loses his/her senses and becomes an instrument of the spirit.
- The spirit speaks through the medium and reveals information on lost property or enemies in society.
- The spirit may make certain demands on the living e.g. sacrifices and offerings be made by the living.
- It may advise and give a warning on impending danger.
- It may make certain promises of blessings to a given family or clan.

AFRICAN MORAL AND CULTURAL VALUES

MEANING OF LIFE AND ITS WHOLENESS IN THE TRADITIONAL AFRICAN SOCIETY

- All African communities believe that God is the source of life.
- Africans believe that life is a rhythm which recycles itself.
- There are several dimensions of life which include physical, social, spiritual and environmental.
- The physical dimension refers to the material state of human beings. It covers the human beings and the physical environment.
- The social dimension of life comprises of relationships of the living with others in a community. Life can only be experienced through living in a community.
- The spiritual dimension of life links human beings with the spiritual powers like God, spirits and ancestors.
- The environmental dimension refers to the surroundings such as plants and animals and non-living things.
- African communities promote life through the observance of rituals, taboos and other community regulations.
- It is also continued through various stages in human growth such as the rites of passage e.g. birth, initiation, marriage and death.
- Life in traditional African community is promoted and continued through marriage and bearing of children.
- Death, which is the final stage of life transforms one from the physical to the spiritual life.

Explain the traditional African practices which show that life is sacred

- Greetings which express a state of life and prolonged prosperous life.
- Taking care of the physical body through feeding, protecting it, nurturing and taking medication when sick.
- Establishing a good relationship with God and the ancestors through worship, prayers and veneration.
- Seeking God's protection all the times especially in times of crisis.
- Taking care of ancestral land which links the living and the dead.
- Taking care of both domestic and wild animals by providing food and protecting nature.
- Protecting human life including the unborn.
- Respecting sexual intercourse for married couples only.
- Obeying the rules and taboos that govern the well-being of the community.

THE AFRICAN CONCEPT OF COMMUNITY AND KINSHIP SYSTEM

Meaning of Community

- A community is a group of people occupying one geographical location, speak one language and are guided by common values, interests and goals.

- The African community consists of the living, the living dead and the yet to be born.
- Each community is governed by specific rules, regulations and traditions.
- The survival of the community depends on God and other spiritual powers.
- Each African community has a social and political organization based on the smallest unit, the family. The family consists of the father, who is the head, wife/wives and the children.
- Members of a family originate from the same ancestor and they form an extended family.
- A number of related families who share the same ancestor make up a clan. The clan is bound by certain rules, regulations and taboos.
- Several clans brought together formed a community.
- Members are expected to show concern for one another and provide cooperation in times of need e.g. misfortunes, sicknesses, marriage e.t.c.
- The community provides a sense of belonging and identity for its members thus making individuals feel secure.

African concept of Kinship
- Kinship refers to the relationship between people through either blood or marriage.
- Blood kinship refers to the relationship where people share the same ancestor, are from the same family and share in the life passed on to them from previous generations of their families, including the living and the dead.
- Marriage kinship is the relationship brought through marriage. These are referred to as in-laws. A wife joins the husband's family and becomes a new member. The two families of the bride and bridegroom develop new relationships, the ties grow strong and binding.
- Kinship ties are strong bonds that exist among members of a community.

What is the significance of blood kinship in traditional African communities?
- It promoted harmonious living as related people respect each other.
- Kinship system determines how members relate to one another, thus controlling behaviour of one person towards another.
- It provides a sense of security to members since relatives assist each other in times of need.
- It helps maintain culture of the people (Religion, customs, traditions and beliefs).
- It helps members to face challenges and hardships together.
- It binds together the entire life of a community
- It helps regulate marital customs, rules and regulations since people related in one way cannot be allowed to marry.
- It gives individuals a deep sense of belonging since they feel part and parcel of the community.
- It determines the punishment for the offenders.
- It instils team-spirit and collective responsibility
- It defines the roles played by each member in the community.
- It promotes cooperation during communal work.

- It contributed to traditional education since the young were taught and guided by the elders.

FACTORS CONTRIBUTING TO HARMONY AND MUTUAL RESPONSIBILITY IN THE AFRICAN COMMUNITIES

Explain the factors that contributed to harmony and mutual responsibility in the traditional African communities

- **Political ties** – Refers to the way power and authority are exercised in a community. Power is allocated among clan elders according to one's status, hence individual families fit in this political set up. People in such a set up live together obeying unwritten laws and the elders have authority to discipline errant members.
- **Division of labour** – work was shared according to age, gender and social status. Division of labour made all members of the community to participate in work.
- **Communal worship** – community members gathered to pray and offer sacrifices to thank God for a good harvest, victory in a battle e.t.c. common religious beliefs and practices create a sense of oneness especially with the living and the departed.
- **Leisure activities** – during leisure time people come together to be entertained through singing, dancing, sharing stories, and sports which enhanced cohesion in the community.
- **Rites of passage** – there were ceremonies to mark the rites of passage such as birth, naming, initiation, marriage and death, in which all the people participated. This enhanced unity.
- **Observance of taboos/norms** – taboos guided behaviour and the relationship between community members. Everyone was encouraged to develop virtues such as friendship, love, honesty, courage
- **Sharing** – all resources were shared e.g. land, food, work were shared and owned by the community, which kept the community united.

What methods were used in acquiring moral values in traditional African society?
- Through teaching/ informal education.
- Through administration of punishment.
- Social role models.
- Through guidance and counselling.
- Involving them in constructive/meaningful activities.
- Rewarding morally acceptable behaviour.

THE RITES OF PASSAGE AND MORAL VALUES
RITES OF PASSAGE
- Rites of passage are the stages through which a person goes in life.
- They include birth, initiation, marriage and death.
- During the rites of passage there are ceremonies and rituals conducted to mark the events. Most of the ceremonies are religious and have the following characteristics:
i. Separation – the initiate is separated from the community and is placed in seclusion for a period of time. In the case of death, the person is secluded forever.

ii.   Transition – in this stage an individual undergoes physical, social and emotional changes as they move from the previous stage to another.

iii.   Incorporation – after seclusion, the person is received back to the community and is given full rights in his/her new status.

I)BIRTH AND NAMING
Birth

-    It is the first stage in a person's life.
-    The birth of a child in a family is a time of great rejoicing and celebration.
-    During pregnancy, the expectant mother is accorded a lot of respect and is given special treatment. There are certain rules and regulations she is expected to observe e.g.

i.   Eating special food and avoiding some e.g. eggs and fatty meat.
ii.   Avoiding heavy duties e.g. splitting firewood or carrying heavy loads.
iii.   Abstaining from sexual intercourse because pregnancy is believed to make the woman ritually unclean.
iv.   Wearing protective charms against evil spirits.
v.   Not using sharp tools in the house for fear that such tools would attract lightning.
vi.   Not speaking to the husband directly, can only do so through an intermediary.
vii.   Returning to her parents' home to give birth there and coming back home after weaning the baby.

-    During birth of a baby, elderly women who act as mid-wives witness the delivery. Men are not allowed to go near the delivery place.
-    After delivery, certain rituals are performed to mark the birth of the child e.g.

i.   The umbilical cord is cut and disposed off ceremoniously to ensure continued fertility.
ii.   The sex of the child is announced in various ways such as shouts and ululations.
iii.   Sacrifices and prayers of thanksgiving are offered to God and the ancestors.
iv.   Medicinal herbs or waters are administered to the baby to protect her/him from evil.
v.   Both the mother's and baby's hair are shaved after some time as a sign of purification and newness.
vi.   Both the mother and child are secluded for a certain period of time in order to:
   a. Protect them from evil.
   b. Give the mother time to recover.
   c. Train the mother on the skills of nursing the baby.
   d. Give time for preparation for other rituals.

What was the importance of seclusion period after child birth in traditional African societies?

-    It enables the mothers to regain the lost energy during child birth.
-    It enables the mother to rest after nine months of pregnancy.
-    To keep the mother and the baby away from evil-eyed people.
-    To enable the mother to be trained on how to feed, hold and bath the baby especially if it's the first birth.
-    It was a traditional way of dedicating the baby to the ancestors.

- The mother was still regarded as ritually unclean after birth hence it was a way of keeping her away from the rest of the people.
- To ensure proper feeding of the mother.
- Feast and celebrations are held to welcome the baby into the community and to congratulate the parents.
- The child is given a name to give her/him identity.

Naming

A name is given immediately after birth. Names in traditional African communities are given depending on the following:

- Prevailing weather conditions to the time of birth.
- The time of the day when the baby was born.
- The circumstances surrounding the birth.
- The gender/sex of the child.
- The physical traits of the child.
- After an important historical event.
- The ordained position of the child in the family.
- The wishes of the ancestors in a dream.
- Twins had special names.
- To honour community heroes.
- The name of their god.

The role of birth and naming in inculcating moral values

Morals deal with issues of what is right and wrong. Morals are concerned with goodness or badness of human character or behaviour.

Values are principles or standards that govern human conduct or behaviour.

In traditional African communities, people learn the moral values through every day activities and through the education provided.

Some of the moral values learnt during birth and naming include:

- Birth and naming earn the couple respect in the society because of their new status.
- It promotes love between the husband and wife.
- It enhances truthfulness and acceptance in the community.
- It promotes care and responsibility as parents are equipped with skills of bringing up children.
- It instils obedience to the customs and traditions.
- It promotes unity as members come together to celebrate.
- It promotes patriotism through naming the child after heroes and important historical events in the community.

Reasons why naming ceremony was important in traditional African communities

- It was a ceremony for thanksgiving for the new child.

- It was a sign of acceptance of the child as a full member of the community.
- It gave identity to the child.
- It helped to remember important events in society e.g. Kiprop, Kipkemei, Akoth, Osebe e.t.c.
- For blessing the child.
- It was a way of welcoming the baby to the community.
- It offered security to the child.
- It showed a link between the living and the dead.
- It brought unity to the people as they came together to celebrate.

II) INITIATION

- This is the second major stage in a person's life when an individual moves from childhood to adulthood.
- During this stage, a person undergoes physical, emotional and psychological changes.
- Most Kenyan communities carry out initiation for boys by circumcision and clitoridectomy for girls.
- Some communities e.g. Luo remove the six lower front teeth removed and others carry out tattooing.
- The whole community was involved in the initiation rites and everyone had to undergo the rite, failure to which the person will be looked at as an outcast and as a child, no matter how old (s)he is.
- Those circumcised at the same time form an age-set and acquire a special name.

The rituals connected with initiation rites include:
- Sacrifices were offered
- Shedding of blood
- The initiates were secluded from the community.
- Singing and dancing to arouse spirits.
- Giving gifts or presents are given to the initiates.
- Washing and shaving of the hair.
- The initiate is given new names and wear of new attires.

Importance of the initiation rites in traditional African communities

- The initiate becomes a full member of the community and is considered mature.
- The initiate acquires new rights and privileges e.g. (s)he is allowed to marry and can own property.
- The initiates receive special education during the seclusion period and are taught the secrets and traditions of the community.
- It trains the initiates to acquire new virtues of endurance and courage in order to face challenges in life.
- The initiates are linked to the ancestors through the shedding of blood.
- Members of the community get united through the participation in the rites.
- The prayers and sacrifices are offered, which serve as acts of worship.

In what ways did initiation prepare the initiates into adulthood in Traditional African community?
- They were made to endure pain in order to develop perseverance.
- They were assigned duties similar to those performed in adult life.
- It exposed them to hardship in order to help them develop coping mechanisms.
- They were taught moral values to help them develop deductive thinking.
- They were punished for disobedience to learn about the consequences of their actions.
- The initiates were made to share the belongings to teach them communalism.
- They were taught the history of community to help them trace their ancestry and the society's secrets.
- Grouping into age set and age groups helped them develop collective responsibility.
- They lived in seclusion in order to develop independence.

Moral values acquired during initiation
- Respect for others is taught to the initiates during the seclusion period.
- Loyalty to the traditions of the community is taught.
- It teaches endurance in all situations.
- Sharing of food and other basic necessities is taught.
- Chastity is acquired from sex education which is taught during seclusion.
- Self-control is learnt when the initiates are taught to control their feelings and emotions that may be destructive.
- Solidarity which is seen in the singing and dancing of the initiates and which creates a sense of security and feeling of oneness.
- Courage to face life's challenges without fear is learnt.

What challenges are facing the rite of initiation today?
- Female circumcision is now discouraged by the government.
- Elaborate ceremonies have been stopped in some communities since they do not serve any purpose.
- Seclusion period has drastically reduced (weeks not months) since the initiates have to go back to school.
- It is no longer a preparation ground for marriage – since the initiates are too young today.
- Christianity condemns the rituals associated with initiation.
- Rural-urban migration has led to mixing of various cultures causing a decline in people's participation in cultural practices.
- Modern medical technology has attracted many initiates than the traditional surgeons.

Give the reasons why initiation rites are still practiced today.
- To uphold traditional values, customs and culture.
- To provide an occupation for initiators/surgeons.

- In order to please/appease ancestral spirits.
- To ensure acceptability by those who have undergone the initiation rites.
- To prepare one for marriage.
- To promote African languages through songs and dance.
- To create a new age-set.
- To raise one's social status.
- To provide an opportunity for leadership.
- To help one inherit property.
- To create identity and a sense of belonging into the community.

III) MARRIAGE RITES

- Marriage is the third rite of passage that an individual is expected to go through in life.
- In traditional African communities, marriage is looked at as sacred and ordained by God.
- It is a requirement and an obligation for every normal person to get married and have children.

Why is marriage considered important in traditional African communities?

- It expands kinship since new social relationships are created between families.
- It brings the community together in feasting and rejoicing and everyone has a role to play.
- It promotes mutual love and companionship between a man and woman.
- It raises the social status of the couple since they earn respect.
- It leads to procreation and passing on the gift of life from one generation to another.
- Polygamous marriages earn wealth to the family since many wives are considered as wealth.
- It promotes unity between the families of the bride and the groom.

Rituals connected with marriage

- The marriage partner is chosen carefully, considering the qualities such as kindness, hospitality, faithfulness e.t.c.
- Marriage negotiations are carried out between the families of the bride and groom in preparation for the formal marriage and to strengthen relations between the families.
- Courtship period follows, in which the bride and groom are allowed to familiarize themselves with one another.
- Dowry is paid to seal the marriage. Dowry is important for the following reasons:
  i.   It acts as compensation to the girl's family for the loss of their daughter.
  ii.   It seals the marriage covenant.
  iii. It is an appreciation for the coming of a new wife and mother into the man's family.
  iv.   It is a symbol of the girl's presence in her home.
  v.   It promotes friendship and cements relationship between the two families of the bride and groom.
  vi.   Payment of the bridewealth shows that the man is serious with his intention to marry.

Explain the moral values acquired during marriage in traditional African society

- Friendship i.e. couples end up being friends as they share the family duties.
- Love- couples end up being affectionate towards each other as they also establish love to other family members.
- Responsibility – married members take up new duties in a community which calls for their accountability.
- Respect – married couples are respected because of their status.
- Co-operation – they learn to work with other members in the society.
- Hardwork – they are expected to be dedicated in their work.
- Patience – they learn to exercise patience in case of differences in marriages.
- Honesty – they learn to handle family resources in a trustworthy way.
- Self-control – they learn to refrain from quarrels and fights.
- Mutual concern and care – they are required to work for the wellbeing of their partners and other family members.
- Obedience – they should follow rules and regulations of the community.
- Generosity – they are expected to assist members of the community when called upon.
- Humility – they should humble themselves before their seniors and in laws.
- Courage – they should face challenges of marriage with a lot of determination to succeed.

What precautions were undertaken by Africans to ensure that marriage was permanent?

- Dowry was paid to seal the marriage.
- Members of the community were involved in all stages of the marriage.
- Parents from both sides consulted frequently to ensure that minor problems in marriages are solved in good time before they blow out of proportion.
- People were allowed to engage in marriage at a mature age especially after initiation.
- Unfaithfulness was heavily punished.
- There were go-betweens who were always handy when problems cropped up in marriages.
- Women were taught by their responsibilities by their grandmothers before marriage to be subordinate.

Reasons that explain why polygamy is still practiced in our society today

- Parents are assured of security in their old age because of their children.
- Parents are assured of continuity of their lineage when they die.
- It enables parents to have many children.
- It acts as a source of wealth to the family when children get employed.
- In case of death the gap created is easily filled by other partners in marriage.
- The problem of childlessness is easily contained as other partners can solve the problem.
- The problem of orphanage is curtailed as the remaining parents take care of the children.

State the reasons why unmarried people were undermined in African traditional society

- Marriage was compulsory for everyone.
- An unmarried person was regarded as a child and not a grown up.
- They lacked experience in sex, responsibilities and family matters.
- Such a person was considered impotent.
- Once he died, his place was forgotten.
- It is seen as a fight against community expansion.
- It is only parents who were highly valued.

IV) DEATH RITES

- Death is the final stage a person goes through in life.
- It is a sorrowful event because the dead person is physically and permanently removed from among the living members of the family.
- Rituals associated with death vary from one community to the other and are taken seriously by the family and community members.
- All the rituals are done to maintain a good relationship between the living and the dead.
- It is believed that death is not the end of life, but the dead continue to live in spirit-form.
- It is believed that death is caused by something or someone and that there is no natural death in the African understanding. Some of the causes of death include:
  i. Sorcery
  ii. Witchcraft/magic
  iii. Curses by elders.
  iv. Evil spirits
  v. Breaking a binding taboo or oath.
  vi. Disrespect for ancestors.
  vii. Old age.
  viii. God's will.
- The death rituals that are carried out are determined by the cause of death, age of the deceased person, one's social status, the gender and the will/wishes of the deceased e.g. children and unmarried people had simple funeral ceremonies and attended by few people while those of the rich, heroes and leaders are elaborate and attended by many people.

The death rites carried out and their significance include:

- Mourning and wailing to announce the death and as a sign of sorrow.
- There is singing and dancing to comfort the bereaved, praise the dead and request the spirits and ancestors to receive the dead.
- Washing the corpse using water and herbal medicine to preserve it and send it clean to the spirit world.
- Burying the dead with their property which is believed to assist the dead in the next world.
- The burial site is carefully selected in the ancestral home so that the spirit of the deceased does not haunt the living members.

- Pregnant women and children are not allowed to touch or come to close contact with the corpse so that misfortunes do not befall them.
- The body is carefully placed in the grave facing the appropriate direction according to the customs of the community.
- There is feasting and drinking of beer to encourage, strengthen the bereaved and as farewell meal with the dead.
- Sharing of the deceased's property among the relatives as a sign of solidarity with the dead and the care given to his/her property.
- Lighting of fire symbolizes the chasing away of spirits associated with death.
- After burial, close relatives shave their hair as a sign that a member has been separated from them and for cleansing impurities.

The role of death in inculcating moral values in traditional African communities

- Promotes the virtue of solidarity as members join to participate in the burial rites.
- The living members develop a sense of responsibility as they take the roles of the deceased and care for his/her property.
- The spirit of mutual concern for others is cultivated as the community members join to support those who are bereaved.
- The virtues of honesty and righteous living are acquired as one tries to avoid the possible causes of death.
- The respect given to the ancestors and the deceased is extended to other members.
- Obedience to the customs and traditions of the community is learnt as members observe the burial rituals.
- Patriotism is cultivated as members observe all customs and traditions related to death in the community.
- The members develop the moral value of thankfulness as they appreciate the role played by relatives, friends and the ancestors.

Give reasons why death was feared in traditional African community.

- It disrupts the rhythm of human life.
- It is irrevocable, one cannot escape it.
- It brings impurity to the family.
- It deprives the community of individuals.
- It involves very many rituals.
- It comes unannounced and unexpectedly.
- It separates one from the loved ones and end of life on earth.
- Nobody knows about the after-life.
- It may cause misunderstanding in the community.
- Death rites reveal people's characters.
- It brings poverty to the family involved.

Explain how Africans demonstrated their belief that death was not the end of life.
- Africans bury the dead with their property.
- Pouring libation to the dead.
- Ancestral veneration.
- Talking to the dead during funeral.
- Inheriting the dead man's wife and bearing children for him.
- Africans believe in rebirth or reincarnation of the dead.
- Seeking advice from the dead.
- Seeking communication from God through the ancestors.

THE ROLE OF RELIGIOUS SPECIALISTS IN THE AFRICAN COMMUNITIES AND THEIR RELEVANCE TODAY

Specialists are people with special skills and talents that are necessary in serving the community. These skills may either be social or spiritual.

Religious specialists in traditional African communities include:
- Herbalists
- Diviners.
- Prophets
- Priests
- Medicine-people
- Rainmakers
- Elders
- Kings

Members of the community consult these religious specialists on various issues and occasions e.g. birth, sickness, marriage, death, drought, sickness, installation of a leader, when going to war or in cases of barrenness e.t.c.

These specialists acquire their skills through the following ways:
- Through apprenticeship/learning the art of diviner.
- Through inheritance.
- Through visions.
- Through dreams.
- Being possessed by the spirits.
- Receiving a call from God and ancestors.

a. Priests
The duties of priests involve both spiritual and social aspects e.g.
- They mediated between the people and God.
- They lead in prayers and offer sacrifices.
- They guide and counsel people.

- The carry preside over cleansing ceremonies.
- They reconcile warring parties.
- They take care of sacred places e.g. shrines and temples.
- They are custodians of the community's traditions and customs.
- They bless community members e.g. before going to war.
- They intercede for people's needs to God.

b. Healers/medicine-people

These are men and women who have deep knowledge of herbs, roots, or other objects in the environment for curing people. Their roles include:

- Establishing causes of a diseases.
- Treating illnesses.
- Giving charms to protect people from charms illnesses or evil.
- Providing aid to increase productivity of the people, animals or farms.
- They dispelled witchcraft and magic.
- They guided and counselled people.
- They presided over religious functions.

Give the occasions when the services of medicinemen are required in Traditional African Communities.

- When there was sickness/illness.
- During rites of passage.
- When the community is struck by misfortunes.
- Before warriors go for war.
- When property is lost/stolen.
- During religious functions.
- When there are mysterious occurrences.
- When reconciling two warring parties.
- During disputes in the community.
- When there is witchcraft.
- During installation of community leaders.
- When there is barrenness/childlessness.

c. Rainmakers

Rainmakers have special knowledge of the environment that enables them to predict weather conditions.

Rainmakers perform the following duties:

- They cause rain by performing certain rituals.
- They stop rain.
- They predict weather conditions.
- They guide and counsel the community.

- They bless the community.
- They are mediators between God and the people.

d. Diviners

Diviners find out hidden secrets or seek solutions to problems.

Diviners perform the following roles:

- They foretell occurrences.
- They warn people on future misfortunes.
- Preside over religious functions e.g. offering sacrifices.
- Mediate between the people and God and ancestors.
- Diviners guide and counsel people on various matters.
- They bless warriors before going to war.
- They perform cleansing rituals.
- They settle disputes among the people.
- They reveal secrets and expose wrongdoers in the society.
- They cure illnesses.

e. Prophets/seers

African communities have prophets and prophetesses who have the ability to read and interpret events and predict the future. Some of the prophets receive revelations about the future through visions and dreams. They perform the following duties:

- They predict/foretell future events in the community.
- They warn people on the impending danger.
- They act as mediators between human beings and spirits and ancestors.
- They lead the community in prayers.
- They settle disputes in the community.
- They guide and counsel people on religious matters.
- They bless the people.
- They perform cleansing rituals.
- They are the guardians of the community's customs and traditions.
- They are mediators between God and people.

f. Elders

These are people who are advanced in age and have acquired immense experience, wisdom and knowledge since they have passed through various stages of life.

They must be credible and morally upright people and have families and grown up children.

In every community, a council of elders is established and is endowed with the responsibility of providing law and order.

The council of elders performs the following roles:

- Settling disputes.
- They give direction and guide the community on various issues.
- They oversee the sharing of property.

- They are custodians of the customs and traditions of the community.
- They make peace on behalf of the community in case of disputes.
- They preside over religious functions.
- They guide and counsel the community members.

g. Mediums

Mediums are religious leaders who when possessed interact with the spirit world. They perform the following roles:

- Reveal and interpret messages from the spirit world.
- Give solutions to people's problems.
- Reveal cure for sicknesses to the medicine-people.
- Reveal secrets about stolen property.
- Reveal the causes of sicknesses or death.

The relevance of the Religious specialist in the society today

The African religious specialists still feature prominently in day-to-day lives of the people. This is seen in the following areas:

Medicine-people

- They have been licensed by the government to operate herbal clinics.
- They diagnose diseases.
- They offer treatment for different diseases where modern drugs may have failed.
- Their services are cheap and easily in the reach of patients.

Diviners

- They establish the causes of illness, barrenness or any misfortunes.
- They serve as fortune tellers in getting employment and passing examinations.
- They exorcise evil spirits.

Rainmakers

- They are consulted during community ceremonies to stop the rains during those occasions.
- During severe droughts they perform rituals aimed at causing rain.

Priests

- They are still called upon to lead in prayers during public functions.
- They preside over religious ceremonies.

Elders

- Are consulted by both the community members and government to solve disputes.
- They serve on land boards.
- They guard the traditions of the people e.g. on inheritance, marriage, death rites e.t.c.

Factors that have undermined the role of the religious specialists today

- Christianity discourages consulting traditional religious specialists by associating their practices with witchcraft.
- Christian leaders are also given more prominence over traditional priests.

- The new government structures and political systems have taken over the role of traditional elders.
- The level of education is used as a tool in choosing leaders as opposed age, wisdom and experience that were used in traditional African communities.
- Through migration people from different communities mix up and therefore they may not recognize the traditional African leaders and religious specialists.
- Modern medicine has replaced the role of traditional healers.

State the reasons why witchcraft is feared in Traditional African Communities.
- Many deaths are attributed to witchcraft.
- Witchcraft leads to suffering of individual community.
- People suffer mysterious illnesses due to witchcraft.
- It causes hatred/disunity.
- It causes fear/suspicion/mistrust among people.
- It carries severe punishment from ancestors, spirits, God and the community.
- It leads to poverty.
- It leads to destruction of property.
- It is full of mysterious happenings.
- It forces people to migrate from their homestead and ancestral lands.
- Those associated with it are regarded as evil/outcasts.

AFRICAN MORAL VALUES HOSPITALITY, HONESTY, COURTESY, INTEGRITY TOLERANCE/PERSEVERANCE, LOYALTY, CHASTITY, RESPECT, RESPONSIBILITY, LOVE, CO-OPERATION, AND UNITY

Morals – these are principles or ideas of what is right or wrong in society.

Morality – It is a set of social rules and norms intended to guide the conduct of people in a society. These rules and norms emerge from and are based on people's beliefs about what is right and what is wrong.

Moral values – these are the forms or patterns of conduct or behaviour that are considered worthwhile by a society. They are the factors that influence one to choose what is good over evil. Moral values are also related to moral virtues, which are admirable traits of character.

Examples of African moral values
- Hospitality: it refers being welcome to visitors and strangers, and sharing food, drinks and shelter to them.
- Honesty: it is the practice of being truthful and trustworthy.
- Loyalty: it refers to devotion to a person or faithfulness.
- Respect: it is the ability to show regard for other people and recognize their rights, status and circumstances. Children are taught to respect elders, parents and leaders.
- Cooperation: refers working together for a common purpose or benefit.

- Obedience: means following instructions given by someone in authority e.g. parent, elder, teacher, pastor, chief e.t.c. and following laid down rules and regulations.
- Humility: it is refers to adhering to moral and ethical principles and being honest. Such a person is described as being humble.
- Integrity: it is the quality of always behaving according to the laid down moral principles that one believes in. It promotes respect and trust from others because one can be relied on.
- Sharing: it refers to using resources such as land, food and jointly with other people.
- Responsibility: it refers to the act of being caring about others and their wellbeing. A responsible person is able to carry out his/her duties effectively with minimal supervision or guidance.
- Love: it refers to the deep and tender affectionate feelings towards other people.
- Unity: it is the state of togetherness and oneness in the community. It is a moral value that fosters harmony and togetherness.

PAPER TWO

Topic 13: OLD TESTAMENT PROPHECIES ABOUT THE COMING OF THE MESSIAH

- The word messiah means "the anointed".
- It is used in the Old Testament to refer to people in Israel because God chose them to serve him e.g. kings and priests like David was anointed with oil to serve as king.
- Many prophets in the Old Testament prophesied the coming of a messiah. These prophecies describe the Messiah as a righteous king, who would rule over Israel according to the will of God.
- The beginning of these prophecies about the messiah in the Old Testament is prophet Nathan's prophesy to David.

Nathan's prophecy (2 Samuel 7: 3 – 17)
- ❖ After David had built a beautiful palace for himself, he felt that it was not in order for the Ark of the Covenant to continue dwelling in the Tent of Meeting.
- ❖ He therefore wanted to build a temple for God, to house the Ark of the Covenant.
- ❖ However, God told Nathan that David's son would be the one to build Him a temple. God also gave David divine promises through Prophet Nathan.
- ❖ These promises contain prophesies concerning the messiah.

Nathan's prophesies concerning the Messiah include:
- Be a descendant of King David.
- Establish an everlasting kingdom.
- Rule over Israel forever.
- Deliver Israel from her political enemies.
- Always be supported by God.
- Be a great king, whose kingdom will be kept strong.
- He will rule according to the covenant way of life.
- He will make David's name great and famous.

Isaiah's prophecy (Isaiah 7:10 – 16; 9:1 – 7)
Prophet Isaiah made the prophecy about Immanuel, which means God with us.
- He prophesied that the messiah will have supernatural titles such as: Immanuel, Wonderful Counsellor, Mighty God, Eternal Father/Everlasting Father, Prince of Peace.
- The messiah would be a descendant of David/rule of the throne of David.

- The messiah will rule forever.
- He would be despised or rejected by many.
- He would be born of a young woman/virgin.
- Messianic reign/rule will bring happiness and joy to the Israelites.
- The messiah would suffer for the sins of human beings.
- Peace and prosperity will prevail during his messianic reign.
- He will rule with justice and righteousness.
- He would have characteristics of normal human being/child.
- His suffering will be through the will God.

Jeremiah's prophecy (Jeremiah 23: 5 – 6)

According to Jeremiah, God would raise up a messiah who would:

- Be a righteous descendant of King David.
- Rule wisely.
- Do what is right and just.
- Protect Judah from all her enemies and establish peace.
- Be called 'The Lord our Salvation'
- Carry out the will of God.
- Rule on behalf of God.

Micah's prophecies concerning the messiah (Micah 5: 2 – 5)

Micah prophesied the following about the messiah:

- The messiah will be born in Bethlehem.
- He will rule over Israel.
- His origin is from the Old/ancient days.
- He will be born of a woman.
- He will feed his flock.
- He will rule in the power of God.
- In his time, Israel will be secure.
- He shall be great to the ends of the earth.
- Israel will have victory over her enemies/there will be peace in Israel.

The Psalmist Prophecy (Psalms 41:9; 110: 1 – 2)

The Psalmist's prophecies include:

- The messiah will be betrayed by a close friend.
- He will rule from Zion.
- The messiah will rule in the midst of his enemies/will be given victory over his enemies.
- The messiah will be honoured by God.
- The messiah will sit at the right hand of God.

Deutro-Isaiah's prophecy/Suffering Servant (53; 61: 1 – 2)

Deutro-Isaiah's prophesy refers to the messiah as the suffering servant of Yahweh. The prophecies about the Suffering Servant include:

- The servant will succeed in his work and will be highly honoured.
- Many who have witnessed his suffering will be surprised at his success and honour.
- The servant will be despised, rejected and ignored by those who are with him.
- The servant is has nothing attractive, he is ordinary and simple.
- He will be harshly treated, arrested, sentenced to death and killed.
- His body will be buried in a rich man's tomb.
- He will endure all that is done to him in humble silence.
- He will suffer and die for the salvation of human beings.
- His suffering is according to the will of God.
- He will be filled with the spirit of God.

THE CONCEPT OF THE MESSIAH IN THE NEW TESTAMENT
(Luke 1: 26 – 38; 2: 1 – 23; 23:1 – 35; 24: 50 – 51)

The Jews were under the rule of the Roman Empire at the time of Jesus' birth. To them, the Messiah, who was prophesied by the Old Testament prophets, would deliver them from the rule of the Romans.

They therefore were expecting a political and military messiah, who would defeat the Romans and lead them to prosperity.

They had the following expectations about the messiah:

- The messiah will be a military ruler who would conquer the enemies of Israel.
- He would be from the dynasty of David.
- He would be born in from a royal family.
- He would lead Israel to political and economic prosperity.
- He would appear in Jerusalem in full glory.
- He would perform miracles and mighty deeds.
- He would not associate himself with the outcasts e.g. poor, sinners and Gentiles.
- He would uphold Judaism.

❖ Jesus was the Messiah, but not the type that the Jews were expecting. He was not a political or military Messiah. Jesus was a spiritual messiah.

❖ Jesus fulfilled the Old Testament prophecies concerning the messiah. Therefore, Jesus is the messiah who came to deliver people from the slavery and bondage of sin, and not from political oppression.

The ways in which Jesus is the fulfilment of the Old Testament prophecies about the messiah are:

- Jesus was born of a young woman called Mary, who was engaged to Joseph, a descendant of King David as prophesied by Nathan, that the messiah would be a descendant of David.
- The angel announced to Mary that Jesus will rule over the house of Jacob forever, which fulfils Nathan's prophecy that David's descendant will rule over Israel forever.
- Isaiah's prophecy of a virgin conceiving is fulfilled when Mary is told by the angel that she would conceive by the power of the Holy Spirit.
- Jesus was born in Bethlehem, which is also the birth place of King David, as prophesied by prophet Micah about the ruler whom God would raise up from Bethlehem.
- Angel Gabriel announced that Mary's son would be called Immanuel, which fulfils Nathan's prophecy that the messiah would be called Immanuel.
- The blind beggar in Jerusalem referred to Jesus as son of David, which fulfils Isaiah's prophecy that the messiah will be a descendant of David.
- In the synagogue in Nazareth, Jesus says that he was the fulfilment of Isaiah's prophecy of the messiah who would liberate the captives.
- In the temple, Simeon testified that Jesus would bring salvation to the whole world, which was prophesied by Prophet Isaiah that the messiah would bring salvation to the whole world.
- Jesus was betrayed by Judas Iscariot, his disciple, which fulfils Micah's prophecy that the messiah would be betrayed by a close friend.
- Jesus performed miracles in his ministry such as healing the sick, raising the dead, and casting out evil spirits as prophesied by Isaiah, that the messiah would work miracles.
- Jesus also fulfilled the prophecy of the Suffering Servant through his passion and death for the salvation of humankind.

Jesus fulfilled the messianic prophecies about the suffering servant in the following ways:

- He died on the cross in order to deliver the whole world from sin.
- He submitted himself willingly to suffering and eventual death by crucifixion.
- He was despised and rejected.
- He was spat on and mocked.
- He was crucified in the thieves even though he was innocent.
- His sides were pierced and wounded.
- He was buried in a rich man's tomb.
- Through him, God's everlasting kingdom was established.

THE ROLE OF JOHN THE BAPTIST (Isaiah 40:3 – 5; Malachi 3: 1; 4: 5 – 6; Luke 7:20 – 35)

- The prophets in the Old Testament such as Malachi and Isaiah predicted the coming of a messenger who would prepare the way for the messiah.
- Prophet Malachi foretells that the messenger who would prepare the way for the messiah would be Elijah.
- Christians believe that God sent Elijah in the person of John the Baptist to prepare the way for Jesus Christ, who is the Messiah.
- John had all the characteristics of Prophet Elijah that made him be referred to as Elijah e.g.
    i. He appeared in the wilderness.
    ii. He lived a simple life.
    iii. He wore camel's skin.
    iv. He ate locusts and wild honey.
    v. He was courageous just as Elijah e.g. he condemned King Herod for marrying his brother's wife.
    vi. John was filled with the Holy Spirit of God and he proclaimed God's message to the people of his time.

- John the Baptist acted as a link between the Old Testament and the New Testament. He marked the end of the Old Testament and introduced the New Testament in the following ways:
    i. He asked people to repent in preparation for the coming of the messiah.
    ii. He preached baptism for the forgiveness of sins.
    iii. He baptized Jesus in the River Jordan to prepare him for his mission.
    iv. He introduced Jesus to his disciples as the messiah and surrendered them to Jesus.
    v. He warned people of God's coming judgement which would be effected by the messiah.
    vi. He acknowledged Jesus' greatness over him.
    vii. He baptized those who repented and asked them to live holy lives.

Topic 14: THE INFANCY AND EARLY LIFE OF JESUS

THE ANNUNCIATION (LUKE 1: 5 – 56)
Annunciation of the birth of John the Baptist (Luke 1: 2 – 25)
- The birth of John the Baptist was announced to Zechariah, a priest.
- Zechariah was performing his priestly duties of burning incense in the temple while the rest of the people were praying outside the temple
- The angel of the Lord appeared to Zechariah, standing on the right hand side of the altar.
- Zechariah was troubled and was overcome with fear when he saw Angel Gabriel.
- The angel told Zechariah not to be afraid for his prayer had been heard.
- The angel informed Zechariah that his wife Elizabeth will bear a son.
- The angel gave the name of the son as John.
- The angel said that the son would bring joy and gladness to his parents, be great before the Lord, not drink wine or strong drink, will be filled with the Holy Spirit, and that he would turn the sons of Israel to the Lord.
- Zechariah could not believe the angel's message since he was an old man and his wife was barren and so he asked for a sign.
- The angel answered that he was Gabriel, standing in God's presence and sent to bring the good news.
- When Zechariah refused to believe the angel, he was struck dumb until the day when the angel's message comes to pass.
- The people who were waiting outside wondered why he had taken too long in the temple.
- When Zechariah came out, he could not speak to them and they realized he had received a vision in the temple.
- He made signs to them and he remained dumb.
- He went home and after some time his wife conceived.

Annunciation of the birth of Jesus (Luke 1: 26 – 38)
- Angel Gabriel appeared to Mary, a virgin, who was engaged to Joseph from the house of King David to announce the birth of Jesus.
- The angel of the Lord addressed Mary as the favoured one and said that the Lord was with her and that she was blessed among women.
- Mary was troubled and was filled with fear about the angel's greetings.
- The angel told her not to be afraid and told her that she was going to conceive and give birth to a son.
- The angel said that the child will be called Jesus and that the child will be great.
- Then Mary wondered how it would happen and yet she did not know a man.
- The angel assured her that she would conceive by the power of the Holy Spirit.
- Mary accepted the angel's message by saying that she was the handmaid of the Lord.

Lessons that Christians learn about God from the annunciation of the birth of John and Jesus
- God answers the prayers of the righteous.
- What is impossible with men is possible with God.
- God uses those who are humble to carry out his will.
- God fulfils his promises.
- God fulfils both spiritual and physical needs of the people as brought out in the angel's message.

The message of angel Gabriel about John the Baptist
- John the Baptist was to be a son.
- His name was to be John.
- He will bring joy or gladness to his parents.
- He will be great in the sight of God.
- He will be the forerunner of the messiah.
- He would lead a Nazirite lifestyle and therefore he will drink no wine or strong drink.
- He will enjoy greatness similar to that of Elijah.
- He will be filled with the Holy Spirit from his mother's womb.
- He will turn many of the sons of Israel to the Lord their God.
- He will turn the hearts of the fathers to the children.

Identify the characteristics of Jesus as announced by Angel Gabriel to Mary.
- He will be great.
- He is a descendant of King David.
- He shall inherit David's throne.
- He will rule over the house of Jacob forever/his kingdom will be eternal.
- He will be called the Son of the Most High.
- He will be holy.

Mary visits Elizabeth (Luke 1: 39 - 56)
- After the angel left her, Mary went to visit her cousin Elizabeth, Zechariah's wife.
- Mary entered her house and greeted Elizabeth.
- When Elizabeth heard Mary's greeting, the baby leapt in her womb with joy.
- She was filled with the Holy Spirit.
- Elizabeth said that Mary would be mother of the Messiah and that she was most blessed among women.
- Mary's responded to Elizabeth's remarks with a hymn called the Magnificat.
- Mary stayed with Elizabeth for about three months then returned home.

Main teachings in the Magnificat/the song of Mary

- God is holy.
- God shows mercy to the righteous.
- God rejects the proud and uplifts the lowly.
- God feels the hungry with good things.
- He denies the rich.
- God is faithful to his promises.

Ways in which Christians show appreciation of God's favour to them.

- By worshipping God through prayers.
- By praising Him through songs.
- By serving God by preaching the Good News.
- By sharing generously what they have with those who don't have/helping the needy.
- By giving tithes and offerings.
- By helping in the building of the church.
- By preaching repentance of sins or calling people to repent their sins.
- Having faith in God.
- Obeying the teachings of God.
- By showing compassion to others.
- By showing love to their enemies.

THE BIRTH OF JOHN THE BAPTIST (LUKE 1: 57 – 80)

- The time came for Elizabeth to have her baby, and she gave birth to a son.
- Her neighbours and relatives joined her in celebration.
- On the eighth day the baby was to be circumcised according to the Jewish tradition.
- They wanted to name him after his father Zechariah, but his mother said the son would be called John.
- They argued about the child's name then they made signs to Zechariah and he wrote the name John on a writing tablet.
- Immediately Zechariah regained his speech.
- He praised God for what He had done.
- Zechariah sang the song Benedictus in praise of God.

Message about God and John the Baptist as revealed by Zechariah in the Benedictus

- God is a redeemer.
- God has brought salvation through Jesus.
- God fulfils his promises.
- John the Baptist will be a prophet of the Most High God.
- John would prepare the way for the messiah.
- John would give the knowledge of salvation to his people.
- John would call people to repentance and forgiveness of their sins.
- John would give light to those who sit in darkness and the shadow of death.
- John would guide the people in the way of peace.

135

THE BIRTH OF JESUS (LUKE 2: 1 – 20)

- The birth of Jesus took place in Bethlehem, in Judea, during the reign of Emperor Augustus Caesar, who had ordered a census to be carried out.
- Joseph travelled to Bethlehem with Mary, where they were supposed to be counted from.
- While in Bethlehem, the time came for Mary to deliver her child.
- The baby was born in a stable and Mary wrapped him in swaddling clothes and laid him in a manger because there was no room for them in the inn.
- The angel of the Lord appeared to the shepherds who were in the fields, watching over their flock and announced to them about the birth of Jesus.
- The angel gave them a sign on how they would find the baby wrapped in swaddling clothes and lying in a manger
- A great multitude of other angels appeared singing praise to God.
- The shepherds went to visit the baby after the angel departed from them.

Describe the events that took place when the angel of the Lord visited the shepherds on the night when Jesus was born

- The shepherds were looking after their flocks in the field at night.
- The angel appeared to them.
- The glory of the Lord shone around them.
- They were filled with fear.
- The angel told them not to fear.
- He told them of the good news of the birth of Jesus.
- The angel told gave them a sign that they would find the baby wrapped in swaddling clothes and lying in a manger.
- A group of other angels appeared praising God.
- The shepherds went to Bethlehem and found the baby as they had been told by the angel.

Lessons that Christians learn about the stories of the birth of Jesus

- Jesus is the son of God and therefore, he is the messiah.
- The birth of Jesus was God's plan, which fulfils of the Old Testament prophecies.
- Jesus was born to bring salvation to humankind.
- God uses the humble and the weak to fulfil his obligations.
- His birth was extraordinary and mysterious.
- The birth of the Messiah was a joy to all, including those who are unborn e.g. John the Baptist leapt with joy in her mother's womb.

How was the birth of Jesus extra-ordinary?

- He was born of a virgin.
- He was conceived by the power of the Holy Spirit.
- He was given the name by an angel of the Lord even before he was born.
- He was born and laid in a manger.
- A group of angels appeared praising God at his birth.
- The shepherds in the field were given the message of Jesus' birth by the angel.
- His birth had been foretold by prophets in the Old Testament.

Evidences from St. Luke's Gospel that Jesus came for the poor

- The parents of Jesus were from a poor background.
- He lived in Nazareth, a town of the poor.
- He was born in a cowshed and laid in a manger.
- His birth was revealed by to the shepherds.
- At dedication, his parents offered a pair of doves.
- In his ministry, Jesus associated more with the poor and those who were suffering.
- Some of his apostles were from poor backgrounds e.g. fishermen.
- In his teachings he said that the kingdom of God is for the poor.
- In his teachings, he challenged the rich to share their wealth with the poor.

DEDICATION (LUKE 2: 21 – 40)

- Jesus was circumcised on the eighth day, according to the Jewish tradition, and was given the name Jesus as was suggested by the angel.
- When the time came for the dedication, Mary and Joseph brought Jesus to the temple to present him to the Lord as required by the Mosaic Law.
- Mary went for purification in the temple as demanded by the law.
- The parents of Jesus offered a sacrifice of a pair of turtle doves.
- In the Temple, there was an upright and righteous man who had received a revelation, from the Holy Spirit, that he would not die until he had seen the messiah.
- When Jesus was brought to the temple, Simeon took him in his hands and praised God.
- He asked God to rest him in peace now that he had seen the Messiah.
- Simeon blessed the parents of Jesus and made prophecies about of the child, Jesus.
- A prophetess Anna also gave thanks to God and testified about the child.
- The parents returned to Galilee with the child after performing the rituals.

Explain Simeon's prophetic messages about Jesus during His dedication (Luke 2:21-40).

- That Jesus was the son of God and therefore the promised Messiah.
- He would bring salvation to all/he is the saviour of the world
- He would be the light of revelation to Gentiles/non-Jews.
- He would liberate the Israelites from oppression.
- He would cause the rise and fall of many in Israel.
- He would face opposition and his mother would suffer great pain due to this.

Lessons that Christians learn about Simeon's prophecy

- God keeps his promises.
- Jesus is the messiah that people were waiting for.
- Jesus brings universal salvation.
- Jesus will suffer and die for the sins of mankind.
- All Christians are witnesses to the salvation brought by Jesus Christ.

THE BOY JESUS AT THE TEMPLE (LUKE 2: 41 – 52)

- At the age of twelve years, Jesus accompanied his parents to Jerusalem for the yearly Passover festival.
- When the festival ended, Jesus remained in the temple as his went back home in Galilee.
- In the temple, Jesus sat with the elders and teachers of the Law asking and answering questions.
- The elders marvelled at his intelligence and knowledge of the scriptures.
- His parents were not aware that he stayed behind for they assumed that he was among the travellers.
- After a whole day's journey, they discovered Jesus was missing, and they searched for him among friends and relatives.
- They travelled back to Jerusalem in search of him.
- He was found in the temple, after three days, seated and engaging the teachers of Law in the Mosaic traditions.
- When Mary and Joseph saw Jesus they were surprised and his mother asked him why he had caused them so much anxiety.
- Jesus answered them, "didn't you know that I had to be in my father's house?"
- Mary and Joseph took Jesus back to Nazareth and Jesus increased in years and wisdom.

Explain what Jesus meant when he said "didn't you know I must be in my father's house?"

- Jesus was already aware of his unique relationship with God, whom he calls his father.
- Jesus was already aware of his divine nature.
- Jesus is the Son of God.
- He was asserting that he was ready for his mission as demanded by his father.
- The temple is God's house.
- It was a fulfilment of Malachi's prophecy.
- The family should not hinder one from serving God.

Give reasons why Mary took Jesus to the temple.

- To be dedicated before God as a first born male Jewish child.
- To fulfil the vows made by the Israelites before God.
- To be given a name according to the Jewish culture.
- To be circumcised on the eighth day according to Jewish traditions.
- To be able to learn the Jewish religious traditions just like other youths.
- To fulfil the annual pilgrimage to Jerusalem for Passover.

Why should children be introduced to the worship of God?

- To create in them an awareness of God early.
- To enable them learn the teachings of the church at an early age.
- To make them familiar with the religious practices of the church.
- To enable the child master the meaning of church rituals e.g. prayers and songs.

- To ensure they undergo all the relevant rituals of the church in order to become full members of the church.
- To imitate and emulate the life of Jesus in the child.

State the ways in which parents develop their children's spiritual life.
- By having the children baptized and participate in the sacramental life of the church.
- Leading righteous lives for the child to copy/being good role models.
- Taking children to church for dedication and thanksgiving.
- By allowing them to interact with others e.g. during Sunday school.
- By praying to God to guide the child.
- By exposing the child to church activities.
- By condemning the child's evil activities and correcting them.
- By offering counselling services on spiritual matters.
- Teaching them to read the Bible.

State the challenges that parents experience in bringing up children.
- Parents are too busy in their work that they have no time for their children.
- Disintegration of African traditional morals e.g. obedience.
- Poverty.
- Negative western influence.
- Sickness/pandemics e.g. HIV/AIDS.
- Immorality and corruption in the society.
- Negative peer influence/pressure.
- Generation gap.
- Influence/access to pornographic literature.
- Urbanization and modernity.
- Permissiveness.

Explain the ways in which the early childhood of Jesus prepared him for his future ministry.
- Jesus assisted his parents with work e.g. carpentry which enabled him to carry out his duties of healing and preaching in his ministry.
- Jesus was taken to the temple by his parents where he learnt the Mosaic Law, which he later challenged, modified and accepted some in his ministry.
- He interacted with the teachers of the Law and discussed with them scriptural issues which enabled him become a great teacher in his ministry.
- He was filled with the Holy Spirit which led him in performing miracles.
- Jesus was obedient to his parents which assisted him to respect all elders and people.
- Many people such as Zechariah and Prophetess Anna identified Jesus as the Saviour and throughout his ministry, he was identified as the Son of God.
- Jesus was dedicated in the temple by his parents and circumcised according to the Jewish Law making him grow up to respect the Jewish Laws.
- Jesus was born under humble circumstances i.e. in a cowshed which made him a humble and peaceful messiah.

Ways in which the church trains the youth to be part of the church community.

- They are taught the best rules of the church.
- They are assigned roles in the church.
- They are made to accompany their parents to the places of worship.
- They are guided and counselled.
- They are encouraged to join youth groups in the church.
- They are rewarded for good conduct.
- They are asked to observe the activities performed by elders in church.

Topic 15: THE GALILEAN MINISTRY

JOHN THE BAPTIST AND JESUS
a) The Teachings of John the Baptist (Luke 3: 1 – 20)
- He demanded that people should repent their sins and be baptized.
- He urged people to show charity and compassion to others by sharing with the needy
- He told tax collectors to be honest, not to collect more than what was required of them.
- He told soldiers not to abuse their power by robbing and accusing others falsely.
- He warned the sinners about God's coming judgement.
- John the Baptist announced the coming of the messiah and said that he was not the messiah.
- He condemned King Herod's immoral behaviour of marrying Herodias, his brother's wife.

For having condemned Herod fearlessly, John the Baptist was put in prison by Herod Antipas.

Give the teachings of John the Baptist about the Messiah.
- The Messiah will be greater than John the Baptist.
- He will baptize with the Holy Spirit and fire.
- He will bring God's salvation.
- He will proclaim judgment.
- He will punish sinners and reward the righteous.

Relevance of John's teachings to daily life
- Christians should be fair, honest and just in their dealings with other people.
- Christians should avoid being hypocrisy.
- Christians should acknowledge their sinfulness and repent their sins.
- Christians should avoid sexual immorality.
- Christians should share what they have with the needy.
- Christians know that they will be judged for their sins.

Give the similarities between the role of Jesus and that of John the Baptist.
- Both called sinners to repentance.
- Both proclaimed judgment on sinners.
- Both faced political leaders with courage.
- Both led exemplary lives.
- Both taught about nature of God.
- Both condemned the evil ways of people.

Outline the differences between the work of John the Baptist and that of Jesus Christ.
- John the Baptist preached mainly in the wilderness/the desert of Judah, while Jesus preached in the synagogues, homes, cities and towns and in the temple.
- John the Baptist called people to repentance, while Jesus forgave/died for their sins.
- John the Baptist baptized people with water, but Jesus baptized with the holy spirit/fire.
- John the Baptist lived a Nazarite life, while Jesus mixed freely with all people.
- The emphasis of John the Baptist's preaching was in the promised Messiah, while that of Jesus was about the kingdom of God.
- John the Baptist's message was direct whereas Jesus preached in parables.
- While John the Baptist's disciples fasted, the disciples of Jesus ate and drank.
- John the Baptist did not perform miracles, but Jesus ministry was full of signs and wonders.
- John the Baptist was the fore runner/prepared the way while Jesus fulfilled/was the messiah.

Identify the ways in which Christians play the role of John the Baptist today.
- They call people to repentance.
- They baptize the converts.
- They condemn the evils of their day.
- They remind people to prepare for the second coming of Christ.
- They advise the political leaders of their day.
- They announce the coming of divine judgement.
- They give practical moral advice on sharing and honesty.
- They preach Christ as the promised Messiah.

b) The baptism of Jesus (Luke 3: 21 – 22)
- All the people had been baptized by John the Baptist.
- Jesus was also baptized.
- Jesus then started to pray.
- The heavens opened.
- The Holy Spirit descended on him in form of a dove.
- A voice came from heaven.
- Jesus was described as the Son of God.

Jesus was baptized even though he had no sin because of the following reasons:
- Jesus wanted to confirm and show his approval of the ministry of John the Baptist.
- He wanted to identify himself with humankind.
- He was baptised to fulfil the Old Testament prophecies concerning the Messiah.
- Through baptism he received the Holy Spirit who was necessary for his mission.
- It was part of God's plan for the salvation of human beings.
- It was a sign of his death and resurrection for the salvation of humankind.
- It demonstrated Jesus' humility.
- It showed Jesus' willingness to obey God and to carry out his mission.

Importance of Jesus' Baptism to modern Christians
- Through baptism Christians identify themselves with Jesus.
- Christians receive the power of the Holy Spirit through baptism.
- Baptism unites Christians as members of the body of Christ, that is, the church.
- Baptism signifies the end of the old life and the beginning of a new life in Christ.
- It signifies the complete forgiveness of sins.
- Baptism makes Christians children of God.
- Through baptism Christians become full members of the church and the Christian community.
- Baptism prepares Christians for the Kingdom of God.
- It acts an outward sign of their inner faith as it is done publicly.
- It is a sign of a new covenant with God.

Problems faced by new converts in the church today
- They are sometimes not fully accepted and integrated in the church.
- The older Christians may not serve as role models.
- They may not be involved in church activities/not given responsibilities.
- They are tempted to backslide and go back to their previous lifestyle.
- Older Christians expect them to change faster than they possibly can.
- Some experience problems of communication or language barrier.
- They may lack Christian literature to strengthen their faith/guidance and counselling.
- In a large church, they get lost in the crowd and are not identified or recognized.
- The financial demands of the church may be too much for them.
- Lack of assistance and concern when a new member is in need of material and social needs.
- Some get frustrated when their expectations are not given or not met.
- They are assigned duties which they can't manage.

THE TEMPTATION OF JESUS (LUKE 4: 1 – 13)
Describe the temptations of Jesus in the wilderness as recorded in Luke 4: 1 – 13
- After baptism Jesus was led by the Holy Spirit into the wilderness where he stayed for forty days and nights praying and fasting.
- He ate nothing and so he felt hungry.
- The devil asked him to command stones to become bread if he was the son of God.
- Jesus answered saying that man does not live by bread alone.
- Satan then led Jesus to a high place and showed him all the kingdoms of the world and promised to give Jesus everything if he worshipped him.
- Jesus said that it is written that, you shall worship and serve only the Lord your God.
- The devil then took Jesus to the pinnacle of the Temple and told him to jump down since God would send angels to ensure that he did not get hurt.
- Jesus responded that it is written that you shall not tempt the Lord your God.
- After the devil finished tempting him, he left Jesus for a while.

These temptations were meant to test Jesus' obedience to God. They were meant to prepare Jesus for his mission, since in his ministry he faced various forms of temptations.

The relevance of the temptations of Jesus to Christians today
- Christians should accept temptations so that their faith may be strengthened.
- They should use the word of God to challenge the devil.
- Christians should not be worried about material things but trust in God's providence.
- Christians should lead a prayerful life in order to be blessed and overcome temptations.
- Christians should worship one God and avoid anything that will interfere with their faith.
- Christians should remain faithful and obedient to God during temptations.
- Christians should not misuse their God-given power for their own material gains.

Give ways in which Christians overcome temptations.
- Christians can overcome temptations through prayer.
- By reading the Bible frequently to help them choose the right thing to do.
- Seeking the help of the Holy Spirit.
- Keeping away from tempting situations.
- By fellowshipping with other Christians to get encouragement.
- Christians can overcome temptations by having strong faith in God.

JESUS BEGINS WORK IN GALILEE AND IS REJECTED AT NAZARETH (Luke 4: 14 – 30)
- Jesus started his ministry in Galilee, his own home district.
- Having been filled with the Holy Spirit, Jesus understood the nature of his mission which involved preaching the Good News and performing miracles in various towns of Galilee.
- His teachings and works brought conflicts between Jesus and his disciples and the religious leaders.

Jesus' ministry in Galilee and his rejection at Nazareth (Luke 4: 14 - 30)
- On the Sabbath day, Jesus went to the Synagogue in Nazareth, his own village.
- He was given the scroll/book of Isaiah to read.
- He opened and read the message about the messianic prophecies in Isaiah 61, which says that "the Spirit of the Lord is upon me."
- Jesus then told the multitude that the scripture had been fulfilled in him on that day.
- The people became hostile to him for they realized that he was claiming to be expected Messiah.
- Jesus responded telling them that a prophet is never accepted by his own people.
- He gave two examples of non-Israelites who had received God's favours during the time of Prophets Elijah and Elisha.
- This made his listeners rage the more and they tried to kill him by throwing him down a hill.
- Jesus passed in their midst and went on his way.

Outline the mission of Jesus as outlined in Luke 4: 18 – 19.

Jesus read that the Spirit of the Lord was upon him, and was sent to:

- Preach the good news to the poor.
- Proclaim the release of captives.
- Restore sight to the blind.
- Set at liberty those who were oppressed.
- Proclaim the acceptable year of the Lord.

Give reasons why Jesus was rejected at Nazareth.

- Jesus claimed to be the messiah, fulfilling Isaiah's prophecy.
- He did not perform the miracles he had performed in Capernaum.
- He told his listeners that their forefathers had killed God's prophets, which annoyed them.
- He compared them unfavourably with the Gentiles.
- He challenged them and their unbelief.
- They knew he was from a humble family and a carpenter's son.

Jesus heals in Capernaum (Luke 4: 31 – 44)

a) Jesus heals a man with an evil spirit (Luke 4: 31 – 37)

- Jesus went to Capernaum, in Galilee, and on the Sabbath he taught the people with authority.
- In the synagogue there was a man who was possessed by an unclean spirit.
- The man cried out in a loud voice identifying Jesus as the "Holy one of God".
- Jesus rebuked him and commanded the evil spirit to leave the man.
- The demon threw the man down and went out of him without hurting him.
- The people were amazed at Jesus' power to command the unclean spirits and they obey.
- The news about Jesus spread into all the places neighbouring Capernaum.

b) Jesus heals Simon's mother-in-law (Luke 4: 38 – 44)

- After Jesus left the synagogue, he went into Simon's house.
- Simon's mother-in-law was suffering from fever and Jesus was asked to heal her.
- Jesus commanded the fever to leave her.
- She was healed immediately, and she rose up and served the visitors.
- On that evening Jesus healed several other people suffering from various diseases and cast out demons from the demon-possessed.
- The people were impressed by Jesus' authority and power and wanted to keep Jesus in their own area.
- However, Jesus told them that he had to proclaim the Good News of the Kingdom of God to other towns too.

What lessons can Christians learn about Jesus' healing in Capernaum?

- Jesus is the Son of God and, therefore, he is the promised Messiah.
- Jesus has power over evil spirits or demons.
- Jesus has power to heal all kinds of sicknesses.

- Jesus came to save human beings from sin, therefore Christians should turn to him for healing.
- Jesus' mission is to liberate people from both physical and spiritual suffering.
- Jesus is merciful and compassionate to those who are suffering.

Ways in which the church continues with the healing ministry of Jesus.
- By praying for the sick for spiritual healing.
- By setting up health facilities for treatment of the sick.
- By advocating for balanced diet.
- By encouraging the use of traditional herbs
- By taking care of the orphans.
- By reconciling the warring communities

Jesus calls the first disciples (Luke 5: 1 – 11)
Describe the call of the first disciples in Luke 5: 1 – 11
- Jesus was standing on the shores of Lake Gennesaret, teaching the people the word of God.
- He saw two boats close to the shore, but the owners had gone to wash their nets.
- Jesus got into one of the boats that belonged to Simon.
- He taught the crowd from the boat.
- When he had finished teaching he asked Simon to cast the net into the deep water for a catch.
- Simon was reluctant to do so for they had worked all night without any catch.
- Simon eventually together with John and James, the sons of Zebedee cast the nets into the sea as commanded by Jesus.
- They caught a very large number of fish that the nets almost broke.
- They called their partners in the other boat to assist them, they filled both boats, which were about to sink.
- Simon Peter fell on his knees before Jesus and urged Jesus to go away from him for he was a sinner.
- Jesus told Simon not to be afraid for from that time on he would be catching people.
- When they came to the shore, they left everything and followed Jesus.

Lessons that Christians learn from the call of the first disciples
- Christians should be ready to serve God, since He still calls people today to serve Him.
- Those called to serve God should humble themselves.
- Christians have to respond to God's call in obedience.
- Christians should acknowledge their sinful state and repent.
- Christians should embrace togetherness in their mission, and work as a team.
- Christians have to renounce their families and occupations in order to serve God.
- Christians should use their talents to serve God.

JESUS FACES OPPOSITION (Luke 5: 12 – 6: 11)

Opposition to the preaching and teaching of Jesus about the Good News came mainly from the Jewish religious leaders e.g. the Pharisees, Scribes and the Sadducees.

a) Pharisees

The word Pharisee means 'separated ones', since this group of people separated themselves from the common people.

They also called themselves the 'righteous' to mean they had a close relationship with God.

The Pharisees had the following characteristics

- Pharisees believed in the Mosaic Law and accepted the first five books of the Bible as God-inspired.
- They observed the law strictly.
- They upheld and observed the oral traditions of the elders.
- They believed in the teachings of the prophets and other writings in the Old Testament.
- They taught the young generations the religious traditions of the Jews, as a way of preserving them.
- They believed in the prophecies of concerning the messiah, and waited for their fulfilment.
- They believed in the resurrection of the dead.
- They believed in the judgement of God.

b) Scribes

- The word scribe means 'a writer'. Their work was to re-write copies of the hand-written manuscripts of the Jewish scriptures.
- Scribes either belonged to the Pharisees or to the Sadducees. However, most scribes at the time of Jesus were Pharisees.
- Some scribes ran rabbinical schools where Jewish male youth went to learn the Mosaic Law from the age of 13.
- They were represented in the Jewish Religious Council called the Sanhedrin which was the Jewish Court of Justice that tried those who committed religious sins.

c) Sadducees

Sadducees were very influential and wealthy. They performed priestly duties like maintenance of the temple in Jerusalem and offering sacrifices. Chief Priests were chosen from this group.

The characteristics of the Sadducees include:

- They only believed in the Mosaic Law or the Pentateuch and rejected all other books of the Old Testament as not being inspired.
- They did not believe in the resurrection of the dead.
- They did not believe in the coming of the Messiah.
- They rejected the idea of judgement.

- They rejected the oral traditions of the Pharisees.
- They were enemies with the Pharisees particularly on religious matters, however, they united together to oppose Jesus.

Why did the Pharisees, Scribes and Sadducees oppose Jesus?

- Jesus healed on the Sabbath saying that he is the Lord of the Sabbath yet the Mosaic Law stated that no work should be done on the Sabbath day.
- Jesus claimed to have power to forgive sins during the cure of the paralytic, which the religious leaders viewed as blasphemy because only God has power to forgive sins.
- Jesus associated with outcasts e.g. poor and sinners yet the Pharisees reasoned that a holy person cannot associate with the outcasts.
- In his teachings, Jesus attacked the hypocrisy of the religious leaders calling them blind leaders, which made them hate him.
- Jesus claimed to be the Messiah yet they were expecting a political and conquering messiah. Jesus was a spiritual messiah, and so they failed to believe Jesus to be the messiah.
- The growing popularity of Jesus brought him into conflict with the religious leaders who did not want to lose their own authority.
- Jesus did not observe the law on fasting.

Ways Christians can use to solve conflict in the society.

- Through prayers to bring about proper understanding.
- Guiding and counselling those involved.
- Holding seminars to listen to the views of each side.
- Using Biblical teachings to correct the misunderstanding.
- By setting good examples or being role models to those affected.
- Preaching about peace and reconciliation to the affected parties.
- Advocating for joint activities between the reconciled parties.
- Writing literature materials on conflict management.
- By use of the mass media e.g. TV Video/Radio programmes on conflict/misunderstanding management.

THE CHOOSING OF THE TWELVE DISCIPLES AND JESUS' TEACHING ON TRUE DISCIPLESHIP (Luke 6: 12 – 16, 27 – 49)

- Jesus, having gotten into conflict with the Jewish religious leaders, knew he would not be able to complete his mission since the Pharisees and scribes were plotting to kill him.
- He therefore, decided to choose a special group of disciples who would learn from him and continue with his mission.
- After the night in prayer, he called his disciples and chose 12 upon whom he conferred his authority.
- The 12 were to accompany him, teach his word and be witnesses to the Good News.

The twelve were:

Simon Peter	Bartholomew	James, son of Alphaeus
Matthew	Thomas	Simon the Zealot

Andrew	James	Judas, son of James
John	Philip	Judas Iscariot

- Jesus called the 12 disciples the name 'apostles' meaning he had anointed them for a special mission.

Jesus chose the 12 disciples for the following reasons:
- They were to give him company during his public ministry.
- He wanted reveal to them the nature of his messiahship, which was misunderstood by the people.
- So that they can be witness to others after his departure through spreading the Good News.
- The disciples came from different backgrounds which symbolized that Jesus' ministry was universal.
- To assist him in the day-to-day activities during his ministry.
- For them to be role models around whom the Kingdom of God would be built.
- He wanted to train them to carry on his mission after his death.

Jesus teaching on the qualities of true discipleship (Luke 6: 20 – 49)
- In the Sermon on the Plain, Jesus taught the 12 apostles the qualities of true discipleship.
- In the sermon, he first addressed the 12 disciples in the presence of all the people who included the apostles, disciples and other people who had come from different parts e.g. Judea, Jerusalem, Tyre and Sidon.
- Jesus told the disciples what he expected of them in the new community and assured them that despite the problems they were going to encounter, they would be rewarded.

True disciples according to Jesus, should have the following qualities:
- They should persevere in the face persecution for the sake of the Good News.
- They should have unwavering faith in Jesus.
- True disciples have love for their enemies.
- They must obey and implement the teachings of Jesus.
- They were to be generous to all, and share with the needy.
- They were to exercise self-criticism or self-examination before judging others.
- The disciples should show compassion to others, that is, they should to be merciful like God.

Outline the qualities which true Christians should possess.
- They should persevere in the face of persecution.
- They should have strong and unwavering faith in God.
- They must love their enemies.
- They should obey the teachings of Jesus.
- They should put into practice or implement the teachings of Jesus.
- They should be generous and share with the needy.
- They should exercise self-criticism and not to judge others.

- They must show compassion to others.
- They should confess their faith.

List ways in which the church prepares people to serve God today.
- Preparing new converts for baptism.
- Baptizing the new converts.
- Teaching them new Christian doctrines.
- Encouraging them to read the bible.
- Organizing seminars for specific groups of people.
- Sending those willing to training institutions e.g. Theological colleges, seminaries e.t.c
- Continuous religious training in spiritual and social matters.
- Being role models for converts.
- Guiding and counselling them when they are faced with challenges.

THE SERMON ON THE PLAIN (Luke 6: 17 – 49)

After Jesus chose his apostles, he came down the hill and stood on a level place from where he taught the people. This teaching is referred to as the Sermon on the Plain.

The sermon on the plain consisted of five major themes:

i. **Blessings and woes (Luke 6: 20 - 26):** these are referred to as beatitudes. The poor, hungry and those who are weeping refer to those who cannot afford their basic needs. Jesus gives them hope by assuring them that they will get blessings and peace.
Jesus warns rich and those who have already received their fill. He warns them of the dangers associated with wealth, for it can distract them from serving God.

ii. **Love for enemies (Luke 6: 27 – 37):** Jesus taught the qualities of a true disciple, that is, true disciples should be kind, generous, forgiving and should avoid revenge.

iii. **Judging others (Luke 6: 37 – 43):** disciples are expected to exercise self-criticism and appreciate their own weakness before they can condemn faults in others, in order to avoid hypocrisy.

iv. **Evidence of good discipleship (Luke 6: 44 – 46):** He says that the actions of a person will reveal whether he or she is a true disciple. a true disciple should therefore live an exemplary or morally upright life.

v. **Hearing and doing (Luke 6: 47 – 49):** Jesus expects obedience to his teachings. He also teaches true disciples should have unwavering faith.

Relevance of the Sermon on the Plain to Christians today
- Christians are taught to love their enemies just like God loves them unconditionally.
- Christians should examine their shortcomings before passing judging others.
- Christians should practice what they preach and live exemplary for others to emulate.
- Christians should be generous and share with their possessions needy.
- Christians should be firm in their faith and never give in to temptations.
- A Christian should be willing to hear God's word and proclaim it.
- A Christian should promote peace, and should not seek revenge.
- Christians should aim at inheriting the kingdom of God.

Why do Christians find it difficult to apply the teachings of the Sermon on the Plain in their lives?

- Lack of faith to obey Jesus teachings.
- Desire to revenge against their enemies.
- They do not devote time to pray so as to be empowered by the Holy Spirit.
- Lack of love for others hence they cannot forgive.
- Hypocrisy as many Christians are persecuted for their own wrongs.
- Lack of endurance or perseverance.
- They fear to face persecutions or they lack of courage.
- There is greed/selfishness among some church members.
- Poor role models on the part of church leaders.

JESUS' WORKS OF COMPASSION

- Works of compassion refer to the works of mercy that Jesus carried so as to take away suffering from people e.g. healing those who were seek, raising the dead e.t.c.

a) The healing of the Centurion's servant (Luke 7: 1 – 10)

- After the Sermon on the Plain Jesus went back to Capernaum, a city in Galilee.
- In the town, there was a centurion, whose servant that he really loved, was sick. (A Centurion is an officer in the Roman army, in charge of one hundred soldiers).
- The Centurion sent Jewish elders to request Jesus to go and heal his slave who was sick.
- The elders pleaded with Jesus to heal the slave since the centurion had built a synagogue for them.
- When Jesus was about to get to the Centurion's house, he sent his friends to tell Jesus not to trouble himself going to his house.
- The centurion believed that just a word from Jesus would heal his slave.
- The centurion said that he was not worthy to have Jesus in his house.
- Jesus marvelled at the centurion's faith.
- Jesus told the crowd that he had not found such faith in Israel.
- When those who were sent returned to the house, they found the slave already healed.

From this incident, the centurion portrayed the following qualities:

- The Centurion had great faith in God that he believed just a word from Jesus would heal his slave.
- He showed humility by accepting that he was not worthy to host Jesus.
- He had great love for his slave.
- He was generous and had built a synagogue for the Jews.
- He had great value for human life hence he did not want his slave to die.
- He recognized the Lordship of Jesus.
- He was persistent, having sent two different groups to Jesus to ask for the healing of his slave.

The main teachings of the healing of the centurion's servant are:

- A Christian must have faith in Jesus like the centurion believed Jesus' word could heal.

- Christians should know that Jesus has power to heal all forms of illnesses.
- Christian employers should treat their workers well like the centurion who loved his slave.
- Christians should avoid discriminating against others on the basis of race, gender, tribe and religion like Jesus accepted the Centurion's request yet he was a Gentile and not a Jew.
- Christian leaders should humble themselves and seek help from God when they are in need like the centurion did.
- Christians should show compassion to the needy.

b) The raising of the son of the widow of Nain (Luke 7: 11 – 17)

- Jesus went to the city of Nain with his disciples and a large crowd.
- At the gate of the city he met people carrying a dead man.
- He saw a widow weeping since the dead man was her only son.
- Jesus felt pity for the widow and told her not to weep.
- Jesus moved forward and touched the coffin in which the body lay.
- He told the dead man to get up.
- The dead man sat up and began to speak.
- Jesus gave the man to his mother.
- All the people who were around were filled with fear.
- The people glorified the Lord, saying a great prophet had come.
- Jesus' fame spread in Judea and the surrounding region.

Lessons that Christians learn about Jesus from the raising of the widow's son in Nain

- Jesus has power over death.
- Jesus is a great prophet.
- Jesus is a fulfilment of the Old Testament prophecies for he works miracles.
- Jesus has empathy/pity for those who are suffering.
- Jesus is above ritual uncleanliness.
- Jesus is the Son of God and therefore the Messiah.

c) Assurance to John the Baptist (Luke 7: 18 – 35)

John the Baptist condemned King Herod for marrying his brother's wife, Herodias. For this reasons, Herod had John the Baptist put to prison. This incident took place while John was in prison.

- The disciples of John the Baptist went and reported to him about the miracles of Jesus.
- John sent two of his disciples to go and ask Jesus if he was the messiah who he had been foretold. He wanted to reassure his disciples that Jesus was the expected messiah.
- In response to John's question, Jesus performed miracles e.g. healed the sick, cast out evil spirits and restored sight to the blind.
- Jesus told them to inform John what they had seen and heard.
- After the disciples of John had left, Jesus paid tribute to John, acknowledging that John was the greatest of all the prophets.
- Jesus went on to portray John as his forerunner.

- He described John as a man of strong character who could not be swayed like a person who lived in luxury like a prince in a palace.

d) Forgiveness of the sinful woman (Luke 7: 36 – 50)
- One of the Pharisees invited Jesus for dinner to his house so Jesus went and sat at the table.
- A sinful woman came to Jesus weeping on his feet and wiping him with her hair.
- She kissed his feet and anointed him with perfumed oil.
- The Pharisee wondered why Jesus could allow a sinner to touch him.
- Jesus knew what he was thinking and he told him a parable of the debtors.
- In the parable, one debtor owed five hundred silver coins and the other fifty. When they could not pay, he forgave them.
- Jesus used this parable to teach that the debtor who was forgiven more loved more.
- Jesus told the Pharisee that the woman loved more by her actions which he had not done e.g. she wet Jesus' feet with tears and wiped them with her hair.
- He forgave her sins which were many since she loved Jesus more.
- Those who were present wondered who Jesus was that he even forgave sin, which only God could.
- Jesus told the woman to go in peace for her faith had saved her.

Lessons that Christians learn from the forgiveness of the sinful woman
- Christians should seek Jesus for forgiveness.
- Christians should not discriminate against others on any basis like race, tribe, gender e.t.c.
- They should avoid condemning those working for God like the Pharisees did.
- Christians should be tolerant of sinners and encourage them to repent.
- Christians should recognize their own sinfulness and repent.
- Christians should avoid self-righteous which leads to hypocrisy.
- Christians should humble themselves before God when seeking for forgiveness.

JESUS TEACHES IN PARABLES (LUKE 8: 4 – 21)
A parable is a short simple story which intends to illustrate a religious or spiritual lesson.
Jesus used many parables in his teachings to try and give moral lessons and explain unfamiliar concepts, such as, the nature and growth of Kingdom of God, which is unseen.

Reasons why Jesus used parables
- He wanted to distinguish serious listeners from the casual onlookers.
- He wanted to attract listeners since his stories were enjoyable.
- It was a common method of teaching at the time.
- He wanted to make his listeners think for themselves and make moral judgements by themselves.
- He used them because he was a gifted teacher.
- He wanted to make it easy for his listeners to understand about the kingdom of God, which was unseen.
- He wanted to keep his identity a secret till he completes his mission.

- He used them to avoid direct confrontation with the Pharisees.
- It was a fulfilment of the Old Testament prophecies.

a) The Parable of the Sower (Luke 8: 4 – 15)

- A great crowd came together with the people from different towns and Jesus told them the parable of the sower.
- A sower went out to sow his seeds.
- As he sowed, some seeds fell along the path were stepped on and the birds ate them.
- Some seeds fell on rocky ground, sprouted but dried soon due to lack of adequate moisture.
- The seeds that fell among the thorns grew but were chocked.
- Then some seeds fell on good soil, grew and yielded plenty harvest.
- The disciples of Jesus asked him what the parable meant since they failed to understand its meaning.
- Jesus explained that the seeds that fell along the path are people who hear the word of God, but the devil comes and takes away the word from their hearts.
- The seeds that fell on rocky ground are Christians who receive the word with joy but lose it when temptations come since their faith is shallow.
- The seeds that fell among thorns represent the people who hear the word of God and become believers for some time but are choked by the cares and pleasures of the world.
- The seeds that fell on good soil are people who hear God's word, believe in it with an honest and good heart, and bear fruit with steadfast endurance.

b) The parable of a Lamp under a Bowl (Luke 8: 16 – 18)

- Jesus said that no one lights a lamp and cover it with a bowl or hide it under the bed.
- Instead, they put the lamp on a stand so that it can illuminate the room.
- For nothing is hidden that will not be revealed and nothing concealed that will not be made known and brought to light.
- So listen carefully, for whoever has will be given more.
- Whoever does not have, even the little he thinks he has will be taken from him.

Lessons learnt from the parable

- Christians should to listen to the word of God.
- They should preach to others the word of God and bear fruit.
- Christians should be faithful in order to be blessed.

c) Jesus' True Family (Luke 8: 19 – 21)

- Jesus' mother and brothers came to see him.
- They could not get near him because of the huge crowd.
- Jesus was told that his mother and brothers were standing out, wanting to see him.
- Jesus said that his mother and brothers are those who hear the word of God and do it.

From Jesus' response, he meant that:

- His family includes all people and not only blood relatives.

- His family comprises those who hear and implement his teachings.
- His family is spiritual and not earthly.
- Following Jesus means forsaking all earthly attachments.
- Christians are a family whose home is in the kingdom of God.

THE MIGHTY WORKS OF JESUS (Luke 8: 22 – 56)
- The mighty works of Jesus are called miracles. A miracle is an extraordinary event or action, which appears to be contrary to the laws of nature.
- The mighty works of Jesus reveal his person and his mission.

Types of Jesus' miracles
i. Nature miracles e.g. the calming of the storm (Luke 8: 22 – 25)
ii. Raising the dead e.g. raising Jairus' daughter (Luke 8: 46 – 56)
iii. Healing miracles e.g. healing of the centurion's servant (Luke 7: 1 – 10), the cure of the paralytic (Luke 5: 17 – 41)
iv. Exorcism/casting out of evil spirits e.g. the cure of the Gerasene Demoniac (Luke 8: 26 – 39)

a. The Calming of the Storm (Luke 8: 22 – 25)
- Jesus was crossing the Lake of Galilee with his disciples in a boat.
- Jesus was asleep as they sailed.
- There occurred a violent windstorm and the boat started filling up with water.
- The disciples were afraid that they would drown.
- They woke Jesus and asked him to save them before their boat capsized.
- Jesus woke up and rebuked the winds and the waves.
- He challenged them on their faith.
- The disciples were amazed by Jesus' power to command the storm and it obeys.

Lessons learnt from the calming of the storm
- Jesus has power over nature.
- Jesus came to destroy the evil forces that are against human beings.
- The word of God is powerful.
- Jesus demands faith from those who follow him.
- Jesus is the messiah who was to perform miracles.
- Christians should rebuke the evil forces in the name of Jesus.
- Christians should depend on Jesus to help them overcome temptations.
- Christians should not to give up their faith in the face of persecution.
- Christians should have complete faith in Jesus.

b. The Healing of the Gerasene Demoniac (Luke 8: 26 – 39)
- At the shores of Lake Gerasa, Jesus was met by a man possessed by demons.
- For a long time the man wore no clothes and had been living in the graveyard.
- The man fell at Jesus' feet begging Jesus not to torment him.
- He recognized Jesus as the Son of the Most High God.

- The demons in the man requested Jesus not to destroy them but allow them get into the pigs that were nearby.
- Jesus allowed the demons to enter the pigs, which drowned in the lake.
- The herdsmen reported the incident in the town.
- The people came out to see what had happened and they found the man seated at Jesus' feet, well-dressed and in sound mind.
- They went and testified what they had seen.
- Then all the people of the surrounding country of the Gerasenes asked Jesus to leave the area since they were afraid of further losses.
- The man requested to follow Jesus but was told to go and testify to others what God had done for him.

Lessons learnt about Jesus from the miracle
- Jesus is the son of God, and therefore, he is the Messiah.
- Jesus faced opposition in his mission.
- Jesus has power over Satan.
- Jesus came to destroy the kingdom of Satan in the world and establish God's Kingdom.
- Jesus is also concerned with the psychological welfare of human beings.
- Jesus came to liberate those living in captivity.

Christians learn the following from the miracle
- Christians should rebuke Satan using the name of Jesus.
- Christians should pray to be liberated from the bondage of Satan.
- They should value human life because it is superior to that of other creatures.
- Like Jesus commanded the man who was cured of the evil spirits, Christian should to declare the wonderful deeds of God.
- Christians should support the work of spread the gospel, and avoid being an impediment.

c. The Raising of Jairus' Daughter (Luke 8: 40 – 56)
- After healing the Gerasene Demoniac, Jesus returned to Galilee.
- Jairus, an official at the local synagogue asked Jesus to heal his twelve year-old daughter who was very sick.
- On the way Jesus delayed and reports reached Jairus that his daughter had already died.
- Jesus overheard this and told Jairus have faith and the daughter would be healed.
- On arrival at Jairus' house, Jesus assured the people that the girl was only sleeping and not dead as they thought.
- He went into the house with Peter, James and John together with the girl's parents.
- Jesus took the girl by hand and told her to get up.
- Her spirit was restored and she was given food to eat.
- The girl's parents were amazed but Jesus instructed them not to reveal what had happened.

Lessons learnt about Jesus from the miracle
- Jesus is the son of God, and therefore, he is the messiah.

- Jesus came to uplift the lowly, for example, women.
- Jesus has power over death and is the Lord of resurrection.
- Jesus empathises with those who are suffering.
- Jesus is a universal saviour, who heals both Jews and non-Jews, and people of all walks of life.

Christians learn the following from the miracle
- Christians should show compassion and assist the needy and those undergoing suffering.
- Christians should believe in Jesus, who is the son of God.
- Christians should have hope for eternal life through Jesus Christ.
- Christians should depend on God in times of trouble, and approach Him through prayer.
- Christians should be humble for them to witness the power of God in their lives.

d. The Healing of the Woman with the Flow of Blood (Luke 8: 43 – 48)
- On the way to Jairus' house, a large crowd followed Jesus and pressed against him.
- In the crowd was a woman who had suffered from haemorrhage for twelve years without cure.
- She believed that by touching the cloak of Jesus she would be healed.
- Moved by her faith, the woman touched the edge of Jesus' cloak.
- She got cured immediately.
- Jesus demanded to know who had touched him, for he had felt some power leave him.
- The crowd could not tell who touched him since many people pressed against him.
- The woman came to Jesus trembling and fell before Jesus.
- She explained why she had touched Jesus before the people.
- Jesus told her to go in peace for her faith had made her well.

From the miracles of Jesus, outline the qualities of Jesus / what lessons do Christians learn about Jesus from his miracles?
- Jesus has compassion for those who are suffering.
- Jesus is the Lord of life since he brings back to life those who have died.
- Jesus is the Son of God and therefore he is the promised messiah.
- Jesus came to save the world from sin.
- Jesus is a universal saviour since he healed both Jews and Gentiles, men, women, children and adults.
- Through Jesus' miracles, God's love for human beings is manifested.
- Miracles are an important part of the ministry of Jesus and they supplement his teachings.
- Jesus is concerned about the total well-being of human beings apart from just spiritual aspects.

JESUS AND THE TWELVE DISCIPLES
a) The commissioning of the twelve disciples (Luke 9: 1 – 9)
- Before Jesus ended his ministry in Galilee, he called the 12 disciples and sent the on mission to do the following:
i. To preach the gospel of the Kingdom of God.

ii.   To heal the sick

iii.   To cast out demons.

iv.   To cure diseases.

v.   To give hope to the hopeless.

-    In their mission, the disciples were to depend on God to take care of them. Jesus therefore gave them the following instructions:

i.   Not to carry anything for the journey, that is, no bag, no money, no staff, no bread e.t.c.

ii.   To stay in the homes where they were welcomed until when they depart from the area.

iii.   To shake dust off their feet, where they were not received.

iv.   To eat and drink anything that they were given.

Lessons that Christians learn from the commissioning of the twelve
-    Church leaders should visit Christians in their homes and encourage them.
-    Christians should welcome church leaders in their homes.
-    Christians should care for the sick e.g. by visiting, paying medical bills for them e.t.c.
-    Christians should be ready to undergo persecution and opposition as they spread the gospel.
-    Christians should take care of church leaders by providing their upkeep.
-    Christians should continue with the mission of Jesus by preaching the gospel.

Give the reasons why Christians find it difficult to spread the word of God
-    There is a lot of permissiveness in the society.
-    The environment is hostile.
-    Leadership wrangles in the church.
-    Lack of funds to purchase necessary equipment.
-    Corruptions/greed for material wealth.
-    Christians face opposition/threats from other faiths.
-    Lack of knowledge/skills.
-    Technological advancements.
-    Lack of co-operation.

b) Jesus feeds the 5000 (Luke 9: 10 – 17)
Narrate the feeding of the five thousand as recorded in Luke 9: 10 – 17
-    After the return of the 12 disciples from their mission, Jesus took them Bethsaida to rest.
-    A crowd followed them keen to listen to Jesus.
-    Jesus turned and preached to them about the kingdom of God and healed the sick.
-    At the end of the day, the disciples were worried about what the people would eat.
-    They asked Jesus to release the people to go look for food.
-    Jesus told the disciples to give the people what to eat.

- They answered Jesus that they only had five loaves and two fish which could not feed the people who were about five thousand.
- Jesus asked the disciples to make the people sit down in groups.
- He took the five loaves and two fish, looked up in heaven and thanked God.
- He then broke the bread and asked his disciples to share it out.
- All the people ate and were satisfied.
- The disciples collected up what was left and the filled twelve baskets of broken pieces.

Lessons that Christians learn about Jesus from the feeding of the 5000
- Jesus is the messiah, the Son of God.
- Jesus is the bread of life.
- Jesus has divine power, which is seen in his ability to multiply bread and fish.
- Jesus fills cares not only for the spiritual needs, but also the physical needs of people.
- Jesus has trust in God, which is portrayed by him looking up in heaven and praying.
- Jesus had compassion for the needy, he could not allow the people to go hungry.

Lessons that Christians learn from the Feeding of the 5000
- Christians should trust in God's providence, and pray before their undertakings.
- Christians should be generous, and share what they have with others.
- Christians should preach about the kingdom of God to others.
- Christians should show compassion to those who are undergoing suffering.
- Christians should be courageous, to face challenges in life.
- Christians should assist church leaders in their work, like the disciples assisted in distribution of food.
- Christian should take good care of resources and avoid wastage.

c) The person of Jesus and His destiny (Luke 9: 18 – 27)
- Jesus asked his disciples who the people said he was.
- The disciples answered saying, John the Baptist, others say Elijah, while others say that one of the prophets of old.
- But then Jesus asked them, who they say he was.
- Peter answered that, he is the Christ of God, which means that, Jesus is the son of God, the Messiah. Jesus told his disciples not to mention it in public.
- Jesus explained the nature of his messiahship, that he would suffer, be rejected, killed and on the third day he would be raised.
- Jesus then told his disciples, that anyone who wanted to be his follower must deny himself, and take his cross and follow.

This was the first time that Jesus talked of his passion, death and resurrection.

Jesus was talking about God's plan of salvation, which would be effected through his suffering and death.

d) The transfiguration (Luke 9: 28 – 36)

The term transfiguration refers to change or transformation in one's appearance. The transfiguration of Jesus took place during the last days of his public ministry.

He knew that he was going to be arrested and crucified according to God's plan.

Account for the events that took place during the transfiguration in Luke 9: 28 – 36.

- Jesus went with his disciples Peter, John and James, to pray up the mountain.
- As he was praying, his face transformed, and shone like the sun and his clothes became very bright, dazzling white.
- The disciples were asleep and when they woke up, they saw Jesus' body transformed.
- Moses and Elijah appeared with Jesus talking about his passion and death.
- When Peter saw Jesus, Moses and Elijah talking, he suggested that the disciples make three tents, one for Jesus, one for Moses and one for Elijah.
- While he was still speaking, a cloud came and covered them.
- From the cloud came a voice that said "this is my chosen son, listen to him".
- After the voice had spoken, Jesus was found alone.
- The disciples kept silent and told no one what they had witnessed.

Explain the ways in which the transfiguration of Jesus was important.

- Moses and Elijah appeared to Jesus to confirm his coming suffering and death.
- Elijah's presence symbolizes the Old Testament prophecies which are fulfilled in Jesus.
- The appearance of Moses shows that Jesus came to fulfil the Law.
- The voice from heaven confirmed Jesus as the Son of God, doing His will.
- The transfiguration strengthened the faith of Jesus' disciples, who were to continue with his mission, after his death and resurrection.
- The cloud symbolized God's presence, and signified that Jesus' mission was no longer a secret.
- The transfiguration marked the beginning of his suffering which would lead to his death.

e) Jesus teaching on faith and humility (Luke 9: 37 – 50)

- Jesus came down from the mountain and was met by a huge crowd.
- A certain man from the crowd asked Jesus to heal his son who had been possessed by an evil spirit which threw him into convulsions.
- The man reported that the disciples had been unable to cast out the evil spirit.
- Jesus was disappointed at the disciples' lack of faith.
- Healed the boy of the evil spirit and gave him to his father.

- He told them that He would be betrayed into the hands of men, but the disciples did not understand His words.
- They started arguing and competing among themselves each wanting to be the greatest.
- Jesus taught them that greatness was the ability to welcome the lowliest in the society because it was like receiving a small child.
- One of the disciples said that they had stopped a man from casting out demons in Jesus' name since he was not a disciple.
- Jesus told them to accept the man's work because the man was not against them.

Topic 16: THE JOURNEY TO JERUSALEM

- Jesus was aware that He would be arrested and killed in Jerusalem, but his did not stop him from going there. This was part of His ministry, and according to the will of God, and so He was determined to fulfil it.
- He went through towns and villages on his way to Jerusalem, performing miracles and teaching on various themes such as discipleship, the Kingdom of God, wealth, poverty e.t.c.
- His teachings encouraged his disciples to grow in faith.

a) Duties and privileges of discipleship (Luke 9: 51 – 62).
- Jesus taught those who followed him on his way to Jerusalem about the duties and privileges of discipleship.

Outline Jesus' teaching on the duties and privileges of discipleship in Luke 9: 51 – 62
- Discipleship requires total commitment and dedication to Jesus.
- A disciple has to sacrifice family commitments for the sake of Christ.
- A disciple should be ready to deny himself/herself and accept suffering.
- A disciple has a duty to be loyal to Jesus without giving excuses or turning back from his/her faith.
- A disciple has to put all his/her intellectual resources to building the church.
- A disciple has a duty to spread the Good News.
- A disciple has the priviledge of attaining eternal life.
- Disciples have the priviledge of becoming members of the kingdom of God.
- Disciples have the joy of winning others to the kingdom of God.

Relevance of Jesus' teachings on the cost of discipleship today
- Christians are motivated to sacrifice comfort in order to serve God.
- Christians are reminded to have strong faith.
- Christians are discouraged from desiring any aspect of their past sinful lives.
- The teachings guide Christians to forsake anything that is an obstacle to salvation.
- It teaches Christians to give Jesus priority over everything else.
- It encourages Christians to accept suffering and rejection for the sake of Jesus.

b) The mission of the seventy two (Luke 10: 1 – 24).
- On his way to Jerusalem, Jesus chose 72 disciples and sent them in pairs ahead of him to preach the Kingdom of God and heal in every town and place where he was about to go.
- In his instructions, Jesus informed the 72 that the harvest is plenty, but the workers are few. This meant that there were many people waiting to hear the Good News, but the disciples were few.
- He told them to expect opposition and persecution, and gave them instructions not to carry provisions for the mission.

Jesus gave the 72 the following instructions

i. They were to preach peace in the houses they entered.
ii. They were to shake dust off their feet where they were rejected.
iii. They were not to carry money, food or clothing, but were to depend totally on the hospitality of the people.
iv. They were not to waste time on long and unnecessary salutations on the way, accepting many invitations and moving from one house to another.
v. They were to heal the sick.
vi. They were to preach the kingdom of God.

- The success of the 72 disciples' mission made Jesus happy; he described it as a complete destruction of Satan's kingdom.
- Jesus told the 72 to rejoice that their names were written in heaven. This is an assurance of eternal life to the disciples.
- Jesus rejoiced in the power of the Holy Spirit and praised God for the divine revelation, which He had made to those who are humble.

Relevance of Jesus' teaching on discipleship to Christians

- Christians have a task to spread the word of Go to all nations.
- Christians should persevere in as they face of opposition in their mission.
- Christians should be hospitable to church leaders.
- Christians should heal the sick in the name of Jesus.
- Christians should humble themselves in order to receive God's grace and witness the power of God in their lives.

What should a Christian do when offered a responsibility?

- A Christian should accept it and not to turn down the offers.
- They should pray for God's guidance as they undertake their responsibility.
- One should show total commitment to it.
- One should seek advice from others.
- One should observe the ethics surrounding the responsibility.
- A Christian should thank God for it.

c) A committed follower of Jesus (Luke 10: 25 – 11: 1 – 13).

Commitment refers to the responsibility, devotion or dedication that one has in carrying out a certain task.

The parable of the Good Samaritan, the story of Martha and Mary and Jesus' teaching on prayer bring out the qualities of a committed follower of Jesus.

i. **The parable of the Good Samaritan (Luke 10: 25 – 37)**
- A teacher of Law came to test Jesus and asked Him what he should to receive eternal life.
- Jesus told him to love God and his neighbour.

- He wondered who a neighbour was.
- Jesus told the story of a man who was travelling from Jerusalem to Jericho.
- He fell among robbers who attacked him, beat him up and left him half dead.
- By chance, a priest was passing by, and when he saw the man, he passed on the other side.
- A Levite also found him and he too, passed on the other side.
- A Samaritan came across the injured man, he felt compassion for the wounded man.
- He dressed his wounds, set him on a donkey and took him to an inn.
- The Samaritan paid for the expenses and left him in the care of the inn-keeper.
- Jesus asked the teacher of Law who among the three was a good neighbour.
- The teacher of law said it was the Samaritan who was a good neighbour.
- Jesus told him to behave like the Good Samaritan and help those in need.

From the parable of the Good Samaritan, who is a committed follower?
- A committed follower is a person who understands and obeys the law.
- A committed follower uses his resources to help those in need.
- He/she understands a neighbour as anyone who is in need of help, regardless of their social status.
- A committed follower if one who has compassion for those who are suffering.
- One who is does not discriminate against others on the basis of race, religion, status or gender.
- A committed follower should be ready to assist those in need of help.

State the factors which hinder Christians from practicing Jesus' command to love one's neighbour.
- Inadequate resources.
- Inaccessibility of the needy.
- Language barrier.
- Adverse environmental conditions.
- Cultural beliefs and traditions.
- Insecurity.
- Lack of technical know-how/knowledge.

ii.   Jesus and Martha (Luke 10: 38 – 42)
- On his way to Jerusalem, Jesus visited Martha and Mary who were sisters.
- Martha went to prepare a meal for the visitors.
- Mary on the other hand sat at Jesus' feet listening to his teachings.
- Martha complained to Jesus that Mary had left her to do all the work.
- Jesus told Martha not to be worried and troubled about many things.
- He told her that Mary had chosen the right thing, and it will not be taken away from her.

Jesus in this incident is encouraging Martha to strive to listen to the word of God, than be distracted by the things of the world which shall be taken away from her.

From this incident, a committed follower is one who:

- Listens to the word of God.
- Does not allow the cares of the world to distract him/her from serving God.
- Calls other people to the Kingdom of God and avoids leading others away from it.
- Welcomes the servants of God to their homes.

iii. Jesus' teaching on prayer (Luke 11: 1 – 13)

Prayer is a way of talking to and with God.

Reasons why people pray

1. To honour God.
2. To request for favours.
3. To thank God
4. To confess sins and seek forgiveness.
5. To seek God's protection.
6. To intercede or pray for others.

- Jesus often retreated to a quiet place, like on a mountain, to pray.
- One day after Jesus had stopped praying, one of his disciples asked him to teach them how to pray, the way John taught his disciples.
- Jesus taught them the prayer, which is referred to as the Lord's Prayer.

The Lord's Prayer has six petitions:

a. God is addressed as "Father"
b. Honouring God's Holy Name – Hallowed be thy name.
c. Declaring the kingdom of God – Thy kingdom come.
d. Asking God to provide for our daily needs – Give us each day our daily bread.
e. Asking God for forgiveness of sins as we forgive others – Forgive us our sins as we forgive everyone who is indebted to us.
f. Pleading with God not to bring temptations – and lead us not into temptations.

From the parable of the friend at midnight, Jesus teaches about persistence in prayer. He emphasizes that prayer should be said at all times without ceasing for God will grant your request.

From the Lord's Prayer and the parable of the friend at midnight, a committed follower of Christ should:

- Acknowledge God as father.
- Honour God's name.
- Declare the kingdom of God.
- Ask God for daily needs.
- Seek forgiveness of sins.
- Request protection from temptation.
- Seek deliverance from evils.
- Pray persistently.

- Have faith that God answers prayers.
- Forgive others who sin against us.

Why do some Christians find it difficult to pray?
- Dwindling faith in God.
- Laziness.
- Frustration at family or personal level.
- Sin in their lives.
- Loss of hope due to unanswered prayers.
- They are short of knowledge of the scripture.
- Shyness.
- Trusting wealth and education instead of God.
- Poor training from early life.

USE OF GOD'S POWER TO OVERCOME EVIL (Luke 11: 14 – 36)
a. Jesus and Beelzebul (Luke 11: 14 - 23)
- Jesus cast out a demon that had made a man dumb.
- When the demon came out, the man began to talk.
- The people were amazed.
- However, some doubted and accused Jesus of using the power of Beelzebul, the chief of demons to cast out demons.
- The people asked Jesus to perform a miracle to prove that he was using God's power to drive out demons.
- Jesus refused to perform miracles and asked his accusers to use common sense.
- He argued that Satan cannot fight against himself and therefore their accusation was false.

b. The Return of the Unclean Spirit (Luke 11: 24 – 28)
- Jesus explained that when an evil spirit is cast out, it travels across the country looking for a resting place.
- If it fails to find someone to possess, it returns to the person from whom it came.
- When it finds the person clean, it goes and brings seven other spirits which are more evil than itself.
- When this happens, the person becomes worse than he/she was before.
- While Jesus taught this, a woman praised Jesus' mother for bringing him to life and nursing him. The woman was commending Jesus for his great power to drive out demons.
- Jesus advised that it was more valuable to hear and obey God's word.

Christians learn that they should not allow Satan to occupy their hearts, instead, they should let God rule their hearts permanently through the Holy Spirit. They should do this by listening and obeying the word of God.

c. The sign of Jonah (Luke 11: 29 – 32)

- Jesus told the crowds that gathered that there generation was wicked, since they were asking for a sign to show that Jesus was the messiah.
- He told them that no miracle would be given to it except the sign of Jonah.
- He added that just as Jonah was a sign to the people of Nineveh, so was the Son of Man was the sign to that generation.
- Jesus warned them of judgement, saying that the Queen of Sheba would condemn them, for she had come from the south to hear the wisdom of Solomon.
- Jesus is greater than Solomon and should be words should be listened to.
- Jonah preached to the people of Nineveh and they and they repented, but now a person greater than Jonah had come.

Jesus challenged the unbelief of the people who were asking for a sign to prove that Jesus is the Son of God. He told them that sign of Jonah, which made the Ninevites to repent was enough even for their generation.

He used the example of the Queen of Sheba who travelled from the South to hear Solomon's wisdom.

Christians should have faith in Jesus, who is greater than both Solomon and Jonah.

d. The Light of the Body (Luke 11: 33 – 36)

- Jesus said that no one lights a lamp and then hides it.
- Instead, it is put on a lamp-stand to provide light for people.
- The eye is like a lamp of the body.
- When one's eyes are okay, the whole body is full of light.
- If the eyes are poor, the whole body will be in darkness.

The word of God is the light. Those who refuse to believe, live in darkness. The word of God is a light to the whole world, so it should be spread to all people.

From the four incidences about Use of God's power to overcome evil, Christians learn that:

- Jesus has power to drive out demons, which comes from God and not from Beelzebul.
- God's power is greater than Satan's power.
- When a demon-possessed person is healed, (s)he should be filled with the Holy Spirit to avoid being re-possessed.
- Christians are called the light of the world as Jesus is, hence they should transmit God's word to everybody with courage.
- Christians are also called to listen and accept God's word so that when the day of judgement comes, they will be saved.

JESUS' TEACHING ON HYPOCRISY, WEALTH AND WATCHFULNESS
a) Fearless Confession without Hypocrisy (Luke 11: 37 – 12: 1 – 12)
Definition of terms

Confession – It refers the act of a person admitting that he/she has done wrong or committed a mistake, and then asking for forgiveness.

Hypocrisy – It means being insincere or pretending to have certain admirable qualities.

Honesty – It refers to the state of being sincere, truthful or morally upright. An honest person is fair and just in character and behaviour. Such a person always tells the truth.

Jesus' teaching on the Hypocrisy of the Pharisees (Luke 11: 37 – 12: 1 – 3)

Jesus was invited to a Pharisee's house to eat with them. He took his place at the table and the Pharisees observed that Jesus ate without washing his hands. Jesus used this incident to teach the disciples on the hypocrisy of the Pharisees.

He attacked their hypocrisy by stating that:
- They neglected the needy and the poor but stress on the external observance of the Law e.g. washing hands.
- They paid tithe, and give offerings but they don't do justice and show love for God.
- They loved being exalted and honoured e.g. by having the best seats in the temple.
- They demanded public recognition e.g. being greeted with honour in market places.
- They overburden the people with too many laws which they don't observe themselves.
- he accused them of killing the prophets of God

Jesus' teachings on Confession (Luke 12: 8 – 12)

Jesus taught his disciples to be fearless in their testimony about God, and in their mission. He stated that:
- They should acknowledge Jesus before other people and Jesus would acknowledge them before God's angels.
- They should be bold and witness to Jesus before all the people and avoid denying Him.
- They should not sin against the Holy Spirit, for such sin is not forgiven.
- They should confess their loyalty to him publicly without fearing the consequences.
- When they are persecuted, they should trust in the Holy Spirit, who will give them what to say.

b) Jesus Teaching on Material Possessions (Luke 12: 13 – 34)
The Parable of the rich fool

Jesus warned his disciples to guard themselves from all types of greed using the parable of the rich fool.
- He said that the land of a certain rich man produced plenty harvest.
- The man wondered what he could do, for his stores were not enough to store the produce.
- He decided to pull down the barns and build bigger ones.
- He then would store all his grain goods in the new barns.
- The man would relax and celebrate for he had plenty of goods stored to last many years.

- Unfortunately, he did not live to enjoy his wealth because that same night God told him that he would give up his life and everything he had kept for himself.

Jesus teaches his disciples not to put their trust in wealth, but to trust in God's providence. The emphasis that Jesus makes is on how his disciples use their wealth. It is not evil to have wealth, but wealth should be used to serve God.

From the Parable of the rich fool, Jesus taught the following about material possessions:

- God gives and takes away life, so disciples should trust and depend on God, and not in material wealth.
- Disciples should trust in God to give them provisions e.g. food, clothing and what to drink.
- They should seek the kingdom of God first, and all other things will be given to them.
- Disciples should seek God's kingdom for them to be rewarded in heaven.
- Disciples should avoid greed for material possessions which are temporary, but seek God.
- Disciples should use their wealth to spread the Good News of the Kingdom of God.

Jesus' Teaching on Watchfulness and Readiness (Luke 12: 35 – 59)

Watchfulness means being alert, and on the lookout. Readiness is the condition of being prepared or willing to do something.

Jesus used various illustrations to show how important it was to be ready and watchful.

i. **Watchful servants (Luke 12: 35 – 40)**

Jesus told His disciples that:

- They should get dressed for service and keep their lamps burning
- They should be like people waiting for their master to come back from the wedding celebration, so that when he knocks, they can open the door for him.
- Blessed are the slaves whom their master will find alert, for he will have them take their place at the table.
- If the owner of the house had known the hour when the thief was coming, he would not have let his house be broken into.
- They must also be ready because the son of Man will come at an hour when they do not expect.

Jesus used the two examples of the servants waiting for their master, and that of the thief, to explain that the Son of Man, that is, Jesus, will come at an unknown hour, so disciples should be ready at all times. This would be on the day of judgement, so disciples should prepare by living exemplary lives.

ii. **The Faithful or unfaithful servants (Luke 12: 41 – 48)**

- Jesus said that blessed is the servant who the master finds at work when the master returns.
- The master will put that servant in charge of all his possessions.

- But if the servant beats the other servants, eats and gets drunk when the master has delayed to return, the master of the servant will return when he/she least expects and punish him severely.

Disciples should therefore be responsible and do what is right so that when the Son of Man comes, He should find them ready and doing what is right.

iii. Jesus, the cause of divisions (Luke 12: 49 – 53)
- Jesus said that His coming brought division.
- He said that there will be five in one household divided, three against two and two against three.
- They will be divided father against son and mother against daughter e.t.c.

Jesus' coming brought division, those who believed him and those who were against him. Disciples should be watchful for the divisions that may arise because of their faith and mission.

iv. Understanding the signs (Luke 12: 54 – 56)
- Jesus said that when one sees clouds rising, they can tell that it will rain.
- And when they see the wind blowing, they know it will be sunny and hot.
- Jesus tells the disciples that in the same way they observe the signs of the weather, they should see and interpret the signs of the Kingdom of God.

v. Making peace (Luke 12: 57 – 59)
- Jesus tells his disciples to judge what is right by themselves.
- He said that before going to court, they should make an effort to solve their dispute with their accusers.
- This is because the judge will have them arrested and they will not be released until they have paid in full.

Christians should therefore repent their sins to God, and be in the right relationship with God before the day of judgement

Relevance of the teachings of Jesus on watchfulness and readiness
- Christians should obey the teachings of Jesus, in order to escape judgement.
- Christians should know that Jesus is the Son of God and saviour of the world.
- They should ready to suffer for their faith in God through Jesus Christ.
- They should make honest confession of sins to be forgiven.
- They should be responsible in their mission and always be ready for the coming of the Lord.
- Christians are the disciples of Jesus, who should continue with His ministry of spreading the Good News.
- Christians should be able to identify the signs of God's presence among them.

THE KINGDOM OF GOD

THE GROWTH OF GOD'S KINGDOM (Luke 13: 1 – 35)
The Kingdom of God is manifested in the teachings and the works of Jesus e.g. the miracles he performed and casting out demons.
Some of the parables that Jesus used in his teachings had illustrations of the characteristics of the kingdom of God e.g.

i. The parable of the mustard seed (Luke 13: 18 - 19)
ii. The parable of the yeast (Luke 13: 20 – 22)
iii. The parable of the sower (Luke 8: 14 – 15)
iv. The parable of the treasure and the pearl

a) A call to Repentance (Luke 13: 1 – 5)
- Some people told Jesus of how Pilate killed some Galileans and mixed their blood with their sacrifice.
- Jesus told those people that, it doesn't mean that those Galileans were worse sinners than all other Galileans.
- He warned them that unless they repent, they will also perish just like the Galileans.
- He also gave the example of the eighteen people who died when the tower of Siloam fell on them.
- Those people were not worse sinners too.
- He insisted that they should repent in order not to perish.

b) The Parable of the Unfruitful Fig tree (Luke 13: 6 - 9)
- A man had a fig tree that planted in his vineyard.
- For three years the fig tree bore no fruits.
- So he told his gardener to cut it down.
- The gardener pleaded with him to allow it one more year, and not to cut it.
- The gardener promised to dig around it and put some fertilizer on it.
- If it did not bear fruit the master can cut it.

In this parable, the gardener if Jesus, and the owner of the vineyard is God. Christians are expected to bear good fruits by obeying the teachings of Jesus. Jesus uses this parable to warn his disciples that they have another chance to repent.

c) Jesus Heals a Crippled Woman on a Sabbath (Luke 13: 10 – 17)
- One Sabbath, Jesus was teaching in a synagogue.
- There was a woman who had an evil spirit that had kept her sick for eighteen years.
- She was bent over and could not straighten herself up completely.
- When Jesus saw her, he called her out and told her that she was free from her illness.
- Jesus placed his hands on her and she was healed.
- She straightened herself up and praised God.
- The official of the synagogue who witnessed this miracle was annoyed told people to work and go for healing on those days.

- Jesus called him a hypocrite arguing that if people could untie their oxen or donkeys and feed them on the Sabbath, why not do good to a human being?
- He further explained that the woman was a descendant of Abraham whom Satan had bound for 18 years.
- As a daughter of Abraham, she had to be released from this bondage on a Sabbath.
- Jesus' response made his enemies ashamed while other people rejoiced over all the good things Jesus had done.

From this incident, Jesus shows that he came to destroy the Kingdom of Satan and liberate people from it. Through this, the Kingdom of God is established. In the kingdom of God, saving human life is more important than the demands of the Law.

d) The Parable of the Mustard Seed (Luke 13: 18 - 19)
- Jesus compared the growth of the Kingdom of God to a mustard seed.
- He said that when a man plants a mustard seed in his field.
- The seed grows and becomes a tree and birds make their nests in its branches.

Jesus used this parable to explain how God's Kingdom grows from a small beginning to become great, attracting many people.

e) The Parable of the Yeast (Luke 13: 20 – 21)
Jesus told the parable of the yeast to illustrate how the kingdom of God grows in an unseen manner.
- He said that the Kingdom of God is like yeast that a woman took and mixed with flour until all the dough had risen.

Yeast was fermented dough which was kept over from the previous baking. Some little yeast was spared and used to ferment freshly-prepared dough.

f) The Narrow Door (Luke 13: 22 – 30)
- On his way to Jerusalem through the towns and villages, a person asked Jesus whether just a few people would be saved.
- Jesus told him to strive to go through the narrow door, for many will try to enter, but will not be able.
- Once the head of the house locks the door, those outside will not be able to enter.
- Once the door is locked, no amount of persuasion will make the master to open it.
- This will make many to cry, especially when they see Abraham, Isaac and Jacob and all the prophets in the kingdom of God.
- People from all directions who will have strived to enter through the narrow will sit down at the feast of the kingdom of God.
- He added that those who are now last will be first and those who are now first will be last.

Jesus used this illustration to portray how difficult it is to attain the Kingdom of God.it involves making many sacrifices, and has various moral demands. So the disciples of Jesus have to be committed to work for the attainment of the Kingdom of God.

g) Jesus Anticipates His Rejection (Luke 13: 31 – 35)
- Some Pharisees warned Jesus to go elsewhere, for Herod wanted to kill Him.
- Jesus told them to inform Herod that he would continue with his journey to Jerusalem, performing miracles, healing and driving out demons for the next three days.
- He added that it is not right for a prophet to be killed anywhere except in Jerusalem.
- Jesus also lamented over Jerusalem for killing the prophets that God of God.
- He added that God wanted to protect them like a hen gathers her chicks under her wings.
- Since Jerusalem will reject Jesus, God will abandon them until they say "Blessed is the one who comes in the name of the Lord".

This illustration confirms Jesus as the Son of God, who will die after the completion of his mission, in Jerusalem. He laments over Jerusalem, who kill the messengers of God and foretells that God would abandon her, until they acknowledge Jesus as the Son of God.

From the above illustrations, the following is Jesus' teaching about the Kingdom of God
- The Kingdom of God can only be attained after one repents sin.
- The Kingdom of God grows when people are saved from the bondage of Satan.
- In the Kingdom of God, saving human life is important than the demands of the law.
- The Kingdom of God starts from a humble beginnings and grows to greatness.
- The Kingdom of God grows secretly in people's hearts and in an unseen manner.
- The Kingdom of God has many moral demands and challenges for those striving to enter.
- It is for those who are committed and dedicated to work for Jesus.

State the ways in which Christians prepare themselves for God's Kingdom.
- Repenting.
- Forgiving others.
- Obeying God's commands/leading holy lives.
- Taking part in the Lord's table/Holy Eucharist.
- Praying and fasting.
- Evangelization.
- Bible study.

A GREAT FEAST FOR ALL WHO ARE PREPARED (Luke 14: 1 – 35)
a) Jesus Heals the Man with Dropsy (Luke 14: 1 – 6)
- One Sabbath Jesus went to have dinner in the house of a leading Pharisee.
- The Pharisees watched Jesus closely to see what he would do.
- While in the house, a man whose limbs were swollen came to Jesus for healing.
- Jesus asked the Pharisees and teachers of the Law whether the law allowed healing on a Sabbath or not.
- The Pharisees and scribes did not answer him because, if they said yes it would show they were not observing the law strictly, and if they said no it would have shown that they were insensitive to human suffering.
- Jesus healed the man and sent him away.

- He reminded them that if any of them had a son or an ox that had fallen in a well on the Sabbath day they would fail pull him out.

This healing is a manifestation of the Kingdom of God present through Jesus Christ. The Pharisees were not happy for they considered Jesus as having broken the law on the Sabbath observance by healing the man suffering from dropsy. This put Jesus in conflict with them.

b) The Invited Guests (Luke 14: 7 – 14)
- Jesus noticed how the guests at the Pharisee's house chose the best seats and told them a parable.
- He told them that when invited to a wedding feast, they should not choose the place of honour, because host may have invited a more distinguished person.
- The host may come and ask you to give your place to the distinguished guest, leading to embarrassment as you move to the least important place.
- He told them that when invited, one should take the least important place.
- You will be honoured when the host tells you to move to a better place.
- Such an act would exalt an invited guest.
- He added that those who exalt themselves will be humbled and those who humble themselves will be exalted.
- He also told his host that in a feast, one should not only invite one's relatives, friends, neighbours or the rich who are likely to invite them back.
- He advised them to invite to their houses the poor, crippled, lame and the blind.
- By inviting the less priviledged who cannot repay, you shall be repaid in the resurrection.

Jesus used this incident to teach about humility, as a requirement to enter the Kingdom of God.

c) The Parable of the Great Feast (Luke 14: 15 – 24)
- One of the men sitting at the table with Jesus said that blessed are those who will feast in the Kingdom of God.
- Jesus told them a parable of a man who invited his friends for a feast.
- When the time for the feast came, he sent his servants to those he had invited to come, for the feast was ready.
- All the invited guests sent apologies and did not come.
- The master was furious and sent his servant to go out to the streets and alleys of the city to invite the poor, the crippled, the blind and the lame.
- The servants did as commanded but the hall was not full.
- He sent the servants to the highways and country roads to invite more people to the feast.
- The master said that none of those invited earlier would be welcome to the feast.

Jesus used this parable to suggest that the Jews who were given a chance to the kingdom of God but they declined, hence God gave the chance to the Gentiles and the poor. Jesus is God's servant who was sent to invite the Gentiles to the kingdom of God.

Lessons that Christians learn about the kingdom of God
- The kingdom of God is like a great feast.
- The kingdom of God is universal, meant for all people, regardless of the social status.

- Those who respond to the invitation to the kingdom of God will share it with God, the host.
- Those who make a personal decision will attain the kingdom of God.
- We respond to God's kingdom through repentance.
- There is no second chance for those who give excuses when invited.
- The invitation to the kingdom of God is done by God and his servants.

Why did Jesus refer to Pharisees as hypocrites?
- They considered themselves self-righteous.
- They despised others/looked down upon others.
- They lacked humility and they exalted themselves.
- They knew the commandments but did not apply them.
- They followed rules made by human beings/traditions of elders opposed to God's law.
- They emphasized outward cleanliness as opposed to purity of heart.
- They altered the Law of Moses to suit their selfish motives.
- They misled people and had bad influence on the people.
- Their effect on the people was hidden yet widespread.

d) The Cost of Discipleship (Luke 14: 25 – 36)
Jesus turned to those who followed him and taught them what it takes to be a disciple. To follow Christ does not only entail repentance and forgiveness of sins, but it also calls for total commitment.

To be a disciple of Jesus, one has to:
- Renounce his family and love Jesus more than his father, mother, wife and children.
- Deny himself/herself and accept to suffer for the sake of Christ.
- Give up all his/her possessions to the growth of the kingdom of God.
- Be totally committed to the word of God such that one cannot turn back.
- Be ready to preach the gospel and heal the sick.
- Lead an exemplary life.

RETRIEVING THE LOST (Luke 15: 1 – 32)
a) Parable of the Lost Sheep (Luke 15: 4 – 7)
The Pharisees were complaining that Jesus welcomed sinners and outcasts and eats with them. He told them this parable:
- A shepherd had a hundred sheep.
- He lost one sheep and was left with ninety nine (99).
- He abandoned the 99 and went in search of the lost one that had gotten lost.
- When he found it, he placed on his shoulders rejoicing.
- He invited the friends and neighbours to celebrate the finding of the lost sheep.
- Jesus said that in the same way there will be more joy in heaven over one sinner who repents than 99 respectable people who do not need to repent.

Jesus is therefore a good shepherd who seeks the sheep who are lost.

b) Parable of the Lost Coin (Luke 15: 8 – 10)

- Jesus said that, if a woman has ten silver coins and loses one of them, she lights the lamp and sweeps her house looking carefully in the whole house until she finds the lost coin.
- Once she finds it, she will call her friends and neighbours to celebrate.
- She will be overjoyed to find the lost coin.
- Jesus said that in the same way, the angels of God rejoice over one sinner who repents.

Just like the woman diligently and carefully looks for her lost con, so does God look for the sinner. Jesus is the light of the world and is making every effort to seek the lost until he finds them. God and the angels in heaven are overjoyed when one sinner repents.

c) Parable of the Lost Son/The Parable of the Prodigal Son (Luke 15: 11 – 32)

- A man had two sons.
- The younger son asked his father for his share of the inheritance.
- The father shared out his property between the two sons.
- The younger son left home for a far off country and spent all the wealth on careless lifestyle.
- A severe famine took place in that country after he had spent everything, and he was needy.
- No one was willing to share with him anything, including his friends.
- He was employed to herd pigs, and was so desperate that he ate the food that pigs ate.
- He came to his senses and thought of his father's servants who had more than enough to eat while he was dying of hunger.
- He decided to go and apologise to his father, and ask to be employed as one of the servants.
- When the lost son got home, his father received him with great joy.
- He ordered the servants to dress him with the best robe, a ring on his finger give him shoes.
- The father killed a fattened calf to celebrate for his son was dead but he was then alive, he was lost but had been found.
- When the older son came home and realized what was going on, he got angry and refused to go join the celebration.
- His father explained to him why he had to hold the feast for his brother.
- The father assured him that everything he had belonged to the older son.
- The father explained that the celebration was necessary because his brother was alive and had come back home.

In the same way the father of the two sons, God's kingdom brings joy and happiness to those who are lost and are ready to repent.

Application of the teachings from the Parables of the Lost

- God is ready to forgive sinners who repent.
- God rejoices and is overjoyed when a sinner returns to Him through repentance.
- God puts in effort to search for those who are lost in sin, too bring them back to His Kingdom.

- God is provider of all the needs of humankind.
- Christians should forgive others like the father of the prodigal son.
- Christians should seek and preach to the sinners to bring them to God's Kingdom.
- Christians should rejoice when sinners repent.
- Christians should avoid self-righteousness.
- Christians should avoid jealousy.
- Christians should not judge others for God is the final and true judge.

WEALTH, POVERTY, FAITH AND PRAYER

JESUS' TEACHINGS ON WEALTH AND POVERTY (Luke 16: 1 – 32)
a) The Parable of the Shrewd Manager (Luke 16: 1 – 13)
- Jesus told his disciples of a rich man who was told of that his manager was wasting his assets.
- The rich man told the manager to submit to him a complete account of how he was handling his property.
- The rich man wanted to sack the manager.
- The shrewd manager, knowing that he would be sacked decided to make friends with some debtors so that they could take care of him when his master sacked him.
- He asked the debtor who owed his master a hundred barrels of olive oil change the figure to fifty barrels.
- The second debtor owed a hundred bushels of wheat and the manager asked him to change it to 80 bushels.
- The master commended the dishonest manager because he acted shrewdly.
- Jesus also praised the shrewd manager not because of his dishonesty but because he acted promptly and with wisdom in a moment of crisis.
- Jesus told his disciples to make friends for themselves by how they use their worldly wealth.

Jesus teaches his disciples to make wise decisions, on how they use their wealth, for them to attain the Kingdom of God. For example, they should use wealth to assist the needy, or to proclaim the word of God.

b) The Rich man and Lazarus (Luke 16: 19 – 31)
- There was a rich man who feasted sumptuously and dressed in expensive clothes.
- At the gate of the rich man, there lay a poor man called Lazarus, whose body was covered with sores, which dogs would lick
- Lazarus ate what fell from the table of the rich man.
- The poor man died and was carried by the angels to heaven, at Abraham's side.
- The rich man died, was buried and went to hell.
- The rich man pleaded with Abraham to send Lazarus to dip his finger in water to cool his tongue.
- Abraham denied him his request.
- He reminded him that while he was alive, he had all the good things while Lazarus had nothing but the rich man did nothing to help Lazarus while he was alive.

- The rich man further pleaded with Abraham to send Lazarus to his brothers to warn them so that they could live a righteous life and not suffer the way he was suffering in hell.
- Abraham declined once more telling him that his brothers have Moses and the prophets to warn them.

This parable is used to teach about sharing. Those who are rich should help the poor, the needy, orphans e.t.c.

With reference to the parable of the shrewd manager and the parable of the rich man and Lazarus, outline Jesus' teaching on wealth
- Those who have wealth should share it with the poor and the needy.
- The rich should not love their riches more than they love God.
- Wealth should be used to maintain God's work.
- Those who have wealth should use it wisely.
- The poor should accept themselves as children of God and humble themselves to realize God's love for them.
- Wealth is temporary, and therefore no one should put their trust in material possessions.
- People should avoid misusing their wealth, because its misuse leads to suffering.

Give the ways in which Christians use their wealth today
- Promoting the spread of the gospel.
- Assisting victims in places where disasters occur.
- Building homes for the poor, orphans e.t.c.
- Providing medical services.
- Promoting education and training.
- Giving offerings and tithes to the church.
- Creating employment opportunities.
- Investing money in community development projects.

Why do some Christians find it difficult to share their wealth with others?
- There is selfishness or individualism in the modern society.
- The high cost of living has led to economic constraints.
- Some only share with members of their tribe, race, clan or family.
- Denominational differences hinder the spirit of sharing.
- It can encourage dependence and laziness.
- It is difficult to identify those who may genuinely require help or assistance.
- Those receiving help may be suspicious.
- Those receiving the assistance may not show appreciation.
- They have not understood the biblical concept of sharing.

JESUS' TEACHING ON THE POWER OF FAITH (Luke 17: 1 – 37)
a) Jesus' teaching on sin (Luke 17: 1 – 4)
- Jesus taught that sin can lead to loss of faith.

- He told the disciples that people are likely to commit sin, however, if a person makes others to commit sin, it would be better for the person if a large stone was tied round his neck and he were thrown into the sea.
- This is a warning to those who lead others to sin hence making their faith weak.
- Jesus also told his disciples to forgive those who wrong them constantly.
- To be able to forgive another person many times in a day requires strong faith.

Give the teachings of Jesus on sin
- Jesus has power to forgive sin.
- God forgives people's sins on condition that they also forgive other people's sins.
- We should ask God to forgive our sin/should repent.
- We should ask God to protect us against sin.
- Sin comes from the heart.
- Sin is not only the act but evil thoughts too.
- Those who cause/lead others to sin will be severely punished.
- Forgiveness should be limitless.
- Sins that are forgiven on earth also forgiven in heaven.
- Sin leads to death.
- All sins are forgiven but not blasphemy.
- Sin should be condemned /rebuked.

Identify the ways through which Christians can avoid sin.
- By resisting temptation from the devil.
- By obeying God's laws.
- By being prayerful/fasting.
- Avoiding selfish desires.
- Using free will/freedom given to us properly.
- Seeking guidance and counselling.
- Avoid bad company/peer influence.
- Avoid drugs and alcohol abuse.
- Avoid places that make them vulnerable e.g. discos/bars parties held at night e.t.c.

b) Jesus' Teaching on Faith (Luke 17: 5 – 6)
- The apostles asked Jesus to increase their faith.
- Jesus responded by telling them that if they had faith as big as a mustard seed, they could command a mulberry tree to uproot itself and be planted in the sea.
- Jesus therefore taught that faith makes even the weakest strong.

c) A Servant's Duty (Luke 17: 7 – 10)
- Jesus also told his disciples that if any of them had a servant who had come from ploughing the field or shepherding sheep, they would command the servant to prepare dinner for them.
- The master will then ask the servant to serve him as he eats and drinks.
- The master will not thank the servant, since the servant did what he/ she was told.

- Jesus told the disciples, that they too should do what they are commanded to do and appreciate that they do not deserve special praise for doing what is their duty.

Jesus therefore teaches that a servant can only rest when there's no work to do. Similarly, disciples, should serve God tirelessly, and should not expect to be thanked for performing their God-given responsibilities.

d) Jesus Heals Ten Lepers (Luke 17: 11 – 19)
- On His way to Jerusalem, Jesus passed along Samaria and Galilee.
- As He entered a village, He met ten men who were suffering from leprosy.
- The men stood at a distance and called Jesus 'master' and asked him to have mercy on them.
- When Jesus saw the lepers, he told them to go and show themselves to the priests.
- As they went to the priests, they were healed and made clean.
- One of them on realizing that he had been healed, came back praising God.
- He threw himself at the feet of Jesus and thanked him.
- The man who came back was a Samaritan and Jesus wondered why only the foreigner came back to give thanks to God.
- Jesus pointed out to him that his faith had healed him and told him to get up and go.

e) The Coming of the Kingdom (Luke 17: 20 – 37)
- Some Pharisees asked Jesus when the kingdom of God would come.
- Jesus told them that the kingdom of God does not come with signs that can be seen.
- He added that the Kingdom of God was in their midst.
- Jesus told his disciples that a time would come when they would wish to see one of the days of the Son of Man.
- He told the disciples that before the coming of the Kingdom of God, the Son of Man will suffer and be rejected by their generation.
- Jesus said that the day of the Son of Man will be a day of suffering like during Noah's and Lot's time.
- He added that on that day, whoever will try to keep his life will lose it, but whoever loses his life will preserve it.
- He taught his disciples that they would require strong faith to overcome the trials that they were likely to experience until the second coming of Jesus

From the above illustrations, Jesus taught the following about faith
- Faith strengthens one to overcome temptations.
- Faith makes disciples to forgive those who wrong them.
- Faith gives disciples the power to perform miracles in Jesus' name.
- Faith enables disciples to carry out their mission without expecting rewards.
- Faith in Jesus effects healing.
- Faith in God enables us to show gratitude to him for blessings.
- Faith enables us to witness the kingdom of God in our hearts.
- Lack of faith in Jesus leads to God's punishment while faith in Jesus leads to eternal life.

Why do Christians practice forgiveness?

- It shows love for others.
- It creates and promotes peace.
- It is a way of attracting more converts.
- It shows obedience to God's commandments.
- In order to follow the example of Jesus or emulate Jesus.
- In order to be forgiven by God.
- It strengthens relationships with others.
- It lengthens life and promotes healthy living.

PERSISTENCE IN PRAYER (Luke 18: 1 – 14)

a) The Parable of the widow and the unjust judge (Luke 18: 1 – 8)

- Jesus told the disciples a parable to show them they should pray persistently and not lose heart.
- In a certain town there was a judge who neither feared God nor respect people.
- There also was a widow who kept going to the judge asking him to grant her justice against her opponent.
- For a while the judge refused, but he later granted her justice.
- The judge said to himself that if he failed to help the widow, she would keep pestering him.

The parable teaches that:

i. Prayer should said with persistence.
ii. Prayer should be offered in faith.
iii. Prayer should be said with courage.
iv. We should pray boldly.

b) The Parable of the Pharisees and the Tax collector (Luke 18: 9 – 14)

- Jesus told the Pharisees this parable, since they were confident of their righteousness and therefore looked down upon other people.
- He said that two men, a Pharisee and a tax collector went to pray.
- The Pharisee stood and prayed praising himself.
- He thanked God for not being greedy, dishonest or an adulterer or even like the tax collector.
- He told God that he fasts twice a week and pays tithe.
- The tax collector stood at a distance and would not even raise his head to heaven.
- He beat on his chest and told God to have pity on him for he was a sinner.
- Jesus told his disciples that the tax collector and not the Pharisee was in the right relationship with God.

The parable teaches that:

i. Prayer should be said in humility.
ii. Prayer should be addressed to God.
iii. Prayer should be brief and precise.
iv. Prayer should be said with sincerity.

Relevance of the parable of the Pharisee and the tax collector to Christian life today
- Christians should approach God with humility.
- Christians should avoid pride and self-righteousness.
- Christians should honestly confess their sins and ask for God's forgiveness.
- Christians should be persistent in prayer.
- Christians should not condemn others as sinners.

THE WAY TO SALVATION (Luke 18: 15 – 19: 1 – 27)

The way to salvation refers to the act of seeking to be delivered from sin and its consequences through Jesus Christ.

Those who have received salvation are assured of receiving eternal life through Jesus Christ. Jesus used various illustrations to teach about the way to salvation.

a) Jesus Blesses Little Children (Luke 18: 15 - 17)
- Some people brought children to Jesus so that he could bless them.
- When the disciples saw this, they reprimanded them for doing so.
- But Jesus called the children to himself telling the disciples that the Kingdom of God belongs to such like them
- He told the disciples that whoever does not humble himself cannot enter the Kingdom of God.

Christians should therefore humble themselves and trust in God to enter the Kingdom of God, that is, salvation.

b) The Rich Man (Luke 18: 18 – 30)
- A rich man came to Jesus and asked Him what to do in order to receive eternal life.
- He addressed Jesus as 'Good Teacher' but Jesus refused to be called good because only God is good.
- Jesus told the rich man to obey the Ten Commandments.
- The rich man said that he had kept the commandments since when he was youth.
- Jesus told him to sell everything he had, give to the poor and then follow Him.
- The rich man was very sad to hear this for he was extremely wealthy.
- Jesus observed that it is very hard for the rich to enter the Kingdom of God.

Jesus, in this parable, was teaching his disciples that wealth can be a barrier to entering God's kingdom. Wealth should not prevent one from serving God. It should be shared with the needy.

c) Jesus Speaks a Third Time about His Death (Luke 18: 31 – 34)
- Jesus took his disciples aside.

- He told them that they were heading to Jerusalem where everything written about him would be fulfilled.
- Jesus explained that going to be handed over to the Gentiles.
- He would be mocked, spat on, mistreated and be killed.
- He said that He would rise again on the third day.
- The disciples did not understand what Jesus said, for it was hidden from them.

Jesus was predicting his suffering and death, which would take place in Jerusalem. It is through this, that humankind would attain salvation. He also said that He would resurrect after three days.

d) Jesus Heals a Blind Beggar Near Jericho (Luke 18: 35 - 43)
- Jesus came to Jericho and met a blind man sitting by the road begging.
- When the blind man heard the crowd passing, he sought to know what was happening.
- The people told him that Jesus of Nazareth was passing by.
- He shouted calling Jesus son of David.
- He told Jesus to have pity on him.
- The people in told him to be quiet but he shouted even more.
- Jesus stopped and ordered that the beggar be brought to him.
- Jesus asked the blind man what he wanted and he answered that he wanted to see again.
- Jesus commanded him to see and told him that his faith had healed him.
- He regained his sight and followed Jesus, giving praise to God.

The blind beggar referred to Jesus as "Son of David", which confirms Jesus as the Messiah. Restoring sight to the blind is part of His mission.

Lessons that Christians learn about salvation from the Healing of the Blind beggar
- Christians must make an effort to seek God for them to attain salvation like the blind beggar.
- Christians should have faith in Jesus for them to attain salvation.
- Christians should pray persistently like the blind beggar for them to attain salvation.
- Christians should help the needy in order to attain salvation.
- Christians should not be a hindrance to those seeking salvation.

e) Jesus and Zacchaeus (Luke 19: 1 – 9)
- As Jesus was passing through Jericho, Zaccheus wanted to see him.
- Zacchaeus, a rich tax collector, wanted to see Jesus, but he was short and could not see Jesus because of the crowd.
- He ran ahead and climbed up a tree to see Jesus.
- When He reached that place, Jesus looked up and told Zacchaeus to come down for He was going to stay at his house on that day.

- Zacchaeus welcomed Jesus joyfully to his house.
- The people complained that Jesus had entered the house the house of a sinner.
- Zacchaeus declared that he would give the poor half his wealth, and pay back those he had cheated four times.
- Jesus was pleased with Zacchaeus' decision and told him that salvation had gotten to his house on that day.
- He said that the Son of Man had come to seek and save the lost.

Zachaeus became a changed man due to his encounter with Zacchaeus. He repented and paid back those he had cheated, and shared his wealth with the poor. Jesus assured him of salvation.

Lessons that Christians learn from Jesus' encounter with Zaccaheus
- Christians should humble themselves like Zacchaeus to attain salvation.
- Christians should confess their sins to attain salvation.
- Christians should share their wealth with the poor to attain salvation.
- Christians should have faith in Jesus, though whom salvation comes.
- Christians should invite Jesus in their hearts for them to attain salvation.

f) The Parable of the Gold Coins (Luke 19: 11 – 27)
- When Jesus was about to enter Jerusalem, he told his disciples and the people listening the parable of the gold coins.
- He said there was a nobleman who was going to a far country to be made a king and then return.
- He called his servants and gave them each a gold coin.
- He asked them to trade with the gold coins.
- After the man was made king, he returned and ordered his servants to appear before him and account for how much they had gained by trading.
- The first servant had gained gold coins more, and was made to rule over ten cities.
- The second one had earned five gold coins, and was made to rule over five cities.
- The third servant returned the gold coin intact, for he had not invested it.
- The master was very annoyed with this servant for failing to invest the money in a bank so that it could earn interest.
- The master ordered that the one gold coin be taken away from him and be given to the one who had ten gold coins.

This parable teaches the need for people to use their talents and abilities.

What lessons do Christians learn from the parable of the ten pounds? (Luke 19: 11 – 27)
- Christians should use their abilities that God has given them for the benefit of others.

- Christians will be rewarded according their performances.
- Christians have been given different gifts and abilities by God.
- Christians will give an account of how they used their abilities.
- Christians need to be honest and obedient.
- God expects Christians to use opportunities provided for his glory.
- Christians will lose their abilities if not put to use.

Topic 17: THE JERUSALEM MINISTRY

THE TRIUMPHANT ENTRY INTO JERUSALEM (Luke 19: 28 – 40)

- When Jesus approached Bethphage, Bethany at the Mt. Olives, he sent two of his disciples to the village ahead to bring him a donkey which no one had ridden.
- The disciples were to find the colt tied.
- They were to say that the Lord needed it, if asked why they were untying it.
- They disciples found everything exactly as Jesus had told them.
- They brought the donkey to Jesus and cast their garments upon it.
- Jesus rode on the donkey as people spread their clothes on the road.
- The multitude of his disciples began to rejoice and praise God.
- The crowd hailed Jesus as the king of Israel.
- Some Pharisees asked Jesus to rebuke the disciples to keep quiet.
- He responded that if the disciples kept quiet the stones would cry out.

Lessons that Christian learn from the triumphant entry

- Christians should prepare and be ready to receive Jesus in their lives like the crowds that escorted him to Jerusalem.
- They should emulate Jesus and be channels of peace in their communities.
- Christians should be humble like Jesus in their service to others.
- Church leaders should be servants of their followers.
- Christians should expect opposition and resistance as they evangelize, but they should not give up hope.
- Christians should thank and praise God for his intervention in their lives and as the crowds that followed Jesus.
- Christians should be bold as they witness to Jesus like the crowds that followed Jesus and declared him king.

THE CLEANSING OF THE TEMPLE (Luke 19: 41 – 48)

a. Jesus weeps over Jerusalem (Luke 19: 41 – 45)

- As Jesus entered Jerusalem, he wept over the city. He wept over Jerusalem for the following reasons:

i. The people of Jerusalem did not realize his arrival.

ii. They did not recognize him as a peaceful Messiah.

iii. They were engaged in sinfulness and had forgotten the covenant way of life.

iv. They had forgotten that they were a chosen people with the role to serve God's will to other nations.

v. Jerusalem was the centre of worshipping God yet it was spiritually dead.

vi. Religious leaders had forgotten the laws that they kept and taught.

vii. Jesus had foreseen that he would be rejected in Jerusalem.

viii. Jerusalem was going to be destroyed as a punishment for forsaking God's covenant.

b. Jesus cleanses the temple (Luke 19: 45 - 48)

- Jesus then entered the temple where He found people buying and selling.
- He drove them out and overturned their tables.
- He accused them of turning his father's house into a den of robbers.
- Jesus began to teach in the temple daily.
- The Pharisees sought to destroy him but they were unable because the crowds followed him and were attentive to his teachings.

Give the reasons that led Jesus to cleanse the temple

- He was disappointed with the hypocrisy of the Jewish religious leaders.
- The temple was being used to oppress the weak by overcharging them.
- The worshippers in the temple had not reorganized themselves for his messiahship.
- To show that he was the new temple in whom Christians worship.
- The temple was being used to discriminate against the gentiles and women.
- To show that he was the son of God/messiah.
- By cleansing the temple Jesus was asserting his spiritual authority over the spiritual heritage of the Jews.
- He cleansed the temple to show his followers an example of keeping God's house clean.
- As the messiah, Jesus could not tolerate to see evil.
- The temple had become a centre of sin/had lost its holiness

JESUS CONFLICTS WITH THE JEWISH LEADERS (Luke 19: 47 – 48, 20: 1 – 47, 21: 1 – 4)

- After cleansing the temple, Jesus taught in the temple daily.
- The Jewish religious leaders, that is, the Chief Priests, scribes, Pharisees and elders wanted to kill him but they feared the people, who kept listening to him keenly, not wanting to miss a word.
- Jesus expected to be rejected, and be put to death, which was part of his mission and according to God's plan. Jesus was the Messiah, and also the Suffering Servant.
- The Jewish religious leaders tried to find fault with Jesus by asking Him testing questions meant to challenge Him. However, Jesus gives skilful responses which they cannot find fault with him.
- Jesus conflicted with the Jewish religious leaders in the following ways:

a. The Question about Jesus' Authority (Luke 20: 1 – 8)

- Jesus was teaching in the temple one day when the chief priests, scribes and elders came to him.
- They asked where he got his authority from.

- Jesus asked them where John's baptism was from, whether from heaven or from men.
- The leaders could not answer because if they said it was from heaven, Jesus would ask them why they did not believe him. And if they said it was of men the people would stone them, since the people knew John was a prophet.
- They therefore said they did not know.
- Jesus answered that he would not tell them by whose authority he was teaching and preaching.

b. The Parable of the Wicked Tenants (Luke 20: 9 – 18)

- Jesus then told them the parable of the wicked tenants.
- He said that a man planted a vineyard and leased it to tenants, and travelled to another country for a long time.
- When the time for harvest came, he sent his servant to the tenants, that they may give him some of the fruits of the vineyard.
- The tenants instead beat him up and sent him away empty-handed.
- He sent another servant whom they beat, treated shamefully and also sent him empty-handed.
- He sent yet a third one whom they wounded and threw him out.
- The owner of the vineyard decided to send him only son, thinking the tenants would respect him.
- However, the tenants beat him up and killed him.
- Jesus then asked what the owner of the vineyard would do to the tenants.
- The owner will destroy those tenants and give the vineyard to others.
- Jesus concluded the parable by saying that the stone which the builders rejected has become the cornerstone.

The Jewish religious leaders wanted to arrest Jesus and put him to death for they realized that He was attacking them in this parable. He accused them of rejecting God's prophets and messengers. The killing of the son represents how Jesus would be killed in the hands of the Jewish religious leaders.

c. Paying taxes to Caesar (Luke 20: 19 – 26)

- The Jewish religious leaders were annoyed that Jesus attacked them in the parable of the wicked tenants.
- They wanted to arrest him but they feared the people.
- They therefore sent spies to him who pretended to be sincere, so that they could find fault in his words and accuse him before the governor of Judah.
- They asked him whether it is lawful to pay taxes to Caesar.
- The question posed a dilemma to Jesus since if he answered that it was right to pay taxes, the people would oppose him since the Jews did not like paying taxes to Caesar,

but if he opposed the payment of taxes he would be accused of treason by the government.

- Jesus asked his questioners to produce a silver coin and state whose image was on it.
- When they said the emperor's, Jesus told them to give to Caesar the things that are Caesar's, and to God the things that are God's.
- They were unable to trap him with his own words, and they remained silent.

d. The Question about the Resurrection (Luke 20: 27 – 40)

- The Sadducees who did not believe in resurrection came to Jesus with a question about the resurrection.
- They said that in the Law of Moses, if a man's brother dies leaving a wife without children, that man must marry the widow and bear children for his brother.
- There were therefore seven brothers, and the first took a wife and died without children.
- And the second took her as wife and died childless.
- And the third took her and in the same way all the seven died without children.
- The woman died too, finally.
- They asked Jesus whose wife the woman would be between the seven brothers in the resurrection.
- Jesus told them that in the resurrection there is no marriage
- Jesus added that in the resurrection no one dies again because they are equal to the angels and are children of God.

e. The Question about the Messiah (Luke 20: 41 – 44)

- Jesus asked the Jewish religious leaders how it could be that the messiah will be a descendant of David.
- He observed that in Psalms, David says that the 'Lord said to my lord, sit on my right', which means that David himself referred to the Messiah as his Lord.
- Jesus observed it is not enough to describe the Messiah as the Son of David. The messiah is the Son of God, who will suffer, die and resurrect on the third day.

f. Jesus warns against the hypocrisy of the Teachers of Law (Luke 20: 45 – 47)

Jesus warned his disciples to beware of the hypocrisy of the Jewish religious leaders for the following reasons:
- They walked around in long robes.
- They loved being greeted with respect in market places.
- They took the best seats in the synagogues and in feasts.
- They made long prayers intended to make people notice them.
- They robbed widows of their property.

g. The Widow's offering (Luke: 21: 1 – 4)
- Jesus watched the rich giving their offering in the temple.
- And he saw a certain poor widow giving her offering of two little copper coins.
- Jesus praised the widow for giving all she had.
- He said that the rich offered what they spared from their wealth, but the widow gave all that she had.

Describe the seven causes of conflict between Jesus and the Jewish religious leaders in his Jerusalem ministry.
- They questioned the authority whose which Jesus was using to teach (Luke 20: 1 – 8).
- In the parable of the tenants, Jesus accused the Jewish leaders for rejecting God's prophets and plotting to kill him. (Luke 20: 9 – 18)
- They conflicted on the issue of whether to pay taxes to Caesar or not. (Luke 20: 19 – 26)
- In the question about resurrection, the Sadducees did not believe in resurrection. He challenged them that they did not understand the resurrection life yet it was in the writings of Moses whom they quoted. (Luke 20: 27 – 39).
- He claimed to be the Messiah and said that even David called Him Lord in the book of Psalms. (Luke 20: 4 – 44)
- Jesus openly condemned the hypocrisy and arrogance of the leaders because they loved the best seats in the synagogues, made long prayers and put on robes. (Luke 20: 45 – 47).
- He condemned the offerings of the rich Jewish leaders which were meant to show off but praised the widows offering which was made out of self-sacrifice. (Luke 21: 1 – 4)

JESUS' TEACHING ABOUT ESCHATOLOGY (Luke 21: 5 – 38)
- Eschatology is the study of the events that will occur during the end times.
- Jesus' teaching on eschatology was to encourage his disciples to face persecution and other difficult situations with courage and hope.
- Jesus taught that the end times will be accompanied with signs such as:
  i. The temple of Jerusalem would be destroyed.
  ii. People will come claiming to be the Messiah.
  iii. There will be wars between nations.
  iv. Natural calamities will occur.
  v. Strange and celestial beings would come from the sky.
  vi. Jesus' disciples would be arrested, persecuted and imprisoned.
  vii. The disciples will be persecuted.
  viii. The disciples would be hated because of Jesus' name.
  ix. The city of Jerusalem would be destroyed
  x. There will be disruption in the sky and in the sea.
  xi. People will be in despair.

xii.   People will faint due to them witnessing the signs of the end times.

After these signs, the Son of Man will appear in power and glory to take his faithful ones.

The parable of the Fig Tree (Luke 21: 29 – 33)

- Jesus then told the disciples the parable of the fig tree to explain the reality of his coming.
- When the fig tree and other trees shed their leaves, people know that the summer is near.
- Jesus said that in a similar way, when the disciples see the signs, they should know that the Kingdom of God is near.
- Jesus added that this generation will not pass away till all he said had been fulfilled.

The parable of the fig tree teaches the disciples the need to be aware of the signs of the end times and to give them hope.

The Need to be Watchful (Luke 21: 34 – 38)

- Jesus concluded his teaching about eschatology by encouraging his disciples to lead a moral life.
- He told the disciples to avoid drunkenness and being preoccupied with the worries of this world.
- He advised them to be careful that the coming of the Son of Man may not catch them unaware.
- They were to keep alert by praying, so that they can have strength to go safely through all the things that will happen before the Son of Man.
- Jesus continued teaching in the temple daily, and many people kept coming to listen to him.

The relevance of Jesus teachings on eschatology to Christians

- Christians look forward with hope to Jesus' second coming, as Lord and judge.
- Christians should live a prayerful life in order to overcome difficult situations.
- Christians should live moral lives as they wait for the second coming of Christ.
- Christians should have unwavering faith so as not to be swayed by the cares and pleasures of life.

How do Christians today prepare for the second coming of Jesus?

- Living holy lives.
- Repenting their sins.
- Preaching the good news.
- Helping the poor and needy.
- Condemning evils in the society.
- Praying and fasting.

Topic 18: JESUS' PASSION, DEATH AND RESURRECTION

- The Jewish religious leaders were determined to arrest Jesus, and put him to death, for they were convinced that He was inciting people against them.
- Jesus was aware of this, but He also knew that He had to suffer and die in order to accomplish His mission.
- Before his death, Jesus had the Last Supper with His disciples and prepared them for his death.

THE LAST SUPPER (Luke 22: 1 – 30)

a. The plot against Jesus (Luke 22: 1 – 6)

- As the feast of Passover was approaching, the chief priests and the experts of the Law were trying to find a way of putting Jesus to death secretly.
- However, they were afraid of the crowds who came to listen to Jesus' teachings.
- They were aware that if they arrested Jesus in public the people would riot and cause unrest.
- Then Satan entered Judas Iscariot, one of the twelve disciples, and he went to discuss with the Jewish religious leaders how he could betray and hand Jesus over to them.
- They were happy and they offered to give him money.
- Judas accepted their offer and started looking for an opportunity to hand Jesus over to them when Jesus was not with a crowd.

By accepting to betray Jesus, Judas Iscariot had broken the relationship of friendship and trust between him and Jesus.

b. The Lord's Supper

i. Preparations for the Lord's Supper (Luke 22: 7 – 13)

- Jesus sent Peter and John to go and prepare the Passover that he and the disciples may eat.
- The disciples asked Him where He wanted them to prepare the it.
- He instructed the two to go into the city of Jerusalem where they would meet a man carrying a jar of water.
- Jesus told them to follow the man into the house he would enter.
- Once they enter in the house, the disciples were to ask the owner to show them the guest room where Jesus and the disciples would celebrate the Passover.
- Jesus told them that the owner would show them an upper furnished room.

- He told them to prepare the room.
- The disciples went and found as Jesus had told them and they prepared the Passover.

ii. The Last Supper (Luke 22: 14 – 38)

- When the time came for Jesus and his disciples to eat the Passover meal, he sat with them at one table.
- He told them that he had desired to have the meal with them.
- He took the cup, gave thanks and asked the disciples to share.
- He also took bread, gave thanks, broke it and gave them.
- He explained to them the meaning of the bread and wine.
- He commanded the disciples to hold the celebrate the feast His memory.
- He informed them that he would be betrayed by one of them.
- He taught the disciples the qualities of good leadership e.g. humility and service to others.
- He told Simon that he would be tested by Satan.
- He assured Simon that he had prayed for him that his faith does not fail him and asked him to strengthen others in their faith.
- Jesus told Peter that he would deny him three times before the cock crowed that very day.
- He commanded the disciples to acquire money bags, travellers bags and swords.

What is the significance of the symbolic acts that happened during the Last Supper?

- The bread represented his body would suffer for the sake His followers and die on the cross.
- The wine represented the blood of Jesus which would be shed for the salvation of the humankind.
- The cup represented God's new covenant with his people, established through the death of Jesus Christ.
- The offering of His body and blood means that Jesus is the new sacrificial lamb replacing the old Passover lambs that were sacrificed on the night of the exodus.
- The command to his disciples "do this in memory of me" implied that the disciples were to continue to celebrating the Lord's Supper.
- Foretelling his betrayal was a fulfilment of the Old Testament prophecies about the messiah.
- The argument on greatness by the disciples meant that the disciples did not understand the passion of Jesus.
- The prediction that Peter would deny him was a fulfilment of the Old Testament prophecies.

- By commanding the disciples to purchase a sword, Jesus was preparing them for hostility.

Give the names used to refer to the last supper
- Lord's Supper.
- Holy table.
- Holy Communion.
- Holy Sacrament.
- Great banquet.
- Lord's meal.
- Last Supper.

The significance of the Lord's Supper to Christians
- Christians renew their faith in God when they celebrate the Lord's Supper, which represents God's New Covenant.
- Christians prepare for the second coming of Jesus and the establishment of God's kingdom when they celebrate the Lord's Supper.
- Christians receive assurance of the forgiveness of sins when they celebrate the Lord's Supper.
- Jesus is present is present the sharing of the bread and the wine when celebrating the Lord's Supper.
- The Lord's Supper is a symbol of the heavenly banquet which Christians will partake of in God's Kingdom.
- The Lord's Supper is also a sacrifice of praise and thanksgiving to God.
- It reminds Christians of Christ's death and resurrection for their sins.

PRAYER ON MOUNT OLIVES (Luke 22: 39 – 46)
- After celebrating the Last Supper, Jesus went to the Mt. Olives.
- His disciples followed Him to the mountain.
- When he got there, he told his disciples to pray so that they do not fall into temptation.
- Jesus moved a distance away from the disciples and knelt down and prayed.
- An angel from heaven appeared to Him and strengthened Him.
- In His anguish, Jesus prayed earnestly and His sweat was like drops of blood falling to the ground.
- When He got up from prayer and came to the disciples, He found them asleep.
- He again told them to pray so that they do not enter into temptation.

The Betrayal and arrest of Jesus (Luke 22: 47 – 53)

- While Jesus was still talking to his disciples, a crowd, led by Judas Iscariot, came to arrest Him.
- Judas moved up to where Jesus was kissed him to identify Him to the crowd.
- Jesus asked Judas "are you betraying the Son of Man with a kiss?"
- One of the disciples struck off the ear of the chief priest's slave.
- He told the disciples not to resist.
- Jesus healed the ear of the slave.
- Jesus asked the chief priests and officers of the temple why they had come to arrest him with swords and clubs as if he was a criminal.
- He also asked them why they had come to arrest him while he had been in the temple with them daily.

Reasons that made Judas Iscariot betray Jesus
- Greed for money and material possession.
- It was God's will for the fulfilment of the scriptures to be realized.
- Judas was unable to overcome the temptation by Satan.
- Judas was looking for fame or recognition.
- He was unhappy with Jesus' activities.
- He was an informer of the Jewish religious leaders.
- He was expecting a political messiah yet Jesus was a spiritual messiah.

The Denial of Jesus by Peter (Luke 22: 54 – 65)
- After he was arrested, Jesus was taken to the High Priest's house.
- Peter followed him at a distance.
- Fire was lit in the courtyard and Peter sat among the people who were warming themselves.
- A maidservant saw Peter and looked up saying that he was also with Jesus.
- Peter answered by saying he did not know Jesus.
- After a while another servant saw Peter and told him that he was one of the disciples of Jesus.
- Peter denied that he was not among them.
- After about one hour another man also identified Peter that he was one of the disciples and Peter denied knowing Jesus.
- As he spoke the cock crowed.
- Jesus looked at Peter and he remembered what Jesus had said.
- Peter went out and wept bitterly.
- Those who were holding Jesus began to mock and beat Him.
- He was blindfolded and asked him repeatedly to prophesy who had beaten him.

By denying Jesus, Peter had broken the promise that he made to Jesus earlier when he said that he was ready to go with Jesus to prison and to death. Peter may have denied Jesus for the following reasons:

i.   He lacked moral courage in times of trouble.
ii. He acted on impulse at the time when Jesus predicted his denial.
iii. He was over-confident of his loyalty to Jesus.
iv. He lacked the support of the other disciples, most whom had run away.
v.   He feared that he would be arrested for being a disciple of Jesus.

Peter wept bitterly after Jesus looked at him, and he remembered Jesus' prediction that he would deny Him. This is a sign of repentance brought on by having recognized his failure and his love for Jesus.

THE TRIAL OF JESUS (Luke 22: 66 – 71; 23: 1 – 25)

The trial of Jesus took place in different places, before the Sanhedrin, before Pilate, before Herod and then the judgement was made by Pilate. The trial before the Sanhedrin was aimed at gathering evidence which would be used to accuse him before Pilate.

a. Jesus' trial before the Sanhedrin (Jewish Council) (Luke 22: 66 – 71)

- In the morning after Jesus had been tortured throughout the night at the High Priests' house, he was brought before the council of the Chief priests and scribes.
- They asked him if he was Christ.
- He responded that they would not believe him and that if he asked, they would not answer.
- He added that soon the Son of Man would be seated in the right hand of the God.
- They asked him if he was the son of God.
- He responded that they had said so.
- They concluded that they needed no more testimony since they had heard it from his lips.

b. The Trial before Pilate (Luke 23: 1 – 5)

- And the crowds of the Chief Priests and scribes led him to Pilate.
- They accused him of inciting people to rebel against the emperor, opposing the payment of taxes to the Caesar and claiming to be the King of the Jews.
- Pilate asked Jesus if he was the King of the Jews.
- Jesus responded by saying that he had said so.
- Pilate told the chief priests and the people that he had found no fault with Jesus.
- The people protested saying that Jesus incited the people, teaching throughout Judea beginning from Galilee up to Jerusalem.

c. Jesus before Herod (Luke 23: 6 – 12)

- When Pilate heard of Galilee, he asked if Jesus was a Galilean and sent Jesus to Herod, who was in Jerusalem at that time.
- When Herod saw Jesus he was so happy, for he had heard many things about Jesus and he desired to see him perform a miracle.
- Herod asked him several questions but Jesus never answered any of his questions.
- When he failed to get a miracle from Jesus, Herod and the soldiers in ridiculed and mocked him.
- They dressed him in a fine robe and sent him back to Pilate.

d. Pilate's judgement (Luke 23: 13 – 25)

- Pilate called the Chief Priests and other Jewish leaders and told them that he had not found Jesus guilty of any of their accusations against Jesus.
- He observed that Herod too had not found Jesus guilty.
- He proposed that Jesus be whipped and released.
- However, the Chief Priests and other Jewish leaders insisted that Jesus was guilty and had to be killed.
- The crowd insisted to have Jesus crucified and have Barabbas released instead.
- After failing to convince them, Pilate gave in and passed a death sentence on Jesus by crucifixion.

Jesus was before the Sanhedrin calling himself the "Son of Man" which was interpreted by his accusers to be the Son of God. They considered him to be guilty of the sin of blasphemy or disrespect of God. According to the Jewish law, the penalty for blasphemy was death. Jesus was therefore was condemned to die for claiming to be the Son of God.

Even though Pilate found Jesus innocent, he was intimidated release Barabbas, who had been imprisoned for murder and sedition against Rome. It was a tradition for a convicted person to be released during the Passover. Jesus, who was innocent was convicted and sentenced to death, at the expense of Barabbas, a guilty person.

In what ways was the trial of Jesus unjust?

- Jesus was not told the reason for his arrest.
- He was mocked and beaten even before trial
- False accusations were brought against him.
- The Sanhedrin insisted on his death after Pilate found him innocent.
- The crowd intimidated Pilate to put him to death.
- Though innocent Pilate was to have him whipped.

- A criminal/Barrabas was released to pave way for his death.
- Peter who followed him was treated with threats and intimidation on the night before trial.
- Herod treated him with contempt and ridicule at the trial.

The Crucifixion of Jesus (Luke 23: 26 – 43)

- As Jesus was led away to face death, a man called Simon of Cyrene was forced to Him Jesus carry the cross to the place of crucifixion.
- The women of Jerusalem followed Jesus and mourning and wailing for him.
- Jesus turned to them and told them not to weep for Him but for their children.
- He cautioned that God's judgement would be so terrible, that those who had no children would be counted as being blessed.
- Jesus was crucified in Calvary, at a place called Golgotha.
- His hands and feet were nailed on the cross.
- He was crucified with two criminals, one on his right and the other on his left.
- Jesus asked God to forgive them, for they did not know what they were doing.
- After Jesus was crucified, the soldiers cast a dice to divide his clothes.
- The Jewish leaders and soldiers mocked him asking Jesus to save himself if he was truly the Messiah.
- The soldiers also mocked him and gave him vinegar.
- An inscription reading "This is the King of the Jews" was placed above his head.
- One of the criminals crucified with Jesus also mocked Jesus and challenged him to save himself and them.
- But the other criminal rebuked him explaining that they were guilty but Jesus was innocent.
- The repentant criminal asked Jesus for a place in the Kingdom of God.
- Jesus promised him eternal life in heaven.

What actions were taken by the Jewish leaders to ensure that Jesus was put to death?

- They paid Judas Iscariot to betray Jesus.
- They brought false witnesses to accuse him of blasphemy.
- They hurriedly tried him at night before people knew what was happening.
- They framed a treason charge against him.
- They employed armed people and Roman soldiers to deal with those who fought for Jesus.
- They blackmailed Pilate into accepting their demands to have Jesus crucified.
- They organized a mob to shout for the death of Jesus.
- They crucified him when they got permission from Pilate.

d. The Death and Burial of Jesus (Luke 23: 44 – 56)
The Death of Jesus (Luke 23: 44 – 49)
- At the sixth hour, there was darkness over all the earth until the ninth hour.
- The curtain of the temple tore into two.
- Jesus committed His spirit into God's hands.
- Jesus breathed the last and he died.
- When the Roman centurion saw what has happened, glorified God saying that Jesus was an innocent man.
- The crowds who watched the death of Jesus returned home beating their breasts, which is a sign of mourning.
- All his friends and women that had followed him watched the events from a distance.

The Burial of Jesus (Luke 23: 50 – 56)
- After Jesus died, Joseph of Arimathea, a rich righteous member of the Sanhedrin, requested Pilate to allow him bury the body of Jesus.
- He hurried to wrap Jesus' body in linen and lay him in a tomb that had never been used. This was in fulfilment of Isaiah's prophecy concerning the suffering servant of Yahweh who was buried in a rich man's tomb.
- Joseph hurried to bury Jesus because it was the eve of the Sabbath.
- The women who had accompanied Jesus from Galilee followed Joseph and saw the tomb where Jesus's body was laid.
- They went back home to prepare spices and perfumes which they hoped to use to treat Jesus' body after the Sabbath, in obedience to Sabbath observance.

By giving Jesus an honourable burial, he confirmed that Jesus was the Son of God and King of the Jews.

Give the ways in which Jesus prepared his disciples for his death.
- He talked about it in advance in the temple.
- He called and assigned them duties.
- He trained the disciples for the future roles in spreading the gospel.
- He appointed Peter to take over Jesus ministry and leadership.
- He promised them the Holy Spirit.
- He had the Last Supper with them in which he pointed out that one of them was to betray him.

What roles do Christians play in a burial ceremony?
- They read scriptures/the Bible.
- They officiate the burial ceremony.
- They sing gospel songs or relevant hymns.

- They preach about death and God's Kingdom.
- They provide counsel and hope to bereaved members.
- They give company, console the bereaved family.
- They participate in the reception and serving visitors.
- They offer prayers for the bereaved and the deceased.
- They provide burial necessities e.g. casket, food, attire.

How is Christian persecution carried out today?
- Their message may be rejected.
- They are arrested and put in custody.
- Christian are scorned upon by non- believers.
- They are harassed by political systems.
- They face opposition from other religious.
- They are beaten up by rival groups and undergo physical torture.
- They may be denied public audience.

THE RESURRECTION (Luke 24: 1 – 49)

a) Witnesses to the Resurrection
- The rising of Jesus from the dead is referred to as the resurrection. This took place on the third day after His death.
- Witnesses to the risen Christ include the holy women, the disciples of Emmaus and Jesus' other disciples and apostles.

Testimony of the Holy Women (Luke 24: 1 – 12)
- On the first day of the week, early at dawn, Mary Magdalene, Salome and Mary mother of James, Joanna and the other women went to the tomb to prepare Jesus' body.
- They found the stone rolled away from the tomb.
- They went into the tomb but they did not find Jesus' body.
- Two angels appeared and informed them that Jesus had risen in line with what he had taught.
- They went and informed the eleven disciples about the resurrection.
- However, the disciples did not believe them.
- But Peter got up and ran to the tomb and confirmed that it was empty.
- As he was looking in, he saw the linen clothes by himself.
- He went home wondering what had happened.

The Disciples on the Way to Emmaus (Luke 24: 13 – 32)
- On the same day, two of the disciples were going to a village called Emmaus.
- They were talking about Jesus' suffering, his death and the empty tomb.
- As they were talking, Jesus joined them but they did not recognize him.

- Jesus asked them what had happened that they were talking about.
- They told him what had happened to Jesus of Nazareth, how the holy women had found the tomb empty.
- They also told him the angel's message to the holy women about Jesus' resurrection.
- Jesus then explained to them the scriptures which say that the messiah had suffered to reach his glory.
- They invited Jesus to dine with them.
- While they were at the table, Jesus took bread, said blessings and broke it and handed it over to them.
- At this point they recognized Jesus but the He vanished out of their sight.
- After this, they went to the eleven apostles in Jerusalem to testify about their encounter with the risen Lord.
- They told them all that happened on the road to Emmaus and how they had recognized Jesus at the breaking of the bread.

Appearance to the disciples (Luke 24: 33 – 49)
- As the disciples of Emmaus narrated their encounter with Jesus to the apostles, they were also told that Jesus had appeared to Simon.
- As they were still talking, Jesus appeared to them.
- The apostles were frightened and thought that they had seen a ghost.
- However, Jesus invited them to examine and touch his hands and feet which had the marks of the nails.
- He asked them for food and they gave him fish which he ate.
- Jesus then commissioned his disciples to preach the gospel to all nations but asked them to wait for the Holy Spirit first.

Give reasons why Jesus appeared to his disciples after his resurrection.
- To prove to them the power of God.
- To make them realize and understand the fulfilment of Old Testament prophecies.
- To comfort and bless them.
- To prove that He was alive.
- To prove the prophecies that on the third day Jesus would rise again.
- To promise them the Holy Spirit.
- To strengthen their faith.
- To enable them understand His mission.
- To commission them to be sis witnesses and continue his work of preaching, repentance and forgiveness of sin.

Give evidence to show that Jesus resurrected
- The testimony of the holy women.
- The appearance of Jesus to the two disciples on their way to Emmaus.
- His appearance to the disciples.
- Peter's testimony on the day of Pentecost.
- The empty tomb.

- The confirmation by the angel to the holy women.
- Jesus ascension as witnessed by the disciples.

b) JESUS ASCENSION TO HEAVEN (Luke 24: 50 – 53)

Ascension is derived from the word ascend which means going up. For Christians, this means the passing from the earth to heaven.

- Jesus then led His disciples to Bethany.
- He lifted up his hands and blessed them.
- As he blessed the disciples, He departed and was taken to heaven.
- The disciples returned to Jerusalem with joy and stayed in the temple praising God.

The disciples were joyful and thanked God because their blindness and disbelief had been overcome. The redemption of humankind had been accomplished.

Significance of passion, death and the resurrection of Jesus to daily Christian life

- Through the suffering, death and resurrection, humankind is saved from sin.
- There's hope of life after death, which is seen through the resurrection of Jesus.
- The resurrection of Jesus and the sending of the Holy Spirit gave rise to Christianity, the universal religion.
- Through His resurrection, Jesus was glorified and became Lord and Christ.
- It makes Christians have the courage to face persecution in their ministry.
- The death and resurrection of Jesus reconciled human beings to God.
- Through His ascension, Christians are assured that Jesus will come again as Lord and Christ.
- The resurrection of Jesus is a sign of victory over sin and death.
- Christians have hope for eternal life in Christ.

Topic 19: THE GIFTS OF THE HOLY SPIRIT

PETER'S MESSAGE ON THE DAY OF PENTECOST (Acts 2: 1 – 40)

Meaning of Pentecost

- Pentecost was one of the Jewish yearly festivals.
- It was the day that the Jews commemorated God's giving of the Law of Moses on Mt. Sinai.
- The Feast of Pentecost took place exactly 50 days after the Passover festival and it was also referred to as the Feast of Weeks.
- It was celebrated at the end of the harvest to thank God for granting them a good harvest and the Israelites offered their first fruits to the Lord.
- During Pentecost, all the Jews, those living in Palestine and those in diaspora, went to Jerusalem to celebrate the festival.
- It is during the Day of Pentecost that the disciples received the Holy Spirit.

Events that took place on the day of Pentecost

- The disciples of Jesus were all gathered in a room for prayer.
- A sound came from heaven suddenly like a rush of a mighty wind and filled the house in which the disciples were.
- The Holy Spirit descended in form of tongues of fire and rested on the heads of each of the disciples.
- Filled with the Holy Spirit, the apostles began to speak in different tongues.
- Each one of the visitors gathered there was able to hear the disciples in their own native language.
- However, while some of the people were amazed at what was happening, others accused the disciples of being drunk.
- Peter, full of the Holy Spirit, took his leadership role and courageously explained to the crowd what was happening.
- He explained that the disciples were not drunk as it was still very early in the morning, but were filled with the Holy Spirit.
- The people were moved by Peter's speech and they asked what they were to do to escape God's judgement.
- Peter invited them to repent and be baptized in the name of Jesus for the forgiveness of sins.
- About 3000 people accepted Peter's message and were baptized on this day.

*This marked the birth of Christianity.

Peter's message

After the disciples were accused of being drunk, Peter defended them and explained that:

- The disciples were not drunk as the crowds thought, but they were filled with the Holy Spirit of God which is His gift to them.

- He said that they were filled by the Holy Spirit as a fulfilment of Prophet Joel's message of what would take place in the last days.
- Jesus was made the Lord and Christ and this was seen in his great works and ministry.
- He said that Jesus of Nazareth is the son of God.
- He told them that Jesus was from Jerusalem.
- The suffering, death and resurrection of Jesus happened according to the plan of God.
- The death, resurrection and ascension of Jesus was real and that they were living witnesses to it.
- God had raised Jesus from the dead and he's seated at the right hand-side of God.
- The great King prophesied by Prophet Nathan to David who would rule with justice was Jesus Christ.
- That Jesus brought life and salvation and so they needed to turn from their evil ways in order to receive it.

Importance of Pentecost to Christians
- Peter's bold preaching is a challenge to Christians to continue the preaching God's word.
- Speaking in tongues signifies the multiplicity and variety of people, which means that Christianity is a universal religion.
- Pentecost affirms the significance of vernacular as the best means through which the gospel should be spread. It explains the importance of bible translations into vernacular languages.
- The Holy Spirit is given to anyone provided that he/she is a believer.
- Like Peter, Christians should witness to others what Jesus has done to prove that he is Lord.
- Pentecost day assures Christians that God keeps his promises.

Give ways in which the Holy Spirit manifested himself on the day of Pentecost.
- The Holy Spirit manifested himself in form of a mighty wind.
- It manifested in the form of tongues of fire.
- The disciples spoke on behalf of the community of believers.
- It enabled Peter to remember the Old Testament scripture (Joel's prophecy).
- The Holy Spirit convicted the listeners of their sins.
- It enabled the listeners to repent and be baptized.
- It enabled the apostles to recall what Jesus had taught them.

Identify the leadership qualities portrayed by Peter on the day of Pentecost, which can be learnt by Modern church leaders.
- Christian leaders should be courageous like Peter.
- They should be principled decision makers.

- They should have the ability to protect and defend their colleagues.
- They should be focused and committed.
- They should be authoritative like Peter.
- They should be knowledgeable of the scriptures like Peter.
- They should be God fearing and faithful to God.
- They should eloquent speakers and charismatic.

THE TEACHING OF JESUS ON THE ROLE OF THE HOLY SPIRIT (John 14:15 – 26; 16: 5 – 15; ACTS 1: 7 – 8)

In his ministry, Jesus taught that the roles of the Holy Spirit include the following:

- The Holy Spirit will be a counsellor to Christians who would advise and guide them on worldly and spiritual matters.
- He will reveal and teach the disciples all that they need to know concerning Jesus.
- He will ensure believers speak and live for truth.
- He will remind disciples everything that Jesus taught.
- The Holy Spirit will convict people of their sins by working in their conscience and so enable them to see the need for salvation.
- He will be a companion to the disciples in their entire mission.
- He will strengthen the faith of the disciples and give them courage to face persecution.
- The Holy Spirit will enable believers to be witnesses of Jesus all over the world.
- The Holy Spirit glorifies the name of Jesus through what he enables the believers to do.
- The Holy Spirit enables believers to perform miracles and prophesy the truth about God.
- He will give the disciples wisdom to discern and expose the secret hearts sinful people.
- He will enable the disciples to predict future events.

What is the work of the Holy Spirit in the church today?

- To strengthen the Christian faith.
- It bestows various gifts on Christians.
- It gives believers guidance when making decisions on various church matters.
- It helps believers pray.
- It gives the Christian the ability to perform miracles.
- It gives believers boldness to witness to the risen Christ.
- It helps the church expand and grow all over the world.

THE GIFTS OF THE HOLY SPIRIT (1 Corinthians 12, 13, 14)

Spiritual gifts are special powers, abilities, and talents to carry out special tasks given by God to Christians to be used for the service of others and one's personal benefit. They include:

- **The gift of wisdom** – This enables Christians to make right judgments and decisions.

- **The gift of knowledge** – This enables believers to get a revelation that is hidden from others. It also enables one to understand issues which cannot be comprehended by others.
- **The gift of faith** – This is undivided trust or unquestioned confidence in God. It is different from the faith you receive after acknowledging God. This gift enables one to believe that all things are possible with God.
- **The gift of healing** – This is a gift of enabling one to heal many kinds of sicknesses. It determines the time and kind of healing to be given.
- **The gift of performing miracles** – this is the gift of performing all kinds of extra-ordinary acts including healing in Jesus' name.
- **The gift of prophecy** – It enables Christians to interpret and foretell future happenings.
- **The gift of discernment** – This enables believers to distinguish between the Holy Spirit and evil spirits.
- **The gift of speaking in tongues** – This gift enables one to speak in other languages as the Spirit gives them utterance. The language is foreign even to the speaker.

Saint Paul explained that all the spiritual gifts are from the same Holy Spirit and are important. He explained that all the gifts of the Holy Spirit should be demonstrated with love. He stressed that love as a fruit of Holy Spirit, is supreme over all other spiritual gifts possessed by Christians.

He explained that love is the greatest spiritual gift and possesses the following characteristics:

- Love is patient and kind.
- Love is not jealous or boastful.
- It is not arrogant or rude, hence it is not ill-mannered or selfish.
- Love does not insist on its own way.
- It is not irritable or resentful.
- Love is not disrespectful in dealing.
- It does not rejoice at wrong but rejoices in the truth.
- Love bears all things, hopes all things, and endures all things.
- Love is eternal/never ends.

Comparison between Prophecy and Tongues

After demonstrating the supremacy of love over other spiritual gifts, Paul advised that if love is remained their principal goal, Christians should strive for other spiritual gifts but should realize that the gift of prophecy is more desirable than tongues. This is so because:

- Speaking in tongues is impossible to understand to those who are not able to interpret the tongues.

- Tongues are used to address God and so whoever speaks in tongues only benefits himself/herself unless s/he interprets to the others.
- Prophecy on the other hand is easy to understand and hence it benefits other Christians by strengthening and encouraging them in their lives. A prophet's message may touch a sinner who may repent and turn back to God.
- Therefore, while speaking in tongues contributes to the development of the individual, prophecy contributes to the common good of the church.
- Paul therefore advised that the person who speaks in tongues should pray for the power to interpret God's message that other Christians present can benefit from the experience.
- This is because lack of interpretation could lead the non-Christians judging those who speak in tongues as mad since the language sounds unintelligible.

How to use spiritual gifts

Paul provided practical regulations for the use of spiritual gifts, so that they can be exercised in an orderly manner in order to contribute to the common good of the church. He instructed that:

- In any one meeting, not more than two or three people may speak in tongues.
- Those who speak in tongues should do so one after the other, and not at the same time.
- Then person who has the gift of interpretation should explain the message to the congregation.
- If there is no interpreter available, the person with the gift of tongues should not speak to the assembly and if s/he must speak, s/she should do so in private.
- On prophecy, only two or three prophets should speak in the same meeting.
- The other members should listen and assess the message in the prophecy.
- If any other person in the congregation receives a revelation, s/he should be given a chance to speak to the congregation as the other listen.
- Prophets should speak one at a time and in an orderly manner for the purpose of instructing and encouraging all those present.
- Paul stressed that everything must be done decently and in an orderly manner during worship, since God is a God of order and not disorder.

State the ways in which Christians use the gift of wisdom in their daily lives.

- In making their day-to-day decisions.
- In handling leadership in the church.
- When arbitrating between two parties in controversial issues.
- In making difficult choices in their lives.
- In handling the church's financial matters.
- In preaching the word of God.
- In understanding and interpreting God's message.
- In guiding other Christians on spiritual matters.

- When choosing leaders.
- When praying so as to be able to pray wisely.

Give Paul's teaching on the importance of the gifts of the Holy Spirit.

- All gifts come from the same Holy Spirit and the same God.
- All the spiritual gifts serve the same God.
- All gifts are used for the benefit of the community.
- Their respective values have to be judged.
- Love is the greatest of all gifts.
- Spiritual gifts help Christians distinguish good from evil and live righteous lives.
- They are used to glorify God.
- They are used for instructing and encouraging the church.

THE CRITERIA FOR DISCERNING THE GIFTS OF THE HOLY SPIRIT (1 Corinthians 12: 1 – 3; Matthew 7: 15 – 20; Galatians 5: 16 – 26)

This is the way in which one is able to differentiate those gifts that come from the Holy Spirit and those that do not.

Saint Paul gave some guidelines on how one would be able to identify the source of the spiritual gifts and they include the following:

- One with the gifts of the Holy Spirit recognizes Jesus as the Lord and saviour.
- A person filled with the Holy Spirit will bear the fruit of the Spirit e.g. love, joy, peace, patience e.t.c.
- Those filled with the Holy Spirit will live and act according to the teachings of Jesus.
- A person filled by the Holy Spirit does not condone the desires of the flesh e.g. sexual immorality, idolatry, sorcery jealousy, selfishness e.t.c.
- They live a life of honesty and sincerity and accept the demands of the spirit.
- A true prophet speaks the truth and calls sinners to repentance to avoid God's judgement.

THE FRUITS OF THE HOLY SPIRIT (Galatians 5: 16 – 26)

St. Paul taught about other gifts that last e.g. faith, hope, and love, but the greatest of the gifts is love.

- He said that faith and love are the guiding principles of the new life of Christians.
- Those who have faith in Jesus do not need the Law of Moses to justify them.
- Those who live by the spirit through faith in Christ produce the fruits of the spirit which are:
a) **Love** – This is the affection towards another person regardless of sex, race or religion.
b) **Kindness** – This is showing mercy and care for the needy.
c) **Patience** – This is waiting upon God as much as He may take long to answer prayers. We must not give up even when the circumstances are discouraging.

d) **Goodness** – This is leading life that can be of value to others, like reaching to those who do not know God.

e) **Self-control** – this is being disciplined and having strong control over one's actions. Christians should strive for righteousness even if they are under force to do wrong.

f) **Peace** – it is where people live harmoniously with others and strive at all times to be calm in all situations.

g) **Faithfulness** – it means trusting and believing in God. Christians should not be hypocrites before other people.

h) **Gentleness** – This is the ability to be moderate in all situations. Christians should not be violent or cause violence.

i) **Joy** – This is a state of being happy which is sourced from salvation. Christians are expected to share their joy with others.

MANIFESTATIONS OF THE GIFTS OF THE HOLY SPIRIT IN THE CHURCH TODAY (Galatians 5: 16 – 26)

The gifts of the Holy Spirit are seen among believers in different ways today.

Show the Manifestation of the Holy Spirit in the church today (Galatians 5: 16 – 26).

- Speaking in tongues is manifested in most Pentecostal churches of today. It enables Christians to communicate to God intimately.
- The gift of love enables Christians of today to show compassion to the less privileged.
- The gift of prophecy has enabled Christians to tell the people what God intends to do.
- Prophecy helps Christians give warnings to the people to change from their evil ways and turn to God.
- The gift of healing is witnessed in church today whereby various diseases are being cured.
- The gift of wisdom and knowledge is seen when making right decisions and enable people in the congregation to develop a sense of conscience.
- The gift of distinguishing spirits is emphasized to avoid the manifestation of false spirits and also be able to tell those who go to church with evil intentions.
- The gift of faith gives Christians the courage to condemn evils in the society and be ready to endure persecution for the sake of the gospel.
- The gift of distinguishing spirits helps Christians to differentiate between the Holy Spirit and evil spirits.

How can Christians prove that they possess the Holy Spirit?

- By recognizing Jesus as their personal Saviour.
- They should not condemn Jesus.
- They should bear the fruits of the Holy Spirit in their lives.

- They should be trustworthy and righteous in their lives.
- They should help in the growth of the church.
- They should lead pure lives and be good examples to others.
- They should possess the gifts of love which is the greatest of all.

How are spiritual gifts misused in churches today?
- Those who have the gift of speaking in tongues and that of prophecy develop pride.
- Those with the gift of healing misuse it for material gain by demanding payment.
- Those who believe in faith-healing stop members from seeking medical treatment.
- Some Christians pretend to have a certain gift so that they may be recognized as full members of a particular church.
- Misunderstanding of how spiritual gifts should be used in the church has led to division and creation of splinter groups.
- Some misuse the gift of prophecy to prophesy false messages.
- Some Christians misuse the gifts of the Holy Spirit to compete for followers.

Topic 20: UNITY OF BELIEVERS

Unity is the idea of bringing people together.

Unity of believers therefore refers to the oneness of Christians who have faith in Jesus Christ as their saviour and have surrendered their lives to him.

In the New Testament, those who believe in Jesus Christ as their saviour are referred to by various titles e.g.

- Christians
- Disciples
- People who belonged to the way.
- The faithful
- Brethren.
- The church
- The saints.

St. Paul stressed on the unity of believers because they come from different social and cultural backgrounds hence it was necessary for them to learn how to accommodate and tolerate one another.

The early Christians in Jerusalem saw themselves as an assembly of the Lord and demonstrated their unity by:

- Praying together.
- Sharing the Eucharist/Lord's Supper
- Sharing their possessions.

- Meeting to receive the apostolic teachings.
- Sharing meals.

The unity of believers can be compared to how people from different backgrounds are united in a country for a common good e.g. Kenyans are united by factors such as:
- The National language.
- Education
- The constitution.
- One government.
- Games and sports.
- National symbols such as coat of arms, national flag.

In the New Testament, the concept of unity of believers is demonstrated using various images/symbols
- The People of God.
- The Body of Christ.
- The Vine and the Branches.
- The Church
- The Bride.

a) THE PEOPLE OF GOD (1 Peter 2:9-10)
In the Old Testament, the Israelites were united by factors such as:
- The covenant between God and Abraham.
- The leadership of Moses during the Exodus.
- The Ten Commandments.
- The Promised Land.
- The circumcision rite.
- The prophets.
- The kings.
God had promised that he would make the Israelites his people and he would be their God.

In the New Testament, the perception of the People of God is different. The people of God are not just descendants of Abraham, but those who follow Jesus and his teachings.
In 1 Peter 2: 9 – 10, the people of God are:
- They believe in God and lead a life of worshipping God.
- Are a chosen race so that they proclaim God's wonderful works to the world.
- They are a royal priesthood and serve the greatest God.
- They are a holy nation living exemplary or righteous lives.
- They belong to God and are God's own people.
- They were called from darkness to light.
- They were once not a people, but now are God's people, a people of the covenant.

- They are led by the mercies of God and have received God's grace.

b) THE BODY OF CHRIST (1 Corinthians 12: 12 – 27; Ephesians 4: 1 – 12)

St. Paul described the unity of believers using the symbol of the human body to explain the importance of all who belong to the church. He taught that:

- Jesus is the head of the church.
- The Christians/believers form the many body parts.
- The church like the human body has many parts that function for the good of the whole body.
- They all need to work together for the well-being of the church.
- All parts are interdependent and one part cannot do without the other.
- As the body of Christ, the church has many members from different backgrounds but all have been united through baptism in one spirit.
- Different church members have different spiritual gifts that are used for God's work.
- Members of the church should be united in Christ for the prosperity of the church.

Saint Paul further lists the elements of unity centred on the Trinity of God that should exist among the believers. These are:

- One body which is the universal church.
- One spirit that dwells in the church.
- One Lord, Jesus Christ, the head of the church.
- One faith in the Lord Jesus.
- One baptism.
- One God and Father of all believers.

c) THE VINE AND THE BRANCHES (John 15: 1 – 10)

- In the New Testament, Jesus is the vine planted by God and God is the vine dresser.
- The Christians are the branches of the vine tree.
- The Christians/believers are encouraged to bear much fruit by remaining faithful in Christ.
- The unfaithful Christians will be pruned and burnt just like the dead branches are pruned and burnt.
- Christians are to remain faithful and united in Christ so that whatever requests they make will be granted.
- Christians are also expected to obey God's commandments just as Christ was obedient to his Father.
- Christians have to show that they belong to Christ by loving one another just as Christ loved the church.

d) THE CHURCH/THE ASSEMBLY OF GOD (Ephesians 5:21-32)

Paul discusses the unity of the church by using the theme of marriage. He teaches that:

- Just as the husband and a wife come together from different backgrounds, so do members of the church.
- Christians must live in harmony with one another.

- Jesus Christ is the head of the church just as the husband is the head of the home.
- Just as wives are subject to their husbands, Christians should be subject to Christ, their Lord.
- Just as the husbands love their wives, so did Christ love the church and gave his life for her.
- The union between the church and Christ is supposed to last just as a marriage is meant to be a lifelong union.

e) THE BRIDE (Revelation 21:1-12;2 Corinthians 11:2)

- In the New Testament, Christians are the bride or the New Jerusalem, married to Christ.
- Christ is the bridegroom who seeks his bride.
- The bride is God's own choice.
- Christians as the bride should remain pure and not be corrupted in sin.
- God's relationship with Christians is perfect and will last eternally.
- Christians should prepare themselves to receive Christ who will return for his bride, the church.
- Christians' patience as they wait for Christ, the bridegroom will not be in vain because shall wipe every tear from their eyes and there will be no death or pain.

Ways in which the church today demonstrates the New Testament teaching on unity

- Praying and worshipping together.
- Correcting each other in love.
- Helping the needy amongst them.
- Visiting each other in homes.
- They observe a day of worship to honour God.
- They share the Holy Communion/meals.
- They solve problems affecting the church members.
- They cooperate by providing Christian programmes in the mass media/resource materials.
- They speak in one voice to condemn evil in society.

THE CAUSES OF DISUNITY IN THE EARLY CHURCH AND SOLUTIONS OFFERED (1 Corinthians 1: 4 – 21)

- **Church leadership**: Disputes arose on who was the leader of the church amongst Paul, Peter and Apollos. Paul emphasized on the unity of the church through Jesus. He dismissed the argument regarding human leader as their leader because the focal point was Jesus who had died for all. He said the church is led by the Holy Spirit.
- **Eating meat offered to idols**: Believers who were strong in faith ate food offered to idols arguing that the idols were powerless. The weak believers argued that these meals made those who ate them impure. Paul advised those who are strong in faith should stop eating meat offered to idols for the sake of the weak ones so as not to lead them astray.

- **Misuse of spiritual gifts**: Some Christians boasted over the gift of speaking in tongues as being more important than gifts. Paul taught them that all gifts are given by God for the good of all. He emphasized on the need for love which is the greatest of all.
- **Sexual immorality**: Christians in Corinth had become more immoral than non-Christians even to the extent of committing incest. Paul advised them to excommunicate such people from the church.
- **Dispute over marriage:** Some believers avoided marriage because they expected the second coming of Jesus soon. Paul taught that people should live in a state they thought they could serve God better. He discouraged divorce unless the marriage between a believer and non-believer becomes unbearable.
- **Abuse of the Lord's Supper:** The original meaning of the Lord's Supper had been forgotten. The Christians grouped themselves according to their status in the society. The rich ate and drank while the poor watched with embarrassment. Paul asked the rich to eat and drink at home before having the Lord's Supper in order to avoid greed. He reminded them its meaning, which is, sharing in remembrance of Jesus.
- **Misunderstanding of the resurrection of the body**: Some Christians believed in the resurrection of the body after death while others doubted it. Paul reminded them that resurrection is real and that Jesus was a living proof and he even appeared to his disciples.
- **Dispute over covering of the head during worship**: Some women had stopped pactising the traditional way of covering their heads during worship while others maintained it. Paul reminded them of the requirement for women to cover their heads during worship and men were advised to keep their hair short. He advised both genders to be decently dressed as an honour to Christ, the head of the church.
- **Christians settling disputes in courts** – Christians in Corinth were taking one another to courts of law to settle disputes. However, these were pagan courts hence incompetent to handle disputes arising from Christian issues. Paul told them that it was wrong for them to take their disputes to be solved by pagans. He advised them to solve problems peacefully because they are empowered to judge the world.

State the reasons why the use of the gifts of the Holy Spirit brought disunity in the church at Corinth.
- There was competition in speaking in tongues.
- There was disorder and confusion in worship as people with different gifts tried to outdo one another.
- People did not use their gifts for the benefit of the church and one another.
- Some gifts such as prophecy were looked down upon, hence there was pride and boasting.
- There was no interpretation of tongues when the gift of speaking in tongues was in use, hence messages were not understood.

- People did not show love for one another.
- Those with the gift of speaking in tongues despised those who did not have/some members thought they were too spiritual.

Give and explain the causes of disunity in Kenyan church today

- Leadership roles - Some churches do not allow women to take leadership positions. This marginalizes the women who are denied a chance to exercise their roles.
- The Lord's Supper or the Holy Communion is conducted differently, with each church having their own practice.
- Formation of splinter groups - These are smaller groups who break away from the main church. It may be as a result of different opinions.
- Baptism - Some churches baptise by complete immersion of the person being baptized in water while others baptize by sprinkling.
- Doctrinal differences whereby some issues are interpreted differently. For example the gifts of the Holy Spirit and salvation are not emphasized in all churches.
- Leadership - Some church leaders feel superior to others and so want to be recognized. If they are not, they break away from the church.

State the factors that contribute towards Christian unity.

- Believing in Jesus Christ.
- All are guided the same Holy Spirit of God.
- They have received the same baptism.
- Dependency on one another for spiritual nourishment.
- Participation in the Holy Communion.
- All Christians have a common goal and destiny i.e. Kingdom of God.
- Teachings of Jesus about love.
- Use of the Bible as God's word.
- Fellowshipping together.

Why is unity still important to the Kenyan churches?

- This ensures that the teaching of Jesus is followed.
- To promote the oneness of Christ.
- To share natural and artificial resources given to us by God.
- To fulfil the needs of evangelism.
- To reduce religious conflicts.
- To avoid many issues that may cause disunity experienced in Christian service today.

Identify the instances when the unity of believers becomes threatened in Kenya today.

- During political elections when church members support different candidates.

- During constitution making when members hold different views.
- Interpretation of various doctrines e.g. baptism and celibacy.
- When war breaks out that makes believers to be in opposing or enemy camps.
- Financial constraints that make various church denominations not extend help to other denominations.
- Limited vacancies in learning institutions or work places by various denominations.
- When Christians form tribal affiliations.

Give reasons why Christians should be in unity today.
- To effectively evangelize.
- To set a good example for others to follow/be role models.
- To prevent formation of splinter groups within the church.
- To take a common stand on matters affecting the society.
- To share resources equally.
- To promote oneness in Christ.
- To reduce internal fighting and wrangles.
- To emulate Christ who promoted unity of mankind through His teachings being for all nations.

Topic 21: INTRODUCTION TO CHRISTIAN ETHICS

Definition of terms
- **Ethics** is derived from the Greek word 'ethikos' which means custom or conduct. It is the systematic study of human actions to determine their rightness or wrongness.
- The word ethics is related to the term morals, both of which refer to human character and its inclination to behave in one way or another.
- Ethics therefore is the study of moral life.

The Basis of Christian Ethics
- The Bible – in making moral decisions, Christians are guided by God's revelation to them in the Bible.
- Integrity/Conscience – This is being responsible for whatever action a person takes. When one's conscience is right, his/her mind will not allow such a person to do something wrong. The vice versa is true.
- Christian community – Christian communities rely on the teachings of Jesus which they receive through their religious leaders.
- African traditional culture which was incorporated in Christianity – Some values which were stressed upon in African societies were carried on into Christianity e.g. respect and obedience.

- Government/Civil law – Every political government is guided by a constitution which stipulates various laws. Christians do follow these laws hence a guide to their behaviour.
- Christian Literature – Christians have written Christian articles and books which inspire and give moral guidance the Christian community.
- God's messengers – God talks to his servants in form of visions and dreams to give them his revelations.

Christian values that enhance creation of a just society

Christian moral values enhance the formation of a Christ-like character and the creation of a just society.

A just society is one where there is peace and harmony and people are governed by moral values and the rule of law.

Some Christian moral values include:

- Love – it refers to affection and tender devotion to something, and a deep concern for the welfare of others. It includes the virtues of mercy, loyalty and service.
- Honesty/reliability/faithfulness – honesty is to tell the truth and to carry out one's commitment without deceit. An honest person is reliable and can be trusted to carry out tasks with faithfulness.
- Justice/fairness – justice refers to being fair. It is observed in situations in which people are treated equally and without discrimination.
- Respect – it is the quality of recognizing other people's rights, status and circumstances. It includes self-respect and respect for others.
- Humility –It refers to accepting oneself with his/her strengths and weaknesses. A humble person is not proud or boastful of his/her achievements and uses his/her qualities to serve others. Humble people are sensitive to the feelings of others and do not hurt them deliberately.
- Perseverance – to persevere is to show determination and endurance in pursuing a good goal. A person who perseveres does not give up however challenging a situation or task may be.
- Chastity – it is the state of being pure physically, spiritually and mentally. It also implies having good sexual morals, avoiding sex before marriage and remaining faithful in marriage.

LIFE SKILLS

- These are abilities that help people to develop positive behaviour and also to effectively deal with the demands and challenges of everyday life.
- They assist people to deal with issues in a constructive and effective way and it also helps them to gain confidence in themselves, with other people and with the community.

Life skills are important since they help people to:

- Live positively and actively with themselves and with others.
- Practise healthy behaviour.
- Recognize and assess risky behaviour.
- Avoid risky situations and behaviour.
- Make informed choices and decisions.

Life skills include:

- Critical thinking – it is the ability to analyse and make value judgements about a situation. It enables one explore the possibilities of doing a task in more than one way.
- Creative thinking – it enables a person to come up with new ways or ideas of dealing with situations or issues. It requires one to be imaginative and original in their thinking.
- Decision making – it is the process of making up one's mind in order to reach a conclusion or resolution. It involves making a choice among several options.
- Self-esteem – it refers to how we respect and admire ourselves as individuals and the confidence we have. Self-esteem influences our actions towards others and our achievements in life.
- Assertiveness – it is a way of expressing one's feelings or desires openly. It is knowing what you want and why and the ability to take the necessary steps to achieve what you want.

Topic 22: CHRISTIAN APPROACHES TO HUMAN SEXUALITY, MARRIAGE AND FAMILY

- Human sexuality is the physical or physiological characteristics that make one a male or female.
- This is determined by the roles and cultural factors of an individual society.
- Sexuality is not sex, although sex is an integral component of sexuality.
- Human sexuality expresses itself in the way people behave, that is, their thinking, attitudes, feelings and appreciation of self, others and the world around.

Traditional African understanding of human sexuality

- Sex is regarded as sacred because it is a gift from God and also because it is a means through which life is transmitted.
- Sex is highly valued and so the elders offered sex education to the youth to avoid its misuse.
- During initiation the youth were taught that the function of sex was for procreation and so was to be practiced in marriage only.
- Virginity was highly valued among girls and those who lost it before marriage were either punished or disowned by their people.
- It was a taboo to talk about sex unless the forum was suitable.
- Taboos/rules were enforced to curb irresponsible sexual behaviours. This included discipline when one related with another person of the opposite gender.
- The societies also nurtured girls and boys to grow up knowing their roles. Girls were taught how to become responsible wives and mothers. Boys were taught how to become responsible husbands and fathers.
- Performance of duties or division of labour was defined in relation to one's sex. Women had their tasks clearly defined from those of men.

Explain and appreciate the Christian teaching on human sexuality

- Like in the African societies, sex in Christianity is holy and sacred because it is God-given.
- Human sexuality originates from the Biblical story of creation when God created man in his own image.
- Christian teachings show that men and women are equal before God. They have a common destiny in the Kingdom of God.
- Sex is mainly meant for procreation which is fulfilled in marriage. God allowed man to multiply and subdue the earth.

- Both men and women have complimentary roles which neither of the two can fulfil on his/her own. For example in child bearing the two need each other.
- Both the New and Old Testament emphasize responsible sexual behaviour.
- In the Old Testament, the Law of Moses stipulates regulations of sex whereby incest, sodomy e.t.c. were forbidden. Those who committed adultery were to be stoned to death.
- In the New Testament, Jesus forbade adultery by forbidding looking at a woman with lustful eyes.
- St. Paul in the New Testament forbids both pre-marital and extra-marital sex. He teaches that the body is the Temple of God and so the body should not be for immoral practices.
- Christianity values virginity by teaching the youth to abstain until marriage, Christians have the capacity to exercise self-control in order to save it for its main function which is fulfilled in marriage.

Traditional African practices related to male/female relationships
- The way in which male and female related with one another depended on age and taboos.
- Children imitated their parents with girls imitating their mothers and boys imitating their fathers.
- At a tender-age children are unaware of their sexuality and so the parents socialize them on who to become in future.
- At puberty the boys and girls become aware of their sexuality.
- Sex education is given at this stage to prepare them for marriage.
- In marriage, the couples are free to engage in sex both for procreation and companionship.
- The couple relates as a husband and wife.
- In old age the couple becomes less sexually active.
- They become the elders and are respected by the community.
- The elders become the decision-makers and chief-advisers.

Christian teaching on male/female relationship at various levels
The Christian view on male/female relationship is that men and women were created as equal human beings. Both were created in the image and likeness of God.
The Bible teaches that:
- Both man and woman have a common origin.
- Man was created from the soil and the woman was created from his flesh.
- Both man and woman are co-creators with God.
- Both man and woman are created to complement and be companions to one another.
- The two, male and female unite in marriage, which is meant to be a lasting union.
- The New Testament states that the man is the head of the family. A husband loves the wife who in turn submits to him.
- The Bible condemns all forms of immorality and people should respect their bodies as Temples of the Holy Spirit.
- Depending on a particular church, the roles of men and women vary. Some churches discourage women from taking leadership positions.

- Jesus recognizes leadership with women such as his mother Mary, the Samaritan woman, e.t.c.
- The emphasis on equality of both male and female is to maintain peace and love for each other.

RESPONSIBLE SEXUAL BEHAVIOUR
Christian teaching on responsible sexual behaviour
Responsible sexual behaviour refers to a healthy social relationship between people of different or the same gender at all ages, including those who are married. Christianity teaches the following on responsible sexual behaviour:
- Sex is only to be practised in the setting of marriage. It's for procreation and companionship.
- Sex therefore should not be practised outside marriage.
- St Paul teaches that to reduce immorality, each person should have their own partner and should not deny each other unless they want to pray.
- Paul continues to teach the need of respect for the marital bed hence discouraging adultery and Christians to uphold chastity.
- The Old Testament states that the woman was created to be man's companion. It therefore condemns same sex marriages.
- The Bible recognizes the need of discipline concerning sexual matters and control over sexual desires.
- Responsible sexual behaviour is one way of obeying God's law on sex.
- Our bodies being the Temple of the Holy Spirit, our sexual behaviour must be responsible to uphold respect and dignity.

The following are the guidelines that may help the boys and girls to lead responsible sexual behaviour:
i. Avoid physical contact such as kissing and hugging.
ii. Avoid conversations on topics that are sexually suggestive.
iii. Controlling your desires by dwelling on positive thoughts about your special friend.
iv. Avoid meeting in lonely and isolated places.
v. Avoid social functions e.g. discos and parties that may open room for sexual abuse.
vi. Avoid visiting each other frequently.
vii. Avoid all kinds of pornographic literature.
viii. Seek advice from Christian leaders and counsellors about your relationship.
ix. Study the Biblical teachings on sex.
x. Pray for God's guidance.

In what ways can the youth cope with their sexual emotions?
- Praying/studying God's word.
- Discussing sexual matters with counsellor/parents.
- Engaging in wholesome recreational activities.
- Occupying themselves with household chores.
- Keeping away from opposite sex until ready for marriage.
- Avoiding pornography or any place that intensify sexual emotion

- Engaging in educational activities.
- Avoiding heavy petting and hugging with opposite sex.

Christian teaching on irresponsible sexual behaviour and their effects

Irresponsible sexual behaviour refers to the perversion, misuse and abuse of sex. Some acts of irresponsible sexual behaviour include incest, rape, fornication, adultery, homosexuality, prostitution, concubinage, masturbation, bestiality, trial marriage, child marriage.

a) **Incest -** This is having sexual relationships among or between blood relatives.
- Lev 18: 6 – 18 forbids sex between relatives and refers to it as disgrace against God.
- In 1 Cor 5:1-5- St Paul condemns incest and provides for the excommunication of such a person.
- Gen 19: 30-36 and 2 Samuel 13:12-21 give examples of incestuous practices which were condemned at the time.
- Incest is a defilement of the body which is the Temple of the Holy Spirit.

Consequences of the incest
- Family conflict and psychological trauma to the victims.
- It lowers human dignity of the victims.
- The children born out of such relations may have genetic complications.
- May lead to pregnancy and sometimes abortion.
- The victims may be infected with sexually transmitted diseases and HIV/AIDS.
- It may lead to pregnancy and abortions.
- It destroys family relationships and leads to divorce.

b) **Rape -** This is forceful sex without the consent of one of the partners. It is a form of sexual violence. It is a crime committed on women, girls, boys and even men.
- Sex is sacred and so rape is a misuse of sex and against God's teaching because it does not fulfil the law of love.
- Like other irresponsible sexual behaviours, rape is a perversion.
- The church condemns rape as both a crime and sin.

Consequences
- It lowers the dignity of the victim.
- It can lead to contraction of STIs and HIV/AIDS.
- It causes physical and psychological trauma to the victim.
- It leads to fear and distrust of men in future.
- Can lead to the death of the victim or permanent disorder
- Can lead one into depression.
- May cause pregnancy, abortion hence deaths sometimes.
- It causes hatred between families of the perpetrator and the victim.

Explain the reasons that discourage victims of rape from reporting rape cases.
- They feel ashamed or shy to reveal it to other people.

- They fear the stigma associated with rape.
- Some fear to be abandoned by their partner especially married women.
- The authorities might be far from reach.
- Some are ignorant of their rights/they might not know whom/how to report the cases.
- Laxity in punishing sexual offenders e.g. rape cases take long.
- Rape is agonizing/traumatizing therefore the victims feel depressed/withdrawn and they will not want to talk about it.
- Families may discourage it especially if a relative is involved.

c) **Fornication** - This is pre- marital sex.
The Bible teaches condemns sexual intercourse before marriage because it defiles the body which is the temple of the Holy Spirit.
Fornication may be caused by the following:
- Lack of self-control.
- Peer pressure.
- Lack of role models.
- Permissiveness in the society.
- Ignorance about human sexuality.
- Lack of firm Christian teachings.
- Unemployment/poverty.
- Drug and alcohol abuse.
- Influence from the media.
- Availability of contraceptives
- Drug and alcohol abuse.

Consequences
- It can lead to pregnancy outside marriage and abortion sometimes.
- Can cause guilty feelings because the practice is against the teachings of God.
- Can lead to unfaithfulness in marriage if the partner persists with the behaviour.
- Contraction of STIs and HIV/AIDS.
- Loss of self-respect and dignity.
- Early and forced marriages.

d) **Adultery** - This is extra-marital sex. It refers to illicit sexual intercourse between a man or woman who is married and someone else other than his/her marriage partner.
In traditional African communities, adultery was punished. The forms of punishment administered to an offender include:
- Whipping.
- Paying fines.
- They were divorced, especially the adulterous wife.
- One was cursed and excommunicated from the community.
- Loss of respect and leadership positions in society if he was an elder.
- The adulterer had part of his/her body mutilated.
- Stoning to death.

- Sent back to her parents for re-education on the importance of faithfulness in marriage.
- The adulterer was mocked and ridiculed in songs and dances.

In the Bible adultery is highly condemned:
- In Deut 2: 22 the bible states the stoning of those involved in adultery.
- Exodus 20: 14 states that people should not commit adultery. It is therefore a sin.
- Prov 5: 15 states that unfaithfulness is betrayal of the love between husband and wife.
- Jesus in Matt 5: 27 – 28 condemns adultery and advocates for purity in heart and mind.
- Adultery is punishable. 2 Sam 12: 15 – 19 gives an example of the punishment of King David.

Consequences:-
- Unplanned pregnancies which leads to abortion.
- Contraction of STIs and HIV/AIDS.
- It violates conjugal rights of the offended partner.
- It can lead to divorce and separation.
- Leads to mistrust between the couple.
- It may lead to violence e.g. the betrayed spouse may be bitter and start a fight which may result in injury and damage.
- It can lead to feelings of guilt and regrets by the unfaithful partner.
- It can lead to neglect of family responsibilities and sometimes abandoning one family to live with another man or woman.

e) **Prostitution (commercial sex work)** – refers to the offering of one's body for sexual purposes in return for money or other favours.

This may result due to:
- Poverty/unemployment
- Drug and alcohol abuse.
- Stress.
- Adventure/peer pressure.
- Rejection at home.
- Broken families/lack of role models.
- Uncontrolled sexual desires.
- Pornography on the media.

Consequences
- Can lead to break up of families.
- It lowers human dignity.
- It causes unplanned pregnancy leading to abortion.
- Contraction of STIs and HIV/AIDS.
- Large numbers of crimes are committed in areas where prostitution is rampant.
- Misuse of money to please a partner.
- It undermines the purpose of sex

f) **Homosexuality** – This is having sexual relations between people of the same gender. Sexual intercourse between men is referred to as sodomy. The same kind of sexual relationship between women is called lesbianism.
- Lev 20: 13 condemns sexual relations with another man.
- St. Paul in Romans 1 teaches that suppression of truth leads to perversion of which homosexuality is one.
- Paul condemns homosexuality and says it is incompatible with the teachings of God.
- It is a lack of Christian moral principles and a sin before God.

Consequences:
- It is a punishable sin.
- Lowers the dignity of the victims.
- Can lead to contraction of STIs and HIV/AIDS.
- Can cause psychological problems e.g. stress, depression and suicide thoughts.
- Can't lead to procreation.
- There's no fulfilment of sexual urge.

Give the reasons why the church in Kenya is opposed to same sex marriage.
- It is sinful.
- It undermines human dignity.
- It undermines the use of sex/procreation.
- It is against Biblical teachings.
- It is against the law of the Land.
- It is against the African culture.

g) **Abortion: -**This is the termination of pregnancy before it is due for birth. This is done to pregnancies which result after irresponsible sexual behaviours.

Effects include:
- Can lead to death
- Encourages irresponsible sexual behaviours.
- May cause barrenness.
- Causes shame and guilt to the victim.
- Can cause depression.

Reasons why the Christian church is opposed to abortion
- Abortion is murder which is against God's commandment (Exodus 20: 13).
- Life is sacred hence God alone has a right to take it.
- A human body is the temple of the Holy Spirit. Abortion interferes with the mother's body and destroys that of the victims.
- The victim risks death.
- It may result into barrenness.
- It leads to the feeling of guilt/depression/stress/bitterness to the victim/family.

h) **Divorce /separation:** Divorce is a permanent separation of married couples while separation is temporary. This may result from irresponsible sexual behaviour and other conflicts.

The causes of divorce among couples include:
- Unfaithfulness in marriage.
- Extreme poverty.
- Domestic violence.
- Misuse of family resources.
- Childlessness
- Interference from in-laws and members of the extended family.
- Religious differences between the spouses.
- Abuse of drugs and alcohol.

The Bible condemns divorce and emphasizes that marriage is a permanent union. Jesus taught that divorce is wrong and anybody who divorces his wife commits adultery.

Its effects include:-
- Single parenthood.
- Depression and suicide thoughts.
- Frustration and lack of security for children.
- Psychological problems to both parents and children.
- Divorcees may be tempted to turn to prostitution for example for economic needs and to satisfy their sexual desires.
- It may lead to abandonment of the church by the couple.
- If the woman remarries, the children from the previous marriage may experience rejection in the new home.

i) **Sexually Transmitted Infections (STIs) and Human Immuno-Deficiency Virus (HIV) and Acquired Immune Deficiency Syndrome (AIDS)**

The most common diseases that are sexually transmitted are Gonorrhoea, Syphilis and Acquired Immune Deficiency Syndrome (AIDS)

(i) Gonorrhoea

It is caused by bacteria called Neisseria gonorrhoea/gonococcus.

Symptoms

Signs show after seven days after intercourse with an infected person e.g.
  i. Feelings of discomfort inside the penis.
 ii. Pain when passing urine.
iii. Headache.
 iv. Severe pain in the lower abdomen for women.
  v. Frequent urination.
 vi. Fever.

Effects

- It leads to sterility in both men and women. Germs infect the fallopian tubes in women causing them to block.
- It can cause blindness in a new born baby if the mother was infected with the disease.
- It causes arthritis, which is an infection of the bones.
- Ectopic pregnancy due to narrowing of fallopian tubes as a result of scars formed after infection.

(ii) Syphilis

It is caused by bacteria which only survive in moist conditions e.g. in the vagina, urethra, anus, mouth and in sores.

Causes

- Sexual contact with an infected person.
- Kissing an infected person.

Symptoms

- A painless sore or pimple appears on the man's penis or woman's vulva and also under the tongue between 2 to 6 weeks after infection.
- A swelling of the glands in the groin.
- A feeling of being unwell.
- Appearance of rashes, sores and spots on the face, armpits, under the breast, mouth or throat.

Effects

- It leads to the infection of the liver.
- It causes the destruction of testicles.
- Paralysis due to infection of the spinal cord.
- It attacks the placenta and the foetus causing miscarriage, still birth, premature birth or the baby being born is infected with the disease if the mother is infected.
- Madness.
- Death of the victim.

(iii) HIV/AIDS

How is HIV/AIDS transmitted/spread?

- It is transmitted through sexual intercourse with an infected person.
- From an infected mother to her child while in the womb, during birth or while breast feeding.
- Blood transfusion from an infected person.
- HIV contaminated instruments used for cutting and piercing e.g. needles, razor blades and knives.

What are the symptoms of HIV/AIDS?
- Swelling of the glands in the neck, arm pit and groin.
- A feeling of tiredness lasting for weeks without apparent cause.
- Loss of appetite and weight.
- It causes fever, which may last for several weeks.
- Sweating at night.
- Diarrhoea lasting for weeks.
- Skin diseases.
- Growth of fungus in the mouth.
- Prolonged cough and shortness of breath.

What is the impact of HIV/AIDS?
- It leads to death of the victims hence increasing the number of orphans and bringing sorrow.
- It leads to increased medical expenses.
- The financial expenditure is high because of the need for drugs, balanced diet and frequent medical check-ups.
- It reduces population growth with an increase in the number of orphans.
- It leads to recurrent illness due to reduction in immunity.
- Loss of labour because the victim later on dies.
- Misery and stress on the family of the victims who later on die.
- Family structure changes with the orphans being left under the care of elder siblings or grandparents.

Mention the ways in which Christians can help people living with HIV/AIDS.
- To love and care for them.
- By guiding and counselling them on positive living.
- Treating them with dignity by not discriminating against them.
- Praying for them.
- Visiting them to give them hope, comfort and encouragement.
- Preaching the word of God to them for spiritual nourishment and repentance.
- Providing them with material support like food, shelter and clothing.
- Advocating for the protection of their rights as human beings.
- Providing job opportunities or income generating projects for them to support themselves.
- Providing adequate medical care for them in terms of medicine and paying hospital bills.
- Taking care of their children and or dependents where necessary.

Reasons why the church should participate in the fight against HIV/AIDS
- As a continuation of Jesus work of healing.

- As a duty to guide and counsel the society.
- As a duty to promote moral values in society.
- To cater for infected members in society.
- To cater for the affected members in society.
- To conserve or preserve God's creation.
- To help reduce human suffering.
- To promote economic development.
- To promote peace in the family/co-existence

MARRIAGE

- Marriage is an agreement between a man and a woman who decide to have a lasting relationship as husband and wife.
- Marriage is a union between a man and woman who have attained reasonable age and are willing to live together.
- The purpose of marriage is to establish a permanent relationship between husband and wife.

People marry for the following reasons:
- To express mutual love and comfort.
- To procreate and start a family by bringing up children.
- To enhance the unity of the couple and the families involved.
- To promote the social status of the couple.
- To provide happiness to the husband and wife.
- To experience personal fulfilment through sexual union.

TRADITIONAL AFRICAN UNDERSTANDING OF MARRIAGE

- The traditional African marriage is referred to as a customary marriage.
- Marriage is a union of a man to a woman or women, in which procreation is promoted.
- Marriage may be monogamous, polygamous or levirate.
- Marriage without procreation is incomplete since children have roles to play for example; promote social status of the parents, bind the family, source of labour and security to the family.
- Polygamy was valued because through it, the social status of the family is raised, gives opportunity of getting more children, and reduces unfaithfulness among others.
- Marriage extends kinships ties by including the parents, sisters and brother- in-laws.
- Marriage is a communal affair which involves communities of either side of the two partners.
- Marriage is a permanent agreement and must not be broken due to divorce or separation. It's binding.
- Marriage is a covenant relationship because it fulfils all the elements of a covenant.
- Marriage partners are not a personal choice rather they must be approved by members of the respective families.
- Dowry is mandatory which may be paid in form of livestock, honey, grain, beer etc.
- Marriage recognizes the husband as being superior to his wife who is expected to be submissive to him.

What is the importance of children in traditional African marriage?

- Children promote the social status of their parents since the more the children a man has the more the respect a man earned.
- Children provide a bond of unity between the husband and wife.
- They are a source of labour to the family, assisting with tasks such as cultivating the land, babysitting and household chores.
- They are a source of wealth e.g. daughters fetch a lot of bridewealth for their parents when they get married.
- Sons are heirs to the family's wealth.
- Children take care of their parents when they get old and have a duty to give them a decent burial.
- They are a source of security to the family.

Reasons why polygamy was allowed in the traditional African communities

- Polygamy raises the social status of the family.
- The husband can still get children from the other wives if the first wife was barren.
- It ensures that every woman has an opportunity to get married.
- It ensures that there is always someone around to help in times of need.
- It helps to prevent or reduce cases unfaithfulness especially on the part of the man.
- It contributes to effective family planning, particularly in the spacing of children.

Why is marriage considered as a covenant?

- It binds the husband and wife together.
- During the marriage ceremony the couple makes vows, promising to be loyal to each other.
- There are witnesses to the couple taking vows.
- There is a ceremony where people eat and share a meal as a sign of friendship and unity.
- There are obligations or conditions to be fulfilled by each party e.g. payment of bridewealth and bearing of children.
- Breaking of marriage vows has serious consequences on those who break the covenant.
- God and ancestors are invoked to bless and protect the marriage.

What is the significance bridewealth in traditional African marriages?

- It acts as compensation to the girl's family for the loss of her help and contribution in the homestead.
- It seals the marriage.
- Its acts as an appreciation of the girl by the man's family.
- It is a symbol of the girl's presence in her home.

- It cements the relationship and friendship between the families of the man and woman.
- It shows that the man is serious with his intention to marry.

CHRISTIAN TEACHING ON MARRIAGE
- Marriage is a divine institution ordained by God.
- Marriage is for procreation since God commanded Adam and Eve to multiply and fill the earth.
- It is meant for companionship.
- Marriage if for fulfilment of mutual love through mutual forgiveness, being faithful to one another, praying together, consulting one another in decision making and complementing each other in roles.
- Marriage is a remedy against sin since it provides people with the opportunity to express their sexuality and avoid premarital and extramarital sex, which are condemned in the bible.
- A Christian marriage should be monogamous, which was the original plan of God.
- Marriage should be permanent, since it is sacred and a life-long union.
- A Christian marriage is complete with or without children.

SECULAR APPROACHES TO MARRIAGE
- In the modern world, marriage is not given prominence as such since one has a choice either to marry or not to marry.
- Today it is common to find young people choosing to live together by following either the traditional African practice or Christian teachings.

The following are the changes that have taken place in marriage:
- Some people decide not to marry for personal or social reasons as opposed to the traditional African practice where marriage was compulsory.
- Today marriage is complete with or without children, unlike in the traditional African practice where procreation was the purpose for marriage.
- Today monogamy is practiced because of economic and religious reasons.
- In the modern practice of marriage, the husband and wife are equal partners in marriage unlike in the traditional practice in which the wife was subordinate.
- The choosing of a marriage partner today has become an individual affair unlike in the traditional practice where such was a collective affair.
- Today, payment of dowry has been commercialized and is negotiated in reference to factors such as the educational level of the girl and the kind of career/job she is pursuing, unlike in traditional practice in which value was attached to bride-wealth.
- In the traditional practice, qualities considered in a prospective bride and groom such as industrious, honesty, hospitality, kindness and health do not feature prominently in the

choice of a marriage partner today. Instead, external beauty, financial and social status are considered.

- In traditional African practice, once marriage has been formalized, it is extremely difficult to dissolve it unlike today where cases of divorce and separation have risen.
- Today many couples prefer few children due to economic and social factors as opposed to the traditional African practice in which many children were highly valued.
- Today inter-ethnic marriages are common because of migration and interaction in schools, colleges, work place and churches.

PREPARATION FOR MARRIAGE

a. Traditional African practice

- Preparation for marriage in the traditional African communities is a long process, with the key moments marked with rituals.
- It involves several processes such as choosing a marriage partner, betrothal and courtship, and the wedding.

i. Choosing a marriage partner

A marriage partner is chosen through the following ways:
- Chosen by the parents particularly from two families that have friendly relations.
- A partner himself chose the bride.
- Chosen through an intermediary who is a close or a trusted relative.
- A senior wife or first wife of the polygamist may choose a wife for her husband.
- Levirate marriage/widow inheritance where a widow who lost her husband is inherited by the husband's brother or a close relative.
- There are cases where a debtor gives his wife to a creditor in order to repay a debt.

The traditional qualities of a good wife and husband
Qualities of a good wife

Hardworking	Morally upright	Generous
Fertile	Kind	Warm-hearted
Faithful	Obedient	Welcoming to guests
Beautiful	Polite	Clean

Qualities of a good husband
- Able to provide good leadership for the family.
- Aggressive.
- Courageous/brave.
- Wise.
- Responsible.
- Good manager of property.

Betrothal and courtship
- Betrothal refers to the formal engagement between a boy and a girl.
- Courting means wooing with an intention to marry. Courtship is therefore the period between engagement and the time when the actual wedding ceremony takes place.
- The main objective of courtship is to make friendship.
- Courtship in traditional African society was initiated by the groom to be.

Reasons why courtship is important include:
- It helps the groom to identify a suitable marriage partner.
- The two families involved in the marriage negotiations establish a firm relationship.
- It enables the boy and girl to learn each other and their families.
- It helps the two to check out if they are related.
- It gives the two families time to negotiate and pay the bridewealth.
- Boys and girls are instructed on family life education where they are taught their duties and responsibilities.

Wedding ceremony
- A wedding ceremony varies from one community to another.
- The bride is brought to the groom's home, there is feasting and celebration.
- During this time, the couple is visited by relatives and friends from both sides.
- Part of the celebrations have a religious dimension as prayers are offered for the couple and God is called upon to bless them in all ways and especially with children.
- In some communities, the marriage ceremony involves some rites which are performed by an elder.
- During the ceremony, relatives gather together to witness the couple making promises and vows to one another.
- An elder then blesses the couple.

- Virginity is highly valued so if the girl is a virgin, great celebrations are carried out and this enhances the status of the girl's family.
- If the girl has lost her virginity, the marriage may be dissolved and this brings shame to her parents.

b. Christian preparation for marriage

- Preparation for marriage in the Christian context is based on the teachings of the Bible and the church.
- The youth in the various churches are taught how to grow in their faith, how to relate with the opposite sex, how to pray and study the Bible.
- Most preparations for marriage occur after a couple announces to the church authorities their intention to marry.
- The Christian preparation for marriage follows the stages such as choosing the partner, courtship, and marriage ceremony.

i. Choosing a marriage partner

The following are some of the guidelines the church gives on choosing a marriage partner:

i.   Commitment to one's faith – churches advise Christians to marry fellow Christians.
ii. Moral uprightness – young men and women are encouraged to study the character of a possible marriage partner. The partner should possess qualities such as kindness, politeness, reliability, hardwork, hospitality, trustworthy, responsibility, generosity, and integrity.
iii. Common interest – common interests deepens a relationship. When people differ in perception of issues can lead to unnecessary quarrels and tensions.
iv. Ability to provide for the family – the man and woman should show commitment in providing for the family in terms of leadership, shelter, food, clothing, education, healthcare and security for the marriage to be stable.
v.   Education – the level of education of a prospective partner should be considered so that there is no great disparity between the two.
vi. Management of family finances – it is important for the prospective marriage partners to understand the importance of being open and accountable in earning money, making decisions together on how to spend it.
vii. Health status – the prevalence of HIV/AIDS today has made it necessary for prospective partners to consider health status of their partners.

ii. Betrothal and courtship

- After betrothal, courtship starts and this period which may last a few months or a few years is important in the sense that it gives the couple time to study each other and make necessary preparations before the actual wedding.

The following are the guidelines on how the couple should relate during the courtship period:

- To remain chaste until the time they formally wed in church.
- To avoid visiting each other frequently.
- To be civil and friendly to those people they have known before.
- To avoid jealousy when one's special friend mixes with the opposite sex.
- To seek good and objective advice from those who are older and from church leaders.
- To commit themselves to prayer and the power of the Holy Spirit in their relationship.
- Seek advice on issues like number of children, spacing, and use of contraceptives e.t.c.

During the courtship period, the bride and groom to be agree on the date of the wedding.

Three weeks before the wedding ceremony, banns (public announcements) are made to ensure that there are no obstacles to the marriage taking place.

The wedding ceremony

- The Christian wedding ceremony takes place in a church building.
- The wedding is presided over by an ordained clergy such as a priest or pastor.
- On the wedding day the bride is escorted by her parents and relatives and is officially handed over to the groom and his relatives.
- During the ceremony, hymns are sung, relevant Bible passages are read and the sermon delivered by the presiding priest/pastor.
- The couple exchanges vows in which they promise to be loyal and faithful to each other and to live together permanently.
- The couple also sign a marriage certificate to signify their commitment to each other.
- After the ceremony in church, the couple hosts a reception for invited guests and relatives, where there is feasting and merry making.
- The groom and the bride receive gifts from parents, relatives and friends.
- Afterwards, the couple may go on honeymoon or move to their home immediately to begin their married life.

CELIBACY AS AN ALTERNATIVE TO MARRIAGE

- Celibacy means the unmarried state.
- It is commonly used to refer to the unmarried state for religious reasons such as taking vows as a nun, monk, priest or bishop who take vows of chastity.
- The practice of celibacy is derived from the scriptures and Jesus' teachings.
- John the Baptist is depicted as an ascetic who did not indulge in strong drink, shave his hair or marry.
- Jesus taught that celibacy is a gift from God and cannot be imposed on anybody.
- Jesus gave reasons why some people do not marry e.g.

i. Due to natural causes, that is, there are those who were born eunuchs.
ii. Some have been made eunuchs by other men e.g. through castration.
iii. Others decide not to marry and dedicate their lives to the kingdom of God.

- Jesus assured those who have left everything for the sake of following him that they will be rewarded in God's kingdom.
- Saint Paul taught that celibacy is good only for those who have received it as a gift from God.
- He advised married Christians that temporary sexual abstinence is good for religious reasons and it may be permitted in marriage, but only if both partners agree to it.
- He advised the Christians that it was better not to marry.
- He advised the widows or unmarried to remain single but if they could not, they should marry to avoid falling into sin.

Other reasons why some people do not marry

- Some people delay marriage in order to pursue education.
- Some fail to marry because they hold careers that are too demanding and would keep them from their families for long periods e.g. soldiers, pilots e.t.c.
- Due to lack of guidance and counselling on marriage and family.
- Discouragement from failing marriages.
- Economic reasons e.g. being unable to raise bridewealth.
- Poor health and sicknesses e.g. epilepsy, mental diseases and impotence may stop some people from getting married.
- Economic independence e.g. a girl in a high paying job may opt not to marry.
- Disappointing relationships may discourage a girl from getting married.
- Interference from parents may have a negative impact on a relationship between two young people.

What is the view of St. Paul on marriage according to 1 Corinthians?

- It is not sinful to get married.
- Christians can practice celibacy to serve God better.
- He discouraged divorce in marriage and maintained that marriage is permanent.
- He encouraged reconciliation in case of divorce.
- Divorce can only be allowed between believers and non-believers whose marriage relationship has become unbearable.
- He encourages the remarrying of widows and widowers in case they can't control their sexual desires.
- Marriage partners should not deny each other the conjugal rights.
- Paul allows abstinence only for the sake of prayer.

What is the importance of the virtue of faithfulness in a Christian marriage?

- It earns one respect in the society.
- It enhances peace and harmony in the family.
- It boosts trust between the couple.
- It prevents the spread of STDs and HIV/AIDS.
- Prevents divorce and separation which may result due to unfaithfulness.
- It keeps stress and depression away.

Outline the importance of marriage in Traditional African Societies.

- Marriage is mainly for procreation and continuation of a clan/community.
- It promotes one's social status.
- It extends kinship ties.

- It provides a basis on which a family, which is the basic unit of a society could be laid down.
- It is meant for prestigious reasons.
- To provide happiness to the husband.

What was the importance of giving bridal wealth in traditional African marriages?
- It compensates the girl's family.
- It seals the marriage.
- It is a sign of appreciation to girl's family.
- It shows that she dwells with her family symbolically.
- It binds the two families.
- It shows that the man is responsible and he is serious with the marriage.

In what ways is a modern marriage different from the African and Christian Marriage?
- Marriage is not a priority since some people fail to marry because of various reasons.
- Procreation is not a must in modern marriage whereby some people see children as a burden.
- Gender equality is stressed upon whereby the superiority of man is not guaranteed and is seen as a violation of women's rights.
- Marriage is an individual affair where a person chooses his or her partner without necessarily involving the parents.
- Dowry has been commercialized in that the amount given is negotiated in proportion to one's status.
- Divorce/separation is common today due to high level of extra-marital affairs and other reasons.

Why is polygamy discouraged by the Christian church?
- Polygamy creates rivalry which leads to dishonesty and disrespect.
- It was not instituted by God in the creation story.
- It may lead to a web of STDs in case one of the partners may have it.
- The man may not love the women equally.
- The children may not receive the basic human needs adequately.
- It is against the teachings of St. Paul who relates marriage with the relationship of church and Christ.
- It undermines the role of a woman as a partner.
- It sets a bad example to the children who later can choose to become polygamous as their father whom the society views as a hero.

FAMILY

Definition

- A family is the basic social unit of human society.
- In all human societies, a family consists of the parents, children relatives and other members living together.
- A family is founded in marriage, where a husband and wife begin a new life with the aim of starting a family through children born to them.

Types of families

a. Nuclear family

- This is a family that is comprised of the mother, father and children.
- Nuclear families are monogamous.

Most people in modern life prefer a nuclear family because:

i. The man gives undivided attention to his wife and children.
ii. There is mutual love, peace and harmony at home.
iii. There is sexual satisfaction between the couple

b. Polygamous family

It is a family in which a man marries more than one wife. This type of family is commonly found in traditional African communities.

The reasons why men get married to more than one wife include:

i. Polygamous families have many children who provide labour, security and defence.
ii. The many family members provide mutual help and assistance to each other.
iii. The husband continues to get sexual satisfaction as the wives give birth at different times.

The disadvantages of a polygamous family include:

i. The many wives compete for attention from the husband leading to tension and hostility in the family.
ii. The man may be unable to provide basic needs adequately for the large family.
iii. A husband may fail to satisfy his wives sexually.
iv. He may fail as a father to provide love and attention to the children.

c. Single-parent family

This is a family in which only one parent lives with the children. Single-parent families result due to the following reasons:

i. Due to the death of one of the parents.

ii.   Separation of the parents due to misunderstanding or divorce.

iii.   When one of the parents is imprisoned for a long period, such as, life imprisonment.

iv.   When a girl is rejected by a man after she gets pregnant.

v.   Some women who are not interested in marriage get children out of the wedlock.

d. Extended family

It consists of parents, children and other relatives such as grandparents, cousins, nephews, nieces, uncles and aunties. It is more common in Traditional African society.

TRADITIONAL AFRICAN UNDERSTANDING OF THE FAMILY

- African communities believe that a family is founded family through marriage and procreation, hence formation of a family is a sacred duty instituted by God.
- The family in traditional African societies consists of both the living, the yet to be born and also the dead. Therefore, the family comprises of both the living and non-living members.
- Regulations and taboos are put in place to guide and regulate behaviour in a family setting.
- The African family extends past the nuclear family whereby an individual has many mothers, fathers, sisters and brothers within the clan and the rest of the community.
- Polygamous families are highly valued since the more the wives one has, the more respected one becomes. Children also become many and so offer labour and security to the family.
- The husband is the head of the family who takes care of it. Their wives take care of the homes and are subordinate to husbands. They also perform household duties while men maintain the homes.
- The family is a socio-religious institution since important religious and social activities take place in the families, such as, rituals related to naming, initiation, marriage and death are undertaken by all members.
- Family relationships are strong in traditional African society and entail obligations and rights which extend to all members of the family both dead and living e.g.
  i.   Burying the dead.
  ii.   Arranging for marriages for the young people and those remarrying.
  iii. Paying bride-wealth.
  iv.   Raising children and caring for them.
  v.   Providing security for the family and the vulnerable members.
  vi.   Providing for the economic needs of the family.
  vii. Providing leadership in the family and the community.

What are the advantages of traditional African family?

- It enhances responsibility among members of the family.
- It provides a sense of belonging to members since there is mutual caring and provision of material and moral support to individuals.
- It enhances the stability of marriage since the extended family participates in the selection of spouses.
- It facilitates a meaningful employment for everyone since everybody is a worker and work is divided according to gender, age, and status.
- It fosters unity among all members since members are bound by kinship ties, they cooperate in economic, social and political activities.
- It promotes collective responsibility, for example, it is the duty of every family member to punish errant members.
- It trained members on how to live in a community with others.
- It encouraged family virtues among its members e.g. tolerance, respect, love etc.

Disadvantages of a traditional African family

- It promotes exploitation of the responsible individuals who may be pressurized to support many needy members of the family.
- It encourages dependency on responsible members and discourages initiative and hard work.
- Managing large families is a problem especially when a man lacks leadership qualities.
- It may lead to conflicts that destabilize the family especially due to feelings of jealousy, hatred and competition among wives and children.

CHRISTIAN UNDERSTANDING OF THE FAMILY

- In Genesis 1: 28 the family is instituted by God hence it is divinely ordained by God, when He blessed Adam and Eve and commanded them to be fruitful and multiply.
- A Christian family is monogamous whereby it has one father, one mother, and children who are related by blood, marriage or adoption. Polygamous family is not recommended.
- The Christian family is complete with or without children because God is understood to be the provider. Children are a gift from God.
- The cornerstone of a family is love. St. Paul compares the love of Christ for the church to the love of a husband to the wife in the New Testament.
- Both husband and wife should fulfil their conjugal rights towards each other. They should have mutual understanding and not deny one another.

- The husband is the head of the family who is expected to love his wife and provide for the family. Parents should not provoke their children and children should respect their parents.
- The family is the source of Christian values and teachings and so parents have the responsibility of training and disciplining the children. This should be done in accordance to Christian ethics.
- Parents have complementary roles in a family which are achieved through mutual love and understanding.

THE VALUE OF RESPONSIBLE PARENTHOOD

Once a couple is married and has children, the husband and wife become parents. As parents, the couple is expected to behave according to the expectations of the community and bring up their children in a responsible way.

Responsible parenthood is a way in which parents ensure that they bring up their children well so that they can be all-round people. They ensure that children are properly nurtured in every stage of their lives and create families in which everybody feels secure and wanted.

Responsible parenthood in manifested in some of the following ways:
- Responsible parents understand and perform their roles. That is, the father loves and provides for the family as its head, and the mother too takes care of the children and gives them security and a sense of belonging.
- Responsible parents educate and train their children and nurture them into social beings besides taking them to school to gain formal education.
- Responsible parents provide religious education to their children to strengthen their faith in God. This ensures strong spiritual foundation for them.
- Responsible parents help their children to grow physically, socially, psychologically and emotionally from childhood through puberty and into adulthood.
- Responsible parents teach their children morals and right behaviour so that they know what is right and wrong, good and bad.
- They teach the children how to relate with one another as brothers and sisters among themselves and with other people like relatives and peers.
- Responsible parents treat and love all the children equally without discrimination whatsoever. Whatever the weakness or differences, all children are equal.
- Responsible parenthood is creating a peaceful environment for the children to achieve good communication and understanding.
- Responsible parenthood is having the size of a family that can be well taken care of. Parents family plan to avoid getting many children whom they cannot provide for all their needs.

CONTRACEPTION

Contraception is the intentional prevention of a pregnancy. There are two types of contraception:

1. Natural contraception: it involves couples abstaining from sexual contact during those periods of the month when the woman is fertile and is likely to conceive.
2. Artificial contraception: it is a method used to prevent fertilization from taking place by preventing the male sperm egg and a female ovum from meeting after sexual intercourse. Some artificial contraceptives prevent conception by ensuring that the sperm does not fertilize the ovum. Others prevent the sperm from travelling into the uterus by blocking the entrance of the uterus and such contraceptives include diaphragm and cervical caps. Others prevent sperms from spreading in the vagina e.g. condoms. Others kill the sperm e.g. spermicides, sprays and foaming tablets.

Christian views to contraception

Christians oppose the use of artificial contraceptives because of the following reasons:

- Use of contraceptives encourages extra-marital sex.
- It has made couples become suspicious of each other leading to quarrels and divorce.
- They have increased prostitution.
- Some contraceptives can cause actual abortion.
- God has endowed man with the ability to exercise self-control.
- They interfere with the life-giving process, which is sacred.

Discuss problems related to family life today

- Divorce and separation – This is either permanent or temporary separation of married couples due to a certain reason, especially in cases of unfaithfulness of one partner or domestic violence against the other.
- Poverty which may result from either unemployment or underemployment. Employment is the main source of income today therefore joblessness or underpayment means one cannot be able to provide well for the family which results in high levels of poverty.
- Domestic violence may be in form of abusive language, physical assault, brutal killings or psychological torture, sexual assault and child labour and molestations. This is common today whereby the rights of an individual are denied.
- Alcoholism and drug abuse – over-consumption and addiction to drugs and alcohol have led to loose behaviour among the victims, misuse of family resources and instability of families.
- HIV/AIDS and other STIs. These diseases cause death of the victims among other serious permanent problems. There is over-expenditure of financial resources for the upkeep of dietal and medical needs for the victim. In case of death, the family set up is broken and responsibilities are interchanged.

- Generation gap has widened up due to change in dressing, language and fashion. The youth feel the old are old-fashioned while the old feel that the youth are rebellious.
- Cultural and religious differences which have arose through marriage integration. People intermarry with others from different ethnic and religious backgrounds. This creates problems in case of language, customs and the denomination to attend.
- Individualism which has risen due to financial constraints and urban families. It makes one to find it difficult to support their relatives.
- Lack of communication between parents, or children creates mistrust and suspicion between members. Communication creates understanding and so people should strive for it.
- Single parenthood which results from divorce or getting children outside marriage is rampant today. Such parents face financial constraints, depression, loneliness and sometimes irresponsible sexual behaviours.
- Mismanagement of family resources has caused family disputes today. Disputes arise due to ownership of property and management. This causes hatred and jealousy among members.

Explain the traditional African approaches to problems related to family life today.

- Divorce was not allowed in African societies. People were prepared during initiation to understand that marriage was lifelong and was bound by the bridewealth and bearing of children. The roles of each member of the family were clearly defined. With these divorce was rare.
- In African communities family resources such as land, livestock and other main property was acquired through inheritance. It was the responsibility of the father/ husband to take care of this property.
- African communities did not condone single-parenthood. It was the responsibility of everyone to get married and have children. Girls who broke their virginity and became pregnant were disowned by their families and were later married off to older men as second wives.
- The African communities gave the father the responsibility of disciplining the family. Wife-beating was acceptable in many communities as a way of disciplining the wife. Child abuse and molestation was not acceptable.
- It was the role of the children to obey their parents, the wife to submit to the husband, and the husband to provide for the family. In case of disputes arising between the three groups of people, elders solved them, punishment was given whenever need be and reconciled the parties concerned.
- Polygamy was meant to alleviate immorality. At the same time it caused jealousy among the co-wives. However it was the responsibility of the husband to ensure the wives lived to his expectations.

- Individualism was unheard of and there was communal sharing of resources and responsibilities. This was strengthened through the kinship ties which created a sense of belonging to the community.
- African communities didn't allow separation which arose due to other requirements except war. The family stayed together to fulfil its functions of integration.
- African communities valued children as part of the family. In cases of a barren woman, the husband was free to marry another wife but maintain the barren wife. In case of an impotent husband, the wife bears children for him through his brother.

Evaluate the Christian approaches to problems related to family life today.
- Parents are instructed to bring up children in love and fear of God. Jesus said children belong to him. The church also discourages child abuse and asks Christians to live in harmony with each other.
- Concerning diseases, Christians are free to visit medical centres for treatment. Others seek spiritual healing from their leaders who are ordained with the gift of healing. The church also provides training and counselling services to the affected and the infected. The church also teaches people to practice abstinence from sex before marriage and faithfulness in marriage. Some churches have set up children homes and orphanages for children who have lost their parents through HIV/AIDs.
- Christianity does not allow divorce unless on grounds of unfaithfulness of one partner. The Ten Commandments say, you shall not commit adultery. St. Paul teaches that the body is the temple of the Holy Spirit and so it must not be defiled by immorality.
- A Christian family may be complete even without children because children are a gift from God. Childlessness should not be a ground to instability of homes. They could be acquired through adoption.
- Single parenthood should only arise due to death or inevitable divorce. Christianity forbids sex outside marriage. However children who are born out of such settings should not be rejected.
- The bible condemns drunkenness and other immoral activities. This defiles the body which is the temple of the Holy Spirit and also misuses funds which are to be used to promote God's love. Adultery is forbidden and advices people to marry to prevent immorality.

How can children show love and respect to their parents?
- Prov 30: 17 states that children should not scorn their parents.
- They should show their parents joy (Prov 10: 1).
- They must be hardworking. (Prov 22: 13) condemns laziness.
- Exodus 20: 12 asks children to obey their parents.
- Children should listen to the advice and teachings of their parents (Prov 1: 8 – 9).

- 1 Tim 5: 3 – 8 asks children to provide for their parents.

Name the duties of parents to their children.
- Pass spiritual faith and religious teachings to their children.
- Provide basic needs to their children.
- Provide school education and general knowledge to children.
- To be role models to their children.
- Give inheritance to their children.
- To discipline their children.
- To provide security and protection for their children.
- Parents take care of the general welfare of their children.

Explain the problems associated with childlessness in marriage today
- In extreme cases it may lead to divorce.
- It may also lead to suicide in extreme cases especially by the woman if the husband adversely accuses her of barrenness.
- A childless couple may feel incomplete.
- A man in a childless marriage may engage in heavy drinking to cover up his frustration.
- Childless couples may result to unfaithfulness to prove fertility.
- A childless couple may easily be tempted to steal children.
- It is easy for childless couples to hate children or those who have children.
- Many childless couples have constant war amongst themselves because they keep blaming each other.

How should a Christian couple respond to the problem of childlessness?
- They should accept their state.
- They should consult medical experts for advice.
- They should pray to God to help them in their problems.
- They should visit children's home to offer their service to the needy children.
- They can adopt a child through legal procedure.
- Attending guidance and counselling sessions on family life education.
- Reading literature on childlessness as a way of getting a solution to their problems.
- They should love each other dearly.

Give reasons for the increase of abortion today in Kenya.
- Availability of birth control services.
- Improved technology.
- Breakdown of traditional African values and Christian virtues.
- Increase of sexual immorality.

- Influence from the western culture.
- Pursuit of careers and education.

Give seven reasons why it is important for members of the family to discuss how to spend their money.

- It ensures careful use of wealth.
- It gets rid of extravagance or wastage of wealth.
- It creates peace and harmony in the family.
- It creates a sense of responsibility in the family members.
- It prioritizes needs of the family.
- It creates trust especially between the husband and wife.
- It trains family members for future financial management.

TOPIC 23: CHRISTIAN APPROACHES TO WORK

Define the terms work and vocation

Work is a human activity which involves the use of mental and physical energy. Besides mental and physical, work may also involve spiritual, mental, political, social or cultural dimensions. Work is done to facilitate the good running of all the named dimensions.

Give the reasons why people work.

- For personal development. Through work people discover and build their interests, abilities, aptitudes and potentials.
- For self-satisfaction and fulfilment – work is a basic need which is ordained by God. It is natural to work.
- People work to acquire the basic necessities of life e.g. food, clothing, and shelter.
- Work makes people occupied both physically and mentally, hence taking away idleness.
- People work to serve the community, fellow human beings and to care for the environment.
- People work to acquire wealth, which raises one's social status.
- To socialize and grow as a member of the community.
- People work to attain independence, that is, in order not to depend on parents, guardians or other members of the society.

Types of Work done

- Salaried employment – This is where people are employed to work for public or private offices and are given a salary or wage at the end of the month.
- Self-employment – People invest money, time and other resources to set up businesses so as to generate income for themselves and create job opportunities for others e.g. dairy farming, having a salon e.t.c.
- Casual work – This is a temporary job where people are hired when their services are needed but are laid off when their services are no longer needed.

Meaning of vocation

Vocation is a calling. Therefore it is a kind of work that one is called by God to perform for example, in the Old Testament people were called by God to become prophets and in the New Testament Jesus called the disciples to spread his message to the rest of the world. Christians of today have been called to perform different responsibilities in line with the command of God.

Therefore, whatever a person does, can be looked at as a vocation e.g. medicine, teaching, farming, banking e.t.c.

How can a person recognize his/her vocation?

The following factors determine a person's career:

- Available opportunities for future development in a particular job.
- The need to serve others e.g. the church and the needy in society.
- A person's own interests, talents and abilities.
- Attraction to a certain type of work.
- Christian teachings about various jobs are considered so that one does not accept a job that doesn't conform to Christian teachings.

Traditional African attitude towards work

- Work was taught from childhood, and everyone was a worker. Only the very young children, the sick and the old were exempted from work.
- People worked to obtain basic needs. Therefore, work was taken seriously by all members of the community.
- Work is divided according to age, gender and the social status of the individual e.g. the youth looked after livestock, hunted, fishing e.t.c. Women performed household tasks while men performed the heavier tasks.
- Many African communities have predominant occupations depending on the environmental conditions e.g. pastoralism, fishing, hunting e.t.c.
- Work in African community is communal. This enhanced cohesion in the community.
- African communities recognized that work is sacred, hence, they prayed and gave offerings and sacrifices to God to bless their work.
- African communities recognized the work of specialists. These were the people who had special tasks to perform like healers, seers, rainmakers e.t.c.
- Work was integrated with lcisure e.g. people worked as they sang.
- There was no exploitation of one person by another for personal gain.
- Idleness and laziness were condemned and highly discouraged.
- Manual work was highly valued and encouraged.

Secular/modern attitude towards work

- The kind of work that one will do is determined by their level of education someone acquires. The higher the level of education the better the pay.
- People work depending on the availability of job opportunities. Sometimes because of job scarcity, people end up doing jobs that they are not called to do.
- Due to many job seekers and less job opportunities there tends to be stiff competition.

- People work expecting pay at the end of the month. Unlike in the traditional African societies, today work is for personal gain and gratification.
- Some youth consider and value "white collar' jobs than "blue collar" jobs and disregard manual jobs as being old fashioned.
- There is stiff competition in employment due to many job seekers and few job opportunities which often leads to unethical behaviour like bribery and corruption so as to get jobs.

Explain the differences between the traditional African and modern attitudes towards work

- In Traditional African communities, work was an economic activity but today because of the introduction of wage economy where both men and women can earn a salary, the desire for luxuries has increased above the basic necessities of life.
- In Traditional African communities, everybody was a worker and work was divided according to age, gender and status whereas in modern society both men and women can do any type of work.
- In Traditional African communities all forms of work were good but today people regard manual work as dirty and below man's dignity.
- In Traditional African communities work is done in a religious context but today the religious aspect of work has been forgotten.
- In Traditional African communities there was little competition among workers whereas today there is a fierce competition among workers which may open room for unethical means to be used.
- In Traditional African communities work was a social activity and people assisted one another while today the social aspect has been overridden by individualism.

Christian teachings on work

- Work was instituted by God Himself. He created the heavens and earth and all in it. Human beings too must work like God did.
- Human beings are co-creators with God and therefore God continues to create through the work of human beings. Human beings therefore glorify God through work.
- The book of Proverbs recognizes hardwork and condemns laziness. It recognizes that wealth is the fruit of hard work and poverty results from laziness.
- When Christians work they are fulfilling one of their God-given duties. God commanded man to cultivate the Garden of Eden.
- Christians need to share work. Eve was created as a helper of Adam.
- Christians should work but leave some time to rest. God rested on the seventh day after working for six days. (Ex. 20: 9)

- The Bible condemns evils associated with work such as exploitation, slavery and failure to pay wages.
- Christians are encouraged to work so as not to be a burden to others. They need to work to be an example to others. (1 Thessalonians 4:11 – 12)

Why is it necessary that a Christian should work?

- Work was ordained by God.
- They work as a way of continuing with the creation activity of God.
- Work is an important aspect of human life which makes them complete.
- To emulate God since man is created in the image of God, who is presented as a worker.
- Human beings have to work to protect and preserve God's creation.
- Work enables Christians to provide for his life requirements.
- Work enables Christians to become self-reliant and dignified.
- It is the will of God that Christians should work and He blesses those that work hard.
- Work keeps Christians busy and shun away idleness which can lead to sin.
- Through work Christians make a worthwhile contribution to the society.
- Work justifies the existence of Christians.

The role of professional ethos, ethics and code in society

a) **Professional ethos** refers to the unique principles and moral values that identify a particular profession. They regulate the conduct of a particular profession and makes people to have confidence and trust in a professional. Professional ethos also provides the workers with the right attitude towards work and confidence in their work. It also promotes self-discipline because the workers are encouraged to promote the value of their profession.

b) **Professional ethics** is the moral standards expected of members of a particular profession. They are principles of conduct that guide the members of a particular profession. Professional ethics specify the competence expected of its prospective members. It may require a particular level of education. Members who uphold their professional ethics create confidence in the members of the public. Professional ethics protect its members from being emotionally involved with the people they serve.

c) **Professional codes** are the written rules that guide members of a particular profession in upholding the ethos and ethics of their profession. These ensure satisfactory performance in the work of its members as required by the people they serve. The code lay down the guidelines on how workers should relate to one another and the people they serve.

The role of professional code and ethics

- They ensure personal integrity in workers of a particular profession.
- They give guidelines on how and who to employ, promote and terminate employment.

- They protect its members against any form of abuse or misuse by members of public.
- They create confidence and trust in the members of the public.
- They give guidance on how professionals should relate to one another.
- They determine the expected level of performance of a particular job.
- They serve as a measure of competence in performing duties.
- They provide ways of dealing with errant members of the professions.

SOME VIRTUES RELATED TO VARIOUS TYPES OF WORK

A virtue is a behaviour that shows high moral standards. The following are some of the virtues related to various types of work

- **Diligence** is the commitment to hardwork without giving up. Diligent people are self-driven to achieve certain objectives in their work.
- **Honesty/integrity** - Honesty is sincerity and being truthful. Integrity is having good morals irrespective of external pressure. These two virtues ensure that people work without or with minimum supervision.
- **Faithfulness** is the virtue of loyalty or trustworthy. A faithful person does all his work. He can be trusted and keep the secrets of the employer confidential.
- **Responsibility** is the ability to make decisions bearing in mind the welfare of other people. A responsible person is able to account for his/her work and fulfil his duties as required.
- **Loyalty** is being trustworthy and faithful. It entails obedience and devotion to work.
- **Tolerance** is being able to withstand other people's weaknesses even if it's not acceptable. Tolerance overlooks differences and considers the benefits. This helps people to accept and appreciate one another.

THE MORAL DUTIES AND RESPONSIBILITIES OF EMPLOYERS AND EMPLOYEES

(a) Rights of employers

- Conduct their business without unfair external pressures which tend to threaten their work.
- Get loyalty and trust from their employees.
- Have freedom of association with fellow employers.
- Demand good work input from employees as per the contract agreement.
- Enjoy profits from their businesses.
- Opening up and conducting new businesses.
- Employing and dismissing employees in accordance with labour laws.

(b) Duties of employers to Employees

- To respect their employees and their dignity.

- To pay their employees a wage in proportion to the work done. Employees should not be underpaid.
- To motivate their employees by giving incentives to those who deserve e.g. give promotions to the suitable candidate.
- Employers should share their profits with employees and make them feel part of the business.
- Take care of their employees' welfare. For example provide covers, insurance or leave/time off to rest.
- To manage their businesses efficiently to avoid their closure, that may render people jobless.
- Compensate for redundant employees or those who end their contract.

(c) Rights of employees:
- Have a right to receive a wage/salary in proportion with the workload. It should generally be fair.
- Have a right to work in a safe and favourable environment to avoid risking their life.
- Have a right to work for reasonable amount of hours and be given a time to rest.
- Have a right to personal development and training which can give them an opportunity for promotion.
- Have a right to be treated as per the contract agreement in cases of retirement or termination of work.
- Have a right to join or form associations or trade unions.

(d) Duties and responsibilities of employees:
- Be responsible and work diligently so as to provide services of high quality with minimum or no supervision.
- Be honest and a confidant of his employer.
- To respect the enterprisc as though it was his by protecting it.
- Be loyal and promote the interests of the employers.
- Promote dialogue and peaceful resolutions to problems affecting them.
- Be well trained to enable him gain skills that can provide quality work.

Give ways that an employer can use to show respect to their employees:
- Accept freedom of worship.
- Pay the employee a just wage
- Avoid mistreatment of employees
- Respect the religious duties of the employees.
- Avoid over taxation.
- Give the employees a conducive working environment.

- Allow them to rest and give motivation to the employees e.g. salary increments and promotions.
- Also be considerate to the employees' grievances.

CHRISTIAN APPROACHES TO ISSUES RELATED TO EMPLOYMENT

a) Wages are payments made for work done. Other terms used are salary, pay or remuneration. A wage should be fair/just whereby it should correspond to work done.

Factors considered when assessing a just wage include:

- Ability of the employer to pay.
- Number of years an employee has worked or the experience an employee has.
- The skills and training required to do the job.
- Amount of work done should be equivalent to the wages given.
- The wage given should enable a worker to support his/her family and other dependants.
- The value of the work to the community.
- Efficiency with which the work is carried out.

b) Industrial action/strike is a situation where workers refuse to work in protest in order to pressurise for higher wages or better working conditions. Strikes may take various forms e.g. go slow, sit ins, downing tools and violent and peaceful protests.

Conditions under which an industrial action may be justified

- A strike must have a serious cause.
- It should have a reasonable hope of success for it to be justified.
- All other means e.g. negotiation must have been tried and failed before a strike is called.
- There must be no violence or deliberate damage of property, intimidation or bullying by the strikers of those who are not and wish not to strike.

What are the consequences of industrial strikes?

- It may lead to loss of lives where violence is used.
- It creates animosity between the employer and the workers.
- It leads to loss of earnings for the employees if they are sacked.
- it may result in destruction of property if violence is used.
- It may lead to imprisonment of the strikers if they are found guilty.
- It can lead to suffering of the families or dependants of the sacked workers or during the period when they are not working.
- It may lead to the workers losing all their terminal benefits.
- It is very difficult for the workers to get employed elsewhere especially when there is serious unemployment in the country.

c) **Child Labour** refers to the employment of people under the age of eighteen years on a full time basis. The law forbids the employment of children. It requires that one reports to the nearest Labour office if they have a minor in their employment. Children should be respected, protected and given a conducive environment in which they can thrive and develop.

Reasons why children are employed

- They provide cheap labour.
- They cannot join trade unions and therefore cannot fight for proper terms and conditions of service.
- They can be easily hired and fired.
- They do not have qualifications in any skill so as to negotiate for their terms.
- They are looked at as a source of extra income by their guardians.
- High rate of school drop-outs.
- Some children are orphans and destitute hence have no one to take care of them.
- Urbanization and industrialization have led to an increase in child labour.

Rights of children

- Right to live and be loved.
- Right to education and training.
- Right to expression.
- Right to citizenship.
- Right to protection and guidance.
- Right to play and leisure.
- Right to health.

Ways in which Christians deal with the challenges of child labour

- The church condemns child labour since it inhibits a child's growth hence preventing the child from enjoying childhood.
- The church has put up homes for poor children and orphans.
- They provide guidance and counselling to both parents and children on responsible living as parents and children.
- The church provides non-formal education for poor children.
- The church teaches that child labour is against human rights.

Why is child labour morally wrong?

- Children are a gift from God and should not be oppressed.
- It retards the Child's growth and development.
- The child may not develop his talents.

- It makes the child to have a negative attitude to work.
- It shows the parent's irresponsibility.
- It denies them formal education.
- It leads to loss of human dignity.
- Child labour promotes poverty which is a social evil.
- Most of the children are underpaid by their employers.

d) **Unemployment** is a situation where there are not enough jobs for all the people. Unemployment leads to many social evils e.g. idleness, theft, prostitution, jealousy and hatred. People who are unemployed are generally insecure, unhappy and lack basic essentials in life.

Factors that cause unemployment
- Bribery and corruption, nepotism and tribalism.
- Lack of skills and capital to start self-employment.
- Bad governance and poor economic policies by the government.
- Retrenchment/laying off workers in the civil service and private sector.
- Introduction of new technologies sometimes replaces human labour.
- Increased insecurity which discourages investment.
- Gender inequalities make it difficult for some gender groups to find employment.
- Industrial action leads to some people losing jobs.
- Surplus labour where the government trains more people than it needs.

Ways in which Christians can help solve the problem of unemployment
- Christians encourage self-employment by setting up vocational training institutions and polytechnics to encourage people to train in various skills for self-employment.
- Christians encourage community service.
- The church condemns idleness, discrimination and corruption in work and immorality in work relationships.
- Christians advocate for good working conditions and terms of service for those in salaried employment.
- The church offers guidance and counselling to promote positive attitudes towards work.
- The church in collaboration with the government and Non-Governmental organizations give financial and material support to people in order to create job opportunities.

e) **Self-employment** refers to where a person initiates a personal enterprise and manages it with the help of others. It enables one generate income to the owner of the business. Unlike those in salaried employment who earn at the end of the month, a self-employed person owns a business.

Challenges facing self-employment

- Inadequate funds to start and run a business.
- Some people are not able to identify the proper markets.
- Some people lack the necessary skills needed or have inadequate skills.
- Some traders sometimes face ruthless competition from larger firms.
- Extended family commitments might lead a person to become bankrupt.
- There are many risks involved e.g. theft, fire, drought and floods.
- Taxes may be too high.

Christian approaches to self-employment

- The Bible praises hardwork.
- God gives different gifts and so people have to identify their gifts and maximize them.
- The Bible supports self-employment because it promotes values such as creativity, originality, responsibility and self-reliance.
- A self-employed person should choose a job that is approved by Christian morals.
- A self-employed person should be patient and not greedy.
- Christians are supposed to help the poor and needy, and self-employment empowers one to do this.

Give reasons why manual work is important in human life.

- Through manual work human beings emulate God as a worker.
- It is a sign of being obedient to God's instructions to work.
- It enables human beings to look after and preserve the environment thus becoming co-creators with God.
- It keeps the body physically fit.
- Human beings are able to obtain their basic needs and earn a living.
- It is a way of serving others in the community thus contributing to economic development
- It enables human beings to develop their talents and abilities.
- Manual work gives satisfaction and fulfilment of an individual.
- It keeps one busy and active thus avoiding being idle and hence reduces crime rate.

Explain the factors which result to strained relationship between employers and employees.

- Underpayment/delaying payment.
- Employers being insensitive to employees' problems/needs.
- Overworking the employee or giving them no rest.
- Refusing employees to take leave or to observe public holidays.

- Lack of promotions and salary increments/motivation.
- Lack of freedom of expression/association and not communicating with employees.
- Harassment sexually/abuses/quarrels.
- Not following the terms and conditions of service.
- If the employee is not loyal or does not respect the employer.
- Not efficient employee/not diligent in work

Show ways in which Jesus upheld the dignity of work during his life and ministry.
- He was a worker/carpenter.
- He established God's kingdom on earth by doing the work of preaching, forgiving, miracles e.t.c.
- He called different workers to be his disciples e.g. fishermen, tax collectors e.t.c
- He used work to make his teaching clearer e.g. parable of the sower.
- He solved situation that reduced work/healed Simon's mother in law to allow her to work.
- He gave advice that promoted work e.g. paying to Caesar's what belongs to him.
- He discouraged overworking/rested, worshipped on the Sabbath day.
- Promoted division of labour by commissioning the 12 disciples to perform various duties.
- He found fulfilment in his work and he never complained at work.
- He discouraged child labour by even calling adults to be his disciples.

TOPIC 24: CHRISTIAN APPROACHES TO LEISURE

Explain the meaning of leisure

- Leisure is the free time one has at his/her disposal used for both physical and mental relaxation after work, in order to regain lost energy.
- Leisure time gives one an opportunity to develop socially, culturally and spiritually leaving aside the economic aspect.

The traditional African understanding of leisure

- Leisure time was meant for socialization since it was a communal affair. It involved everyone in the community from the young to the elderly.
- Leisure is undertaken after work.
- All leisure activities had an educational aspect whereby after the activity a person could achieve new lessons and morals. For example myths and legends gave the history of their clans.
- Leisure activities were organized along gender and age group lines. For example, wrestling was for men, folk telling was done by the elderly, the youth staged dances e.t.c.
- Leisure was also experienced during rites of passage. They provided relevant education, sharing, drinking, dancing in relation to the rite that was being experienced.
- Leisure time was also meant to develop strong kinship ties hence gave a sense of belonging.
- Leisure activities were performed to give thanks to God for blessings bestowed.
- During leisure time community matters are discussed.
- There are strict rules and regulations that govern participants during leisure time.
- Leisure is sometimes integrated with work e.g. where people sing as they work.
- The most common leisure activities included:
  i.   Wrestling
  ii.   Bull fighting.
  iii. Story telling
  iv.   Dancing and singing.
  v.   Beer drinking.
  vi.   Visiting neighbours, friends and relatives.
  vii. Holding family meetings.

The Christian teaching on leisure

- Leisure is divinely instituted by God when He rested on the seventh day after creation.

- Leisure time allows Christians to rest and worship God.
- Leisure is a gift from God to human beings hence Christians join God in celebrating the work of creation and their own work.
- Christians should make good use of leisure time rather than waste or misuse it.
- Christians use leisure time for personal growth and fellowship with one another.
- Leisure is used to strengthen social relationships through visiting and meeting friends and relatives.
- It is used to bring joy and new hope to those who are suffering as Jesus did during the Sabbath.
- Christians should avoid leisure activities that may compromise their faith and harm their health.
- The most common leisure activities for a Christian include:
  i. Singing in church.
  ii. Praying.
  iii. Attending Christian meetings.
  iv. Listening to Christian music.
  v. Watching Christian movies and films.
  vi. Playing games.
  vii. Reading the Bible and other Christian literature.
  viii. Visiting the sick, relatives and friends.
  ix. Writing Christian literature.
  x. Visiting the sick.
  xi. Caring for the needy.
  xii. Going for retreats.

Give the guidelines that a Christian should follow in deciding on how to spend their leisure time.
- They should know that their bodies are the temple of the Holy Spirit.
- They should avoid actions that would lead others to sin.
- They should not be enslaved by any sought addiction.
- They should be wise to choose between right and wrong deeds.
- They should use their leisure time to glorify God and helping the less fortunate.
- They should engage themselves in productive activities.
- They should avoid actions which may be harmful and cause them regrets.

How can leisure be used by Christians to glorify God?
- By singing Christian hymns, reading the Bible and other religious literature and praying to God.
- Socializing with relatives and friends.

- Preaching the gospel.
- Involvement in community projects.
- Doing charity work.
- Organizing fellowships in the community.

Discuss the importance of leisure

- Leisure gives one an opportunity, to rest and relax. This allows one to regain the lost energy so as to perform better at work.
- Leisure gives as an opportunity to assess the work done.
- Leisure time gives us an opportunity to meet people hence promotes socialization. It may also allow them to attend social gatherings.
- Leisure is a time for recreation which allows people develop and utilize their talents.
- Leisure gives Christians a chance for spiritual development through prayer, fasting and attending Christian gatherings and reading the Bible.
- Educational leisure activities enable one to become more knowledgeable and acquire new skills
- Leisure time gives one a chance to perform acts of charity and worship God, by serving others.

OUTLINE THE VARIOUS FORMS OF LEISURE

a) **Active leisure** – This involves the activity of the whole body. It involves mainly the physical energy alongside mental energy. Examples of active leisure activities include games, tree planting, educational tours etc.

Importance of active leisure

- It strengthens relationships.
- It offers a chance for one to socialize with others who share common interests.
- It develops one's body.
- One builds stamina if involved in sporting activities.
- It enables one to participate in his/her favourite activity.
- Helps one to exercise God-given talents.
- One discovers new places and other ways of doing things.

Disadvantages of active leisure

- Some activities are costly e.g. golf, motor racing.
- It may cause addiction.
- Some active leisure activities are dangerous to one's physical health e.g. motor racing, boxing, wrestling and mountain climbing.
- Some leisure activities make a person to use a lot of energy causing a lot of exhaustion.

- Some leisure activities can lead to loss of life e.g. accidents in motor racing.

b) **Passive leisure** – These are mainly entertainment activities which do not involve physical energy, rather it involves mental energy. Examples of passive leisure activities include listening to the radio, watching television, games or resting in bed.

Reasons why people engage in passive leisure
- It provides an opportunity for people to think and plan ahead.
- It allows people to relax and rest.
- It makes one to recover the lost energy.

Disadvantages of passive leisure
- It can lead to idleness.
- It encourages laziness.
- If allowed to continue, it may kill creativity in an individual.
- People who like passive leisure may become overweight.
- Some of the activities are addictive.
- Some passive leisure activities are expensive and may cause embezzlement of family funds.
- They are not creative in nature.
- Children who continuously watch TVs will not have time for academic work hence deterioration in academic performance.

OUTLINE THE VARIOUS USES OF LEISURE

- Leisure time is used to worship God and seek spiritual nourishment.
- Leisure time gives one a chance to serve others.
- Leisure time is used to meet and socialize with friends and family. This strengthens relationships.
- Leisure can be used to entertain ourselves and relax our mind and body.
- Leisure time gives us a chance to rest from our daily work routine.
- Leisure time is used to discover and develop one's talents and abilities.
- Leisure gives us a chance to know and understand ourselves better.
- It is used to read and acquire more knowledge e.g. reading educational and inspirational books.
- It is used to exercise the body and mind so that one can be physically and mentally fit.

MISUSE OF LEISURE TODAY

Leisure if misused in the following ways:
- Staying idle doing nothing.
- Watching pornographic movies that degenerate morals.
- Gambling, where people use a lot of money in the hope that they will make more.
- Taking alcohol and other drugs like bhang and miraa.
- Gossiping and rumour mongering since it can cause quarrels and conflicts.
- Discos and night dancing which can lead to sexual immorality and drug abuse.
- Spending plenty of time on passive activities.

Outline some of the problems one may face when choosing leisure activities.

- Lack of parental control.
- Financial constraints.
- Inability in choosing leisure activity.
- Commercial exploitation.
- Inferiority complex.
- Lack of time for leisure.
- Lack of a variety of leisure activities to choose from.
- Concentration of leisure activities in towns.

MISUSE/ABUSE OF DRUGS

- A drug is a chemical substance which when taken or gets into the body causes changes in the functioning of the body e.g. a person suffering from malaria feels better after taking certain drugs prescribed by a medical doctor.
- Drugs are mostly used to cure illnesses, but they have also been misused hence causing pain and suffering to their victims and their families.

Types of drugs
a) Medical/curative drugs
- They are used to prevent, treat or cure certain diseases.
- Some medical drugs are also used to relieve pain e.g. Panadol and aspirin. These are known as sedatives.
- Some medical drugs are used to relieve tension and induce sleep e.g. piriton and valium. These are called tranquilizers.
- Some are used to treat chronic diseases e.g. cancer, asthma, diabetes and high blood pressure. These are palliatives.
- Some medical drugs can cause addiction, aggravate/worsen a person's illness or even cause death, hence they should be used carefully with the supervision of the doctor.

b) **Soft drugs**: they categorized into two; stimulants and volatile substances.
  i.   **Stimulants:** these are drugs which increase the activity of the central nervous system e.g. tobacco, caffeine, miraa and amphetamines.

Tobacco – it is taken in the form of cigarettes or snuff. It contains nicotine which causes addiction to smoking. It contains carbon monoxide inhaled during smoking and damages the arteries, heart and lung e.t.c. Tar, a black substance left in the lungs after smoking causes cancer of the throat, heart and lungs.

Effects of smoking
- Causes discoloured teeth.
- Causes bad breath.
- Can cause fire accidents in the homes, forests and industries.
- Can cause miscarriage in pregnant women or cause them to give birth to underweight and unhealthy babies.
- Smoking causes poor blood circulation.
- It also causes chest and respiratory diseases.
- It aggravates bronchitis.

Khat/miraa – it is also known as mairungi. It is a plant whose stalks and leaves are chewed to induce excitement. It interferes with food digestion and sleep.

  ii.   **Volatile substances –** these substances intoxicate the user and distort the user's speech. They are derived from petroleum products, paint thinners and dry cleaning fluids. An example is the glue sniffed by children living in the streets.
       It provides the user with a temporary feeling of happiness but leads to loss of appetite.

c) **Hard drugs/narcotics** – when a narcotic substance is taken, it affects the mind causing drowsiness, sleep, stupor or insensibility. Examples include:

   i. Cocaine is derived from *coca tree*. It leads to addiction, lack of nervous coordination and general rebellion. It causes mental problems and death.

   ii. Bhang comes from a plant called Indian hemp. It is also called *marijuana, cannabis sativa* or hashish. It causes illusions and makes the users excited and aggressive because they feel that they have an extra-ordinary outburst of energy. It causes drowsiness and reduces the user's sense of responsibility.

   iii. Morphine is derived from cocaine. It can be used medically to suppress pain. It may lead to addiction if used outside the doctor's prescription.

   iv. Heroin is a highly addictive analgestic (pain relieving) drug derived from morphine and used as a narcotic. It is used medically by surgeons as a local anaesthetic.

The effects of drug abuse

- Drug abuse destroys the normal functioning of the body leading to disease like cirrhosis, kidney failure, heart damage, lung cancer among others.
- It leads to the death of the user in extreme cases.
- When expectant mothers abuse drugs, their children may have deformities.
- Sometimes they cause hallucinations and reduced reasoning capacity.
- The user becomes irritable and aggressive and leading to violence.
- It can lead to family breakups, separation and divorce due to frustration of the other family members.
- Some drug users commit crimes and other immoral behaviours which are harmful to themselves and others e.g. robbery, prostitution, corruption etc.
- It can cause school dropout due to poor performance and unruly behaviour.
- It can lead to loss of jobs due to the irresponsible behaviours of the person at work.
- It can cause financial problems since the person uses family finances, resources and time to buy and take drugs.

Give possible remedies to drug abuse

- Law enactment and enforcement- Selling of drugs is illegal and so the government should enforce laws and take strict measures against the law breakers.
- Guidance and counselling- Teachers, parents and other rehabilitation centres offer proper guidance to the users and children. They can be guided on the basis of biblical principles and other society's moral values.
- Education – People of all ages and gender should be enlightened on the proper use of drugs. They should be taught on the dangerous effects of drugs.

- Parents have a role to play by setting examples and being role models to their children. They should instil the right values and Christian principles in their children.
- There should be a variety of leisure activities from which the youth can be able to choose from. They should be encouraged to perform recreational activities and other helpful hobbies.
- Besides the school, church leaders should also play the role of leading by example and also provide morals to the youth.

Discuss the abuse of alcohol and its effects

Alcohol is a sedative and it is usually taken during social occasions. It's a product of fermentation and distillation. In African communities alcohol was used for entertainment during various leisure activities. It was mainly taken by elders and drunkenness was not allowed.

In the secular world alcohol is used as either medicine or for entertainment. Alcohol is abused when it is taken in excess or when it is not used for the right purpose. It is also be abused when one becomes an addict and spends all his money and time on it.

Reasons why people abuse alcohol and other drugs

- Peer pressure whereby one takes drugs in order to fit in a particular group.
- Boredom and idleness may push one to use drugs to kill the boredom.
- Drug availability in the market at a fairly cheap price which is affordable to many.
- Commercial advertisement of the substances in the media promotes abuse of the drugs by attaching positive effects on its use.
- Lack of role models from parents and other important people in the society.
- Permissiveness in the society since the modern nation is influenced by the western culture leading to the breakdown of traditional values.
- Greed whereby people look for money by peddling and trafficking drugs.
- Frustration and financial stress which may be as a result of being unable to perform in various ways like poor performance in school or at work.
- Addiction arising from frequent use of certain drugs or alcohol. Addicts have a constant demand for drugs.

The effects of alcohol abuse including following:

- It can destroy one's health intellectually or destroy the liver functioning.
- It can lead to misuse of family resources like money and time.
- It can lead to irresponsible sexual behaviour since one is unable to make moral decisions.
- In case of a pregnant mother the unborn child may experience some deformities.
- It can lead to loss of job and eventually financial problems.

- It can lead to addiction.
- It can cause accidents due to lack of concentration

State ways in which alcohol drinking can lead to family breakdown

- It causes wastage of family resources leading to inability to support one's the family.
- It can lead to quarrels and fights.
- It can cause misunderstandings, suspicion, mistrust in the family.
- It can cause lack of respect in the family.
- It can lead to loss of paternal and maternal love for the children.
- It leads to irresponsible sexual behaviour like unfaithfulness in the family.
- It can lead to diseases, accidents, which can cause death.
- It leads to inability to work and eventual loss of jobs.
- It leads to strained family relationships.
- It retards the mental, spiritual and physical development of a person.
- Failure by an alcoholic partner to give conjugal rights to the partner causes frustration and bitterness.

What is the attitude of Christians towards excessive drinking?

- All Christian communities condemn excessive drinking of alcohol.
- Some Christian communities allow moderate use of drinks.
- Others forbid alcohol completely even light stimulants such as tea and coffee.
- Total abstinence has been undertaken by some religions.
- Moderation and self-discipline is a requirement of Christian life.
- As a Christian one should be made aware of the effects of excessive drinking.
- A Christian should know alcoholism is a disease.
- A Christian should pray for alcoholic persons to return to sanity and sanctity.
- A Christian should encourage the alcoholic to practice his/her religion.
- The alcoholic should avoid bad company that influence them to drink.

Explain the factors that are frustrating the fight against drug abuse in Kenya today.

- Massive corruption in the police force.
- Permissiveness in society.
- Poor investigative skills by the police force.
- Political patronage/protectionism of drug dealers.
- Financial constraints in assisting agents that fight drug abuse e.g. NACADA.
- Light sentences/punishment by the judiciary given to drug dealers.
- Negative mass media influence that portrays drug abuse in positive light.

What is the role of the church in handling social problems associated with misuse of leisure?

- Opening rehabilitation centres.
- Offering guidance and counselling.
- Setting homes for orphaned and destitute children and old people.
- Organizing social functions.
- Running family life programmes.
- Educating the community on how to spend leisure time.
- Seeking divine intervention from God to change those misusing leisure.

Explain the Christian criteria for evaluating the use of leisure.

As Christians choose the leisure activities to be engaged in, they should be guided by the following principles:

- Leisure activities should be used to worship God and develop their spiritual well-being.
- Leisure activities must not lead someone to sin because this will displease God.
- Leisure activities should improve the normal functioning of the body, physically, mentally and psychologically. There should be a balance between passive and active leisure.
- Leisure should only come after work, as a form of rest and relaxation.
- Christians should choose leisure activities that are not harmful to themselves or to others.
- Christians should choose leisure activities that enrich their knowledge of God e.g. reading the Bible and other Christian literature.
- Leisure that makes one to be extravagant should be avoided.
- Christians should avoid leisure activities that lead to addiction hence they should enjoy leisure moderately.
- A Christian should engage in activities that don't lead others to do wrong or lead others to sin.
- Leisure activities should show respect and dignity of the person. They should be worthwhile and not weaken his faith.
- Leisure activities should be moral and within God's laws.

Identify disadvantages of over-indulging in leisure activities.

- A person may easily get addicted to that leisure activity.
- May lead to poor human relations for the sake of leisure.
- They may neglect their families.
- A person may neglect their work and other important activities.
- It may hinder the person from exploiting other leisure activities.
- Can lead to over-spending time on a specific leisure activity.
- Can lead to boredom during leisure time.

- It may lead to health problems e.g. obesity, liver cirrhosis, tremors etc.

TOPIC 25: CHRISTIAN APPROACHES TO WEALTH, MONEY AND POVERTY

Define the concepts of wealth, money and poverty

a) **Wealth** is the total accumulation or possession of economically valuable property or materials by an individual. Wealth may be in form of lots of money, land, animals, buildings, vehicles and other business enterprises. Different communities may value wealth differently because a property may be highly valued in one society and less valued in another.

Wealth is acquired through the following ways:

- Well-paying jobs.
- Successful business careers.
- Commercial farming.
- Inheritance.
- Industrial investment.
- Investment of money in financial firms.
- Exploitation of natural resources.
- Provision of commercial services.

b) **Money** is something that is generally accepted as a medium of exchange. It is used as the legal tender. It is usually in form of coins and bank notes. Money has the following qualities:

   i. Money must be generally acceptable – people must have confidence in its purchasing power since the value of money lies in what it can buy.
   ii. Must be portable – it must be easy to carry about.
   iii. Must be durable/stable – its value should not be subject to deterioration during the time of storage.
   iv. Must be valuable – its value must be maintained through proper control of its circulation.
   v. Must be divisible – it must be easy to divide it into small units.
   vi. Must be relatively scarce in order to maintain its value.

c) **Poverty** is whereby an individual is unable to afford the human basic needs such as food, clothing and shelter. Poverty it brings suffering since it leads to lack of medical facilities, hunger, lack of educational facilities and lack of care for the environment.

Outline the causes of poverty

- Joblessness or unemployment which may be as a result of illiteracy or other causes.
- Political instabilities due to wars which destroy the wealth of individuals and countries.
- Corruption makes the government unable to initiate economic projects that uplift its people.
- Adverse climatic conditions which lower the productivity of land.
- Regional imbalance of natural resources where some regions are endowed more than others.
- Historical and social factors such as family backgrounds e.g. children born in poor families will not secure basic needs and their offspring are likely to follow suit.
- Inflation is another cause whereby the poor may not be able to afford some commodities due to high prices.
- Laziness
- Overdependence on foreign aid.
- Low level of technological advancement has hindered the exploitation of natural resources.

TRADITIONAL AFRICAN UNDERSTANDING OF WEALTH

- Wealth is believed to be a gift from God. Africans made sacrifices to God to thank Him and ask Him not to take it away.
- Wealth also came as a result of hard work. This was achieved by working as farmers or pastoralists.
- Wealth is measured in terms of land, livestock, and the number of wives and children one has.
- Women and children were not allowed to own any property.
- Men who were wealthy were respected and greatly honoured in the society.
- Some forms of wealth are owned communally e.g. land while others are owned communally.
- Those who were wealthy shared their wealth with the poor.
- There were clear guidelines on the ownership and use of wealth.
- Wealth was acquired through ways such as:
  i. Inheritance.
  ii. Payment of bridewealth/dowry.
  iii. Through farming.
  iv. Exploitation of natural resources.
  v. Through barter trade.
  vi. Raids.
  vii. Marrying many wives and having many children.

TRADITIONAL AFRICAN UNDERSTANDING OF POVERTY

- In traditional African communities, poverty is understood as lack of basic needs required to live a decent life and lack of a family.
- Poverty is seen as a curse or a form of punishment for wrong doing.
- Poverty was not embraced and so the youth were equipped with skills to help them acquire wealth.
- Those who were poor as a result of laziness were ridiculed since everyone had to work hard to acquire wealth.
- Poverty was believed to be caused by factors such as:
  i.   Laziness.
  ii.   Lack of inheritance.
  iii. Sickness.
  iv.   Natural calamities.
  v.   Breaking of taboos.
  vi.   Insecurity.
- The poor, orphans and widows were taken care of by the rich since there was sharing and communal ownership of property.
- Ancestral land is held in custody for future generations. The landless are given a portion of land to cultivate and graze their animals.

THE IMPACT OF MONEY ECONOMY IN THE TRADITIONAL AFRICAN SOCIETY

Money economy is a state of using money as the medium of exchange in economic activities such as banking, investment, insurance and payment of goods and services. The use of money in Africa was introduced by European missionaries and the colonial administration.

Before the coming of Europeans, Africans carried out barter trade. The colonial government created a need for money in the traditional African minds due to a number of factors.

Factors which led to the introduction of the money economy in Africa

- Payment of taxes. The Europeans introduced payment of taxes to the government forcing Africans to work in the plantation to get money to pay taxes.
- Introduction of new goods. Europeans brought along with them goods e.g. cloth, soap, porcelain, sugar, matches, which were acquired using money.
- Changes brought by colonization: The Europeans occupied the white highlands and established plantation farming. The labourers on the farms had to be paid in form of money.
- Introduction of formal education. Africans learnt skills in various fields which enabled them to be employed in various sectors where they were paid in the form of money.
- Introduction of modern medical services. Missionaries and colonialists built several hospitals where Africans had to pay for the services in the form of money.

- Emergence of new lifestyles. In Africa missionaries emphasized on the material well-being of the new converts e.g. building good houses. To accomplish this, Africans needed money, hence the use of money was introduced into African societies.

The impact of the introduction of money economy in traditional African society

The introduction of money economy has had both positive and negative effects.

Positive effects

- Money is portable and easier to work with.
- Money is simpler when transacting in trade because it is more efficient.
- Women and children can now own money which is different from African societies whereby only men owned it.
- Money led to introduction of waged or salaried jobs which is different from African societies whereby work was not paid for.
- It has led to emergence of cash crops like coffee, tea, pyrethrum etc.
- It led to higher standards of living for the Africans who were employed.
- Africans were able to interact with the outside world through trade.

Negative effects

- It has led to break up of family ties due to rural-urban migrations in search for employment.
- It has led to crimes and vices as people seek or look for money.
- African subsistence crops were replaced by cash crops.
- Work was not paid for in African societies but now it is, which has led to exploitation of workers by some employers.
- Money has led to the widening of the gap between the rich and the poor.
- Dowry which was one source of wealth has been commercialized.
- Informal education which was available has become scarce due to it being made formal. The poor can't afford it due to the high cost of education.
- Large families are avoided because of the high cost of living and people have resorted to raising smaller families.
- Individualism has been created and communal sharing has been disregarded,
- It has led to destruction of natural resources to create room for money generating projects.
- It has led to the high cost of living because everything is acquired by money.

THE CHRISTIAN TEACHING ON MONEY, WEALTH

- Wealth in the Bible is seen in form possession of money (gold/silver), servants, horses and other livestock, vineyards among others.

- The Bible states that wealth is a gift and a blessing from God. Man is therefore a steward or a caretaker of this blessing.
- Wealth is a result of working hard.
- The Bible condemns evil ways of acquiring wealth but encourages that wealth should be acquired through honest ways.
- Wealth should be used to glorify God and support His work. This can be in form of tithes and offerings.
- Wealth can lead man away from God and create a false sense of independence from God.
- Wealth is not permanent.
- Wealth should be shared and used to help the needy.

In what ways do Christians use their wealth?

- Financing the spread of the Gospel.
- Giving relief aid to drought-stricken areas or to victims of floods.
- Contributing towards the construction of hospitals, schools, churches and homes for the aged and destitute.
- Paying lawful taxes to the government.
- Providing formal education and training.
- Giving offerings and paying tithes.
- Providing for the family needs.

Christian teaching on poverty

- Poverty and laziness are related, both of them are wrong and people are warned against them.
- The Bible also records people who were poor due to misfortunes, judgement or persecution for example God allowed Satan to bring misfortunes to Job.
- Poverty is a punishment from God. Israelites were taken captive when they disobeyed God and He punished them through slavery.
- The Bible emphasizes that the rich should share their wealth with the poor.
- Jesus regards spiritual poverty because such people are blessed.

How do people misuse their wealth in Kenya today?

- Through gambling.
- Heavy drinking of alcohol.
- Drug trafficking.
- Engagement in immorality.
- In promoting crime.
- In corrupt practices e.g. buying leadership positions.

- By being extravagant.
- By not sharing with others.
- Spoiling the youth by giving them a lot of money.
- Using wealth to exploit and frustrate others.

CHRISTIAN APPROACHES TO SOME ISSUES RELATED TO WEALTH

a) Fair distribution of wealth (affluence and poverty)

- Fair distribution of wealth is a situation where the nation's resources are shared equitably among its members.
- Unfair distribution of wealth is a situation where there are two social classes of people, the rich (affluence) and the poor (poverty).
- Affluence is the possession of lots of material and living a luxurious lifestyle while poverty is the inadequacy of resources to cater for basic needs. Poverty on the other hand refers to the state of having inadequate resources to meet one's basic needs.
- Christians believe that God created worldly resources for the benefit of all and so the poor should be assisted to acquire their basic needs.
- Christians should advocate for high taxation of the rich and lower for the poor. The revenue can be used to support all people.
- Christians should advocate for economic policies that will ensure fair distribution of wealth.
- The church and government can help the poor start income generating projects by giving them with soft loans.
- Christians should advocate for good governance which will improve the economy and the living conditions of poor people.
- The government should cut down expenditure of public funds and the money used to start income generating activities.
- The church should encourage its members to work hard and earn a living.
- The people should be educated on the importance of work and redeeming time.

b) Bribery and corruption

- Bribery is the giving of privileges or inducement in form of money and goods to someone so as to receive an undeserved favour. Corruption is the practise of giving a bribe in the form of money, goods or privileges in return for a service. Bribery is a form of corruption.
- The Bible condemns corruption and so Christians are asked to condemn it too.
- Christians who have engaged in corrupt practices are called to repentance like Zacchaeus in the New Testament. They should then repay the embezzled money.
- Christians should promote justice in the society and be role models to others by refusing to give and take bribes.

- Jesus condemned corruption which was a form of exploitation of the poor and misuse of leadership position in the society.
- John the Baptist taught the tax collectors not to collect excess taxes, not to give or take bribes. Instead they should repent.
- The Bible condemns corruption because it is a form of oppression for the poor.
- Corrupt leaders lose their fame, power and authority since the people lose confidence in them.
- Evasion of payment of taxes is a corrupt act and Jesus warned against such people, by teaching that "give Caesar what belongs to him".
- Christians are called to use every means to campaign against corruption. It may be in form of evangelism, seminars, teachings etc.
- Corruption may lead to misfortunes or even death e.g. Judas Iscariot who received a bribe to betray Jesus, he lie later died.

Factors that lead to bribery and corruption in the society
- The high rate of unemployment makes many people desperate hence ready to give a bribe in any form in order to secure employment.
- Those who are greedy for money receive bribes and use their positions to influence official procedures e.g. employment and tenders.
- Fear, especially by traffic offenders and hardcore criminals who choose to bribe police officers so that they are not arrested and charged in court of law.
- Due to ignorance some people receive or give bribes in the form of gifts.
- Disintegration of traditional African values e.g. honesty, mutual concern and respect, which are no longer upheld by most persons.
- Lack of moral integrity.

The bible condemns bribery and corruption as they are sins before God. They are morally wrong because of the following reasons:
- People lose confidence and respect for corrupt leaders.
- They cause discontentment among people who are denied their rights.
- They affect one's family negatively and spoils its reputation since the person may be sacked, hence the family loses the source of income.
- It promotes injustice since giving bribes is an illegal means to win favours.
- Bribery and corruption obstruct the cause of justice.
- They impoverish individuals, families and nations.
- They may lead to collapse of public corporations resulting in mass unemployment.
- They are immoral and sinful acts.

How the Christians can help reduce practice of corruption in Kenya

- Praying for the corrupt people to change.
- Being role models.
- Preaching to the people on the ills of corruption.
- Reporting incidences of corruption to the relevant authorities.
- Encourage people to adhere to stipulated laws.
- Publish magazines, newsletters on negative effects of corruption.
- Organize seminars and conferences to discuss solutions to end corruption.
- Campaigning for better salaries.
- Choosing /electing honest leaders.
- Establish causes of corruption.

Life skills

Life skills are the capabilities that may be used to conquer the challenges of life e.g.

- Decision making is to reach a particular conclusion after careful observation and thinking. A decision is a resolution reached after making careful observations and considerations. Christians are therefore advised to think carefully before making a decision over a particular issue e.g. considering reporting those who are tempting him/her to be corrupt.
- Critical thinking is the ability to make a rational (reasonable) decision before taking any action on a particular issue. A critical thinker does not take things for granted and is responsible for the actions he or she takes. Christians are therefore called to think critically and make critical judgments on ways of acquiring wealth.
- Creative thinking is being able to innovate or come up with new ideas to help one to solve a particular problem. Christians are asked to be creative so that they can come up with ways of eradicating poverty.
- Self-esteem is the opinion one has about himself/herself. Some people may have low opinion of themselves and others regard themselves highly. Psalms 1:26 tells us that we are wonderfully and fearfully made. This should create confidence in everyone and the work or activities we engage in should be able to boost our self-esteem.
- Assertiveness is a skill of expressing oneself without hurting those around you. An assertive person is not influenced by others to do wrong. Such people are confident and have high self-esteem. Christians should therefore be firm and confidence for their faith.

Christian values and virtues that enable Christians to make moral decisions and be different from other people:

- Love is the affection or regard for someone or something. The virtue of love enables Christians to share their wealth with the poor and give help to anyone who needs it.

- Honesty is to be truthful and sincere in everything that one does. As a virtue it guides Christians while acquiring wealth and using it.
- Reliability and dependency - a reliable person is dependable and trustworthy. The Bible gives examples of people who were reliable like Joseph and Daniel. Christians should be people who can be relied upon by others who are in need because of their good character.
- Fairness is treating everyone equally without discrimination because of any difference. This virtue ensures equality between the rich and poor, old and young widows and widowers etc. Christians need to condemn unfairness in the society.
- Justice is the state of being fair to all as it is required by the law. Justice is denied when corruption prevails. Christians should condemn all forms of injustices and observe justice as a sign of love to him.
- Respect is having high regard for someone or something. Christians should respect God and his creation as his stewards.
- Humility is the quality of being humble in that one is able to value other people irrespective of their status. A humble person does not value himself more than others. Christians should follow the example of Jesus and put the interests and welfare of others first.
- Faithfulness is trust and confidence in a person no matter the circumstances. Jesus taught that people should be faithful with their wealth whether little or much. Christians should be faithful with whatever public property they are given to manage.
- Persistence is the determination to do something despite the obstacles or opposition one faces. Jesus uses the parable of the widow and the unrighteous judge to show that persistence finally bears fruit. Christians should be persistent in all they do for they will receive its reward.
- Chastity is the state of purity by avoiding all forms of immorality especially sexual immorality. The body is the temple of the Holy Spirit and so it should be kept clean. Christians should listen to the Holy Spirit in everything they do to avoid impurifying themselves. They should not acquire wealth through unchaste ways.

Give the reasons why corruption is rampant among the Kenyan workers.
- Desire for unmerited promotion.
- Frustration in the place of work.
- Desire for instant wealth/power.
- Low pay/salaries.
- A feeling of inadequate compensation to work done.
- A perverted conscience.
- Poverty among Kenyan workers/High dependency ratio in Kenyan families.

Explain the abuses that may arise from the system of taxation in our society today

- Some government officials may corruptly use the tax money to enrich themselves.
- Making the rich and the poor pay the same amount of money is an abuse.
- The policy of taxing the poor is unjust.
- The tax system may be exploitative and oppressive to the poor.
- Those collecting taxes can be bribed so that others evade paying taxes.
- The government may fail to distribute the resources of taxation equitably in all areas.
- Overpricing of goods, when the government raises indirect taxes like excise duty, the buyer ends up paying more.
- A government may take advantage of the tax system to take too many external loans.
- The government may fear increasing taxes because it may lose the support of the masses.
- Some people may not declare other sources of income for example using two receipts books to avoid paying taxes.

TOPIC 26: CHRISTIAN APPROACHES TO LAW, ORDER AND JUSTICE

Define the terms law, order and justice.

Law refers rules and regulations that have been established by an authority to regulate the behaviour of people in a community or society. Laws protect, direct and determine relationships.

There are different types of laws that affect us in our daily lives:

- **Non-legal laws** are those that operate in schools, clubs and organizations. Those who break them do not face legal action but are punished in a way or expelled from the organization.
- **Customary/traditional laws** are those which have developed around culture and social traditions of different communities e.g. taboos.
- **Statutory/legal laws** are laws made by county or national governments and citizens are required to obey them. When people break these laws they are arrested and arraigned in court.

There are various types of statutory laws:

i.   Civil laws are made in parliament to guide citizens in their activities and in relation to one another. They deal with issues of property, paying taxes, labour, management and divorce.
ii.   Criminal law deals with crime and the punishment for crime e.g. murder, rape, robbery with violence, and assault.
iii. Constitutional law deals with matters of the constitution, concerning the state and governance.
iv.   Company law regulates the affairs of companies.
v.   Religious laws are made by different religions to govern their members e.g. Islamic Sharia Law.

Order is a state of peace, harmony and security which results from obedience of laws.
Justice refers to treating others right and fairly, as per the requirements of the law.

TRADITIONAL AFRICAN PRACTICES THAT PROMOTE LAW, ORDER AND JUSTICE

Law in traditional African communities was inherited from the ancestors. It was passed orally from one generation to the other. Laws existed as taboos, customs and norms.

Some of the practises that promote law, order and justice include:

- Taboos were strictly followed and anyone who broke them was punished by the ancestors.
- Kinship ties defined how people relate to one another in the community.
- Religious and cultural beliefs stipulated rules of worship and practises as a sign of fear of God and respect for one another.
- Their political organization was in such a way that the elders were the ones to implement law, settle disputes and administer punishment.
- Punishment for offenders was severe, which helped to maintain order and justice.
- Oaths were administered by specialists, which helped enhance honesty, respect and unity among community members.
- Covenants and peace treaties were signed between warring parties as a way of reconciliation.
- Emissaries and mediators are sent to resolve issues and unite warring communities.
- Meals and drinks are shared after settling a dispute as a sign of peace.

BIBLICAL TEACHING ON LAW, ORDER AND JUSTICE:

- The creation story in Genesis presents God as a God of order. He created everything in its time and purpose.
- Law was instituted by God. He gave Adam and Eve a law of obedience, He also gave the Israelites the ten commandments which later formed the constitution for Israelites.
- The government of Israel was ruled by God himself through judges and later on through kings. The Kings were expected to rule in obedience to the Law of God.
- Punishment for sin is inevitable. Those who failed to observe the covenant law were punished in form of catastrophes, wars and even deaths.
- Jesus and the apostles taught on the respect for those in authority to show that they recognized law. Jesus obeyed the Jewish law and also came to fulfil it.
- God upholds justice by punishing offenders regardless of their status. He punished King David when he committed adultery and murder though he forgave him. The prophets too condemned all forms of injustices because they make people to suffer.
- The Bible shows the importance of law, order and justice. Rulers are custodians of the Law and Christians are required to respect the Law and Authority to create order and harmony in the society.

THE NEED FOR LAW, ORDER AND JUSTICE IN THE SOCIETY

- Laws ensure the guarantee of security and protection of members, in the society. If this is not done there is exploitation of people and property.
- Law regulates the power of rulers and create a better relationship between the rulers and their subjects. If rulers do not follow the law, then the subjects rebel and create disorder.

- Law and justice enable people to live harmoniously because it stands between their different interests. People are able to respect other people's opinions and interests.
- Law and order promote political stability hence promoting economic growth.
- Law is important in maintaining and regulating relationships between different nations and their citizens.
- Laws ensure that the rights of an individual are protected and create a sense of belonging in that individual.
- Laws ensure the keeping of ethics and fairness.
- Where there is Law, a government is able to implement its policies well. Taxation is done well and the revenue collected is able to finance all public projects.
- Law provides for religious freedom which is an important aspect in a person's life.

Explain how Christians can help promote law and order in society today

- Preaching and speaking out against evil in society.
- Living uprightly and setting a good example by having exemplary behaviour.
- Counselling and guiding wrong doers.
- Settling disputes.
- Advising government.
- Providing for the needy.
- Obeying God's commandments.
- Forgiving those who do wrong.
- Educating people on their rights through civic education.
- Praying for peace.
- Job creation for the unemployed.
- Holding inter-denominational meetings.

Give reasons why Christians should not take law into their hands.

- It does not give room to reason.
- It is impulsive and based on emotions.
- It can lead to destruction of property, life and even cause physical injury.
- It is unbiblical, unethical and it lacks love.
- It can be fuelled by lies, false accusation, malice and incitement.
- The victim is denied a chance of defending himself or herself.
- It is a form of retaliation and revenge.
- It does not give room for forgiveness, reconciliation and rehabilitation.
- It can lead to bitterness, regret and psychological suffering.

Rights and duties of a citizen

- A citizen is a member of a political society called a state, kingdom, nation or empire and is subject to all its laws. One can be a citizen by birth and by registration.
- A right is what is legally due to a citizen on account of being a member of the state.

Rights of a citizen include:
- Right to life.
- Right to education.
- Right to liberty.
- Right of association.
- Right to the freedom of speech and access information.
- Right to freedom of movement.
- Right to freedom of thought, conscience and worship.
- Right to protection and relief.
- Right to health/medical services.
- Right to children for protection from all forms of oppression and exploitation.
- Right to protection from discrimination.
- Right to protection from slavery and forced labour.
- Right to own property.
- Right to work and employment.
- Right to freedom to practice your culture.

A duty is one's moral obligation towards the state. It is what is required of a citizen to deliver to the state by being a citizen of a particular country.

The duties of citizens include the following:
- Respecting authority and the laws of the land.
- Paying taxes to the government.
- Participating in political leadership by voting for and electing leaders.
- Protecting and conserving the environment.
- Condemning injustice and reporting the law-breakers to the authority.
- Supporting economic development by performing work and tasks responsibly.
- Being patriotic and defending one's country against false criticism.
- Respecting the rights of others.
- Promoting peace and harmony in the society.
- Caring for the sick and needy.
- Conserving national resources.

THE CAUSES OF SOCIAL DISORDER AND REMEDIES
Causes of social disorder

- **Discrimination** is treating some people unfairly by denying them their rights due to race, colour, creed, gender, religion, language, profession, age etc. Discrimination causes oppression, wars, revenge, murder, robberies, violence and other forms of disorder.
- **Inequitable distribution of wealth and resources.** This is a situation whereby the resources of a family or state are unevenly distributed. Wealth is usually in the hands of the rich who are fewer than the poor. This may be due to corruption and selfishness. This may cause disorder because those who lack may react violently by stealing or grabbing from the rich.
- **Racism** is a form of discrimination which results from the skin colour of individuals. Some people believe that some races are superior while others are inferior. Those discriminated against become demoralized and may resent and cause disorder.
- **Tribalism** refers to ethnicity, whereby, people pursue their interests along tribal lines. People are discriminated against because of a difference in their ethnic group. Ethnicity is a serious issue because it causes hatred between tribes resulting in wars and deaths of people.
- **Crime** is an anti-social behaviour which interferes with the rights of people and creates disturbance and disorder. It may be as a result of poor economic growth, unemployment, urbanization and drug abuse among others. People who are under such conditions may end up committing crime.
- **Sexism** is discrimination along gender lines. Policies of a particular society may favour one gender against the other. In most cases women are discriminated against in education, employment politics, culture and religion. Those discriminated against will resort to any means that will make them be recognized.

Explain the remedies of social disorder

i.   **Rehabilitation**, which is the restoring back of someone to the original status whereby s/he can re-adapt and lead a normal life.
-   Guidance and counselling can be given to criminals to help them realize the importance of living right.
-   The government and other agencies can start up ways of initiating income generating activities to help alleviate poverty which is one of the causes of social disorder.
-   Prisons should be a place of correction and training so that by the time prisoners leave, they are able to sustain themselves.
ii. **Through punishment,** which is a penalty someone receives for breaking the law. Its aim is to correct, it is an act of compensation for the mistake and also a way to deter people from committing crime.
-   Punishment may come inform of imprisonment, corporal, house arrest, death penalty, capital punishment, community service, payment of fines among others.

- Punishment should be aimed at reforming behaviour so that the person can be useful to the society again.

Types of punishment used in Kenya.
- Capital punishment/death penalty.
- Corporal punishment/caning.
- Imprisonment/jail term.
- Probation.
- Approved school.
- Detention – one is confined away from public.
- House arrest- The punished is confined to his own home.
- Deportation.
- Exile.

Explain ways in which the problem of tribalism can be solved in Kenya.
- The people should be taught and made to appreciate the need to love one another regardless of tribe.
- The government should support education and cultural programmes aimed at promoting national unity.
- The society should encourage inter-ethnic marriages which help in promoting unity.
- Perpetrators of tribalism should be charged and punished according to the law.
- The government should create more national schools so as to admit students from every part of the country.
- The use of common language; Kiswahili should be promoted and used as a medium of communication.
- Encouraging domestic tourism which will enable people to appreciate the different parts of the country together with people living there.

Factors that lead people to commit crime in Kenya
- Extreme poverty can make people result to unlawful means for survival.
- Poor relationship between law enforcers and the public interferes with the fight against crime.
- Rural-urban migration and urbanization has broken down the African Kinship system that dealt with lawbreakers.
- Irresponsible parents have abdicated the duty of bringing up their children to teachers and house helps.
- Greed for money/to get richer.
- Drug abuse has led to loss of sense of judgment leading to engagement in criminal activities.
- Wide gap between the rich and poor
- Unemployment and under employment.
- Covetousness and jealousy.

Ways in which Christians in Kenya help those who have been released from prison.
- Praying for them.
- Visiting them so that they can feel wanted in the society/invite them to their homes.
- Preaching the good news of salvation to them.
- Welcoming them to church.
- Providing them with basic needs/finances/medication.
- Offering them guidance and counselling to help them to fit to the society.
- Involving them in community/church activities.
- Helping them to become self-reliant by giving them jobs.
- Counselling their families to accept/forgive them.
- Listening to them/help them to solve their problems.

How does the church cooperate with state to eradicate social evil in society?
- The church organizes seminars to teach the public about the effects of social evils.
- It educates the public on the dangers of social evils to the society.
- It uses the media to condemn social evils in the society.
- The church acts as a good example to the public.
- It ensures that strict is taken against the offenders.
- It organizes prayers for the doers of social evils and helps to rehabilitate them.

ROLE OF CHRISTIANS IN TRANSFORMING THE SOCIAL, ECONOMIC AND POLITICAL LIFE OF A SOCIETY

(a) Participation in the Social life of the society
Christians participate in the social life of the society in the following ways:
- Providing health and medical services.
- Preaching the gospel to all people.
- Christians facilitate the provision of education by putting up schools.
- Christians condemn injustices and other discriminative practices which are done against others like female circumcision, early marriages etc.
- Churches have started rehabilitative centres for orphans and street children,
- They offer counselling to those with marital problems, drug addicts etc.

(b) Participation in the Political life of the society
Politics and religion are inseparable since politics are activities done by the government, under which religion falls. The church helps transform the political life of a nation in the following ways:
- The church sensitizes people on civic matters to enlighten people, of their political rights and duties.
- Christians criticize their political leaders so that they do not abuse office.

- Christians can participate in politics by standing for elections to be elected.
- Christians respect their political leaders and pray for them.
- Christians obey the laws of a country and lead by example.
- They reconcile warring parties.
- They preach and promote peace, love and unity.
- Participating in state functions and public holidays.

Give the reasons why Christians should participate in voting during general elections in Kenya.
- It's a constitutional right in Kenya.
- To help in establishing a government of integrity.
- To uproot oppressive and corrupt regimes.
- To have their views represented in law making.
- To enhance desired peaceful change.
- To vote in some of their own who will be role models in governance.
- It's submission to secular authority and law.

Reasons why some Christians live in disunity
- Greed for power/competition for leadership positions.
- Some are selfish/greed for money.
- They may not agree on church doctrines/rituals.
- Misinterpretation of the bible/different scriptural interpretations.
- Some Christians are arrogant/proud.
- Some practice nepotism/tribalism in the church.
- Others may feel self-righteousness than others.
- Discrimination along gender /age.
- They may be divided on political grounds.

Explain the role of the church in promoting political reforms in Kenya today.
- Condemning all forms of poor governance.
- Standing for the truth.
- Influencing the removal of a bad and corrupt government by voting it out and voting in new leaders.
- Conducting civic education to enlighten the people on their rights and duties.
- Protesting in a responsible and peaceful manner and not through violent demonstrations which cause loss of lives and property.
- Offering themselves for political seats during election.
- Pointing out the wrongs being committed and encouraging others to obey the law.
- Negotiating for peace during tribal clashes.
- Appreciating the leaders and helping provide solutions where there are problems.
- Participating in various political activities in order to bring positive transformation in the society.

(c) Participation in the Economic life of the society.

The church participates in the economic life of a society in the following ways:

- Christians pay taxes to the government and encourage others to do so.
- Christians invest in various economic activities which help to improve the economy and also create job opportunities.
- Churches alongside the government initiate income generating activities which will improve the living conditions of the people.
- Christians should preach honesty in business which will ensure everyone can be able to afford commodities.
- Churches run polytechnics and other vocational training centres which equip people with skills to become self-reliant.
- They provide basic needs to the poor.

THE CHURCH-STATE RELATIONSHIP

This is the interaction of the church and the state in various aspects of a nation's life such as:

- The two work hand in hand in providing education. There are church-sponsored schools which use the government syllabus.
- The government works with the church to make syllabus and books for use in schools.
- The church helps to rehabilitate prisoners by giving them guidance and counselling to help them fit in the society.
- The church is the 'watchdog' of the government and condemns evils performed by some government leaders.
- The church preaches peace, love and harmony, which enables the government maintain law and order.
- The two work together during state functions where religious leaders are called to make prayers.
- The church participates in economic development of a state by paying taxes, investment and creating job opportunities.
- The state provides for freedom of worship which is enjoyed by the church.
- The state provides land on which the church carries out its activities like construction of churches, schools and hospitals.
- The two sometimes differ when the state goes beyond the principles of the Bible.

Give reasons why Christians obey the laws of their country.

- It helps to promote and maintain justice in their nation.
- In order to promote economic development and encourage foreign investors.
- They obey in order to ensure that there's peace and harmony.
- To be exemplary and be role models to others.

- To protect their lives and property of others.
- The Bible demands them to obey and respect their governing authorities.

Give the factors that make people to commit crime today?

- High levels of poverty.
- Genetic factors where one inherits bad behaviour from his parental lineage.
- Environment whereby one stays with people with bad character.
- Abuse of drugs and alcohol.
- High levels of unemployment.
- Lack of guidance and counselling and poor upbringing of children.
- Greed for wealth.
- Breakdown of African Traditional norms.
- Permissiveness in the society.
- Jealousy against prosperous people.

Explain the ways through which Christians promote social justice in Kenya today.

- Condemning social evils.
- Educating the masses on the importance of social justice.
- Being role models by practicing the rule of law and justice.
- Providing social amenities like schools, hospitals to the under-privileged.
- Fighting for the rights of vulnerable groups like widows, children, the disabled.
- Lobbying for the enactment of laws which promote social justice.
- Participating in electing leaders who have integrity.

TOPIC 27: CHRISTIAN APPROACHES TO SELECTED ISSUES RELATED SCIENCE, TECHNOLOGY AND ENVIRONMENT

Definition of terms

Science is the systematic study of our surroundings and behaviour of materials in the physical world based on observation, experimentation and measurement. Science can be categorized into various branches such as Biology, Physics and Chemistry.

Technology is the systematic application of science in order to produce goods and services e.g. use of technology in the evangelism.

Environment refers to various aspects of matter, living and non-living that surround an organism. The surroundings are both natural and artificial e.g. mountains, lakes, land, forests and animals.

Benefits of science and technology

Explain how modern science and technology has improved human life.

- Mechanization and irrigation in farming has led to improved agricultural productivity.
- It has led to improved transport and communication, hence traveling has been made cheaper.
- It has led to improved medicine has better healthcare and reduced mortality rate.
- Genetic regeneration has improved on crop production.
- It has led to family planning programmes to control population explosion thus raising families that are manageable.
- Development of computers, press and other machines has reduced the world into a global village and enhanced communication.
- Good shelter and housing has improved the living standards of people.
- Discovery of new sources of energy which are renewable and less pollutants has reduced health hazards.
- It has led to the development of textile industries hence enhancing proper dressing.

Christian views on issues related to science and technology

a) Euthanasia

It refers to the merciful or painless killing of a patient to relieve him/her from pain or suffering. It is usually performed in order to relieve suffering from a patient who has an incurable disease. It may be voluntary where the patient gives consent that it should be performed or involuntary where it is not decided by the patient.

Reasons for Euthanasia

Those who support Euthanasia give the following reasons why it should be performed:
- Life is a matter of survival for the fittest.
- Useless and burdensome members should be removed from society.
- Human beings have a right to choose a dignified death instead of a degrading and disgusting twilight life.
- Euthanasia is compassion shown to a person who is hopelessly suffering unbearable pain. This makes euthanasia legitimate.
- People suffering from infectious diseases like HIV/AIDS would rather die than infect other people.
- There may be few births so that the youth generation will be too few to support the elderly and disabled.
- Euthanasia enables the family not to spend the wealth of the family on a dying person and leave the family poor.

Christian views on euthanasia

- Christians are against it because it terminates life which is a gift from God.
- Suffering is part of human life and so Christians should pray faithfully during suffering because it strengthens one's spiritual faith.
- Christians advocate for the will of God and so those in pain should be prayed for and counselled.
- Christians should offer physical and spiritual support to those suffering so that they can have a sense of belonging and not feel rejected.
- Euthanasia is against the medical ethos which demand doctors should help save life and not to terminate it.

Give six reasons why Christians are opposed to Euthanasia.

- God is the only one who gives life and thus should be the one to take it away.
- Euthanasia equals to murder which is Biblically condemned/thou shall not kill.
- It destroys God's image in human beings.
- Human judgement is limited and therefore one cannot make correct decisions on terminating the life of others.
- Medical ethics only allow a doctor to sustain life and not to take it away.
- It is against Jesus' mission on earth to heal the sick.
- Suffering is part of a Christian's life from the teachings of Jesus and therefore it cannot be used to justify euthanasia.
- It is constitutional right to uphold human life.

b) **Blood transfusion**
- It is the injection of blood into the bloodstream of a patient, referred to as a recipient, from a donor.

Blood transfusion may be necessary in cases where:
i. A person is suffering from acute anaemia which means that the blood level is below the required standard.
ii. One is undergoing a major surgery.
iii. One is suffering from chronic blood disorder e.g. leukaemia and lupus.
iv. A person has been involved in an accident and has lost a lot of blood.

When a person donates blood in any hospital, it is mandatory that the blood is screened for various diseases. Blood that is contaminated with diseases e.g. syphilis, hepatitis B and HIV/AIDS is not used.

Christian views on Blood transfusion
- Some Christians oppose blood transfusion since the Bible presents blood as sacred and some people argue that transfusion is like transferring life from one person to the other.
- Other Christians support blood transfusion because it's an act of compassion which saves life.
- Those opposed to blood transfusion state the risks of HIV/AIDS and so give alternatives e.g. use of synthetic blood, balanced diet or drugs.
- Other Christians would prefer one donating his/her own blood (auto-transfusion).

Give reasons why people are not willing to donate blood.
- For some Christians it is against their Christian beliefs e.g. against the biblical teachings.
- Some fear to know their health status e.g. HIV.
- Fear that it will be commercialized.
- Poverty that may result to the feeling of "nothing is for free" hence not willing to donate but to sell their blood.
- Selfishness since some people do not see the importance of donating.
- Due to health problems/poor eating habits.

c) **Genetic engineering**
It refers to the change of biological traits of organisms to eliminate genetic disorders or to add new traits to an organism.

Benefits of genetic engineering to human beings
- It has helped in the production of drugs for treatment of human genetic diseases like sickle cell anaemia.

- It has been used to prolong the lives of patients suffering from cancer or bone marrow disease.
- It has enabled the transfer of genes of human insulin which plays an important role in the regulation of blood sugar levels in diabetic patients.
- Has enabled the manufacture of human growth hormone which is used in the treatment of dwarfism and restoring near-normal heights in children suffering from growth hormone deficiency.
- It has enabled scientists to increase the rate of growth and maturity of livestock.
- It has been used to produce genetically engineered bacteria which are used to clearing up oil-spills and polluted surfaces.
- Used to originate genetic finger printing for forensic work in crime busting and criminal trials.
- Used to increase resistance in crops and altering animal traits in plants and animals.
- Used to classify blood during screening before it is transfused to another person.
- Used to make a blood clotting agent which is usually lacking in patients with haemophilia.

Disadvantages of genetic engineering
- It can introduce cancer-causing genes into a common infectious organism.
- It can be misused by scientists who can come up with ecological imbalances and cause serious environmental pollution.
- Genetically modified foods have toxins that may lead to allergic reactions that are difficult to treat.
- Some genetically modified foods have no nutritional value.

Christian views on genetic engineering
- Most Christians accept genetic engineering procedures that are beneficial to man.
- Other Christians argue that God is the sole creator and genetic engineering is against the power of God and His will.
- The responsibility of man is to procreate through marriage.
- The negative effects of such practice are more and so people should be sensitized about science and technology.

d) Organ transplant
- An organ is any part of the human body that has a particular purpose e.g. eye.
- Organ transplant is the removal and replacement of one organ from one's body to another body.
- Organ transplant is carried out if an organ is defective. The donor of the organ may be alive or dead.

Organs that are transplanted include the kidney, pancreas, small intestine, lungs, heart and eyes.

Christian views on organ transplant

- Some Christians oppose organ transplant arguing that it is transfer of life from one person to the other.
- Christians are opposed to the transplanting of organs from animals to human beings as may lead to transferring diseases from one species to another.
- Other Christians support organ transplant arguing that it is an act of compassion of saving lives.

e) Plastic surgery

- It is a form of surgery which is aimed at repairing or reconstructing the damaged part of the body.
- It is usually performed to enhance or restore an area of the body which has become less attractive due to ageing, sun damage, cancer or injury.
- It includes cosmetic surgery, breast surgery, cancer or injury.

Uses of plastic surgery

- It is used to correct deficiencies caused by congenital abnormalities.
- The skin that is badly damaged is corrected through plastic surgery.
- It is used to correct deformities of the face caused by cancer or accidents.
- Some people who are dissatisfied with their looks go for cosmetic surgery to change them.
- Plastic surgery is done on some individuals so as to help them retain their jobs e.g. in film industry and modelling where old age is considered undesirable.
- Those with excessively large breasts may go for plastic surgery to reduce them.
- To improve one's voice especially for professional singers and film stars.

Christian views on plastic surgery

- Psalms 139 tells us that we all were created wonderfully and fearfully.
- Genesis says that we are created in the image of God.
- Christians need to appreciate and be proud of themselves.
- God is more concerned with someone's soul rather than the physical looks.
- Christians may support plastic surgery which is curative in nature and not for beauty.

Why is the church in Kenya opposed to plastic surgery?

- It can lead to death if the operation fails.
- It interferes with God's image given at creation hence it is morally wrong.

- The costs involved are very high.
- Emphasis on beauty and pleasing appearances may be seen as idolatry. Some people strive for beauty to be adored by others.
- Certain diseases may be transmitted especially where tissues are detached from a donor with an infectious disease.
- Plastic surgery does not stop the ageing process.
- It may lead to increase in criminal activities by the victim.
- It is like the scientists use it to compete with God in creation.
- It promotes vices such as pride.

How can modern science and technology enhance Christian understanding of God's creation?

- Science and Technology has enabled human beings to make tools, which help them to control the universe and rule the environment.
- Through increased experiments, human beings have developed sophisticated technology.
- Both have been used to improve human, animals and plant life.
- Science and technology has been used to serve the material and spiritual needs of human beings.
- Improved means of transport and communication is as a result of science and technology.
- Science and technology is a way of man actively participating in God's creation.
- It has been used to sustain and improve the environment for the benefit of the human race.

Explain how modern science and technology has affected our society today.

- It has led to exploitation of workers by the employers.
- It has caused health hazards and accidents in factories.
- Human labour has been replaced by machines.
- Families are separated due to need for employment in industries.
- It has led to individualism where consideration for the welfare of others is neglected.
- It may lead to breakdown of family ties because time for family is limited by the demands of the job.

Give reasons to why some Christians undermine the use of family planning methods

- Procreation is one of the reasons why people marry.
- Procreation is a God given responsibility and should be respected.
- It is one way of running away from the responsibility of filling the earth.
- God is the controller and can be sought to control his creation for the sake of the human race.

- It is morally wrong for married people to avoid having children because of selfish reasons.
- It makes it easier for extra marital sex because unplanned pregnancies can be curbed.

CHRISTIAN VIEWS ON THE EFFECTS OF MODERN SCIENCE AND TECHNOLOGY ON THE ENVIRONMENT

a) Pollution
- It refers to the contamination or destruction of the natural environment in a way that can be harmful to human health and other living creatures.
- There are various categories of pollution:
  i. Water pollution
  ii. Air pollution
  iii. Land pollution
  iv. Noise pollution

Substances that cause pollution are known as pollutants and they include:
a. Industrial affluents.
b. Pesticides and insecticides.
c. Fertilizers.
d. Ultra-violet rays from nuclear plants.
e. Dust.
f. Smoke.
g. Noise.
h. Waste heat.
i. Exhaust gases from automobiles.
j. Radioactivity and electromagnetic pulses.

i. Water pollution
It is the contamination of water with substances that are harmful. Water that is polluted is not fit for consumption by any living organism.

Effects of water pollution
- Water becomes unfit for human consumption.
- Untreated sewage may contain pathogenic bacteria e.g. those causing typhoid and cholera hence causing epidemics in human beings.
- Water corrodes metal appliances in industries and homes.
- Poisonous heavy metals e.g. Mercury and silver discharged into water bodies kill organisms in water and other food chains.

- Hot water flowing from power stations expels oxygen which causes suffocation of aquatic animals causing death.
- Oil spills from tankers in seas and oceans kill aquatic animals such as fish, birds and whales.
- Soil erosion due to poor farming methods reduces the depth of water bodies thus making them prone to adverse abiotic factors such as high temperatures which are destructive to marine life.

ii.   Air pollution

It refers to the presence of contaminants or objects like metal which can cause harm or injury to human, plant and animal life in the atmosphere.

Effects of air pollution

- It causes depletion of the ozone layer which protects living organisms from ultra-violet and infra-red rays from the sun.
- It causes rusting of roofs and other iron and steel surfaces.
- It leads to the formation of acid rain which damages buildings, destroys trees and causes leaching of magnesium and calcium from soils and from damaged leaves.
- It causes build-up of carbon dioxide in the atmosphere which has led to global warming and greenhouse effect.
- It leads to the formation of smog (thick fog) especially in temperate countries which reduces visibility in cities and urban centres thus increasing chances of accidents by motorists.
- It leads to production of foul smell which is associated with gaseous products in the atmosphere like sulphur dioxide.
- It causes formation of coloured rain as a result of concentration of large amounts of dust in the atmosphere.
- It leads to loss of eyesight as a result of gas leakages from industrial plants.

iii. Land pollution

- It refers the physical or chemical alteration to land which causes change in its use and renders it incapable of beneficial use without treatment.
- It involves misuse and chemical contamination of land.
- Land is polluted when solid and semi-solid waste from industries, commercial, medical and domestic buildings is left on the land surface.
- Such industrial waste corrodes or degrades the land surface and makes it unproductive.
- Garbage heaps spoil the beauty of the environment.

- Land pollution also occurs through the use of chemicals e.g. fertilizers, herbicides and pesticides which make land acidic and eventually infertile.

Christian views on pollution

- Christians should advocate for environment friendly products.
- Christians can also urge the government to enforce policies and laws that help to control and prevent pollution.
- Christians can participate in activities that help curb pollution such as tree planting, cultivation methods which can protect the environment.
- Christians can campaign against the use of pollutants.
- Christians should sensitize people on how to conserve the environment and ways of preventing pollution.
- It is the duty of Christians to protect land, air and water. They should therefore oppose all forms of pollution and preserve God's creation.

b) Desertification

- It is slow encroachment of desert-like conditions on land that was once productive making it desolate, uncultivable and uninhabitable.
- It may be done by cutting down of trees and vegetation without replacement.
- Deserts may form naturally e.g. when rains fail persistently in semi-arid areas.
- The creation of deserts may also be accelerated by human activity.

Human activities which contribute to desertification include:
- Overgrazing which leaves the soil bare, leading to soil erosion.
- Overcultivation leaves soils infertile.
- Destruction of forests by fire from smokers or lightning.
- Shifting cultivation.
- Poor methods of irrigation may lead to soil erosion.
- Continuous use of chemicals which may make the soil infertile.
- Cultivation on steep slopes and water catchment areas.
- Cutting down of trees thus leaving the land bare, causing soil erosion which eventually leads to desertification.
- Soil erosion which may result from poor cultivation methods.
- Over population leads to clearance of forests to create more space for settlement.

Christian views on desertification

- Christians are God's stewards who need to protect creation. They should therefore avoid or campaign against desertification.

- Christians can campaign for policies that govern tree planting and cutting and enforce penalties to tree cutters and senseless environmental degradation.
- Christians should be role models in preservation of environment and advocate for the same.
- Christians should protect the environment for the use by future generations.
- Desertification leads to loss of productive land which causes drought and famine.
- Christians can participate in projects that protect the environment like afforestation and garbage collection.

c) Deforestation
- Deforestation is the cutting down of trees and other types of vegetation without replacing them.
- The destruction of woodlands and forests is usually in response to human needs.

What causes people to cut down trees?
- The need for industrial raw materials.
- The need for herbal medicine.
- The need for more space for settlement and farming.
- To pave way for roads and railway lines.
- For domestic and industrial fuel.
- For construction houses.
- To provide for mining areas.
- For making furniture.

Effects of deforestation
- There is loss of locally available products e.g. fruits, honey and herbs.
- There is a threat to long-term supply of wood products.
- Water catchment areas which are protected by forests are destroyed hence rivers dry up.
- It leaves the soil bare hence exposing it to soil erosion that leads to desertification.
- Increase in global carbon dioxide build-up in the atmosphere causes global warming and greenhouse effects.
- There is the extinction of certain species of plants and animals.
- There is destruction of natural beauty.
- There is desertification.

How can Christians participate in the protection of the environment?
- By participating in projects that protect the environment, like garbage collection and tree planting.
- By condemning the destruction and exploitation of the environment by selfish people.

- Being role models and shunning from activities that destroy the environment.
- Supporting agencies that protect the environment with finance and ideas.
- Sensitizing people on the need to protect the environment.
- Teaching the people on methods of caring for and protecting the environment.

Show some of the ways in which science and technology has undermined human dignity

- It undermines the equality of mankind when countries which have improved technology discriminate against the less developed ones.
- It has led to destruction of life e.g. atomic bombing.
- It has undermined the view that God is the only creator. For example in cases of cloning, transplant of organs.
- The evolution theory is against the creation story which sees man as an image of God.
- It has widened the gap between the rich and the poor.
- It has led to environmental degradation which has affected man negatively.
- It has interfered with the sacred duties of man of procreation in use of contraceptives.

PAST KCSE PAPERS 2006 – 2013

CRE PAPER 1 2006

1. (a) Give reasons why Christians read the bible (8 mks)

   (b) With reference to the Genesis stories of creation in chapters 1 and 2, outline the attributes
   of God (7 mks)

   (c) What are the consequences of breaking taboos in traditional African communities?

   (5 mks)

2. (a) State the problems that God made to Abraham (6 mks)

   (b) What problems did Moses face as he led the Israelites during the exodus? (10 mks)

   (c) Give reasons why circumcision was important to the Jews (4 mks)

3. (a) Give reasons why the Israelites demanded for a king (8 mks)

   (b) State the achievements of Solomon as King of Israel (6 mks)

   (c) Identify the causes of power struggle in the church in Kenya today (6 mks)

4. (a) Explain the role of prophets in the Old Testament (6 mks)

   (b) Give reasons why prophet Amos was against the way the Israelites worshipped God

   (10 mks)

   (c) How does God reveal himself to Christians today? (4 mks)

5. (a) Outline the problems that Nehemiah encountered in rebuilding the wall of Jerusalem.

   (10 mks)

   (b) Identify the symbolic acts used by prophet Jeremiah to demonstrate God's judgment and punishment to the Israelites.

(c) What lessons do Christians learn from prophet Jeremiah to teaching on the new covenant?

6. (a) Explain the importance of rituals performed during a naming ceremony in traditional African communities. (10 mks)

   (b) Identify the moral values acquire during marriage in traditional African communities

    (5 mks)

   (c) Why is death feared in traditional African communities? (5 mks)

CRE PAPER 2 2006

1. (a) Describe the visit of the angel of the Lord to the Shepherds on the night Jesus was born.

   (7 mks)

   (b) State the differences between the work of John the Baptist and that of Jesus Christ (8 mks)

   (c) What lesson do Christians learn about family relationship from the incident when Jesus accompanied his parents for the Passover festival (5 mks)

2. (a) Outline the story of the raising of the widow's son at Nain (Luke 7: 11- 17) (8 mks)

   (b) Identify ways through which the church continues with the healing ministry of Jesus Christ (7 mks)

   (c) Give the lessons that Christians learn from the transfiguration of Jesus. (5 mks)

3. (a) Give reasons why Jesus used the parable of the lost son in his teaching (6 mks)

   (b) Outline the preparations that Jesus made for the last supper.(Luke 22: 7- 14) (6 mks)

   (c) Identify the reasons that made Judas Iscariot betray Jesus (8 mks)

4. (a) Identify the spiritual gifts taught by Saint Paul in the early church (6 mks)

   (b) Explain how the use of the Holy Spirit brought disunity in the church at Corinth (8 mks)

   (c) Outline the contribution of women in the church in Kenya today. (6 mks)

5. (a) What are the advantages of a monogamous marriage? (8 mks)

(b) State the factors that have led to the misuse of drugs in Kenya today (7 mks)

(c) Give reasons why the church is involved in the fight against HIV and AIDS (5 mks)

6. (a) State the rights of citizens in Kenya today (7 mks)

(b) Give reasons why Christians pay taxes to the government in Kenya (5 mks)

(c) How is the church helping to reduce the rate of crime in Kenya? (8 mks)

KCSE CRE PAPER 1 – 2007

1. (a) Outline the differences in the two accounts of creation in Genesis 1 and 2. (10 mks)

(b) From the story of the fall of human beings in Genesis Chapter 3, state the effects of sin. (6 mks)

(c) Identify any four causes of evil in Kenya today? (4 mks)

2. (a) State the characteristics of the covenant between God and Abraham. (5 mks)

(b) Explain the importance of God's covenant with Abraham. (10 mks)

(c) What lessons do Christians learn from the incident when Abraham was willing to sacrifice his son Isaac? (5 mks)

3. (a) Describe the nature of the Canaanite religion.

(b) Identify ways in which King Jeroboam contributed to religious schism between Judah and Israel. (4 mks)

(c) What life skills do Christians need to use in order to fight corruption in Kenya today? (6 mks)

4. (a) Describe the characteristics of false prophets in the Old Testament. (7 mks)

(b)   State the teachings of prophet Amos about the day of the Lord.   (8 mks)

(c)   How can Christians assist the church leaders to perform their duties effectively? (5 mks)

5. (a)   Explain the different occasions when Nehemiah prayed.   (8 mks)

(b)   In what ways did Nehemiah demonstrate qualities of a good leader during his time?
                                        (7 mks)

(c)   What is the importance of prayer in the life of a Christian today?   (5 mks)

6. (a)   What changes have taken place in the rite of initiation in Kenya today?   (8 mks)

(b)   Identify moral values taught to the youths during initiation to adulthood in traditional African communities.   (6 mks)

(c)   Give reasons why female circumcision is being discouraged in Kenya today.   (6 mks)

KCSE CRE 2007 PAPER 2

1. (a) Outline what Angel Gabriel revealed about John the Baptist when he announced his birth to Zachariah. (6 mks)

   (b) From the story of the early life of Jesus up to twelve years, identify ways through which he is seen as coming from a poor background. (8 mks)

   (c) Give reasons why children should take part in church activities. (6 mks)

2. (a) Describe the temptations of Jesus in the wilderness before he began his public ministry. (8 mks)

   (b) What lessons do Christians learn from the temptations of Jesus? (5 mks)

   (c) Identify problems faced by new converts in the church today. (7 mks)

3. (a) Outline the events that took place in the Mount of Olives before the arrest of Jesus. (7 mks)

   (b) Give reasons why Peter denied Jesus. (8 mks)

   (c) Why is the death of Jesus important to Christians? (5 mks)

4. (a) Describe the healing of the Gerasene demoniac in Luke 8:26-39. (8 mks)

   (b) State ways in which the Holy Spirit was manifested on the day of Pentecost. (6 mks)

   (c) How are the gifts of the Holy Spirit misused in the church today? (6 mks)

5. (a) Outline the Christian teachings on marriage. (6 mks)

   (b) How should Christians prepare for marriage? (8 mks)

   (c) Give reasons why some Christians break their marriage vows? (6 mks)

6. (a) Explain how unfair distribution of wealth can lead to social disorder in Kenya today. (8 mks)

   (b) Identify ways through which Christians promote justice in Kenya today. (7 mks)

   (c) Give reasons why Christians in Kenya are against the death sentence. (5 mks)

KCSE CRE 2008 PAPER 1

1. a) Give reasons why the Bible referred to as a Library. (5 mks)

   b) Outline five effects of the translation of the Bible into local languages. (10 mks)

   c) State five ways through which the church is spreading the word of God in Kenya today. (5 mks)

2. a) Outline the activities carried out by the Israelites on the night of the Passover. (5 mks)

   b) Give five reasons why the exodus was important to the Israelites. (10mks)

    c) How do Christians show their respect for God? (5mks)

3. a) Describe the contest between prophet Elijah and the prophets of Baal at Mount Carmel
   (1st Kings 18: 17-40) (7mks)
   b) Give four conditions that made it difficult for Prophet Elijah to stop idolatry in Israel. (8 mks)
   c) Identify five qualities of Prophet Elijah that a Christian leader should possess. (5mks)

4 a) State three differences between prophets in the Old Testament and traditional African
   communities. (6mks)
   b) Outline the teaching of prophet Amos on social justice and responsibility.
   c) How is the church promoting social justice in Kenya today? (6mks)

5. a) Explain the significance of the symbolic act of buying land by prophet Jeremiah. (8mks)
   b) Outline the sufferings of prophet Jeremiah during his ministry. (7 mks)
   c) State five ways in which Christians resolve conflicts among themselves (5 mks)

6. a) Identify practices in traditional African communities that show their belief in life after
   death. (8 mks)
   b) State five ways in which Christians resolve conflicts among themselves. (5 mks)
   c) Identify the factors that are undermining the role of elders in Kenya today. (6 mks)

KCSE CRE PAPER 2 Oct/ Nov. 2008

1. a) Outline the message of angel Gabriel to Mary in Luke 1: 26-38. (6 mks)
   b) Explain what the Magnificat reveals about the nature of God (8 mks)
   c) Identify six qualities shown by Jesus when he accompanied his parents to the Temple at the
   age of twelve (6 mks)

2. a) Describe the baptism of Jesus in river Jordan by John the Baptist in Luke 3:21-22. (5 mks)
   b) Outline four teachings of John the Baptist. (8 mks)
   c) Why Christians finding it difficult to apply the teachings of John the Baptist in their lives today? (7 mks)

3. a) How did Jesus celebrate the last supper with his disciples?   (7 mks)
    b) Outline the lessons that Christians learn from the incident when Jesus went to pray with his disciples on the Mount of Olives.   (5 mks)
    c) Give four reasons why the disciples found it difficult to believe that Jesus had resurrected.   (8 mks)

4. a) Identify the fruits of the Holy spirit taught by Saint Paul in Galatians 5: 22-23.   (5 mks)
    b) Explain what the teaching of Jesus about the vine and the branches in John 15:1-10 reveal about the unity of believers.   (8 mks)
    c) Give seven ways in which Christians prevent divisions in the church in Kenya today.   (7 mks)

5. a) Explain the factors that contribute to unemployment in Kenya today   (7 mks)
    b) Give eight causes of conflict between the employer and employees in Kenya.   (8 mks)
    c) Discuss the role of a Christian during a strike.   (4 mks)

6. a) Give six reasons why it is important to have laws in a country   (6 mks)
    b) Outline eight problems related to maintenance of law and order in Kenya today.   (8 mks)
    c) Identify ways in which Christians in Kenya help those who have been released.   (6 mks)

KCSE CRE PAPER 1 2009

1. (a) From the genesis stories of creation, outline seven teachings about human beings.(7 mks)
    (b) With reference to the story of the fall of human beings in Genesis 3, state four effects of
        sin on Adam and Eve   (8 mks)
    (c) How does the church help to bring back members who have fallen from their faith?
                                      (5 mks)

2. (a) Explain four characteristics of a covenant demonstrated in the covenant between God and Abraham.   (8 mks)
    (b) Give seven similarities between the Jewish and traditional African practice of circumcision   (7 mks)

    (c) Identify five lessons that Christians learn about God from the call of Abraham (5 mks)

3. (a) State seven functions of the temple in The Jewish community   (7 mks)

(b) Identify six ways which show that king Solomon turned away from the covenant way of life (6 mks)

(c) Give seven factors that have led to the increase of Christian denominations in Kenya today (7 mks)

4. (a) Give four similarities between prophets in the Old Testament and traditional African communities. (8 mks)

(b) Outline five teachings of Prophet Amos about the remnant and restoration of the Israelites (Amos 9: 8 – 15) (5 mks)

(c) State the relevance of Prophet Amos' teaching on election of Israel to Christians in Kenya today (7 mks)

5. (a) State four promises that the Israelites made when they renewed their covenant with God

during the time of Nehemiah (Nehemiah 10: 28- 29) (8 mks)

(b) Identify five final reforms carried out by Nehemiah to restore the worship of God in Judah (5 mks)

(c) Write down seven problems that Christian leaders in Kenya face in their work today (7 mks)

6. (a) Outline six rituals performed during the birth of a baby in traditional African communities (6 mks)

(b) Give six reasons why children are important in traditional African communities (6 mks)

(c) Explain four ways children are made responsible members in traditional African communities (8 mks)

KCSE   CRE PAPER 2 2009

1. (a) Outline the prophesies of prophet Isaiah about the messiah (8 mks)
   (b) State six activities that took place when Jesus was born (Luke 2: 6- 20) (6 mks)
   (c) Explain the importance of singing in a Christian service (6 mks)

2. (a) Describe the incident when Jesus was rejected at Nazareth. (Luke 4: 16- 30) (7 mks)
   (b) Give four reasons why Jesus faced opposition from the Pharisees in Galilee (Luke 5: 12- 6: 11) (8 mks)
   (c) State five ways in church leaders can respond to those who oppose them in their work (5 mks)

3. (a) Identify five teachings that Jesus made to the guests at the Pharisees' house (Luke 14: 1– 14) (5 mks)
   (b) Give four reasons why Jesus used the parable of the great feast in his teachings (Luke 14: 15 – 24) (8 mks)
   (c) Write down seven reasons why Christians take part in the Lord's Supper (7 mks)

4. (a) Give seven reasons why Jesus sent the holy Spirit to the disciples after his ascension (7 mks)

(b) Identify four teachings of Saint Paul on the similarities between the church and husband
   – wife relationship (Ephesians 5: 21- 32). (8 mks)

(c) State five ways in which Christians are able to identify those who possess the gifts of the
   holy spirit (5 mks)

5. (a) Outline eight Christians teachings on work (8 mks)

(b) State the role of professionals ethics in a work place (6 mks)

(c) Identify six ways in which the church is helping to reduce the rate of unemployment in Kenya today (6 mks)

6. (a) Explain four negative effects of the introduction of money economy on traditional African Communities (8 mks)

(b) Outline six x teaching of Jesus on wealth (6 mks)

(c) Give six reasons why Christians should not involve themselves in gambling (6 mks)

KCSE CRE YEAR 2010 PAPER 313/1

1 . (a) Identify **eight** historical books in the Old Testament. (8 marks)

(b) Give **seven** reasons why the Bible is referred to as a library. (7 marks)

(c) State **five** different occasions when Christians use the Bible. (5 marks)

2. (a) State **four** ways in which God demonstrated His concern for the Israelites during the Exodus (8 marks)

(b) How did the Israelites worship God when they were in the wilderness? (5 marks)

(c) Identify **seven** challenges that Christians face while practicing their faith in Kenya today. (7mks)

3.(a) From the story of Naboth's vineyard, explain the commandments which King Ahab and Queen Jezebel broke. (8 marks)

(b) With reference to 1st Kings 21: 17 – 29, give the forms of punishment prophesied by Elijah to King Ahab and Queen Jezebel. (6 marks)

(c) Why is killing condemned in traditional African communities? (6 marks)

4.(a) Outline **six** characteristics of true prophets in the Old Testament. (6 marks)

(b) State **four** ways in which the rich oppressed the poor during the time of Prophet Amos. (8 marks)

(c) Give **six** reasons why Christians find it difficult to help the needy in society today. (6 marks)

5. (a)   Give six reasons why Jeremiah was not willing to accept the call of God to become a prophet.   (6 marks)

(b) Explain **four** evils condemned by Prophet Jeremiah during the Temple sermon.   (8 marks)

(c) State **six** ways in which Church leaders communicate God's message to people in Kenya today.   (6 marks)

6 (a) Name **six** places in which sacrifices are carried out in traditional African communities.   (6 mks)

(b) Give **seven** reasons why sacrifices are made in traditional African communities.   (7 mks)

(c) State **seven** roles of ancestors in traditional African communities.   (7 mks)

KCSE CRE YEAR 2010 PAPER 313/2

1. (a)   Describe **four** activities that took place during the dedication of Jesus in the Temple (Luke 2: 22 - 40).   (8 marks)

(b) Outline **seven** lessons Christians learn from the incident when Jesus was left behind by his parents in the Temple (Luke 2: 41 - 52).   (7 marks)

(c) State **five** ways in which Christians show respect to places of worship in Kenya today. (5 marks)

2. (a)   With reference to the sermon on the plain, state **five** teachings of Jesus on how human beings

should relate to one another.   (5 marks)

(b) Describe the incident in which Jesus calmed the storm (Luke 8: 22 - 25).   (10 marks)

(c) Identify **five** virtues that Christians learn from the miracle of the feeding of the five thousand.   (5 marks)

3. (a) State **four** accusations that were made against Jesus during his trial (Luke 22: 66 - 23: 1 - 23).   (4 marks)

(b) Give **five** reasons why Jesus appeared to His disciples after resurrection.   (10 marks)

(c) Why should Christians be discouraged from taking part is mob justice?   (6 marks)

4. (a) Explain the teaching of Peter concerning the people of God (1ˢᵗ Peter 2: 9 - 10). (10 marks)

(b) Give **six** ways through which Christians can promote unity among themselves in Kenya

today.   (6 marks)

(c) State how kindness as a fruit of the Holy Spirit is abused in the Church in Kenya today. (4 mks)

5. (a) State **four** similarities between the Christian and traditional African view on marriage. (8 marks)

    (b) Give **six** reasons why some young people are choosing to remain unmarried in Kenya today. (6 marks)

    (c) Identify **six** ways in which the Church is helping to solve the problem of domestic violence
    in Kenya today. (6 marks)

6 (a) Explain the Christian view on plastic surgery in Kenya today. (10 marks)

    (b) Describe **four** ways through which science and technology has negatively affected the environment created by God. (4 marks)

    (c) How can the youth in the Church carry out environmental restoration in Kenya today? (6 marks)

KCSE CRE YEAR 2011 PAPER 313/1

1. (a) Explain the benefits of learning Christian Religious Education in Secondary schools in
    Kenya. (8 marks)
    (b) Outline the major divisions of both the Old and New Testament. (5 marks)
    (c) Identify seven ways in which the Bible is misused in Kenya today. (7 marks)

2. (a) Describe how God prepared the Israelites for the making of the covenant at Mt. Sinai (Exodus 19). (8 marks)
    (b) Give four reasons that made the Israelites to break the covenant while at Mt. Sinai. (4 marks)
    (c) What do Christians learn about the nature of God from the Exodus? (8 marks)

3. (a) Outline the failures of King Saul. (5 marks)
    (b) Explain the achievements of David as King of Israel. (7 marks)
    (c) Give four reasons why Christians in Kenya should build churches. (8 marks)

4. (a) Outline seven characteristics of the prophets in the Old Testament. (7marks)
    (b) Describe the call of Amos to become a prophet of God in Israel. (8 marks)
    (c) Identify the five visions of Prophet Amos. (5 marks)

5. (a) Outline the stages followed in the renewal of the covenant during of Nehemiah. (8 marks)
    (b) Give six reasons why Nehemiah carried out religious reforms in Judah. (6 marks)

(c) What lessons do Christians learn from the renewal of the covenant by Nehemiah? (6 mks)

6. (a) Describe the traditional African view of a community. (8 marks)
(b) Explain six factors that have affected the traditional African people's dependence on God. (6 marks)
(c) Outline six similarities between the Christian and traditional African ways of showing respect to God. (6 marks)

KCSE CRE YEAR 2011 PAPER 313/2

1. (a) Basing your answer on the infancy narratives in Luke 1: 5 – 56, describe what took place
when Mary visited Elizabeth. (6 marks)
(b) Identify six lessons that Christians learn from the lives of Zechariah and Elizabeth. (6 mks)
(c) State eight ways through which Christians in Kenya express their joy for the birth of Jesus. (8 marks)

2. (a) With reference to the sermon on the plain, outline five teachings of Jesus on how human
beings should relate to one another. (5 marks)
(b) Describe the incident in which Jesus forgave the sinful woman in Luke 7: 36 – 50. (8 marks)
(c) Give seven reasons why Christians should ask for forgiveness from God. (7 marks)

3. (a) Outline the instructions that Jesus gave to the seventy two disciples when he sent them on
a mission. (8 marks)
(b)Relate the parable of the Pharisee and the tax collector in Luke 18: 9 – 14. (5 marks)
(c) Give seven reasons that make Christians pray. (7 marks)

4. (a) Explain how Peter's life was transformed on the day of Pentecost (Acts 2: 1 - 40). (8 marks)
(b) Outline Saint Paul's teaching on how the gifts of the Holy Spirit should be used in the
church. (5 marks)
(c) State seven reasons why some Christians find it difficult to help the sick. (7 marks)

5. (a) Give seven reasons for the importance of manual work in Kenya today. (7 marks)
(b) List seven activities that the youth should engage in during leisure time. (7 marks)
(c) State six consequences of denying employees rest. (6 marks)

6. (a) Explain seven ways in which Christians can contribute towards the maintenance of law and order in society. (7 marks)
(b) State seven methods of disciplining errant members in traditional African communities.
(7 marks)
(c) Identify six obstacles to effective maintenance of law and order in Kenya today.
(6 marks)

KCSE CRE YEAR 2012 PAPER 313/1

1. (a) Identify six literary forms used in the writing of the Bible. (6 marks)
(b) State four reasons why the Bible had to be compiled into its present form by the early Christians. (8 marks)
(c) Outline six ways in which Christians in Kenya use the Bible. (6 marks)

2. (a) Describe the covenant ceremony between God and Abraham in Gen 15:1-19. (7 mks)
(b) Identify four differences between the Jewish and the traditional African practices of circumcision. (8 marks)
(c) Give five reasons why church leaders take vows before starting their mission. (5 mks)

3. (a) Describe six ways that King David used to promote the worship of God in Israel.
(8 marks)
(b) Explain four life skills that Elijah used to fight against false religion in Israel. (8 mks)
(c) What problems do church leaders in Kenya face when carrying out their work? (6mks)

4. (a) Give four reasons why Prophet Amos was against the way Israelites worshipped God.
(8 marks)
(b) State six ways in which God would punish Israel for her evils according to Prophet Amos. (6 marks)
(c) How does the church in Kenya punish errant members? (6 marks)

5. (a) From the call of Jeremiah, identify eight qualities of God (Jeremiah 1). (8 marks)
(b) Give six characteristics of the New Covenant foreseen by Prophet Jeremiah. (6 mks)
(c) Give six ways in which Christians can assist victims of disasters. (6 marks)

6. (a) Describe five ways in which people in traditional African communities communicate with God. (5 marks)
(b) Give eight reasons for singing and dancing during initiation ceremonies in traditional African communities. (8 marks)
(c) Give seven reasons why witchcraft is feared in traditional African communities.
(7 marks)

KCSE CRE YEAR 2012 PAPER 313/2

1. (a) Outline Micah's prophecies about the messiah (Micah 5: 1 – 5).   (7 marks)
   (b) With reference to Luke 1: 13 – 17, outline the message of angel Gabriel about John to
      Zechariah.   (7 marks)
   (c) Give three lessons Christians learn from the incident when Jesus was dedicated. (6 mks)

2. (a) Describe the incident when Jesus was baptized in River Jordan by John the Baptist
      (Luke 3: 21 - 22).   (5 marks)
   (b) Outline seven reasons why Christians undergo baptism.   (7 marks)
   (c) Explain the importance of transfiguration of Jesus to Christians today.   (8 marks)

3. (a) Describe the incident of the healing of the ten lepers.   (7 marks)
   (b) Explain the teaching of Jesus on the power of faith (Luke 17: 1 – 37).   (8 marks)
   (c) What lessons do Christians learn from the parable of the ten pounds? (Luke 19: 11 - 27)   (5 marks)

4. (a) Explain how the unity of believers is expressed in the image of the body of Christ. (8 mks)
   (b) State six reasons why the use of the gifts of the Holy Spirit brought disunity in the church
      at Corinth.   (6 marks)
   (c) In what ways do the Christians in Kenya demonstrate the New Testament teaching on
      unity?   (6 marks)

5. (a) Identify five sources of Christian ethics.   (5 marks)
   (b) Give seven reasons why Christians in Kenya condemn homosexuality.   (7 marks)
   (c) Explain how responsible parenthood is demonstrated by Christians in Kenya today.
      (8 marks)

6. (a) Outline the traditional African concept of wealth.   (6 marks)
   (b) Give eight reasons why corruption is widespread in Kenya today.   (8 marks)
   (c) Explain six ways the church is using to eradicate poverty in Kenya today. (6 marks)

KCSE CRE YEAR 2013 PAPER 1 313/1

1. (a) Identify five poetic books.   (5 marks)

   (b) Outline the translation of the Bible from the original language to local languages. (8 mks)

   (c) Describe seven ways in which Christians use the Bible to spread the gospel today. (7mks)

2. (a) Describe the incident when Abraham was willing to sacrifice his Isaac.   (8 mks)
    (b) Give the differences between the Jewish and the traditional African practises of
        circumcision.   (6 mks)
    (c) State six ways in which Christians identify themselves in the society.   (6 mks)

3. (a) How did Prophet Samuel promote the worship of Yahweh in Israel?   (8 mks)
    (b) Explain six effects of idolatry in Israel during the time of Prophet Elijah.   (6 mks)
    (c) What lessons do Christians learn from about social justice from the story of Naboth's
        vineyard?   (6 mks)

4. (a) Identify six characteristics of false prophets in the Old Testament.   (6 mks)
    (b) Describe the teachings of Prophet Amos on Israel's election.   (8 mks)
    (c) State eight factors that hinder Christians form practising their faith.   (8 mks)

5. (a) Identify the measures taken by Nehemiah to enable him to complete the rebuilding of
    the
        wall of Jerusalem.   (6 marks)
    (b) Explain four activities carried out by the Israelites during the dedication of the wall
    of
        Jerusalem.   (8 marks)
    (c) Six ways in which the government of Kenya assists church leaders in their work
        today.   (6 marks)

6. (a) Outline the causes of death in Traditional African Communities.
    (b) Explain the significance the rituals performed after the death of a person in
    Traditional
        African Societies.
    (c) List seven moral values promoted during funeral ceremonies in Traditional African
        communities.

KCSE YEAR 2013 PAPER 2 313/2

1. a. With reference to Luke 1: 8 – 20, describe the annunciation of the birth of John the
        Baptist.   (6 marks)
    b. What do Christians learn about the person and mission of John the Baptist from the
        message of angel Gabriel to Zechariah?   (8 marks)
    c. State eight ways in which the church in Kenya assists families to cope with the
    challenges

facing them today. (8 marks)

2. a. Describe the call of the first disciples of Jesus in Luke 5: 1 – 11. (8 marks)

   b. Give six reasons why Jesus chose the twelve disciples. (6 marks)

   c. Identify six lessons that Christians learn from the call of the first disciples. (6 mks)

3. a. Outline Jesus' teaching on watchfulness and readiness in Luke 12: 35 – 48. (8mks)

   b. Narrate the parable of the widow and the unjust judge in Luke 18: 1 – 8. (6 mks)

   c. Give six reasons why Christians should have faith in God. (6 marks)

4. a. Identify the gifts of the Holy Spirit according to Saint Paul in 1 Corinthians 12: 7 – 11. (8 marks)

   b. How was the life of Peter transformed on the day of Pentecost? (6 marks)

   c. Explain six in which the gifts of the Holy Spirit are abused in the church today. (6 marks)

5. a. State the importance of leisure. (6 marks)

   b. Identify seven leisure activities common to both Christianity and traditional African communities. (7 marks)

   c. Explain the dangers of using illicit drugs among the youth in Kenya today. (7 mks)

6. a. Explain how science and technology has improved human life. (8 marks)

   b. Give six reasons why Christians are opposed to Euthanasia. (6 marks)

   c. Identify ways through which Christians can help to control desertification. (6marks)

KCSE MARKING SCHEMES

KCSE 2006 CRE PAPER 1 MARKING SCHEME

1. (a) Reasons why Christian read the bible
- It provides Christians with moral values
- It is a source of spiritual growth.
- It is used in Christian worship
- It gives them inspiration/hope
- It helps them to understand their relationship with God
- It is a source of Christian beliefs/ practices
- It reveals God to them and makes them understand the will of God
- It is a source of knowledge
- It is the word of God the authors were inspired by God   **(4 x 2 = 8 mks)**

(b) Attributes of God as portrayed in Genesis story of creation. (chapter 1 and 2)
- God is all powerful/ omnipotent
- God of order/ orderly/ perfect
- He is everywhere/ omnipresent
- He is the provider/ sustainer
- He is the creator
- He is all knowing/ omniscient
- He commands moral (obedient – Adam & Eve) Gen 2: 16
- He is loving (wants personal relationship with man)
- He is everlasting/eternal
- He is a spirit
- God is the source of goodness
- God is holy Gen. 2: 3   **(7 x 1 = 7 mks)**

(c) Consequences of breaking taboos in traditional African communities
- Paying of a fine
- Excommunication/ banishment/ ostracized/ Exile
- Punishment/ ridicule/ pain to the body
- Being killed
- Cleaning/ undergoing rituals
- Making sacrifices to appease the ancestors/ God/ Spirit
- Offering compensation
- Being cursed/ mysterious happenings
- Denial of privileges   **(5 x 1 = 5 mks)**

2. (a) Promises that God made to Abraham
- He would make Abraham's name great/ famous
- God would bless those who bless Abraham/ curse those who curse him/ protect him
- All the families of the world would be blessed through Abraham

- God would give land to Abraham's descendants
- He would give Abraham many descendants/ he would have a great nation
- God will bless Abraham
- God would give Abraham long life/ he would die in peace
- He would give Abraham a son/ heir
- Kings will come from Abraham's descendants   (6 x 1 = 6 mks)

(b)   Problems Moses faced as he led the Israelites during Exodus
- Lack of water for the Israelites
- Lack of food for the Israelites
- Complaints/ grumbling by the Israelites/ refuse to listen to Moses
- Warring tribes in the desert
- Settling of disputes among the people
- Traveling in hostile/harsh climate conditions/ terrain
- Lack of faith from the people/ worship of the golden calf
- Rebellion/opposition from his family
- Threat from the Egyptian army
- Bites from snakes   (5 x 2 = 10 mks)

(c) Reasons why circumcision was important to the Jews
- It was an outward sign of the inner faith in God
- It was a physical badge/identity for all male children
- It showed that one had made a covenant with God.
- It was a sign of obedience to God
- It signified purity/ cleanliness
- Through it, one became a member of Jewish community/ Abraham's family

                                                     (4 x 1= 4 mks)

3. (a) **Reasons why the Israelites demanded for a king**
- Samuel had become old/ unable to rule/ feared he would die.
- Samuel appointed his sons as judges/ made the post hereditary
- The sons of Samuel were corrupt/ his sons had failed as judges
- The Israelites wanted to be like others nations
- They wanted a king who could lead them to war against their enemies
- They wanted a leader whom they could see/ rejected God as their king
- They wanted a political government with national authority/ organized system etc

                                                     (4 x 2 = 8 mks)

(b) State the achievements of Solomon as King of Israel
- He built the temple for the worship of Yahweh
- He established trade links with neighbouring nations
- He built many cities in Israel/ infrastructure
- He organized the central government/ improved tax collection/ established a strong army to maintain peace
- He established diplomatic links with other countries/ nations
- He built a magnificent palace

- He composed proverbs and songs for the worship of Yahweh/ wrote the book of ecclesiastics
- He settled disputes wisely
- He installed the Ark of the Covenant in the temple/dedicated the temple of God.

(c) **Causes of power struggle in the church today**
- Greed for lack material possession/ poverty
- Hypocrisy among the believers/ leaders misbehaviour
- Tribalism/ nepotism/ clanism/ racism/ ethnicity/ all other forms of discrimination
- Gender gap
- Economic status/ rich versus the poor in the church
- Education status
- Differences in interpretation of the Christian doctrine
- Rigidity/ conservatism among leaders
- Political interference in the leadership of the church
- Fighting for recognition/ prestige
- Succession wrangles   (6 x 1 = 6 mks)

4.   (a)   **The role of prophets in the Old Testament**
- They spoke on behalf of God/ God's messengers/ mouth pieces
- They foretold the future events
- They guided counselled the kings
- They called people back to repentance/ gave message of hope
- They reminded the people about the covenant
- They condemned the evil in society
- They warned the people of God's judgment
- They made the people understand the nature of God
- They offered sacrifices to God
- They anointed kings
- They interpret the vision dreams from God/current events   (6 x 1 = 6 mks)

(b)   **Reasons why prophet Amos was against the way Israelites worshipped God**
- They gave empty sacrifices which did not reflect holy lives
- They practiced syncretism
- There was insincerity in worship/ hypocrisy
- They made idols/ worshipped idols
- They built many high places of worship for idols
- They misused the temple by feasting drinking
- They refused to listen to the prophets of God/ listened to false prophets
- They misused the Sabbath
- They practiced Temple prostitution   (5 x 2 = 10 mks)

(c) **Ways through which God reveals himself to Christians**
- Through visions
- Through dreams

- By reading the word of God/ bible
- Listening to preachers/ crusades/ observing role models
- Through answering prayers miracles
- Through nature events/ calamities
- Through the holy spirit/ the gifts of the Holy Spirit   (**4 x 1 = 4 mks**)

5. (a) **The problems that Nehemiah encountered in rebuilding the wall of Jerusalem**
- The officials of Tekoa did not co-operate with him (Neh3:5
- He was ridiculed by Sanballat and Tobiah. Neh 2:17 – 19, 4: 2- 3
- He received threats of violence from the enemies Neh 4: 7 – 8
- A trap was laid to derail his mission of rebuilding the wall. Neh 4: 12
- There was a plot to kill him. Neh 6: 2 -3
- Insecurity from the enemies Neh 4: 11 – 12
- False prophets tried to discourage him. Neh 6: 14
- Opposition from the Jewish nobles Neh 4: 19
- False accusation from his enemies Neh 6: 5-9   **(5x 2 = 10 mks)**

(b) **The symbolic acts used by prophet Jeremiah to demonstrate God's judgment and punishment to the Israelites**
- Buying a new linen waistcloth and burying in a cleft of the rock Jer 13L 1 – 11
- Jeremiah was not to marry. Jer 16: 1- 18
- The reworking of the vessels by the potter. Jer 18: 1 – 17
- The breaking of the earthen flask before the elders. Jer 19: 1 – 15
- He was shown two baskets of figs, one with good figs and another with bad figs. Jer 24: 1-10
- Wearing of the ox-yoke Jer 27: 1 – 15   (**4 x 1 = 4 mks**)

c. **Lessons Christians learns from prophet Jeremiah's teaching on the new covenant**
- They should internalize the Law of God/ laws of God are in their hearts
- They should have personal relationship with God/ know God personally
- There is individual responsibility/punishment when one sins
- There is forgiveness of sins if one repents/ reconciliation
- Christians have an everlasting relationship with God
- Those who repent their sins have a new beginning
- The need to have faith in God
- They should obey practice the law of God
- They learn that the new covenant is fulfilled in the coming of Jesus Christ **(6 x1= 6 mks)**

6. (a) **The importance of rituals performed during a naming ceremony in traditional African communities**
- Bathing of the baby sets in the beginning of new life.
- Shaving of the mother and baby's hair symbolizes new status

- Choosing of the appropriate name to give the baby is for identification/ incorporation into the wider society/ honour to the ancestors
- Feeding of the baby symbolized new life growth
- Holding of the baby by members of the community shows concern for it/shared responsibility by the extended family
- Saying prayer/ words of blessings for the mother and baby signifies long life
- Slaughtering of animals is a way of thanksgiving to ancestors/ God
- Feasting is a sign of joys/ socializing/ welcoming the baby/ acceptance
- Giving of presents to the baby/ mother is a sign of good will/ ownership of property
- Wearing of charms signifies protection for the baby/ mother   **(5 x 2 = 10 mks)**

(b)   Moral values acquired during marriage in traditional African Communities
- Faithfulness/ loyalty/ obedience
- Respect/ courtesy
- Responsibility/ hard work
- Hospitality/ kindness
- Tolerance/ perseverance/ endurance/ patience
- Love
- Co-operation/ unity
- Humility
- Honesty
- Integrity
- Courage   **(5 x 1 = 5 mks)**

(c)   Reasons why death is feared in traditional African Communities
- It disrupts the rhythm of human life/ activity
- It is irrevocable/in escapable
- It brings impurity to the family
- It deprives the community of the individuals
- It involves too many rituals
- It comes unannounced
- It separates one from the loved ones/ marks the end of life on earth
- Nobody knows about the life after death
- It may cause misunderstanding in the community
- Death rites reveal people's characteristics
- It brings poverty to the family involved   **(5 x 1 = 5 mks)**

CRE PAPER 2 313/2 2006 MARKING SCHEME

1. (a)   **The visit of the Angel of the Lord to the Shepherds on the night Jesus was born.**
- The shepherds were looking after their flocks in the field at night
- The angel appeared to them
- The glory of the lord shone around them
- They were filled with fear
- The angel reassured them/told them not to fear
- He told them of the good news of the birth of Jesus

- They were told where to find baby Jesus
- The angels gave them a sign on how they would find Jesus
- There appeared a host of angels singing/ praising God
- The angels left them/went back to heaven
- The shepherds went to Bethlehem/ found baby Jesus **(7 x 1 = 7 mks)**

(b) **The differences between the work of John the Baptist and that of Jesus Christ.**
- John the Baptist preached mainly in the wilderness/the desert of Judah, while
- Jesus preached in the synagogues/ homes cities/ towns/ temple
- John the Baptist called people to repentance, while Jesus forgave/ died for their sins
- John the Baptist baptized people with water, but Jesus baptized with the holy spirit/ fire
- John the Baptist lived the life of Nazarite, while Jesus mixed freely with all people
- The emphasis of John the Baptist preaching was in the promised Messiah, while that of Jesus was about the kingdom of God
- John the Baptist's message was direct whereas Jesus preached in parables
- While John the Baptist disciples fasted, the disciples of Jesus ate and drank
- John the Baptist did not perform miracles, but Jesus ministry was full of signs/ wonders
- John the Baptist was the fore runner/prepared the way while Jesus fulfilled/was the messiah **(4 x 2 = 8 mks)**

(c) **Lessons Christians learn about family relationships from the incident when Jesus accompanied his parents for the Passover Festival.**
- Christians should obey their parents
- Parents should teach their children about God
- Parents should provide opportunities for their children to mix with others
- Parents should love/be concerned about their children
- Family ties should not be broken/families should live in unity
- God's work takes priority over the family
- Parents should recognize their children's talents/ abilities
- There should be open communities among family members **(5 x 1 = 5 mks)**

2. (a) **The story of the raising of the widow's son at Nain (Luke 7: 11- 17)**
- Jesus went to the city of Nain accompanied by his disciples/ crowd
- At the gate of the city, he met people carrying a dead man
- The dead man was the only son of the widow
- The mother/ widow was accompanied by a large crowd
- Jesus felt pity for the widow/ told her not to weep
- Jesus touched the bier (coffin) in which the body lay
- Jesus told the dead man to arise
- The dead man sat up/ began to speak
- Jesus gave the man to his mother
- The people were filled with fear
- The people glorified the lord
- Jesus fame spread in Judea/ in the surrounding region **(8 x 1 = 8 mks)**

(b) How the church continues with the healing ministry of Jesus Christ
- Christians pray for/ preach to the sick
- Laying hands on the sick/ anointing them/ any other miraculous healing
- Providing guidance and counselling services
- Constructing hospitals/ health centres/ rehabilitation centres
- Providing preventive/ curative drugs/ treating the sick
- Paying medical expenses for the sick
- Producing/ disseminating literature/ electronic media on health issues
- Preaching against evil/ causes of ailments that interfere with good health
- Providing food/clothing/ shelter/finances to the sick/ needy
- Visiting the sick
- Training medical personnel
- Educating through seminars/ workshops   **(7 x 1 = 7 mks)**

(c) Lessons that Christians learn from the transfiguration of Jesus
- Christians learn that Jesus is the son of God/ holy
- They should be always alert
- They should not be selfish/share God's secrets with others
- It teaches that Jesus was a fulfilment of the Old Testament law/ prophesies
- They should be prayerful
- They learnt that Jesus is the messiah foretold by the Old Testament prophets
- They should enter the presence of God with great respect/reverence
- They should learn to endure suffering
- They should live with hope knowing that there is life after death
- They should be slow to speak/learn more about Christ before they speak   **(5 x 1 = 5 mks)**

3. (a) **Reasons why Jesus used the parable of the lost son in his teaching**
- To encourage sinners to accept the word of God
- To show consequences of loose living
- To encourage people to realize their sinfulness/be willing to repent/reconcile
- To teach about God's love for all people/kingdom of God is for all people
- To show God's unconditional forgiveness
- To warn against judging others/condemning them
- To teach his audience the need to rejoice for/welcome repentant sinners
- He wanted to encourage families to live in harmony/unity   **(6 x 1 = 6 mks)**

 (b) **Preparations that Jesus made for the last supper**
- Jesus sent Peter and John to prepare for the last supper/ Passover
- He instructed two disciples to go into the city/ Jerusalem
- He told them that they would meet a man in the city carrying a jar of water
- Jesus told them that they should follow the man into the house he would enter
- Once in the house, the disciples were to ask the owner/ householder to show them the guest room

- Jesus told the disciples that the householder/owner would show them a large furnished upper room
- He instructed the disciples to prepare the room
- The disciples prepared the meal
- Jesus together with his disciples sat down in the prepared room **(6 x 1 = 6 mks)**

(c) **Reasons that made Judas Iscariot betray Jesus**
- Greed for money/material possession
- It was God's will for the fulfilment of the scriptures to be realized
- Judas was unable to overcome/conquer the power of evil/he was tempted by Satan (Diabalos).
- He was looking for fame/ recognition
- He was unhappy with Jesus' activities
- He was an informer of the Jewish religious leaders
- He was expecting a political messiah yet Jesus was a spiritual Messiah **(4 x 2 = 8 mks)**

4. (a) **Spirituals gifts taught by St. Paul in the Early church**
- Wisdom
- Knowledge
- Faith
- Healing
- Working miracles
- Prophecy/preaching
- Ability to distinguish between spirits/ discernment
- Speaking in tongues
- Interpretation of tongues **(6 x 1 = 6 mks)**

(b) How the use of the gifts of the Holy Spirit brought disunity in the church at Corinth
- The people who had the gifts of speaking in tongues despised those who did not have
- There was competition in speaking in tongues
- There was no interpretation of tongues hence messages were not understood
- People did not show love to one another as they used the gifts of the Holy Spirit.
- There was disorder/ confusion in worship as people with different gifts tried to outdo one another
- People did not use their gifts for the growth/ development of the church
- Gifts such as prophecy/ teaching/ preaching were looked down upon **(4 x 2 = 8 mks)**

(c) Contribution of women in the church in Kenya today.
- Women engage in preaching the gospel/ evangelism
- They clean/ decorate the church
- Women take care of young children in the church
- They contribute money/clothes/ food to the less fortunate/ needy
- They prepare meals for church leaders/visitors/prepare holy communion

- They act as ushers in the church
- Women run income generating projects/other projects for the church
- Women sing in church choir
- They organize seminars/ workshops in the church/ guide and counsel members
- They are leaders in the church/ participate in choosing leaders
- Women give tithes/ offering to the church
- Women pray/ intercede   **(6 x1 = 6 mks)**

5. (a) **Advantages of a Monogamous Marriage.**
- It enhances intimacy/conjugal rights in the family
- It upholds dignity/ honour of the family members/children respect their father
- Security is enhanced
- Love is not divided
- It eases wrangles on property ownership/ inheritance
- It is a covenant protected by God/ the state
- Law and order prevails in the family/ there is harmony/ unity
- It reduces the risk of being infected with sexually transmitted infection/ HIV and AIDS
- Providing for family needs/ resources is easier
- It is easier to develop mutual confidence/ trust among family members
- It reduces delinquency among the children
- The woman takes pride in the marriage/is able to enjoy privileges

(b) **Factors that have led to the misuse of drugs in Kenya today.**
- Poor role models/ lack of role models
- stress / depression/ rebellion (frustrations)
- Peer pressure/ curiosity
- Influence of mass media
- Availability/cheap cost of drugs / too much wealth
- Irresponsible parenthood
- Lack of guidance and counselling
- Corruption/ greed
- Poverty
- Moral decay/ permissiveness in the society
- Lack of knowledge/ ignorance on the use of drugs
- Idleness
- Urbanization/western culture   **(7 x 1 = 7 mks)**

(c) **Reasons why the church participates in the fight against HIV and AIDS.**
- It is a continuation of Jesus works of healing
- The church has a duty to guide and counsel/promote moral values in the society
- To cater for the infected / affected members within the church
- To conserve/preserve God's creation
- It is the duty of the church to help reduce human suffering
- To promote economic development

- To promote peace in the family/co- existence   **(5 x 1 = 5 mks)**

6. (a) **The rights of citizens in Kenya today**
- Rights to life/ live
- Rights to have basic needs/ food/ shelter/ clothing
- Right to receive education
- Right to marry/raise up a family/belong to a family
- Right to have freedom of association/ assembly
- Right to freedom of speech/receive information/ expression
- Right to own property
- Freedom of worship
- Right to liberty/ movement
- Right to work/earn a living
- Right to medical care/health
- Right to security/ protection by law
- Freedom of conscience/right to vote   **(7 x 1 = 7 mks)**

(b) **Reasons why Christians pay taxes to the government in Kenya**
- To emulate Jesus who paid tax to the Roman authorities
- To heed Jesus instructions to respect the civil authorities
- Christianity pay taxes in order to receive service from the government
- To provide essential services
- Christians pay taxes as a sign of patriotism
- Christians pay taxes as a way of sharing their wealth/ resources with others
- It is their duty to pay taxes to the government
- To enable the government to meet its financial obligations   **(5 x 1 = 5 mks)**

(c) **How the church is helping to reduce the rate of crime in Kenya**
- Providing guidance and counselling
- Preaching about love for one another in the society
- Rehabilitating law breakers
- Providing jobs/offering training opportunities to the people
- Giving loans to people to start/run business
- Providing recreational facilities/organizing recreational activities for the youth
- Reporting criminals to the law enforcement authorities
- Disciplining deviant members of the church
- Participating in government programmes established to fight crime (e.g. community policing)
- Obeying the laws of the country/being role models
- Praying for peace/ harmony
- Teaching responsible parenthood
- Providing basic needs for the needy
- Condemning evil practices in the society/ teaching against crime.

ANSWERS KCSE 2007 PAPER 313/1

1. (a) Difference in the two accounts of creation in Genesis 1 and 2.

- The creation order of everything is mentioned in the first account but no order is given in the second account.
- Male and female are created at the same time in the image of God in the first account while in the second account man is made from dust and the woman from the man's rib.
- In the first account, creation is out of nothing but in the second account man is made out of dust of the ground as plants are made to grow out of a garden.
- In the first account human beings are created last while in the second account they are created first.
- In the first account God gives names to what he orders to be while in the second account man is made to give names to all that God created.
- In the first account human beings are to subdue the earth while in the second account God confines them in the Garden of Eden.
- In the first account creation is completed in six days while in the second there is no number of days given.
- God rested on the seventh day in the first account but there is no day of rest in the second account.
- In the first account there is no forbidden tree while in the second account there is.
- In the first account the Spirit of God was moving over the face of the waters while in the second account the spirit of God is not mentioned.
- In the first account God appreciated everything as good while in the second account he said that it is not good for man to be alone.
- In the first account God creates in unity with the spirit while in the second account he was alone.
- In the first account God created human beings for procreation while in the second account they were created for companionship.

(b) The effects of sin from the fall of human beings in Genesis 3: 7 – 23.

- Both Adam and Eve realized they were naked
- They became ashamed.
- They hid from God/feared to face God.
- They started blaming each other.
- The serpent was cursed.
- Enmity between the serpent and human beings developed.
- The woman was to experience pain in childbearing.
- The man was made to rule over the woman.
- The man was made to toil/sweat in order to eat.
- The ground was made to produce weeds and thorns.
- Death was introduced in their lives.
- They were chased/banished from the Garden of Eden.

(c) Causes of evil in Kenya today
- Poverty/affluence/wealth.
- Corruption/greed/selfishness/lust/desire.
- Disobedience/rebellion.
- Inability to forgive others.
- Influence from media/foreign culture
- Wrong choices/lack of vision/peer pressure.
- Unemployment.
- Permissiveness/too much freedom.
- Influence of drug and substance abuse.
- Poor role models
- Lack of guidance and counselling/poor upbringing.

2. a) **The characteristics of the covenant between God and Abraham.**
- It was initiated by God
- It was solemn/permanent/long-lasting
- It was unconditional/was between two unequal parties.
- There were promises to be fulfilled
- It was sealed through the sacrifice of animals
- The parties entered it willingly/it was voluntary
- It had an outward sign/circumcision

   b) **The importance of God's covenant with Abraham.**
- God established a personal relationship with Abraham.
- It showed that Abraham had faith/trust in God
- It demonstrated Abraham's obedience to God
- Abraham was assured of God's protection
- God revealed to Abraham that he would have a son as his heir/many descendants
- It confirmed Abraham as God's choice through who all nations shall receive salvation
- The descendants of Abraham were promised the land of Canaan.

3 a) **The nature of the Canaanite religion**
- It was based on nature/cosmic/cyclic/changes in seasons.
- It was polytheistic/comprised of many gods and goddesses
- Temple prostitution was part of the worship of gods/goddesses
- Human and animal sacrifices were made to the gods/goddesses
- Festivals/feasts were celebrated in honour of the gods/goddesses
- Rituals were performed to ensure continued fertility and well-being of the community
- There were prophets and prophetesses for each god/goddesses
- Each god and goddesses played a specific role in the community
- There was a chief god and goddesses
- Temples/shrine/high places of worship of gods/goddesses

b) **Ways in which King Jeroboam contributed to religious schism between Judah and Israel.**
- He made two golden calves and placed one at Bethel and another at Dan to represent Yahweh
- He set up two rival places of worship in Israel and ignored Jerusalem
- He made the Israelites to offer sacrifices to the golden calves
- He chose priests from ordinary families to serve at worship centres
- He instituted religious festivals in the months of his choice

c) **Life skills Christians need to fight corruption in Kenya today**
- Critical thinking/creative thinking
- Decision making
- Conflict resolution
- Tolerance, assertiveness, self esteem
- Self-awareness, empathy
- Effective communication

4   a) **Characteristics of false prophets in the Old Testament**
- They asked for payments for their services/material gains
- They were self-appointed/had no call from God
- Their prophesies were not fulfilled
- They spoke what people wanted to hear/wanted to please the people
- They raised false confidence among people
- They did not speak with authority when challenged
- They spoke about doctrines/teachings that were contrary to the covenant
- Their lives were not exemplary/hypocrites
- They wanted favours from the kings
- They were not ready to suffer for the truth
- They undermined the work of the prophets

b) **Teachings of Prophet Amos on the day of the Lord**
- It will be a day of terror and disaster
- God will punish the Israelites for their disobedience/He will remember their evil deeds
- The land shall tremble/there will be earthquakes
- People will mourn/no happiness
- There will be darkness at noon
- The feasts and festivals will not be joyful
- People will thirst/hunger for the word of God
- People will faint in the process of searching for the word of God
- It will be a day of disappointment to the Israelites
- The wicked will not escape Gods judgment

c)   **Ways in which Christians can help the church leaders to perform their duties effectively.**
-   Giving financial/material help
-   Advising/counselling them on various issues
-   Encouraging them in their work
-   Participating fully in church activities/functions
-   Giving tithes and offerings faithfully
-   Praying for them
-   Respecting them
-   Practicing/obeying the word of God
-   Defending them against unfair criticism
-   Providing training opportunities for them

5.   a) **Occasions when Nehemiah prayed**
-   Before asking King Artexerxes to let him go back to Judah
-   When he learnt that the Jews in Judah were suffering and the walls of Jerusalem were in ruins
-   When his enemies conspired to attack Jerusalem to stop the construction work.
-   After he condemned the leaders for oppressing the poor
-   When his enemies planned to harm him
-   When he was frightened by Shemaiah to hide in the temple claiming that there was a plot to kill him
-   When he cleansed and reorganized the temple for worship
-   After cleansing the Israelites of the foreign influence

b) **Ways Nehemiah demonstrated qualities of a good leader**
-   He was hard working/ committed to his work
-   He faced opposition/challenges courageously
-   He prayed and consulted God in all situations
-   He had vision/foresight for the nation/Jews
-   He recognized other peoples abilities/allowed to performed different duties
-   He was concerned about the life of his people
-   He was patriotic
-   He made wise/firm decisions in circumstances
-   He was honest
-   He served as a role mode/participated in the rebuilding of the wall in Jerusalem
-   He endured persecutions

6 a)   **The changes that have taken place in the rite of initiation if Kenya Today**
-   Female circumcision/clitoridectomy has been discouraged
-   Circumcision can be done at any age/time
-   Some communities take their children to hospital for circumcision
-   Education of the initiates is offered by persons/bodies other than traditional sponsors

- Some initiation practices like removal of teeth/tattooing of the body are being discouraged.
- Some communities have stopped elaborate ceremonies/rituals associated with initiation
- People are being discouraged from using the same circumcision instruments
- The role of age set/age group is fading away in some communities
- Initiation practices are no longer a test of courage/bravery

b) Moral values taught to the youth during initiation to adulthood in TACs
- Hospitality/generosity/kindness
- Honesty
- Integrity
- Tolerance /perseverance/endurance
- Chastity/faithfulness/self-control
- Loyalty/obedience
- Love
- Responsibility
- Co-operation,
- unity
- courage
- hard work

c) Reasons why female circumcision is being discouraged in Kenya today
- It can lead to infection/STDs/HIV/AIDS due to use of same instruments
- It can lead to injury/mutilation of the reproductive organs of the initiate
- It is against child/human rights
- It can cause psychological torture/traumatizes the initiate
- It can lead to irresponsible sexual behaviour
- It can lead to early marriages
- It can lead to school dropouts among the girls
- It can lead to bleeding/death
- It can lead to separation/divorce
- It can lead to disagreement/quarrels in families

CRE PAPER 2 OCT/NOV 2007 MARKING SCHEME

1. a) **What Angel Gabriel revealed about John the Baptist when he announced his birth to**

Zechariah
- He would be a source of joy to the parents
- Many people would rejoice at his birth
- He would be great in the sight of the Lord
- He was not to take a strong drink/wine
- He was to be filled with the Holy Spirit from his mother's womb
- Many Israelites would turn to God through him

- He would have the spirit of Elijah/power.
- He was to prepare the people for the Lord/call people to repentance
- He would turn the father's hearts to children/bring reconciliation.   (6x1= **6mks**)

b) **Ways which show that Jesus came from a poor background from his early life up to twelve years**.
- His father was a poor carpenter
- His mother was an ordinary village girl
- He was born in a manger/cowshed
- He was born in a small town of Judah/Bethlehem
- The first people to visit him were shepherds, who were lowly regarded
- He was revealed to Simeon and Anna who were simple
- During his dedication the parents offered birds.
- He grew up in Nazareth a town of low status   (**8 x 1 = 8 mks**)

c) **Reasons why children should take part in church activities**
- They are made in the image of God
- To follow the example of Christ who went to the Temple
- To prepare them for future roles as leaders
- To teach them religious beliefs/practices
- To lay a foundation for Christian morals at an early age
- Jesus taught that the kingdom belongs to them/He appreciate/blessed children
- For the continued growth of the Church
- To help develop improve their talents
- To give them an opportunity to socialize with others
- To help them spend their leisure positively.

2 a) **The temptations of Jesus in the wilderness before he began his public ministry.**
- Jesus was led into the wilderness where he stayed for forty days and nights fasting and praying.
- He ate nothing and therefore he felt hungry.
- The devil asked him to command stones to become bread if he was the son of God.
- Jesus answered that it is written that man shall not live by bread alone but every word that comes from the Lord.
- Satan then led Jesus to a high place and showed him all the kingdoms of the world and promised to give Jesus everything if he worshipped him.
- Jesus responded that it is written that you shall worship the Lord your God and him only shall you serve.
- The devil then took Jesus to the roof of the Temple and told him to jump down since God would send angels to ensure that he did not get hurt.
- Jesus responded that it is written that you shall not tempt the Lord your God.
- After the devil finished tempting him, he left Jesus for a while.

b) What lessons do Christians learn from the temptations of Jesus?

- They should resist the devil
- Temptations are part and parcel of Christian life
- They should have faith in God
- They should worship god alone
- They should not put God alone
- They should not put God to test.
- They should not misuse the power of the Holy Spirit
- They should be content with what they have.
- Fasting is important in their live.

c) Problems faced by new converts in the church today.

- They are sometimes not fully accepted/integrate/discriminated against.
- The older Christians may not serve as role models
- They may not be serve as role models
- They are tempted to backslide to previous lifestyles
- Older Christians expect them to change faster than they can
- Some experience problems of communication/language barrier
- They may lack Christian literature to strengthen their faith
- The financial demands of the church may be too much for them
- Lack of assistance/concern when a new member is in need
- Some get frustrated when their expectations are not met
- They are given/assigned duties which they can't manage
- They may be rebuked/embarrassed in public when suspected to be in the wrong

(7x1= 7 mks)

3. a) **Events that took place on the Month of Olives before the arrest of Jesus.**

- Jesus told the disciples to pray
- Jesus moved a distance away from the disciples
- Jesus knelt down and prayed
- An angel from heaven strengthened him
- The disciples fell asleep
- Jesus awoke the disciples
- There came a crowd led by Judas, one of his twelve disciples
- Judas went to kiss Jesus
- One of the disciples struck off a slave's ear.
- Jesus healed the man's ear.
- Jesus asked the religious leaders why they had come to arrest him as if he was a criminal.

(4 x 2 = 8 mks)

b) **Reasons why Peter denied Jesus**

- Peter was afraid of being arrested/killed.
- He was overcome by the devil/Satan
- The denial had been predicted by Jesus

- Peter was confused by the turn of events
- He was disappointed by the fact that Jesus did not fight back
- He lacked faith in Jesus
- He had the support/solidarity with other disciples   **(4 x 2 = 8 mks)**

c) **The importance of the death of Jesus to Christians**
- Through the death of Jesus, Christians are forgiven their sins.
- Christians are not supposed to make animal sacrifices to God.
- It demonstrates God's love for human beings
- Christians are able to commit themselves to the will of God.
- It enable Christians to face death with courage
- Through his death, salvation/eternal life is availed to all people.
- He has become their everlasting high priest by offering his own body **(5 x 1= 5 mks)**

4. a) **The healing of the Gerasene demoniac Luke 8: 26-39**
- Jesus and the disciples arrived at the land of Gerasene.
- They met a man who was demon possessed and lived among the tombs
- The man fell down and told Jesus not to torment him
- This is because Jesus had commanded the unclean spirit out of the man
- Jesus asked the man his name
- The man replied that his name was legion which meant many demons
- The demons begged Jesus not to let them go into the abyss but into the swine that were nearby.
- Jesus commanded the demons to go into the swine
- The swine rushed and drowned in a nearby lake
- The herdsmen then fled and went to tell people in the city concerning what had happened
- People came and found the man sitting at the feet of Jesus, healed, dressed and in his right mind.
- The people got afraid of Jesus and asked him to leave their territory
- The healed man asked Jesus whether he could accompany him
- Jesus told him to go and tell others what God had done for him
- The man went through the town proclaiming the good news about Jesus

(8 mks)

b) **Ways in which the Holy Spirit was manifested on the day of Pentecost**
- Through a sound from heaven
- Like a mighty rushing wind
- As tongues of fire resting on each disciple
- By the disciples being able to speak in different languages
- By Peter becoming courageous to preach
- By many people being convicted of their sins
- By many people repenting their wrongdoing   **(3 x 2 = 6 mks)**

c) **How the gifts of the Holy Spirit are misused in the church today**
- People demand favours/payment for performing miracles
- People claim to be under the influence of the Holy Spirit when they are not.
- There is too much emphasis on speaking in tongues at the expense of other gifts
- Those who have the gifts of the Holy spirit are proud/boastful/look down upon others
- People misinterpret the Bible/confuse others while claiming to be under the influence of the Holy Spirit.
- Individuals cause divisions/splinter groups in the church claiming that the Holy spirit has inspired them to start new churches/ministries
- Sometimes gifts of the Holy Spirit are expressed in a disorderly manner in the church.
- People use the gifts for self-glorification
- People speak in tongues without an interpreter hence creating misunderstanding
- People use the gifts to instil fear/intimidate others. `   **(6 x 1 = 6 mks)**

5. (a) Christian teachings on marriage.
- Marriage should be between a man and a woman
- Marriage should be monogamous.
- Husband and wife should be complementary/help each other.
- The husband should love the wife.
- Marriage should be for companionship.
- Husband and wife should be faithful to each other.
- Conjugal rights should be enjoyed in marriage/sex should only be for married couples.
- The wife should submit to the husband
- Husband and wife should respect/cherish each other.
- Marriage is permanent/it is a commitment/no divorce.
- Marriage is God's plan for human beings/it was instituted by God.
- The husband and wife should cleave to each other/become one/one flesh.
- Marriage provides for procreation/multiplication.

(b) How Christians prepare for marriage.
- Pray to God for guidance in getting a partner.
- Identify the person to marry.
- Inform the parents/guardians about the person to marry.
- Propose to the would-be spouse.
- Inform the church leaders about their marriage plans.
- Attending seminars/counselling sessions on marriage
- Visit the parents/family of the would-be spouse to discuss marriage arrangements/get consent.
- Make arrangement to give dowry.
- Arrange with the church on when the marriage can take place/fix a wedding date.
- Identify the marriage witnesses best man/maid/best couple.
- Ensure there is availability of finance/resource.

(c) Reasons why some Christians break their marriage vows.
- Due to unfaithfulness/adultery.
- Lust/covetousness.
- Financial constraints/poverty
- Pressure from in-laws.
- Lack of faith in God.
- Influence from friends/peers.
- Lack of guidance and counselling.
- Lack of children/barrenness/having children of one gender.
- Hypocrisy/pretence.
- Effects of mass media/foreign culture.
- Poor role models.
- Denial of conjugal rights/dissatisfaction.

6. (a) How unfair distribution of wealth can lead to social disorder in Kenya today.
- It causes anger/hatred.
- Some people can steal/grab in order to be at per with those who have.
- It widens the gap between the rich and the poor.
- Regional/ethnic clashes can occur because of inequitable distribution of land.
- It can create discontent/dissolution/apathy among the people.
- It forms a basis for oppression of the poor by the rich/those who have.
- It makes those who have look down upon those who don't have.
- It can lead to violence/murder.
- It can lead to sexual exploitation/immorality.
- It leads to strikes/demonstrations/industrial action.
- It can lead to a strained relationship between the government and the people.

(b) Ways through which Christians promote justice in Kenya today.
- Preaching to/teaching people to have fair dealings with one another.
- Living exemplary lives/role models.
- Encouraging the government/leaders to uphold the rule of law.
- Carrying out civic education for the citizens to know their rights and duties.
- Condemning acts of unfairness in society.
- Helping in the rehabilitation of the law breakers/offering guidance and counselling services.
- Praying for people to practice justice.
- Participating in law/constitutional making process.
- Assist the needy to get jobs/offering them jobs.
- Asking those who have wrongly acquired wealth to return it/pay back.
- Using mass media to promote justice.

(c) Reasons why Christians in Kenya are against the death sentence.
- The law of God forbids killing
- Death sentence is irreversible in case an innocent person is killed.

- Life is sacred/belongs to God.
- Killing does not reform the offender.
- The offender's right as a human being is undermined as he/she is used as a means to deter others.
- It is against God's principle of forgiveness
- It undermines Christian virtue of love.
- The victim's dependence/family are denied a chance to be with their loved one.
- It can be misused by those in power to instil fear/discourage opposing views/eliminate others.

CRE MARKING SCHEME PAPER 1 2008

1. **a) Reasons why the Bible is referred to as a Library**
- It has many books
- It was written at different times, circumstances/situations
- It is written by different authors/people
- It is written in different styles
- It is written for different purposes/messages/levels.
- It is written over a long period/span of time
- It is divided into two main parts/old testament and new testament
- It is composed of various sections/divisions/It is arranged in a chronological order
- It is a reference book.   **(5x1= 5 mks)**

b)Effects of the translation of the bible into local languages
- Many people are able to read the word of God/improved literacy of the people
- It led to development of African/Local languages
- It made evangelization easier/growth of church
- It led to the development of African Independent churches
- Many Africans got converted into Christianity
- Missionaries were able to learn African languages thus making Christianity spread faster.
- Development of printing press/church bookshops
- It created job opportunities
- Africans demanded for leadership roles in the church.
- The well to do African Christian community developed which contributed to expansion of the church
- It created more room for further research into African religious heritage/beliefs/appreciation of the African culture/Africanization
- Promoted ecumenical movement.   **(5 x 2 = 10 mks)**

c) Ways through which the church is spreading the word of God in Kenya
- By use of electronic media

- By providing Bibles
- Through publishing/printing Christian literature/magazines/print media
- By carrying out outreach campaigns.
- Organizing youth camps/seminars/retreats/conferences
- Helping the needy/ building homes for the aged
- Supporting the teaching of Christian Religious Education
- By preaching the word/holding crusades
- By sending out missionaries/financing them
- By organizing choirs/singing groups/drama.   **(5 x 1 = 5 mks)**

2 a) Activities carried out by the Israelites on the night of the Passover (Exo 12: 1 – 31)

- Every man chose a lamb or a young goat for his family
- The chosen animal was slaughtered
- Blood was put on the two door post of the house
- The slaughtered animal was to be roasted
- The Israelites ate the unleavened bread/bitter herbs/roasted meat
- They ate while fully dressed for the journey/in a hurry
- They burnt all the leftovers of the meal
- They collected jewellery/clothing from   **(5 x 1 = 5 mks)**

b) Why Exodus is important to the Israelites

- It marked the end of their suffering/oppression in Egypt
- It signified that they were a special nation/chosen by God
- It was a fulfilment of the promises God had made to Abraham
- It proved that God was more powerful than other gods/supreme
- It showed /proved to them that Moses was a chosen leader of God
- The Exodus united the people of Israel as a nation
- It made them to understand the nature of God/provider/protector
- It taught them that God needed obedience from human beings
- They received the Ten Commandments which guided them in their relationships.
                    (5 x 2 = 10 mks)

c)   How Christians show their respect to God often

- They set aside a day of worship
- They do not mention God's name in vain
- They pray to him
- Live exemplary lives/role models
- Giving offering/tithes.
- Praise him for wonders
- Taking care of the environment
- Looking after the needy
- Preaching/spreading his word   **(5 x 1= 5 mks)**

3 a) The contest between prophet Elijah and prophets of Baal at Mount Carmel (1 Kings 18:

17 – 40)

- Prophet Elijah asked King Ahab to assemble all the people at Mount Carmel
- The king summoned all the people including the prophets of Baal to Mount Carmel
- Elijah told the people to choose between worshipping God and Baal
- He suggested to the people that two bulls be brought and each party to offer the sacrifices to their god.
- He challenged them and said whichever party will make their god burn the sacrifice will be the true God
- The prophets of Baal were given a bull which they prepared and called upon the name of their god.
- Elijah mocked them/asked them to shout louder to their god.
- He placed the sacrifice on the alter and asked the people to pour water on it
- He called upon God to prove that He was the living God
- Fire consumed the sacrifice/the wood/stones/the water/dust around it
- The people threw themselves on the ground and worshipped the Lord as true God.
- Elijah killed the prophets of Baal.   **(7x1 = 7 mks)**

b) Conditions that made it difficult for Prophet Elijah to stop idolatry in Israel.

- The existence of false prophets who gave false promises to the Israelites
- King Ahab had allowed his Phoenician wife to bring the worship of the false gods and goddess.
- Jezebel had brought foreign gods and goddess in Israel
- There was persecution of true prophets of God by Jezebel/ordered/killed
- King Ahab had allowed the building of temples/high places for the worship of Baal
- The Canaanite religion had a strong influence on the Israelites
- The king participated in idol worship/Baalism was made an official
- The idol gods could be seen/touched so they appeared real   **(4 x 2 = 8 mks)**

c) Qualities of Prophet Elijah that a Christian leader should possess.

- Truthfulness
- Courage
- Faithfulness/trust
- Kindness
- Loving/caring/compassionate
- Honesty
- Responsible/Commitment
- Loyalty/obedience
- Respectful
- Prayerfulness

4. a)   Differences between prophets in the Old Testament and traditional African Communities.

- The Old Testament prophets stressed the worship of one God/Monotheism while in some traditional African communities, prophets recognized many gods/goddesses.
- The Old Testament prophets received their call from God while the traditional African prophets inherited their work from their ancestors.
- The old testament prophets spoke to the nations God sent them to, while the traditional African prophets were confined to their ethnic communities
- The Old Testament prophets faced opposition from their people while the traditional African prophets were respected leaders in their communities.
- The work of the O.T prophets were recorded and preserved while in A.T.R was passed on through oral traditions   **3x2=6 mks**

b)   The teaching of prophet Amos on social Justice and responsibility

- The righteous could be sold for silver, the needy for a pair of shoes.
- The rich women led luxurious lives and were unkind to the poor. Amos 4.1
- The rich women encouraged their husbands to exploit the poor. Amos 4.1
- The rulers lived luxurious lives in good houses as the poor suffered.
- The rulers were arrogant, trusted in material things, drunk wine when the poor had nothing to eat.
- The judges were corrupt and took bribes from the rich.
- The wealthy merchants cheated the poor by using false scales/selling the refuse.
- The Israelites indulged in wine drinking and forced even those not supposed to drink, to do so.
- Those who spoke the truth were hated.
- Prophet Amos advised the people to seek good and avoid evil.
- The Israelites indulged in sexual immorality that profaned the name of the Lord.
- Amos advised against robbery with violence.   **(8 x 1 = 8 mks)**

c) How the church is promoting social justice in Kenya today.

- Providing education to public on social justice/civic education
- By respecting and following the laws of the country as laid down by the Government.
- By providing shelter to the needy
- It preaches on social justice
- The church gives food/clothing to those affected by calamities.
- It advises the government on the need for the practice of justice in society.
- The church condemns social injustice in society.

                                                        (6 x 1 = 6 mks)

5 a) Significance of the symbolic act of buying land by Prophet Jeremiah.

- It showed the people of Judah still had a future despite the coming crisis/Judah will regain freedom after conquest.
- It was an assurance that people would be restored back to their homeland.
- It demonstrated that the people would resume their normal lives/construct homes/cultivate land/own property.
- Divine judgment was not an end in itself

- Restoration was to take place at God's own time/God was to determine when the people would be restored back
- The people had to wait patiently for their return from exile.
- It showed that God was loving/faithful/was to keep his promise of restoration/bring them back to their ancestral land
- It made them feel secure/they were not to lack anything.

b) The suffering of Prophet Jeremiah during his Ministry
- He was rejected by his own family/relatives.
- People made false accusations against him.
- He was threatened with death because of speaking for God.
- He lived a lonely and solitary life/was commanded to neither marry nor attend any social gathering.
- His message was rejected by the Israelites/his scroll burnt
- He went through spiritual struggle as he saw the evil prosper while the righteous suffered
- He was physically assaulted/beaten.
- The enemies attempted to kill him.
- He was put in a muddy cistern.
- He was humiliated in public/mocked
- He was imprisoned/jailed   **(7 x 1 = 7 mks)**

c) Ways in which Christians resolve conflicts among themselves - Only 5pts
- They pray over the issue/problem
- They offer guidance and counselling to the affected
- Paying visits/talking to the offender/fellowship
- By involving church leaders as arbitrators.
- Forgiving the one who has wronged the other/asking for forgiveness
- Willingness by the offender to accept the mistakes made/accepting liability.
- Withdrawing some privileges for a period of time so that one can reform
- By sharing meals/eating together
- Through shaking of hands/accepting a greeting.   **5x1=5 mks**

6. a) Practices in traditional African Communities that show their belief in life after death
- Naming children after the dead
- Invoking the names of the dead during problems /important occasions
- Burying the dead with some property
- Offering sacrifices to the dead
- Powering of libation to the living dead/ancestors/leaving some food for the living dead
- Taking care of the graveyards
- Fulfilling the wishes/will of the deed/carrying out the demands of the dead
- Talking of the dead as having gone for a walk
- Washing the dead body/oiling/decent burial
- Holding commemoration ceremonies
- Burying the dead in a particular position/direction/ancestral land.

(4 x2 = 8 mks)

b) **The requirements that one had fulfil to be made an elder in traditional African Communities.**
- Being initiated
- Must be married
- Being of good conduct/respected in society
- Should have children
- Having the right/specified age
- Ability to provide for others/wealth
- Should be knowledgeable in matters of the society/confidential/wise
- Having support from leaders of the society
- Be of sound mind/good health
- Be a bona fide member of the community
- By undergoing the rituals of being an elder.

6x1= 6mks

c) **Factors that are undermining the role of elders in Kenya today**
- Modern education/technology
- Urbanization/migration
- Intermingling of different cultures/intermarriage
- Laws are made in Parliament/Constitution of Kenya is applied
- Western way of life tends to promote individualism
- Wealth has taken over 'age' as symbol of status
- Most judicial duties of the elders have been taken over by the courts
- Christianity has influenced the members who listen to their church leaders other than the elders
- Permissiveness/moral decadence.

6 x 1 = 6 mks

CRE MARKING SCHEME PAPER 2 2008

1. a) **Message of angel Gabriel to Mary in Luke 1:26-38**
- She was highly favoured among women
- She will bring forth a son/will be named Jesus
- He will be called the son of highest/son of God /will be great
- He will be given the throne of his father David
- He will reign over the house of Jacob forever
- The kingdom will be everlasting
- The Holy spirit would come upon her
- The child to be born would be holy
- That Elizabeth her cousin had also conceived in her old age
- With God, nothing will be impossible   **(6 mks)**

b) **What the Magnificat reveals about the nature of God. (Luke 1: 46-56)**

- God is a saviour because he remembers the lowly
- God is mighty for the scatters the proud/does great things
- God is holy /Holy is His name
- God is merciful to those who fear him
- God is caring/because He exalts the humble
- He is a provider/sustainer because he fills the hungry
- He is faithful because he keeps his promises
- He is kind/helper to his servant Israel   **(4x2=8mks)**

c) Qualities shown by Jesus when he accompanied his parents to the temple at the age of twelve.
- He was obedient
- He was courageous
- He was knowledgeable/intelligent/wise
- He was respectful
- He was cooperative
- He was patient
- He was honest
- He was assertive/independent/making independent decisions
- He was social/outgoing
- He was inquisitive   **6x1=6 mks**

2. a)   The baptism of Jesus in River Jordan by John the Baptist in Luke 3:21-23
- All the people had been baptized by John
- Jesus was also baptized
- Jesus then started praying
- The heaven opened
- The Holy spirit descended upon Jesus in a bodily form as a dove
- Then a voice came from heaven
- Then it said, 'thou art my beloved son with thee am well pleased

                    (5x1=5 mks)

b) The teaching of John the Baptist
- He told the people to repent and be baptized for forgiveness of their sins/He asked people to prepare the way for the lord.
- He told them to be faithful obedient to God and not to pride in Abraham as their ancestor
- He warned them of God's punishment on sin
- He encouraged the rich to share with the needy
- He told the tax collectors not to steal/be honest
- He told the soldiers to stop robbing/accusing people falsely/should be truthful
- He told them that the messiah who was to come after him was mightier/He was unworthy to untie his sandals
- The Messiah would separate the good from the evil/would be punished

- He condemned Herod for his adulterous life/marrying the brother's wife.

4x2=8 mks

c) Reasons why Christians find it hard to apply the teachings of John the Baptist in their lives

- They lack faith in God's word
- Divisions along tribal/racial/denominational lines affect unity among Christians
- Clinging to the past/inability to abandon the old/previous life style
- Negative attitude by the rich towards the needy/poor
- The influence of the mass media/moral decadence in society
- Some Christians lack what to share with others/poverty
- There is rampant corruption in the society
- The emergency of cult leaders/false prophets in the society/lack of role models.
- Some Christians lead hypocritical life.
- Peer pressure   **(7x1= 7 mks)**

3. a) How Jesus celebrated the last supper with his disciples

- Jesus sat with his disciples at one table
- He told them that he had desired to have the meal with them
- He took the cup, gave thanks and asked the disciples to share
- He also took bread, gave thanks, broke it and gave to them
- He explained to them the meaning of the bread and wine/the covenant
- He commanded the disciples to hold the ritual in memory of him
- He informed them that they would be betrayed by one of them
- He taught the disciples qualities of good leadership/humility/service to others
- He told Simon that he would be tested by satan/He informed him that he had prayed for him that his faith does not fail him.
- He asked Simon/Peter to strengthen others in their faith
- Jesus told Peter that he would deny him three times before the cock crowed
- He commanded the disciples to acquire swords/have their own provisions/personal belongings.

b) Lessons Christians learn from the incident Jesus went to pray with His disciples on Mount Olives

- They should be prayerful
- They should put God's will first/desire God's will to be done in their lives
- They should depend on God for strength /support
- Prayer helps one to overcome temptations/difficult situations
- They should depend on God for strength/support
- They should be ready to suffer for God's sake
- They should be watchful /alert for the enemy strikes when they least expect it.
- They need to have close friends/associates that one can lean on.   **(5x1= 5 mks)**

c) Reasons why the disciples found it difficult to believe that Jesus had resurrected

- The message was first taken to them by women who were regarded lowly in society; hence it seemed an idle talk.
- They had witnessed the helplessness of Jesus at the time of crucifixion, hence had lost hope in him.
- They had witnessed the burial could not imagine how the stone could be rolled away from the tomb
- They felt ashamed for having denied betrayed him, hence wished that it was not true
- They had not understood the teaching of Jesus which indicated that he would resurrect on the third day
- It was a new experience they had never seen heard of people coming to life after death on their own
- They lacked faith in the teachings of Christ
- They had expected a political Messiah who was to die in dignity/would not resurrect.

4x2= 8 mks)

4. **a) The fruit of the Holy spirit as taught by saint Paul (Galatians 5: 22-23)**
- Love
- Joy
- Peace
- Kindness
- Goodness
- Self-Control
- Gentleness
- Patience
- Faithfulness

(5x1= 5 mks)

b) The teachings of Jesus about the unity of believers from the vine and the branches
- God is the vine dresser/Jesus is the true vine
- The followers of Jesus/the Christians are the branches
- Christians are related to God through Jesus
- The unfaithful Christians are the unfruitful branches which are cut away/destroyed
- The faithful Christians/fruitful branches are pruned so as to produce more fruit.
- Christians can only bear fruits/do good things if they remain united to Christ
- Through Christ all Christians are joined to one another
- Christians should rely on God for all providence
- Love is passed on to the Christians from God through Christ
- Christians should observe/keeps God's Commandments

(4x2= mks)

c) Ways in which Christians can prevent division in the church in Kenya today.
- Treat each other with love
- Avoid discriminations/segregations/tribalism in the church
- Preach/teach the word of God/bible truths to believers
- Assist those in problems/poor/the less fortunate/the needy
- Practice humility/avoid arrogance
- Openly discuss issues affecting the church/respect the opinions of other people

- Pray for one another/problems affecting the church
- Practice transparent leadership style
- Follow the church doctrines/education members on church procedures
- Repent/ask for forgiveness whenever they are wrong/accept their mistakes
- Preparing a budget annually/seasonally ensuring that the resources are well utilized
- Guidance and counselling

(7x1= 7 mks)

5. a) Factors that contribute to unemployment in Kenya today
- High population whereby there are too many people for the available job opportunities
- Lack of money to start individual businesses /unavailability of finances
- Some people lack skills which make them not to be absorbed in the job market
- Rural–urban migration- Many people are congested in towns where job opportunities are limited
- Rural migration-Many people are congested in towns where job opportunities are limited
- Foreign aid – dependence on foreign aid causing the donors to give conditions of employment that is lean service
- Selfishness/greed-some Kenyans have more than two jobs, while others lack any.
- Education system-many Kenyans prefer white collar jobs after school and because of still competition for available spaces many remain unemployed.
- Insecurity/increase in crime discourages local and international investors
- Negative attitude towards work-some Kenyans lack the initiative to do or participate in economic activities just idle around.
- Unequal distribution of wealth – some regions have more resources that create employment than other. **4x2= 8mks**

c) The role of a Christian during a strike
- Not to take part in the strike
- Encourage other people to find better means of solving the problem
- To inform the authority of any grievances if they are not aware/mediate
- To pray for a solution to the problem/seek God's guidance for a solution to the problem
- Should not take part in a violent demonstration/Encourage peaceful methods of solving the dispute
- To report the matter to the nearest Police station **(4x1=4mks)**

6. a) Reasons why it is important to have laws in a country
- Laws safeguard people's rights/citizen' rights
- People's property is protected under the law
- They protect the consumer from exploitation
- It allows /provides for economic development/growth
- Individuals are able to enjoy the freedom of worship
- The law outlines how foreigners should be handled
- They control taxation/collection of revenue
- It enables the government to protects its citizens against oppression
- The law determines the type of punitive measure for a crime done/prevents crime

- It ensures political stability in a country/nation. (order/peace/love/Unity)
- It outlines the relationships between different nations/countries.

(6 x1= 6 mks)

b) **Problems related to maintenance of law and order in Kenya today.**

- Some legislators/parliamentarians do not observe law thus serving wrong role models.
- There a lot of unfairness/injustice when settling cases because of tribalism/nepotism/religious affiliation/gender.
- Intimidation/people in high offices use their power to influence certain decisions regarding law breaking
- Poverty makes the poor to resort to lawlessness to meet their needs/unequal distribution of resources
- Availability of dangerous weapons/guns in the wrong hands leads to insecurity/terrorism
- There are a few resources to cater for the ever growing population, thus leading to overcrowding/competition that overwhelms the established machinery
- People lack interest/do not care about others, hence don't report cases of lawlessness in the society.
- Bribery/corruption has destroyed the credibility of the government officials.
- People have lost respect/trust for government machinery/have resigned to a life of hopelessness/fear of victimization
- Interference from the civil society/human rights groups/activists who oppose government initiatives in maintenance of law and order
- Inadequate skilled personnel to handle issues to do with law breaking
- People are not conversant with the laws of the country
- Greed for power/wealth: Some people can go to any extend to acquire wealth even if it means breaking the law.

(8x1= 8 mks)

c) **Ways in which in Kenya help those who have been released from prison**

- Praying for them
- Visiting them so that they can feel wanted in society/invite them to their homes
- Preaching the good news of salvation to them
- Showing them care/concern
- Welcoming them into the church
- Providing them with basic needs(food, shelter, clothing) financial/medication
- Offering guidance and counselling to help them to reform
- Involving them in community/church activities
- By helping them to become self-reliant by giving them jobs/survival skills
- Listening to them/helping them to solve their problems
- Counselling their families to accept/forgive them.

(6 x 1= 6 mks)

KCSE CRE 2009   PAPER 1

1. The teaching about human beings from the biblical creation accounts
- Human beings are created in the image and likeliness of God
- They have been given authority/dominion over God creation.
- They communicate /fellowship with God.
- They are special/the greatest creation of God
- They have the ability to think /reason/make choices/decisions in their lives
- They are blessed by God
- They are given a special place to stay/Garden of Eden
- Human beings are to use other creation/plant for their benefits
- They are to take care of the creation, till the land and work
- Human beings are to procreate/multiply through marriage.
- Man and woman are to compliment/provide companionship for each other.
- Human beings are God's creation/male and female.
- The woman is created out of hetmans rib

                                                      (7x1= 7 mks)

b)   Effects of sin on Adam and Eve
- They started dying yet they were to live forever
- They became afraid of God/they hide when He called them.
- They lost authority over the other creation
- Man was to rule over the woman/inequality between man and woman set in.
- The woman was to be in pain when giving birth
- There developed enmity between the human beings and the serpent
- They became embarrassed because of their nakedness
- They were expelled out of the Garden of Eden /separated with God
- They developed mistrust between man and woman.

                                                      (4x2=8 mks)

c)   How the church helps to bring back members who have fallen from the faith.
- By visiting them/inviting them to their homes
- By being patient/forgiving them
- By evangelizing to them/preach/teaching
- By guiding and counselling them/referring them to experts according to their needs.
- Praying for them
- By inviting them back to church
- By encouraging them to repent/confess
- By offering material needs/aid   **(5 x 1 = 5 mks)**

2. (a)The characteristics of a covenant between God and Abraham.
- A covenant is made between two parties who enter into a mutual agreement. God and Abraham were the two parties that entered into a mutual agreement.
- In a covenant promises are made. God made several promises of what He would do for Abraham.

- The covenants solemnized through rituals. Abraham offered animals/birds as sacrifices to God.
- A covenant has an outward sign. Abraham was to circumcise all his male children/descendants to show that he made a covenant with God.
- Covenant has conditions/obligations to be met. The covenant between God and Abraham was not be broken it bound even his descendants generations later
- During covenant making there were witnesses. God as the sole initiator passed through the sacrifice as the witness to the covenant
- A covenant is sealed. It was sealed through the blood of animal
  - Mark for mention
  - Mark for explanation

(4 x 2 = 8 mks)

b) **The similarities between the Jewish and traditional African practices of circumcision.**
- In both it promotes one into full membership of the community.
- It is a mark of identification of a person to a particular community
- It is carried out on male children
- In both cases circumcision has a religious significance
- In both cases special people/religious leaders/head of the communities carry out the operation.
- In both cases it unites the members with the ancestors
- In both cases members receive new names
- In both cases the rite is carried on from generation to generation.
- In both cases the ritual is a communal affair.
- In both cases it involved the cutting of the foreskin

(7 x 1 = 7 mks).

(c) **Identify lessons that Christians learn about God from the call of Abraham**
- God demands faith/obedience from people.
- God is the provider/sustainer/giver
- God blesses/curses
- God is the protector
- God is the controller of the world
- God is a spirit/everywhere
- God is to be worshiped
- God guides people
- God speaks/makes promises/fulfils promises
- God cares for His people.

3. **(a)The functions of the temple in the Jewish community**
- It was used for worship/prayers
- It was the place where the law was taught to children/people
- Priests burnt sacrifices/offered incense in the temple to God.
- Purification rituals were conducted here

- It was a home for priests/residence for Levites
- Dedications/presentations of the babies were carried out in the temple
- It was the business centre for Jews/Commercial centre
- The Jewish council (Sanhedrin) held their session there/a place where cases were heard/determined/law court
- All the Jewish festivals were celebrated here.

(7 x 1 = 7 mks)

b) **Ways which show that King Solomon turned away from the covenant way of life.**
- He married foreign wives.
- He allowed worship of foreign gods/idols/he worshiped foreign gods.
- He murdered his half-brother Adonijah whom he thought would rival his power
- He taxed the Israelites heavily for his upkeep.
- He disobeyed the instructions given to him by his father David to rely on God.
- He built places of worship for the false gods
- He subjected the Israelites to forced labour/slavery during the construction of the temple/his palace.
- He signed treaties with his neighbours for protection
- He sold land to Hiram, the King of Tyre
- He used more time to build his palace than the temple of God

(6 x 1= 6 mks)

(c) **Factors that have led to the increase of Christians denominations in Kenya.**
- Rivalry for leadership/hunger for power.
- Differences in biblical interpretations.
- Hunger for power
- Resistance to change by the older church members who want to remain as it was/generation gap.
- Material gain/greed selfishness where starting a church has become a business
- Lacks of spiritual satisfaction by some members make them start their own churches
- Lack of good example/poor role model by the leaders/corrupt leaders
- Desire to be free from missionary/foreign control
- Differences in mode of worship/ritual observance/mode of worship
- Nepotism/tribalism/clanism/racialism among Christians
- The Kenya constitution has allowed freedom of worship
- Disagreements in ethical issues/policies in the church regarding how certain matters should be handled e.g. family planning, dressing.

4. (a) **Similarities between prophets in the Old testament and traditional African communities.**   **NB/No contrast**
- Both mediated between God and people.
- Both received revelation from God/they were God's spokespeople/delivered message.
- Both foretold the future/predicted/warned/seers
- Both played religious as well as political role
- Both spoke with authority/were charismatic leaders
- Both acknowledged the presence of supreme being/supernatural power

- In both, there were prophets and prophetesses
- Both prophesied to condemn evil in the society
- In both, their prophecies were fulfilled
- In both they were consulted on various issues in society.

(b) **The teaching of prophet Amos on the remnant and a restoration of the Israelites**

- God would restore the dynasty of David after destruction
- God would bring the people back to their land
- The people would rebuild their cities so that the remnant of Edom can occupy them
- The land would be productive/grapes will be in abundance/wine would be in plenty
- The people would grow food and harvest it
- The people of Israel would be peaceful and prosperous
- The Israelites would never be taken into exile again.   **(5 x 1 = 5 mks)**

c) **The relevance of prophet Amos' teaching on election of Israel to Christians in Kenya today**

- Christians are God's people
- It is God who chooses them to be Christians
- The Christians have been chosen by God to proclaim the good news.
- God protects the His people from their enemies
- Christians should be faithful/obedient to God
- They will be punished by God if they do wrong.
- They should always repent their sins/ask for forgiveness
- The priests/bishops/church leaders are chosen by God

5. (a) **The promises that Israelites made when they renewed their covenant with God during the times of Nehemiah (Nehemiah 10: 28-39)**

- They were to live according to God's law/obey all his commandments/requirements.
- They would not intermarry with the foreigners living in their land.
- They promised not to farm every seventh year/they were to cancel all the debts.
  They would make annual contribution towards temple expenses/not to neglect the house of God.
- They were to provide wood for burnt sacrifices.
- They were to offer the first fruits of their harvest/dedicate their first born sons/flocks as required by the law.
- They would pay their tithes in accordance with the law.
- They will not do any business on the Sabbath day.

                              (4 x2 = 8 mks)

b) **The final reforms carried out by Nehemiah to restore the worship of God in Judah.**

- Cleansing of the temple.
- Reinstating of the Levites and other temple workers.
- He ordered the closure of the gates of Jerusalem for proper Sabbath observance.
- He separated the Jews from the foreigners.
- He purified the priesthood.
- Throwing out the household of Tobiah out of the chamber
- Cleansing the chamber in the temple

- Returning the vessels of the house of God
- Appointing treasurers over the storehouses
- Stopping the buying and selling of wares on the Sabbath day
- He ordered an end to mixed marriages/foreigners.

c) **The problem that Christians leaders face in their work today.**
- Opposition from political leaders/society.
- Lack of cooperation from the members of the church/lack of unity among Christians
- False prophets/cultic affiliation/hypocrisy/black magic/witchcraft
- Misinterpretation of the scriptures
- Drug abuse among the members
- Lack of adequate time for pastoral care
- Poor infrastructure that make it impossible to reach some areas
- Insecurity in some parts of the country
- Lack of resources to enable them spread the good news/poverty
- Lack of professional training to enable them do their work effectively.
- Permissiveness/moral decadence, which has become the order of the day.
- Negative influence from the mass media/pornography.

(7x1= 7 mks)

6. a) **Rituals performed during the birth of a baby in traditional African Communities**
- There is feasting by the family/relatives.
- Prayers of thanksgiving/blessings/protection are offered.
- Protective charms are given to the mother.
- Sacrifices are offered to God.
- The mother/baby is kept in seclusion.
- There is dancing/singing for the new life.
- The umbilical cord is cut to separate the baby from the mother.
- The baby/mother are given gifts.
- The mother's hair is shaved.
- Ululations are made to announce the sex of the baby.
- The baby is washed.
- The baby is given bitter/sweet substance to take.

(6 x1 = 6 mks)

(b) **Reasons why the children are important in traditional African Communities**
- They ensure the continuity of the society
- They inherit the parent property
- They take care of their parents during old age.
- They cement the relationship between the husband and wife/make the marriage stable
- They are a source of labour
- They offer security to the society/act as warriors when they grow up
- They are a replacement of the dead relatives/ancestors
- Children are a source of wealth to the family community
- They run errands for the community.   **(6x1 = 6 mks)**

CRE PAPER II 2009 MARKING SCHEME

1   a) The message of Prophet Isaiah messiah (Luke 1: 26-36)
- The messiah would be a descendant of David/rule of the throne of David
- The messiah will rule forever
- He would be despised /rejected by many/a man of sorrow/suffering servant
- He would be born of a young woman/virgin
- Messianic reign/rule will bring happiness/joy to the Israelites
- He would be wounded for people's transgressions/would suffer for sins of human beings
- Peace/prosperity will prevail during the messianic reign
- He will be called wonderful/counsellor/mighty God/Everlasting Father/Prince of peace/anointed One/Immanuel.
- He will rule with justice/ righteousness
- He would have characteristics of normal human being/child
- His suffering will be through the will God/it will be initiated by God.   **(4   x2 =8mks)**

  b)   The activities that took place when Jesus was born (Luke 2: 6 – 20)
- Mary, the mother of baby Jesus wrapped him in swaddling clothes.
- She laid him in a manger
- A multitude of angels appeared singing the praise of God.
- The shepherds hurried to see the baby
- The shepherds spread the news to many people
- The shepherd sung/praises God after they had seen baby Jesus
- The shepherds returned to their homes/work.

  (6x1 =6 mks)

  c) The importance of singing in Christian Service
- It is an opportunity to praise/adore God
- Christians pass messages/pray through singing
- Singing makes worshippers to relax
- Singing creates an atmosphere of worship
- The singing removes boredom because of the varied activities during the service
- God given talents are portrayed/enhanced during singing.
- Non-members are attracted to church through singing
- Those who feel depressed are encouraged through singing
- Singing unites/brings worshippers together as they all join in chorus/song.
                                                    (6x1= 6 mks)

2 (a) A description of when Jesus was rejected in Nazareth (Luke 4: 16 – 30)
- Jesus came to Nazareth where he was brought up.
- He went to the synagogue as he usually did on the Sabbath day.

- He was given book of prophet Isaiah when he stood up to read.
- He opened the book, found the place that was written about him and read it to the people.
- After reading he closed the book and gave it to the attendant and sat down.
- Everybody in the synagogue looked at him.
- He told them that the scripture he has read was fulfilled in their hearing.
- All people were happy with what he had spoken.
- People wondered aloud saying "is this not Joseph's son.
- Jesus told them that they would ask him to do in his own country things he had done in Capernaum/he told them that a prophet is not accepted in his own country things.
- He told them that there were many widows in Israel during the time of Elijah but God sent the prophet to a widow in Zarephath/God only healed Naaman the Syrian of leprosy during the time of Prophet Elisha.
- They were filled with anger/wanted to throw him head long the cliff.
- Jesus passed through their midst and went away.

(7x1= 7 mks)

(b) **Reasons why Jesus faced opposition from the Pharisees in Galilee Luke 5: 12, 6: 11**
- Jesus touched a man with leprosy which was against the Jewish law.
- He forgave sins which the Pharisees knew only God could do/healed the paralyzed man.
- He mixed/ate with the tax collectors who were known to be sinners.
- Jesus made it clear to them that he had not come to call the righteous but sinners to repentance.
- His disciples did not fast, like those of John the Baptist which annoyed the Pharisees
- He challenged them to move from the old traditional orders to the new ones which he had brought
- The disciples of Jesus plucked and ate grains on the Sabbath day, which was unlawful/he healed a man with a withered hand on a Sabbath.

(4 x 2 = 8 mks)

(c) **5 ways in which church leaders can respond to those who oppose them in their work**
- Find out the causes/reasons for the opposition
- The church leaders should pray for/with them
- Explain to them the Gospel truth in a humble manner/guide and counsel them
- Seek reconciliation through third party/another person
- Involve them in decision making/church activities
- Recognize their efforts in supporting the church matters
- Visit them in their homes/fellowship with them /preaching
- Assist them when in problems (financial/materially)
- Send them messages of encouragement
- Change your approach to issue/reform where necessary.

(5 x 1 = 5 marks)

3 (a) **The teaching that Jesus made to the guests at the Pharisees house in (Luke 14: 1-14)**

- Saving a life can be done on a Sabbath day
- It is good to respond to an emergency even on a Sabbath
- Human life is more important than the animal which the Pharisees accept to rescue on the Sabbath day.
- It is good for to one be humble him/sit in lowly place when invited
- Those who exalt themselves will be humbled those who humble themselves will be exalted.
- It is blessed to invite the poor/maimed/lame/blind to the feast instead if one's relatives/friends who can invite you in return.
- Those who do good for the less fortunate will be repaid during the resurrection of the just.

(5 x 1= 5 mks)

b) Reasons why Jesus used the parable of the great feast in his teaching in Lk 14: 15-24

- He wanted to explain that invitation to God's Kingdom is open to many people.
- He wanted to show that the Jews were given the first chance to be part of God's Kingdom but they rejected.
- He wanted to show that people reject God's call due to material possession/family commitment which can be a stumbling block one's spiritual life.
- He wanted to show that gentiles/outcasts are called to God's Kingdom to replace the non-responding Jews.
- He needed to explain that the God's invitation/call is extended to many people/God offers universal salvation.
- So as to explain that those who refuse/do not accept God's call will not receive blessing of god's Kingdom/will not enter the kingdom of god.
- He wanted to challenge the Jews /Pharisees who counted themselves as righteous yet they failed to respond to God's call.

(4 x 2 = 8 mks)

(c) **Reasons why Christians take part in the Lord's Supper.**

   i. Through it, they remember the death of Jesus as a sacrifice for the forgiveness of sin.
   ii. The ceremony is a form of thanking for God's love/redemption plan
   iii. It is time that Christians reaffirm/renew their faith in God/bind themselves in the covenant
   iv. It gives Christians an opportunity to repent/ask for forgiveness of sin
   v. It unites the believers/they fellowship/share with one another
   vi. The partakers experience the presence of God through the sharing of the bread and wine which represent his body and blood respectively
   vii. It is a sign of obedience to Christ who commanded the disciples to do it in his memory
   viii. Through the Christians participate the second coming of Jesus Christ.
   ix. It is a foretaste of the heavily banquet/heavenly feast which Jesus promised his disciples.

4. (a) Reasons why Jesus sent the Holy spirit to the disciples after his ascension

- The Holy Spirit would comfort the disciples.

- He was to counsel the disciples.
- He would guide the disciples on what is right/God's righteousness
- He was to convict people of their sins
- He will teach the disciples on what is right/God's righteousness
- He was to convict people of their sins
- He was to reveal the future/enable the disciples to prophesy God's will.
- He would glorify Jesus through the work of the disciples
- He would enable the disciples to witness Christ throughout the world.
- He would replace the physical presence of Jesus/stay with the disciple forever
- He would empower the disciples to be able to speak with courage/confidence/authority.

(7 x 1 = 7 mks)

(b) **Teaching of Saint Paul on the similarities between the church and husband-wife relationship in Ephesians 5: 21-32**

- Members of the church learn to live together in harmony/unity just like a husband and wife.
- There is a chain of authority in marriage where the husband is the head of family in the same way Christ is the head of church.
- Just as Christ sacrificially loves the church, husband should love wives.
- The union between a husband and wife is meant to last forever, so Christians are called upon to maintain steadfast faithfulness to Christ.
- Christians are called to submit to Christ just as a wife submits to her husband.
- Just as a husband and wife become one flesh, so Christians are supposed to be united/cling to Christ.
- Just as Christ nourishes/cherishes the church, husbands should care for their wives.

(4 x 2 = 8 mks)

(c) **Ways in which Christians identify those who possess the gift of the Holy Spirit.**

- By listening to their confession. They should confess Jesus as Lord.
- By analyzing the kind of teaching they profess. The teaching should be about Jesus Christ/Christian doctrine
- By examining their life so as to know whether they possess the fruits of Holy Spirit.
- By observing their behaviour. The behaviour should not contradict the teachings of Jesus Christ/ be role models.
- When the Christians notice the victorious life of such people over temptations/works of the flesh.
- If such persons do not use the gift of the Holy spirit for selfish gains/enrich themselves.
- When such believers give glory to God/Jesus after serving performing miracles.

5.   (a)   **Christ's teaching on work.**
- Work is ordained from God/ command from God
- Human beings should work to subdue/conquer the earth
- Work is good/God himself worked
- God blesses a hard worker/worked
- God blesses a hard worker/worker/work is rewarded.
- Christians should work to acquire basic needs/necessities.

- Christians should work to assist these who are needy/less fortunate.
- Christian work as a co-creator with God.
- People should work to emulate Jesus who was a worker/carpenter.
- Work became a curse/unpleasant after human being fell into sin.
- Christians should not overwork/ enslave others.
- Those who work should get a just wage.
- People should take rest.
- People should work faithfully/diligently.
- Work should be done in an orderly manner.

(8x1= 8 mks)

b) **The role of professional ethics in work place.**
- They guide the workers on how to relate with one another.
- They define how worker should handle/relate with their clients.
- They help to create healthy interaction between the workers/employees and their supervisors/authority.
- They help in maintaining the standards of the service offered/goods produced in a work place.
- The determine how one should perform his/her duties/keep up the date with the demands of the profession
- They help to maintain dignity of the profession/integrity of the workers
- They help the public to respect the professional from undue pressures from other interested parties.
- They help to determine the entry requirement/qualifications needed in a given profession.

(3 x 2 = 6 mks)

c) **Ways in which the church is helping to reduce the rate of unemployment in Kenya today.**
- The church encourages people to start income generating activities
- The church provides loans to the unemployed to start small scale business
- The church creates job opportunities through establishing church projects.
- It teaches the youth about the dignity of manual work/encourage the youth to participate in agriculture/technical fields.
- It organizes seminars for the youth/unemployment on how to utilize their potentials.
- It condemns corrupt practices which interfere with the recruitment/economic growth.
- It encourages its members to pay taxes promptly so that the government can have the resources to employ/pay the workers.
- It trains/sponsors the youths on vocational skills that are necessary for employment /self-employment.
- The church tries to be fair when recruiting people for various jobs.

(6 x 1 = 6 mks)

6 (a) **The negative effects of the introduction of money economy on traditional African communities.**
- It has led to introduction of wage labour instead of communal working that existed.

359

- It led to migration to towns as people search for better paying jobs, destroying the closely knit traditional way of life.
- It has led to the formation of socio-Economic classes among the people/rich versus poor thus creating suspicion/insecurity.
- It has created individualism which has destroyed the communal way of living/extended family relationship.
- It has led to vices like bribery/corruption/exploitation which have replaced honesty/fairness in traditional African setting.
- The dependency on money has led to social evils like prostitution, immorality which has destroyed the traditional concept of marriage/value of sex.
- It has led to private ownership of land/land can be bought by those with money one hence destroying the traditional land ownership.
- Dowry has been commercialized thus destroying the traditional African meaning of showing appreciation of the family of the bride/girl.
- Age is no longer a determinant of social status /a rich young man maybe respected by an elder who is not economically stable.
- The type of education one receives is now determined by the amount of money one has unlike in the traditional set up where the elders passed on education to all without being paid.
- Due to the introduction of money economy modern means of transport have been acquired which has led to accidents/pollution of the environment.

(4x2=8 mks)

(b)   **Teaching of Jesus on wealth**
- Wealth should be acquired in the right manner
- Wealth a gift from God/God given
- Wealth should be used to serve God/expand God's Kingdom
- Those who have wealth are only stewards
- Those who have wealth should share it with others/help the needy/poor
- Poverty is not a result of sin/the poor can only enjoy God's blessing
- Wealth can be hindrance for one to enter in the Kingdom of God
- One cannot serve God and mammon/wealth
- Wealth cannot satisfy all human needs/cannot answer human quest for salvation.
- Those who have wealth should avoid extravagance/prodigality/luxury.
- Earth wealth/possession is temporary
- Those who have wealth should use it responsibly.   **(6x1= 6 mks)**

c)   **Reasons why Christians should involve themselves in gambling**
- Gambling enables one to get money/wealth without working for it
- In gambling one's gain leads to another person loss
- It creates bitterness in the one who losses
- The bible condemns gambling/unfair interests
- It involves taking advantage of the ignorant players
- There is no security on the wealth/money one put in gambling
- It is addictive/can become a compulsive habit

- It can interfere with family budget/priorities/ can bring misunderstanding in the family/friends.
- It can lead to violence/loss of life
- It can lead to stress/illness
- It shows lack of trust/ dependence upon God
- It can lead poverty, time wasting at the expense of productive work.   **(6 x 1 = 6 mks)**

CRE MARKING SCHEME PAPER 1 2011

1. (a) Explain the benefits of learning Christian Religious Education in Secondary schools in Kenya.
  (8 marks)
- It equips the learner with an understanding of God/spiritual growth.
- The learner acquires life skills to handle challenges in life.
- It helps one to respect his/her and other people's religion.
- It helps one to acquire basic principles for Christian living moral values.
- It enables one to understand how to relate with other people.
- It gives answers to questions and mysteries of life.
- It explains the origin and purpose of human beings on earth.
- It leads to employment or careers opportunities.   **(4 x 2 = 8 mks)**

(b) Outline the major divisions of both the Old and New Testament. (5 marks)
- Law books
- Historical books
- Poetic books
- Prophetic book
- Gospels/biographical books.
- Epistles/letters.   **5 x 1 = 5 mks**

(c) Identify seven ways in which the Bible is misused in Kenya today.   (7 marks)
- It is used to take oaths in courts/offices by people who may not be believers/not saying the truth.
- It is kept in places associated with evil.
- There is distortion of the Biblical teachings/specific verses are picked to fulfil individual demands.
- Some people use the Bible like an ordinary text book/reference.
- It is being used in witchcraft/cults to mislead people.
- Some people are using it to enrich themselves/it is a tool of trade.
- Some new versions translated have changed the original meaning of the Bible message.
- The Bible is not read for spiritual growth but it is kept for display.
- Some people use the Bible to threaten others/administer curses.   **(7 x 1 = 7 mks)**

2. **(a) Describe how God prepared the Israelites for the making of the covenant at Mt. Sinai (Exodus 19).** **(8 marks)**

- God told Moses to remind the people of Israel of how he had brought them out of Egypt.
- God told Moses that he wanted to make a special relationship with Israel/make them a kingdom of priests.
- God told Moses that he wanted the Israelites to obey him.
- Moses called all the elders/people and told them what God had said.
- The Israelites promised to do all that the Lord had said.
- God promised to come down and meet with the people on the third day.
- The people were instructed to consecrate themselves/wash their garments.
- Moses set boundaries for the people not to go up the mountain.
- The people were to abstain from sexual relationships.
- On the third day, there was a thick cloud upon the mountain/loud trumpet blast/an earthquake.
- Moses brought the people out of the camp to meet with God/they took their stand at the foot of the mountain.
- The Lord called Moses to go up the mountain.   **8 x 1 = 8 mks**

(b) Give four reasons that made the Israelites to break the covenant while at Mt. Sinai.

- Moses their leader delayed to come down from the mountain.
- Aaron who had been left in charge of the people was a weak leader.
- The people demanded for a god they could see and feel.
- The people were still influenced by the Egyptian way of worship/idolatry.
- Moses' teaching and influence had faded/vanished from the people's minds.
- The people had lost faith in their invisible God.   **(4 x 1 = 4 mks)**

(c) What do Christians learn about the nature of God from the Exodus? **(8 marks)**

- God is caring
- He communicates.
- He provides.
- He is powerful
- He guides
- He protects
- He commands
- He is to be obeyed
- He punishes those who disobey him/just.
- He is holy.
- He is faithful/fulfils his promises.
- He is patient/slow to anger.
- He is merciful
- He is jealous   **8 x 1 = 8 marks**

3. **(a) Outline the failures of King Saul.** **(5 marks)**

- He offered the burnt offering instead of waiting for Samuel to do it/assumed priestly duties.
- He lacked patience to wait for Samuel who was to offer burnt offering to God.
- He disobeyed God's command to destroy the Amalekites completely by sparing the life of king Agag.
- He spared the best of the animals instead of destroying them.
- He lost faith in God.
- He wanted to kill David/was jealous of David.
- He was deceitful to the servant of God.
- He committed suicide. **(4 x 2 = 8 marks)**

(b) Explain the achievements of David as King of Israel. **(7 marks)**

- He conquered and defeated the enemies of Israel.
- He expanded the geographical boundaries of Israel.
- He captured Jerusalem from the Jebusites.
- He made Jerusalem the capital city of Israel.
- He made Jerusalem a religious centre by bringing the Ark of the Covenant there.
- He made peace treaties with his neighbours.
- He composed Psalms which are used during worship.
- He united the twelve tribes of Israel under one ruler.
- He made preparations for the construction of the Temple. **(7 x 1 = 7 marks)**

(c) Give four reasons why Christians in Kenya should build churches. **(8 marks)**

- Churches are used for worshipping God.
- They signify God's presence/house of God.
- They are used for meetings/a place of gathering for members.
- Religious functions take place there.
- They are places where members receive religious instruction/preaching.
- As a sign of prestige/recognition/identification.
- To demonstrate their faith in the existence of God.
- To follow the traditions of the Old Testament teachings on the temple as a house of God.
- It can be used as a place of refuge in times of danger/calamity.

(4 x 2 = 8 marks)

4. **(a) Outline seven characteristics of the prophets in the Old Testament.** **(7marks)**

- They were God's mouthpiece/spokespeople.
- They responded to God's call in faith and obedience.
- They were called by God.
- They were given specific tasks to carry out.
- They communicated God's messages with authority/without fear.
- Their prophecies came true/were fulfilled.
- They never worked for material gain/were not paid for their work.
- They called people to come back to the covenant way of life.

- They pronounced God's judgement and punishment.
- They were persecuted for their work.
- They led exemplary lives/role models.

(b) Describe the call of Amos to become a prophet of God in Israel. **(8 marks)**
- Amos was a farmer tending to sycamore trees/shepherd.
- He came from a village called Tekoa in Judah.
- He became a prophet during the reign of King Uzziah and Jeroboam II.
- God called him through a vision.
- He felt a strong compulsion to prophesy.
- He responded to God's call in faith and obedience. **(4 x 2 = 8 marks)**

(c) Identify the five visions of Prophet Amos. **(5 marks)**
- He saw a swarm of locusts.
- He saw a great fire sent by God.
- He saw a crooked wall being measured using a plumb line.
- He saw a basket full of ripe summer fruits.
- He saw the destruction of the altar. **(Any 5 x 1 = 5 marks)**

5. **(a) Outline the stages followed in the renewal of the covenant during of Nehemiah.**
- The people gathered in the public square in Jerusalem.
- The priest Ezra read the law to the people.
- They performed repentance gestures of raising and lowering their heads
- The people constructed makeshift tents/shelters to celebrate the feast of booths.
- There was national day of confession/fasting as they wore sack clothes.
- Ezra led people in prayer of confession.
- They sealed the covenant by signing an agreement under the leadership of Nehemiah and the Priest.
- The people promised not to go against the Mosaic Law.
- There was re-distribution of the people in Jerusalem and the countryside.

(4 x 2 = 8 mks)

(b) Give six reasons why Nehemiah carried out religious reforms in Judah. (6 mks)
- To preserve the identity of the Jews as a people of God.
- To separate the Jews from foreign influence.
- To purify the temple which had been defiled by keeping a foreigner.
- To reinstate the services of the Levites as priests in the temple.
- To restore the tithing system that had been forgotten for the upkeep of the temple.
- To ensure that the Sabbath day was free from business activities.
- In order to cleanse the Jews who had intermarried with foreigners/exposed to idolatry.
- To restore the true worship of God. **6 x 1 = 6 marks**

(c) What lessons do Christians learn from the renewal of the covenant by Nehemiah?
- Christians should ask for their sins to be forgiven.
- They should lead righteous lives.
- Christians should always pray to God.
- Christians should demonstrate humility.
- They should avoid groups that can negatively influence their faith in God.
- They should teach other the word of God.
- They should set aside a day for worship.
- They should respect the church as a place for prayer.   (6 x 1 = 6 marks)

6. **(a) Describe the traditional African view of a community.**   **(8 marks)**
- The members of the community include the unborn, the living and the living dead/ancestors.
- The members speak one common language.
- They are related either by blood, marriage or adoption.
- The community members occupy the same geographical area/region.
- They carry out similar economic activities.
- The community is made up of smaller units/clans.
- Each community has its own distinct rules, taboos, beliefs, customs and cultural practices
- Members of a community are expected to participate in the life of the community.
          (4 x 2 = 8 marks)

 **(b) Explain six factors that have affected the traditional African people's dependence on
God.**   **(6 marks)**
- The introduction of western culture/education which has made people to ignore God.
- Some people rely on witchcraft to solve their problems.
- Greed for power/materialism without fear of God.
- Some people rely on science and technology for the interpretation of day to day events.
- Money economy where success now depends on how much money one earns.
- Abject poverty has made people lose hope/faith in God.
- Negative peer pressure influences the members to rely on themselves other than God.
- Pressure of modern living makes people too busy to serve God.
- Urbanization.   (6 x 1 = 6 marks)

 **(c) Outline six similarities between the Christian and traditional African ways of showing
respect to God.**   **(6 marks)**
- In both members pray to God.
- In both they give offerings.

- In both members sing songs.
- In both members show respect to God by helping those in need.
- In both they use God's name sparingly/avoid mentioning God's name carelessly.
- In both members use the God-given resources/environment carefully.
- In both they build/maintain/honour places of worship.
- In both members take care of religious leaders.
- In both members obey the laws commands of God.　　　　**6 x 1 = 6 marks**

CRE PAPER II 2011 MARKING SCHEME

1.　**(a) Basing your answer on the infancy narratives in Luke 1: 5 – 56, describe what took place when Mary visited Elizabeth.**　　　　　　　**(6 marks)**
- She entered Zechariah's home.
- She greeted Elizabeth.
- When Elizabeth heard Mary's greetings the baby in her womb leaped.
- Elizabeth was filled with the Holy Spirit.
- Elizabeth exclaimed with a loud cry.
- She blessed Mary and the child in the womb.
- Elizabeth wondered why Mary the mother of her Lord has visited her.
- Elizabeth informed Mary that the baby in her womb had leaped for joy in her greetings.
- Mary responded by praising God.
- Mary stayed with Elizabeth for three months.　　　　**(6 x 1 = 6 marks)**

　(b) Identify six lessons that Christians learn from the lives of Zechariah and Elizabeth.
- Christians should be righteous/upright/blameless.
- They should obey God's commandments.
- They should persevere/be patient.
- They should serve God faithfully/commitment.
- They should be prayerful.
- They should depend on God/ask God for their needs.
- They should believe God's word.
- They should thank God for blessings.
- They should praise/worship the Lord.
- They should desire to be led by the Holy Spirit.
- Christians should rejoice at the blessings of others.　　　　**(6 x 1 = 6 marks)**

　(c) State eight ways through which Christians in Kenya express their joy for the birth of Jesus.　　　　　　　　　　　　　**(8 marks)**

- They sing/listen to Christian songs/carols.
- They attend Christmas worship/service/mass.
- They partake of the Holy Communion/Eucharist.
- They exchange gifts /cards/messages of goodwill.
- They visit friends/relatives.
- They decorate their homes/churches.
- They buy/wear new clothes.
- They prepare special dishes/drinks.
- They rest from normal duties.
- They hold Christmas concerts/drama.
- They watch movies films on the birth of Jesus.
- They read the Bible and Christmas stories.
- They help the needy/acts of charity.
- They repent/rededicate themselves to God.   **8 x 1 = 8 marks**

2. **(a) With reference to the sermon on the plain, outline five teachings of Jesus on how human beings should relate to one another.**   **(5 marks)**
- Human beings should love one another/their enemies.
- They should practise sharing/help others.
- They should be merciful to each other.
- They should not judge/condemn others.
- They forgive one another/not to revenge.
- They should pray for those who wrong them/they should do good to those who hate them.
- They should not discriminate against one another.   (5 x 1 = 5 **marks)**

(b) Describe the incident in which Jesus forgave the sinful woman in Luke 7: 36 – 50.
- Jesus had been invited by a Pharisee for dinner.
- While he was at the table a sinful woman came with an alabaster flask of ointment.
- She stood at Jesus' feet weeping and wet his feet with her tears.
- She used her hair to wipe Jesus' feet.
- She kissed the feet of Jesus.
- She then anointed the feet of Jesus with ointment.
- The Pharisee who had invited Jesus questioned in his heart whether Jesus was a prophet.
- Jesus knew the thoughts of Simon and told him the parable of the creditor and the two debtors.
- Jesus asked Simon who of the two debtors would love the creditor more.
- Simon said the debtor with more debt would love the creditor more.
- He told Simon that the woman had shown much love because her many sins had been forgiven.
- Jesus then told the woman that her sins had been forgiven.
- The other guests began to question who Jesus was to have the power to forgive sin.
- Jesus told the woman that her faith had saved her.

- He told her to go in peace. (8 x 1 = 8 marks)

(c) Give seven reasons why Christians should ask for forgiveness from God.
- To be at peace with God.
- To show obedience to the teachings of Jesus.
- To improve their relationship with others.
- It gives them confidence to serve God.
- To acknowledge their weakness/a sign of humility.
- It shows their desire to lead a righteous life.
- It is a sign of appreciation of God's mercy.
- It is a way of self-reproach.
- It is a demonstration of their faith in God.
- So as to be forgiven by God. **(7 x 1 = 7 marks)**

3. **a. Outline the instructions that Jesus gave to the seventy two disciples when he sent them on a mission.**
- The disciples were to pray for more labourers to be sent for the harvest.
- They were not to carry any purse/bag/sandals.
- They were not to salute anyone on the road.
- They were to say peace to any house they entered.
- They were to remain in the same house/not to move from house to house.
- They were to eat/drink whatever was provided.
- They were to heal the sick.
- They were to tell the people that the kingdom of God has come near.
- They were to wipe off dust their feet against the people if not received. **(4 x 2 = 8 mks)**

(b) Relate the parable of the Pharisee and the tax collector in Luke 18: 9 – 14.
- Two men went into the temple to pray, a Pharisee and a tax collector.
- The Pharisee praised himself in prayer.
- He said he was holy/better that others/tax collector.
- The tax collector also prayed but could not lift his eyes to heaven.
- The tax collector beat his breast saying he is a sinner/asked for God's mercy.
- It was the prayer of the tax collector that was accepted/the tax collector was justified.
- Jesus concluded by saying that whoever exalts himself will be humbled/whoever humbles himself will be exalted. **(5 x 1 = 5 marks)**

(c) Give seven reasons that make Christians pray. **(7 marks)**
- To show their dependence on God/faith in God.
- To express the power/greatness of God/adore/honour God.
- They pray to ask for their needs/seek guidance.
- Through prayer, they confess their sins/ask for forgiveness.

- To thank God for his faithfulness/goodness/blessings.
- Prayer helps to relieve fears/anxiety/worries.
- It is an instrument through which the work of Satan is destroyed.
- To communicate with God/have fellowship with God.
- To follow the example of Jesus.
- It is a command from God/a sign of obedience.   (7 x 1 = 7 marks)

4. **a. Explain how Peter's life was transformed on the day of Pentecost (Acts 2: 1 - 40).**
- Peter was filled with the Holy Spirit.
- He started speaking in tongues.
- He became courageous/defended the disciples that they were not drunk.
- He was able to remember the scripture/Old Testament prophecies/teachings.
- He began witnessing the life, death and resurrection of Jesus.
- He called people to repentance.
- He was empowered to perform miracles.   (4 x 2 = 8 marks)

(b) Outline Saint Paul's teaching on how the gifts of the Holy Spirit should be used in the church.
- The gifts of the Holy Spirit should be used for the common good of all.
- They should be used to strengthen/encourage and comfort members.
- They should be used to bring unity but not to discriminate/divide members.
- There is need to appreciate/respect all the gifts.
- They should be used in an orderly way/no confusion.
- The gifts should be used in love.
- The gift of speaking in tongues should be minimized in public.
- There is need to have interpretation of tongues for them to be meaningful/helpful.
- Prophecies should be carefully evaluated/weighted.   (5 x 1 = 5 marks)

(c) State seven reasons why some Christians find it difficult to help the sick.
- Some Christians lack the gift of healing.
- They are afraid of being infected.
- Because of religious/denominational/barriers.
- They lack knowledge/skill of handling the sick.
- They have no time for the sick.
- Lack of faith in healing/miracles.
- Because of poverty/may not have enough resources to share.
- Lack of love for the needy/sick.
- It is difficult for some Christians to determine those who are genuinely sick/needy.
- Due to social differences/status/educational background.
- Due to nepotism/ethnic affiliations.

- Due to gender biases. (7 x 1 = 7 **marks)**

5. **a. Give seven reasons for the importance of manual work in Kenya today.**
- Through manual work human being emulate God as a worker.
- It is a sign of being obedient to God's instructions to work.
- It enables human beings to look after/preserve the environment/be co-creators with God.
- It keeps the body physically fit.
- Human beings are able to obtain their basic needs/earn their living through manual work.
- It is a way of serving others/community.
- It enables human beings to develop their talents/abilities.
- Manual work gives satisfaction/fulfilment.
- It keeps one busy/active. **(Any 7 x 1 = 7 marks)**

(b) List seven activities that the youth should engage in during leisure time.
- Taking part in church choir/singing.
- Helping the sick/needy.
- Taking part in retreats/seminars/camps.
- Reading Christian literature.
- Playing games.
- Planting flowers/trees/cleaning the compound.
- Watching TV/listening to Christian music/messages.
- Taking part in Bible Study.
- Visiting their friends/relatives.

(Any 7 x 1 = 7 marks)

(c) State six consequences of denying employees rest.
- It may lead to poor working relations.
- The organization may realize a low output.
- The workers may resort to a strike action/go slow.
- Some of the employees may lose their jobs through sacking/resignation.
- It can lead to poor health/death.
- It may lead to break up of families.
- It can lead to labour conflicts between the employer and the employee.
- Mistrust may arise leading to close supervision.
- Employees may develop negative attitude towards work.
- Accidents are likely to occur.

6. **(a) Explain seven ways in which Christians can contribute towards the maintenance of law and order in society.**

- By obeying the law of the land/leading exemplary lives.
- By respecting the law/authority.
- Through rehabilitating criminals.

- By condemning acts which violate human rights/unjust laws.
- Through educating the masses on their rights and responsibilities.
- By sharing what they have with the needy.
- By praying for peace/national leaders/citizens.
- By preaching on the importance of law and order/peace.
- Forgiving others freely.
- Reporting criminals to relevant authorities.
- Through reconciling the warring parties.
- Through guidance and counselling services.   (7 x 1 = 7 marks)

(b) State seven methods of disciplining errant members in traditional African communities.
- Paying fines.
- Denying children food for some time.
- Reprimanding wrong doers.
- Giving unpleasant names to reflect the wrong that the person has done.
- Denying culprits access to social occasions/being detained/isolation.
- Summoning an indisciplined member before the council of elders.
- Excommunicating wrong doors from the community.
- Through caning and beating.
- Disowning by parents/relatives/friends.
- Being cursed by elders.
- Refusing to name children after them.   (7 x 1 = 7 marks)

(c) Identify six obstacles to effective maintenance of law and order in Kenya today.
- There is an increase in the rate of crime/the law enforcement officers cannot cope with the workload.
- Due to unequal distribution of resources.
- Permissiveness in society.
- Due to political instability/incitement by politicians.
- Extreme poverty.
- Social discrimination.
- Some cultural beliefs/practises hinder effective maintenance of law and order.
- High rate of unemployment.
- Bribery and corruption.
- Greed for material wealth.
- Inadequate modern equipment to combat crime.
- Delay in the delivery of justice to the offended.
- The citizens lack knowledge on the procedures for the effective maintenance of law and order.

CRE PAPER 1 2012 MARKING SCHEME

1. **(a) Identify six literary forms used in the writing of the Bible.** **(6 marks)**
-   The use of narratives /prose form e.g. Genesis
-   Religious epics e.g. Exodus
-   Legal expressions/legislative texts e.g. Leviticus
-   Prophetic speeches e.g. Jeremiah
-   The use of prayers e.g. Nehemiah
-   The use of poetic devices e.g. psalm
-   The use of wise sayings e.g. Proverbs
-   Philosophical essays e.g. Job
-   The use of love songs e.g. Song of Songs
-   Epistles e.g. Romans
-   Biographies/ Gospel e.g. St. Luke.

(b) State four reasons why the Bible had to be compiled into its present form by the early Christians. **(8 marks)**
-   In order to enable the word of God to reach more people in their own language
-   In order to train local people to take up leadership roles.
-   In order to increase the demand for formal education
-   To facilitate the expansion of the church
-   To indigenize Christianity
-   To encourage research into African language/culture
-   In order to establish local bible translation society e.g. Bible society of Kenya

(c) Outline six ways in which Christians in Kenya use the Bible. **(6 marks)**
-   Christian literature quotes the bible as a reference book.
-   Christian songs/hymns are derived/composed from the bible.
-   Preaching/teaching from the bible by religious leaders.
-   By reading the bible to others.
-   By using it for instructions guidance.
-   By translating it into local languages for people to read/understand it.
-   Distribution of the bible to those who do not have it.
-   The bible is used as a reference /main resource material in search for religious knowledge.
-   The bible is a resource material in teaching CRE in schools and colleges.
-   The bible is used in taking of oaths to prove its authenticity.

2. **(a) Describe the covenant ceremony between God and Abraham in Gen 15:1-19.**
-   Abraham was disturbed because he did not have an heir.
-   He asked God to give him an assurance that his own son will be his heir.

- God responded showing him the stars in the night and the sand on the ground. He told him that the two represent the number of his descendants.
- Abraham wanted further assurance that God will fulfil His promise.
- Abraham was told to bring sacrificial animals a heifer 3 years old, a she goat 3year old, a ram 3 years, a turtle dove and a young pigeon.
- He cut the animals into halves and arranged them opposite each other.
- He drove away the birds of prey that came to the carcasses.
- At sunset Abraham fell into deep sleep and thick darkness came over him.
- A smoking firepot with flaming torch appeared and passed between the pieces of meat.
- Abraham was promised that his descendants would be given the land of Canaan from the boarders of Egypt to River Euphrates.

(b) Identify four differences between the Jewish and the traditional African practices of circumcision.

- Jewish circumcision is performed on an eight day old baby while Africans circumcise an adolescent.
- Initiates acquire new status and responsibilities in African society but not in Jewish, where the initiate is still a small child.
- Only males are circumcised among Jews but some African societies circumcise both male and female.
- African circumcision tests courage and bravery while the Jewish practice tests faith and commitment to God.
- Circumcision for the Jews is in obedience to God's command while in African societies it is in obedience to the customary laws.
- There's seclusion of initiates in the traditional African practice of circumcision but not in Jewish community.

(c) Give five reasons why church leaders take vows before starting their mission.

- To receive God's blessings/guidance
- To get acknowledgement from the people they serve
- To remind the leaders to stick to the church regulations
- To give the leader courage to do his or her work
- To show willingness/acceptance/commitment to serve God
- To emulate the biblical way of commissioning God's servants

3. (a) Describe six ways that King David used to promote the worship of God in Israel.

- David brought the Ark of the Covenant in Jerusalem.
- He made Jerusalem a Holy city by centralizing worship.
- He composed songs and Psalms that are used in worship.
- He respected prophets of God e.g. Prophet Nathan.
- He repented his sins to God whenever he made mistakes.
- He called himself the servant of Yahweh/God.
- He had the initial plan of God to build the temple for God.
- He advised his son Solomon to obey the commandments of God.

- He prayed to God before carrying out any task/exercise.
- He was chosen by God through public ministry.

(b) Explain four life skills that Elijah used to fight against false religion in Israel.

- Assertiveness-Told Ahab that he was the course of trouble
- Creative thinking-Requested for a contest
- Decision making-He killed the prophets and prophetesses of Baal
- Negotiation-Elijah asked the Israelites to choose between God and baal
- Conflict resolution/problem solving-He convinced the Israelites that Yahweh was the true God
- Effectiveness-He explained to the people the procedure of offering the sacrifice
- Self awareness-He knew that he was the prophet of the true God
- Critical thinking-He sought ways to proof that Yahweh was the true God

(c) What problems do church leaders in Kenya face when carrying out their work?

- Threats from opponents/opposition
- Lack of material/financial resources
- Lack of co-operation from church members
- Rivalry among leaders/themselves
- May not be good role models/hypocrites
- May suffer from long separation from their families
- Greed of material things/property
- Misinterpretation of the biblical teachings
- May be posted to a harsh working environment/bad weather/roads/people
- Interference in their work
- May lack adequate skills to carry out their work
- Permissiveness
- May face rejection

4. **(a) Give four reasons why Prophet Amos was against the way Israelites worshipped God.**

- They practiced idolatry by worshipping idols such as Sakkuth and Kaiwan, the Assyrian gods.
- Worshippers went to holy places to satisfy their own desires other than pleasing God.
- Worshippers were making offerings to show off, and not out of love for God.
- The offerings which the Israelites made at the holy places did not reflect holy lives.
- They practiced religious syncretism, where they worshipped idols alongside Yahweh.

(b) State six ways in which God would punish Israel for her evils according to Prophet Amos. **(6 marks)**

- Invasion by the Assyrians who would destroy the people and their land

- Attack by an epidemic.
- There would be an earthquake that would destroy the houses of the rich and the poor
- Famine of the word of God – Spiritual famine or hunger for God's word
- There would be an eclipse and the land would be covered in darkness
- Drought leading to painful thirst
- The altars at Dan and Bethel would be destroyed.
- Those who will hide will be carried to exile in Assyria.

(c) How does the church in Kenya punish errant members? **(6 marks)**
- Suspends them
- Refuse them from participating in church activities /rituals
- May be denied leadership positions/demoted/withdrawal of family
- Maybe denied leadership position/demoted/withdrawal of privileges
- Maybe publicly condemned/asked to repent/apologise
- Some may be transferred to different areas
- They may be sacked from the Job/termination of services
- May be excommunicated
- Charged a fine

5. (a) From the call of Jeremiah, identify eight qualities of God (Jeremiah 1).
- God is holy
- God is beyond human understanding (transcendent)
- God chooses whomever he wills to carry out his plans
- God expects total obedience and faith
- God is all knowing/omniscient
- God uses events to reveal himself
- God punishes the sin.
- He is a just God.

(b) Give six characteristics of the New Covenant foreseen by Prophet Jeremiah.
- The law would be written in people's hearts.
- There would be personal knowledge of God.
- There would be forgiveness of sins.
- There would be personal responsibility for sin.
- It would bring a new community of God's people.
- God would take an initiative of establishing a covenant.
- The new community would be ruled by the righteous one from Davidic family/dynasty
- The Israelites would be given a new heart.
- This covenant would be an everlasting one/would not be broken.
- It would mark a new beginning/ a new era.

(c) Give six ways in which Christians can assist victims of disasters. **(6 marks)**
- Donating food/clothing/any material need for them
- Providing shelter for them

- Offering guidance and counselling to them
- Resettling them in safe areas
- Offering health care
- Re-uniting them with their families
- Provide financial assistance
- Offer them with employment
- Taking preventive measures against future disasters
- Through visiting them
- Praying for/with them
- Preaching to them

6. **(a) Describe five ways in which people in traditional African communities communicate with God.**
- Praying were said while kneeling or facing some natural phenomena e.g. mountains, moon, or while raising hands.
- Singing and dancing to God during worship.
- Through invocations where God's name is called to cause blessing to people. An invocation is a short informal prayer e.g. "Help me, Oh God"
- Consulting prophets about Gods will.
- Pronouncing blessings and curses in the name of God.
- Giving sacrifices and offerings.

(b) Give eight reasons for singing and dancing during initiation ceremonies in traditional African communities.
- Songs informed the participants of the history of their community
- They provided an opportunity for members to socialize
- It diverted the initiate's mood from the impending danger
- They teach participants important moral values
- Enhances the participants' gender roles/inheritance
- Exposes those with leadership roles/qualities
- Encourages them to face the challenges
- Drive away evil spirits
- It is a form of entertainment/happiness/celebration

(c) Give seven reasons why witchcraft is feared in traditional African communities.
- It leads to death/destruction
- It is the work of evil spirits
- It leads to poverty/loss of property
- It involves cheating/telling lies In some cases peoples are feared to leave their homes/migrate to other places
- It can lead to breaking of families/made an outcast

- It leads to underdevelopment
- Can cause physical/psychological injuries
- It may cause suspension/hatred/mistreatment/disharmony/disunity among the people
- May cause embarrassment to an individual/family.

CRE PAPER 2 2012 MARKING SCHEME

1. (a) Outline Micah's prophecies about the messiah (Micah 5: 1 – 5).   (7 marks)
- The messiah will be born in Bethlehem.
- He will rule over Israel.
- His origin is from the Old/ancient days.
- He will be born of a woman.
- He will feed his flock.
- He will rule in the power of God.
- In his time, Israel will be secure.
- He shall be great to the ends of the earth.
- Israel will have victory over her enemies/there will be peace in Israel.

(b) With reference to Luke 1: 13 – 17, outline the message of angel Gabriel about John to Zechariah.
- The child to be born will be a son.
- He will be called John.
- The angel said that the son would bring joy and gladness to his parents,
- He will be great before the Lord.
- He will not drink wine nor strong drink.
- He will be filled with the Holy Spirit,
- He will turn the sons of Israel to the Lord.
- He will prepare the way for the messiah.

(c) Give three lessons Christians learn from the incident when Jesus was dedicated.
- Christians should be righteous before God in order to experience him in their lives.
- Christians should thank God for blessing them.
- They should trust/have faith in God.
- Christians should reach out to all people/preach salvation to them.
- Christians should show compassion to the needy in society.
- Christians should be devoted in their worship of God regardless of the challenges they face.
- Christians should dedicate their children to God/fulfil church obligations.

2. (a) Describe the incident when Jesus was baptized in River Jordan by John the Baptist (Luke 3: 21 - 22).
(5 marks)
- All the people had been baptized by John the Baptist.
- Jesus was also baptized.

- Jesus then started to pray.
- The heavens opened.
- The Holy Spirit descended on him in form of a dove.
- A voice came from heaven
- Jesus was described as the Son of God.

(b) Outline seven reasons why Christians undergo baptism. (7 marks)

- Through Baptism Christians identify themselves with Jesus.
- Christians receive the power of the Holy Spirit through baptism.
- Baptism unites Christians as members of one body of Christ.
- Baptism signifies the end of the old life and the beginning of a new life in Christ.
- It signifies the complete forgiveness of sins.
- Baptism makes Christians children of God.
- Through baptism Christians become full members of the church and the Christian community.
- Baptism prepares Christians for the Kingdom of God.
- It acts an outward sign of their inner faith as it is publicly.
- It is a sign of a new covenant with God.

(c) Explain the importance of transfiguration of Jesus to Christians today. (8 marks)

- It took place when Jesus and the three disciples were praying. Christians should therefore take time off their duties to pray.
- Jesus and his disciples had retreated to a private place/mountain to pray. Christians therefore should have retreats/go to a private place for prayer.
- Resurrection is a reality since Moses who died appeared in transfiguration. Christians therefore should have hope for life after death.
- Moses and Elijah appeared to encourage Jesus about the suffering he was about to face. Christians should therefore learn that they should accept/endure suffering as a way of salvation.
- Jesus came to do the will of his father/fulfil the law/prophecies. Christians are assured of salvation/should believe in the word of God.
- The disciples heard the voice of God which commanded them to listen to Jesus. Christians learn that God speaks to them/they should listen to God's voice/Jesus/the word of God.
- The cloud symbolized God's presence with Jesus. Christians therefore learn that God is always with them/they should call upon Him for help/desire to be in God's presence.

3. (a) Describe the incident of the healing of the ten lepers. (7 marks)

- Jesus was on his way to Jerusalem.
- He met ten men who were suffering from leprosy.
- The men stood at a distance and shouted at Jesus to have mercy on them
- Jesus told them to go and show themselves to the priests.
- On their way to the priests, they were healed and made clean.

- One of them on realizing he had be healed, he came back praising God.
- He threw himself at the feet of Jesus and thanked him.
- The man who came back was a Samaritan and Jesus wondered why only the foreigner came back to give thanks to God.
- Jesus pointed out to him that his faith had healed him and told him to get up and go.
- Jesus commended him for his faith, making him a good example to others.

(b) Explain the teaching of Jesus on the power of faith (Luke 17: 1 – 37). (8 marks)
- Faith strengthens one to overcome temptations.
- Faith gives power to be able to forgive others.
- Faith in Christ can enable his disciples to perform miracles.
- Faith in Jesus enables his disciples to perform their duties freely without expecting any material reward.
- Faith in Jesus enables one to seek help from Jesus.
- Faith leads to healing.
- Faith in God enables us to show gratitude to him for blessings.
- Faith enables us to experience the kingdom of God in our hearts.
- Lack of faith in Jesus leads God's punishment while faith in Jesus leads to eternal life.

(c) What lessons do Christians learn from the parable of the ten pounds? (Luke 19: 11 - 27) **(5 marks)**
- Christians should use their abilities that God has given them for the benefit of others.
- Christians will be rewarded according their performances.
- Christians have been given different gifts/abilities by God.
- Christians will give an account of how they used their abilities.
- Christians need to be honest/obedient.
- God expects Christians to use opportunities provided for his glory.
- Christians will lose their abilities if not put to use/punished.

4. **(a) Explain how the unity of believers is expressed in the image of the body of Christ. (8 mks)**
- St. Paul describes the believers as the body of Christ.
- Christ is the head of the church.
- The believers form parts of the body.
- The body has different organs. In the same way the church has different members.
- They all need to work together for wellbeing of the church.
- Every part of the body is needed to make it whole/all parts are interdependent/one part cannot be without the other.
- The different church members are given different spiritual gifts by the Holy Spirit to carry out God's work.
- There should be no division in the church since all believers are members of the Body of Christ.
- Believers are united through Baptism in the Holy Spirit. **(4 x 2 = 8 marks)**

(b) State six reasons why the use of the gifts of the Holy Spirit brought disunity in the church at Corinth. **(6 marks)**

- There was competition in speaking in tongues.
- There was disorder/confusion in worship as people with different gifts tried to outdo one another.
- People did not use their gifts for the benefit of the church/one another.
- Some gifts such as prophecy/teaching were looked down upon/there was pride/boasting.
- There was no interpretation of tongues of tongues when the gift of speaking in tongues was in use, hence messages were not understood.
- People did not show love for one another.
- Those with the gift of speaking in tongues despised those who did not have/some members thought they were too spiritual. **(6 x 1 = 6 marks)**

(c) In what ways do the Christians in Kenya demonstrate the New Testament teaching on unity?
(6 marks)

- Praying and worshipping together.
- Correcting each other in love.
- Helping the needy amongst them.
- Visiting each other in homes.
- They observe a day of worship to honour God.
- They share the Holy Communion/meals.
- They solve problems affecting the church members.
- They cooperate by providing Christian programmes in the mass media/resource materials.
- They speak in one voice to condemn evil in society.

5. **(a) Identify five sources of Christian ethics.** **(5 marks)**
- Human reasons/experience
- The Bible
- Traditions from Christian community
- Natural law
- Situational ethics

(b) Give seven reasons why Christians in Kenya condemn homosexuality. (7 marks)
- It is a form of sexual immorality
- It is against God's/Biblical teachings/it is a sin.
- It is an abuse to the sacredness of sex.
- It is contrary to the natural order of things.
- Homosexuality does not enable procreation to take place.
- It lowers the dignity of human beings who are created in the image of God.
- It can lead to diseases like HIV/AIDS/leading to human suffering.

- It may lead to psychological problems like stress and depression.
- It leads to rejection/being an outcast.   **7 x 1 = 7 marks**

(c) Explain how responsible parenthood is demonstrated by Christians in Kenya today. Christian parents provide physical/basic needs for the family.
- They provide spiritual guidance to their children.
- They teach their children to live in harmony with others/moral values.
- They provide their children with education in order to acquire necessary skills/knowledge to realize their full potential.
- They act as role models for their children.
- They discipline/correct the children whenever they deviate from norms.
- They provide protection/security to their children, which enables the children deal with situations in life.
- They teach their children how to grow physically, socially/psychologically so as for them to understand changes in their bodies as they develop.   **4 x 2 = 8 marks**

6. (a) Outline the traditional African concept of wealth.   **(6 marks)**
- Wealth is a blessing from God.
- It is part and parcel of human existence.
- It is measured in the amount of property, wives and children one has.
- It can be individually or communally owned.
- Wealth is acquired through hardwork/inheritance/gifts/raids/dowry.
- Wealth determines one's social status.
- Wealth should be used to help the needy in society.
- There are rules governing how it is distributed.
- Wealth is used to worship God/appease ancestors.   **6 x 1 = 6 marks**

(b) Give eight reasons why corruption is widespread in Kenya today.   **(8 marks)**
- Unemployment cases which make an individual desperate to secure an employment chance by engaging in corrupt activities.
- Desire for instant services/wealth makes some people become corrupt.
- Some people feel that they have not been adequately paid for work done hence engage in corrupt acts to compensate themselves.
- Fear of arrest/punishment makes law breakers to engage in corrupt deals.
- Some people engage in corrupt deals in order to be served due to ignorance of their rights
- Lack of moral integrity by some people.
- Greed makes some people engage in corruption.
- Due to tribal/ethnic affiliations.
- There is inefficient machinery to curb corrupt practises.
- The judiciary is not able to deal with injustice/cases take too long to be determined.
- Some government agents abuse the power bestowed upon them.
- The belief of the common person that the government is a master and therefore has to be corrupted before receiving services.

(c) Explain six ways the church is using to eradicate poverty in Kenya today.

- The church preaches/encourages hardwork among citizens which enables them to fight poverty.
- The church speaks against vices like oppression/exploitation of the poor by the rich in society which are promoting poverty.
- It takes care of the poor by providing them with material possessions.
- It has established projects that offer employment to members of the society, this enables them to take care of their needs.
- It gives out bursaries to the needy children enabling them undertake education and get employment.
- The church is offering subsidized medical services which enhances the economic output/productivity of the people.
- The church is working together with the government to create a peaceful society which promotes economic and social development.
- It prays for God's intervention in the lives of the poor which gives them hope in life.
- It offers guidance and counselling to the poverty-stricken thus enabling them to open up to realities of life.
- It offers formal and informal training in various skills.

CRE PAPER 1 2013 MARKING SCHEME

1. (a) Identify five poetic books.
- Job
- Psalms
- Proverbs
- Ecclesiastes
- Songs of Solomon   **(5 x 1 = 5 marks)**

(b) Outline the translation of the Bible from the original language to local languages.
- The Old Testament was originally written in Hebrew.
- The New Testament was written in Greek, the official language in the Roman Empire.
- The Old Testament was translated from Hebrew to Greek, this translation is called Septuagint.
- The entire Bible was translated into Latin by Jerome.
- The Bible was translated directly from Hebrew and Greek into English by William Tyndale.
- The Bible was translated into the national languages of European countries during the period of Reformation.
- It was translated from English into Kiswahili by Dr. Ludwig Krapf.

- The Bible has been translated into other local languages by the Bible Society of Kenya/individuals. **(4 x 2 = 8 marks)**

(c) Describe seven ways in which Christians use the Bible to spread the gospel today.

- The Bible is the main source book for Christian sermons/preaching.
- It is used in the writing of Christian literature.
- The Bible is used when composing songs.
- It is used in the production of Christian movies/videos/radio programmes/plays.
- The Bible id used in swearing/taking of oath of allegiance.
- It is used to organize Bible Studies/teaching Sunday/Sabbath school.
- Verses from the Bible are used for imprinting posters/clothes.
- The Bible is used in writing of doctrines for different denominations.
- Biblical texts are used in teaching of Christian Religious Education.
- It is used to offer guidance and counselling. **(7 x 1 = 7 marks)**

2. **(a) Describe the incident when Abraham was willing to sacrifice his Isaac.**
- God told Abraham to take his son, Isaac, to Mt. Moriah and offer him as a burnt sacrifice.
- Abraham took his son, two of his servants and firewood and went to the place where God told him.
- When Abraham came near the mountain, he told the servants to remain behind, as he went with Isaac.
- Isaac carried the wood and he took fire in his hands and a knife and they went together.
- Isaac asked him where the lamb for the sacrifice was and Abraham answered that the Lord would provide.
- When they came to a place where God had told him, he made an altar, placed wood in order and bound Isaac and laid him on the altar upon the wood.
- When Abraham was about to slay his son, an angel of the Lord called him and told him not to lay his hand on Isaac.
- Abraham lifted his eyes and saw a ram behind him.
- He took the ram and offered it as a burnt offering.
- He called the place "the Lord will provide".
- God promised to bless Abraham because of this.
- He went back to with his servants and Isaac to Beersheba. **(6 x 1 = 6 marks)**

(b) Give the differences between the Jewish and the traditional African practises of circumcision.

- Jewish circumcision is performed on an eight day old baby while Africans circumcise an adolescent.
- Initiates acquire new status and responsibilities in African society but not in Jewish, where the initiate is still a small child.
- Only males are circumcised among Jews but some African societies circumcise both male and female.
- African circumcision tests courage and bravery while in the Jewish community it is a sign of covenant with God.
- Circumcision for the Jews is in obedience to God's command while in African societies it is in obedience to the customary laws.
- There's seclusion of initiates in the traditional African practice of circumcision but not in Jewish community.   **(4 x 2 = 8 marks)**

(c) State six ways in which Christians identify themselves in the society.
- They wear a specific design of clothes.
- They abstain from eating certain kinds of food/taking some drinks.
- By carrying/wearing the rosary/cross/badges/rings/the flag.
- They have special ways of greetings/salutations.
- Through making personal testimonies/pronouncements.
- By owning specific bible versions/literature.
- Through speaking in tongues/performing miracles/faith healing.
- Use of specific church designs.
- Use of different titles/names.
- Through ways in which they worship/prayers/doctrines/sacrament.
- By residing in seclusion/homes/houses.
- By observing specific days of worship/holidays.
- Preaching the good news.
- Songs/hymns.   **(6 x 1 = 6 marks)**

3. (a) How did Prophet Samuel promote the worship of Yahweh in Israel?
- He prayed/interceded for the people.
- He mediated between God and the Israelites.
- He performed priestly duties/made sacrifices.
- He condemned King Saul for disobeying God.
- He warned the elders of Israel against demanding for a political king.
- He anointed kings over Israel.
- He obeyed God's command/instructions.
- He always consulted God.

- He built altars for God.
- He upheld the covenant way of life.

(b) Explain six effects of idolatry in Israel during the time of Prophet Elijah.

- God raised prophets to bring back Israel to the covenant way of life.
- There was persecution/hostility towards Yahweh's people/prophets.
- Baal prophets/prophetesses were brought to Israel.
- There was corruption/social injustices/people rejected the covenant way of life.
- The Israelites practised syncretism/mixed the worship of Yahweh with Baal.
- There was drought in Israel for three years as a divine curse on the nation.
- Israel lost its identity as a nation of God's people.
- A contest was held at Mt. Carmel to prove who the true God was.
- Elijah fled the country/was sustained through God's power during the period of the drought
- God's punishment for Baal worshippers/they would die by sword.

(c) What lessons do Christians learn from about social justice from the story of Naboth's vineyard?

- Christians should not use their positions in leadership to acquire wealth irregularly/falsely
- Christians should protect the poor against corrupt leaders.
- They should safeguard property received through inheritance/according to the law.
- Christian should execute justice/protect rights/freedom of citizens/not to kill.
- They should condemn all sorts of injustice in the society.
- Christians should champion/fight for the rights of the weak in the society.
- Christians should be remorseful/repentant.
- Christians should report/expose corrupt leaders.

4. (a) Identify six characteristics of false prophets in the Old Testament

- They did not have a divine call/raised themselves.
- They spoke falsehoods/lies.
- They prophesied out of their own minds/mandate.
- They prophesied what the people wanted to hear/according to circumstances.
- They misled people from the covenant way of life/promoted idolatry.
- They hindered the work of true prophets.
- They worked for material gain/paid for their services.
- Their prophecies were not fulfilled.

(b) Describe the teachings of Prophet Amos on Israel's election.

- Israel's election was out of God's own initiative/favour or them.
- God delivered the Israelites out of the bondage in Egypt.
- He led them during the exodus.
- He protected them in the wilderness.
- He defeated all their enemies.
- God gave them prophets among them to lead them in their religious life.
- God was to punish the Israelites due to their disobedience.

(c) State eight factors that hinder Christians form practising their faith.

- Lack of role models.
- Job commitment.
- Social injustices.
- Peer pressure.
- False teaching/different interpretation of the Bible/devil worship.
- Greed for power/wealth.
- Permissiveness in the society/moral decadence/corruption.
- Science and technology.
- Poverty/unemployment.
- Sickness/ill-health.
- Influence from the mass media.
- Cultural influence/ethnicity/racism/tribalism.
- Gender bias.
- Generation gap.
- Insecurity.
- Natural calamities/disaster.

5. **(a) Measures taken by Nehemiah to enable him to complete the rebuilding of the wall of Jerusalem.**

- He went sought permission to go back to Jerusalem to rebuild the wall.
- He made personal contribution towards the rebuilding of the wall.
- He organized the Israelites in offering labour during the reconstruction of wall.
- He joined his workers in the rebuilding site and worked.
- He did not give up the tasks despite the obstacles he faced.
- Before embarking on the reconstruction he inspected the broken walls and prepared the materials for work.

(b) Four activities carried out by the Israelites during the dedication of the wall of Jerusalem.

- All the people including the Levites, singers and political leaders gathered.
- Priests and Levites purified themselves, the people, and the walls.
- The gates and the walls were also purified.
- Nehemiah brought leaders (Princes) of Judah upon the wall he then appointed two groups who gave thanks and then went into a procession
- The first group led by Ezra moved towards the right, followed by musicians, civic officials, and half the community leaders and priests blowing trumpets and Levites with musical instruments.
- The second group went to the left led by Nehemiah.
- Two groups finally converged at the temple, where there was singing, sacrifices and rejoicing.
- Nehemiah then chose people to be in-charge of tithes, offerings and contributions and ensure they are handled well.

(c) Six ways in which the government of Kenya assists church leaders in their work today.

- It guarantees freedom of worship.
- In the development of the syllabus, church leaders are consulted and involved e.g. CRE.
- It allows the church to run schools and hospitals.
- The church takes part in national celebrations and events e.g. praying during national days.
- The government registers and gives licences to churches.
- In the drafting and making of laws the church leaders participate.

6. (a) Outline the causes of death in Traditional African Communities.

- Curses
- Witchcraft/bad omen.
- Sorcery/magic
- Breaking of taboos.
- Evil spirits.
- Breaking of an oath.
- Offending the ancestors.
- Natural calamities.
- Wars and raids.
- Old age/God's will.

(b) Explain the significance the rituals performed after the death of a person in Traditional African Societies.

- Mourning/wailing/crying is a sign of sorrow/announcing death.

- Making sacrifices to appease the ancestors/deceased/spirits.
- Prayers are made to ask the ancestors to accept the dead in the spirit world.
- Shaving of members of the bereaved family signifies new life in the community.
- Singing and dancing depicts anger towards death/in praise of the dead.
- Washing/oiling of the body before burial shows respect to the departed.
- Burying the dead in the ancestral land shows that one is still a member of the community.
- Burying the dead with personal belongings symbolizes life after death.
- Driving of cattle/livestock shows chasing away of evil spirits which caused death.
- Feasting and drinking is meant to bid farewell to the dead.
- Breaking of pots/destruction of property symbolizes the disorder brought by death.
- Sharing of the deceased's property among relatives as a sign of solidarity.
- Lighting of fire symbolizes chasing away evil spirits/warning spirits of the deceased.
- Pouring of libation shows continuity of life.
- Burying the dead in a particular position signifies protection/responsibility.

(c) List seven moral values promoted during funeral ceremonies in Traditional African communities.

- Promotes the virtue of solidarity as members join to participate in the burial rites.
- The living members develop a sense of responsibility as they take the roles of the deceased and care for his/her property.
- The spirit of mutual concern for others is cultivated as the community members join to support those who are bereaved.
- The virtues of honesty and righteous living are acquired as one tries to avoid the possible causes of death.
- The respect given to the ancestors and the deceased is extended to other members.
- Obedience to the customs and traditions of the community as members observe the rituals.
- Patriotism is cultivated as members observe all customs and traditions related to death in the community.
- The members develop the moral value of thankfulness as they appreciate the role played by relatives, friends and the ancestors.

CRE PAPER 2 2013 MARKING SCHEME

1. **a. With reference to Luke 1: 8 – 20, describe the annunciation of the birth of John the Baptist.** **(6 marks)**
- Angel Gabriel appeared to Zechariah as he performed his priestly duties in the temple.
- The angel stood by the right side of the altar.
- Zechariah was filled with fear when he saw the angel.

- The angel told him not to be afraid because his prayer had been heard.
- The angel told Zechariah that the wife would bear him a son.
- The son would be called John.
- The angel informed Zechariah the work/qualities of the son to be born.
- Zechariah did not believe the angel's message because he and his wife were advanced in age.
- The angel revealed his identity as Gabriel who had been sent by God to bring the message.
- Because of his unbelief, the angel made him dumb until the baby was born.

6 x 1 = 6 marks

b. What do Christians learn about the person and mission of John the Baptist from the message of angel Gabriel to Zechariah? **(8 marks)**

- John would bring joy/gladness to many people.
- He would be great before God.
- John would be a Nazarite/would not drink any wine.
- He would be filled with the Holy Spirit.
- He would reconcile the Israelites with God
- He would have the spirit/power of Elijah.
- He would bring justice.
- He would prepare people for the coming of the Messiah. **(6 x 1 = 6 marks)**

c. State eight ways in which the church in Kenya assists families to cope with the challenges facing them today. **(8 marks)**

- The church organizes seminars/workshops for different groups of family life.
- Offering guidance and counselling.
- Paying visits to families/fellowshipping with them.
- Producing/disseminating literature on proper Christian living.
- Preaching teaching the importance of helping the needy.
- Giving financial/material support to the needy.
- Praying for the families.
- Providing vocational training.
- Offering employment to jobless people.
- Condemning vices which threaten families.
- Establishing rehabilitation centres/houses for the destitute. **(8 x 1 = 8 marks)**

2. **a. Describe the call of the first disciples of Jesus in Luke 5: 1 – 11.** **(8 marks)**
- Jesus was standing by the Lake Gennesaret.

- He saw two boats without the fishermen.
- He entered Simon's boat/asked them to push it into the water.
- He sat down/taught people from the boat.
- He asked Simon to push the boat into the deep water/cast the nets for a catch.
- Simon told Jesus that they had been fishing the whole night without success.
- He obeyed Jesus' command/let the nets down.
- They caught a lot of fish/asked their partners in the other boat to assist them remove the nets.
- They filled both boats with fish/the boats began to sink.
- Simon Peter and his companions were astonished at the miraculous catch of fish/Peter asked Jesus to depart from him because he was sinful man.
- Jesus told Peter not to be afraid because he was to catch men from then.
- They brought their boats to land/followed Jesus/left everything and followed Jesus.

$$8 \times 1 = 8$$
marks

b. Give six reasons why Jesus chose the twelve disciples. **(6 marks)**

- In order to teach them the secrets of the Kingdom of God.
- To have companions/personal assistants.
- To form an inner group which would assist him during his public ministry/spreading the gospel.
- To be witnesses to his saving acts in the world/his mission.
- To reveal his person /give a new understanding of his messiahship.
- It symbolized the reconstruction of the twelve tribes of Israel.
- To train/prepare them for the mission after his death.
- To lay a foundation for the establishment of the church.
- To continue with the biblical theme of election in which God chooses anyone to serve Him. **6 x 1 = 6 marks**

c. Identify six lessons that Christians learn from the call of the first disciples. (6 mks)

- Christians learn that God chooses anyone regardless of their status in the society.
- He gives them duties/responsibilities to serve him in various capacities.
- They should be obedient to Jesus' instructions/commands.
- Christians should be humble/accept their weaknesses/repent.
- Christians should work together as a team.
- God reveals himself in everyday activities.
- Christians should be ready to abandon/forsake their past lives for the sake of Christ.
- They should respond to Jesus' call instantly/immediately. **(6 x 1 = 6 marks)**

3. **a. Outline Jesus' teaching on watchfulness and readiness in Luke 12: 35 – 48. (8mks)**

- Believers should be dressed for his coming.
- They should keep their lamps burning.
- They should be awake/alert.
- Those who are found waiting will be blessed.
- They should be prepared at all times since they do not know the time for Christ's coming.
- Believers should continue working until Christi comes back.
- The servants/believers who are drunkards/mistreat fellow workers will be punished.
- Those who know what is required of them/their masters will and fail to do it will receive a severe beating.
- Believers are expected to respond to God according to how much they have received from Him.
- Those who do wrong out of ignorance will receive lesser beatings/punishment.

(8 x 1 = 8 marks)

b. Narrate the parable of the widow and the unjust judge in Luke 18: 1 – 8. (6 mks)
- There was a judge who neither feared God nor regarded man.
- There was a widow who kept coming to the judge to settle case between her and her enemies/adversaries.
- The judge at first refused to grant the request of the widow.
- The widow did not give up/persisted on her request.
- The judge was afraid of getting worn out by the widow's insistence.
- The judge finally accepted to grant the widow her request.
- Jesus said that God would vindicate/grant the request of those who pray to him persistently.
- Jesus said that God responds to those who pray to Him in faith speedily. **(6 x 1 = 6 marks)**

c. Give six reasons why Christians should have faith in God. **(6 marks)**
- God fulfils the promises he makes to human beings.
- Faith is a requirement for all Christians.
- Those who pray in faith receive their request.
- Christians are dependent on God for all things.
- Faith is a sign of commitment to God.
- It is through faith in God that Christians can perform miracles/great things.
- Christians who have faith in God can be saved/healed.·
- Faith in God helps Christians to overcome temptations/face challenges/persecutions.

- Faith in God enables the Christians to wait patiently for the second coming of Jesus/Kingdom of God. **(6 x 1 = 6 marks)**

4. **a. Identify the gifts of the Holy Spirit according to Saint Paul in 1 Corinthians 12: 7 – 11.** **(8 marks)**
- The gift of wisdom
- The gift of knowledge
- The gift of faith
- The gift of healing
- The gift of performing miracles
- The gift of prophecy
- Interpreting of tongues
- The gift of speaking in tongues **(8 x 1 = 8 marks)**

b. How was the life of Peter transformed on the day of Pentecost? **(6 marks)**
- Peter was filled with the power of the Holy Spirit.
- He spoke in tongues.
- He defended the apostles that they were not drunk.
- Peter became courageous.
- He preached the word of God.
- He became a witness of the work/death and resurrection of Jesus Christ.
- He was able to remember/narrate Old Testament scriptures.
- He gained wisdom/advised the people on what to do.
- He baptised believers.
- He took up leadership roles. **(6 x 1 = 6 marks)**

c. Explain six in which the gifts of the Holy Spirit are abused in the church today.
- Some Christians pretend that they have a certain gift of the Holy Spirit.
- By asking for payment before healing the sick.
- Christians misuse the gift of prophecy by giving wrong information.
- Some Christians may impart demonic powers on the innocent/ignorant as they claim to perform miracles.
- Some Christians who possess the gift of the Holy Spirit develop pride/arrogance.
- Some use the gifts of the Holy Spirit to bring division in the church/creating splinter groups.
- Some Christians refuse to utilize the gifts they possess/personalize the gifts.

- Speaking in tongues during worship leads to disorder/confusion if the tongues are not interpreted/understood. **(6 x 1 = 6 marks)**

5. **(a) State the importance of leisure.** **(6 marks)**
- Leisure enables an individual to spend time with God.
- It enables one to rest the body/relax.
- It helps one to rejuvenate/regain lost energy.
- It offers an opportunity for one to socialize with friends and family.
- People are able to discover new ideas/information during leisure time.
- It gives one opportunity for one to take care of the environment.
- It helps to maintain/improve one's health. **(6 x 1 = 6 marks)**

b. Identify seven leisure activities common to both Christianity and traditional African communities. **(7 marks)**
- Singing/dancing.
- Storytelling/proverbs/riddles.
- Sporting activities.
- Visiting/travelling.
- Weaving/basketry/crafts.
- Retreats.
- Gardening.
- Buying/exchange of goods.
- Taking siesta.
- Education/training.
- Ceremonies/festivals among the youth. **(7 x 1 = 7 marks)**

c. Explain the dangers of using illicit drugs among the youth in Kenya today. (7 mks)
- There is an increase in rate of crimes committed.
- Use of illicit drugs leads to sexual immorality/contracting of STIs/HIV and AIDS.
- Dependence on illicit drugs depletes resources leading to poverty.
- Illicit drugs can damage vital organs/lead to ill-health.
- Illicit drugs cause indiscipline in institutions of learning.
- The number of street children/families is increasing as a result of using the drugs.
- Use of illicit drugs is illegal/the offenders are liable for punishment.
- Use of illicit drugs can cause employer/employee conflicts.

- Illicit drug users become irresponsible/quarrelsome/irritable leading to family disagreements/break up.
- Use of illicit drugs can lead to murder/death.
- It causes addiction.   **(7 x 1 = 7 marks)**

6. **a. Explain how science and technology has improved human life.**   **(8 marks)**
- Modern means of transport enable human beings to travel faster.
- Use of electronic/print media: human beings are able to access/pass information to large audience.
- Use of industrial machines enables work to be done faster/efficiently.
- Use of fertilizers/agricultural machinery has led to increased production/yields/preservation of food.
- Use of medicine/medical equipment has prolonged human life/reduces suffering.
- Use of equipment related to weather forecast assists human beings in understanding the environment.
- New sources of energy have enhanced human life.
- Scientific devices have enhanced security.   **(8 x 1 = 8 marks)**

b. Give six reasons why Christians are opposed to Euthanasia.   **(6 marks)**
- God is the only one who gives life and thus should be the one to take it away.
- Euthanasia equals to murder which is Biblically condemned/thou shall not kill.
- It destroys God's image in human beings.
- Human judgement is limited and therefore cannot make correct decisions on terminating the life of others.
- Medical ethics only allow a doctor to sustain life and not to take it away.
- It is against Jesus' mission on earth to heal the sick.
- Suffering is part of a Christian's life from the teachings of Jesus and therefore it cannot be used to justify euthanasia.
- It is constitutional right to uphold human life.   **(6 x 1 = 6 marks)**

c. Identify ways through which Christians can help to control desertification. (6mks)
- Christians need to practise afforestation/re-afforestation programmes.
- By practising agro-forestry.
- Using alternative sources of energy as opposed to charcoal/firewood.
- Providing education to the public on how to preserve the environment.

- Participating in environmental conservation programmes.
- Donating/giving financial assistance to bodies that control desertification.
- Protecting all water catchment areas.
- Carrying out/practising better methods of farming.
- Reporting cases of forest destruction to relevant authorities.
- By participating in the enactment of laws on environmental conservation.
- Providing guidance and counselling/advice to those involved in activities related to environmental degradation.
- Using alternative sources of building materials as opposed to natural vegetation.

(6 x 1 = 6 marks)

www.ingramcontent.com/pod-product-compliance
Lightning Source LLC
Chambersburg PA
CBHW062057090426
42741CB00015B/3262

* 9 7 8 9 9 6 6 1 8 1 8 2 4 *